Baseball's Greatest What If

The Story & Tragedy of the
Brooklyn Dodgers' Pistol Pete Reiser

Dan Joseph

Mechanicsburg, PA USA

Published by Sunbury Press, Inc.
Mechanicsburg, PA USA

www.sunburypress.com

Copyright © 2021 by Dan Joseph.
Cover Copyright © 2021 by Sunbury Press, Inc.

Sunbury Press supports copyright. Copyright fuels creativity, encourages diverse voices, promotes free speech, and creates a vibrant culture. Thank you for buying an authorized edition of this book and for complying with copyright laws. Except for the quotation of short passages for the purpose of criticism and review, no part of this publication may be reproduced, scanned, or distributed in any form without permission. You are supporting writers and allowing Sunbury Press to continue to publish books for every reader. For information contact Sunbury Press, Inc., Subsidiary Rights Dept., PO Box 548, Boiling Springs, PA 17007 USA or legal@sunburypress.com.

For information about special discounts for bulk purchases, please contact Sunbury Press Orders Dept. at (855) 338-8359 or orders@sunburypress.com.

To request one of our authors for speaking engagements or book signings, please contact Sunbury Press Publicity Dept. at publicity@sunburypress.com.

FIRST SUNBURY PRESS EDITION: November 2021

Set in Adobe Garamond Pro | Interior design by Crystal Devine | Cover by Lawrence Knorr | Edited by Lawrence Knorr.

Publisher's Cataloging-in-Publication Data
Names: Joseph, Dan, author.
Title: Baseball's greatest what if : the story & tragedy of Brooklyn Dodgers' Pistol Pete Reiser.
Description: First trade paperback edition. | Mechanicsburg, PA : Sunbury Press, 2021.
Summary : The career of supremely talented but ill-fated Brooklyn Dodger star Pete Reiser comes to life in this new biography from baseball author Dan Joseph (*Last Ride of the Iron Horse*). Only a tendency to smash into outfield walls stopped Reiser from earning a spot in baseball's Hall of Fame.
Identifiers: ISBN : 978-1-62006-898-4 (softcover).
Subjects: SPORTS & RECREATION / Baseball / Essays & Writings | SPORTS & RECREATION / Baseball / History | BIOGRAPHY & AUTOBIOGRAPHY / Sports.

Product of the United States of America
0 1 1 2 3 5 8 13 21 34 55

Continue the Enlightenment!

Contents

Foreword and Acknowledgments — *v*
Introduction — *ix*
Testimony — *xv*

CHAPTERS

1. Peak Reiser — *1*
2. Like Father, Like Son — *12*
3. Gentleman's Agreement — *26*
4. "Some Kind of Year, '41" — *48*
5. Hitting the Wall — *81*
6. "A Wild and Frightening Beauty" — *97*
7. Soldiering On — *119*
8. "He's the Difference, Brother" — *138*
9. The Other Great What Ifs — *165*
10. Jackie and the Last Rites — *192*
11. Baseball Afterlife — *224*
12. Legacy — *240*

Bibliography — *249*
Notes — *251*
Index — *279*
About the Author — *282*

Foreword and Acknowledgments

One might think that the author of a book on Pete Reiser spent a slice of his youth at Ebbets Field, or had parents and grandparents who passed down memories of the Pistol slaying opponents in the green pastures of the Dodgers' long-lost home. Not the case. I am far too young to have ever seen a Brooklyn Dodgers game. My earliest ancestors on these shores rooted for the Cincinnati Reds. Me, I was raised in an observant Pittsburgh Pirates home. I do not bleed Dodger blue. I do bleed baseball, though, and that's why this book and my previous one, *Last Ride of the Iron Horse* (on Lou Gehrig), were such a joy to research and write.

I wouldn't have gotten very far on this project without the help of some fine people and institutions:

- The Library of Congress in Washington, D.C., in particular the staff of the Newspaper Periodicals Room. It's one of the few places in the country one can access back issues of defunct New York City papers like the *Herald Tribune*, *World-Telegram*, *Journal American*, and the *Amsterdam News*. The Library also has the full collection of Branch Rickey's papers. They are aging and crinkly, and some of them have that wonderful old-paper smell, which gave me a baseball history high.

- The Society of American Baseball Research. I'm a proud SABR member, and I access back issues of *The Sporting News* through the research portal on the organization's website. The SABR Games Project also published stories I wrote on two of Pete's most famous games as I pressed forward on this book. The positive reaction I got to those helped keep me going.

- Newspapers.com. I'm giving a free plug to a commercial website, but they've earned it. I couldn't have gotten started on this book, let alone finished, without them providing instant access to relevant issues of the *New York Daily News*, *Brooklyn Daily Eagle*, *Brooklyn Citizen*, and many other dailies that covered various aspects of Pete's career.

- Fultonhistory.org. The work of one Tom Tryniski, whom I've never met but greatly admire. Through him, I accessed old issues of the *New York Post*, *New York Sun*, *PM Daily*, and the *Daily Worker*.
- Cassidy Lent at the National Baseball Hall of Fame in Cooperstown, New York. I keep firing questions and requests at Cassidy, and she keeps coming through. Thanks, Cassidy, for player files on so many old-time Dodgers, including Reiser, Pee Wee Reese, Dixie Walker, and Joe Medwick, as well as executives like Rickey and Larry MacPhail.

I also owe a debt of sorts to another person I've never met, Donald Honig. Outside of Leo Durocher, Honig was probably Pete Reiser's number-one fan. He rooted for Pete growing up in New York during the 1940s. He talked to him at length for his absorbing 1975 book of interviews with old-time ballplayers, *Baseball When the Grass Was Real*. He detailed the little-kid excitement he felt at meeting his idol in his 2009 book, *The Fifth Season*. Along with W.C. Heinz's award-winning 1958 magazine article, "The Rocky Road of Pistol Pete," Honig's interviews and observations form the bedrock of common knowledge on Pete—though some of that "knowledge" is not correct, led astray by Pete's own flawed memories and the difficulty of fact-checking before old newspapers were online and one could Google-trace any piece of info in sixty seconds flat.

This might sound strange, but I chose not to contact Honig for this book, not because of any qualms about his research, but because I wanted a fresh, non-nostalgic take on Pete's life and career. That said, those familiar with Mr. Honig's work will recognize snatches of his interviews throughout the text. For baseball historians, his work is invaluable and irreplaceable.

My biggest thanks go to Pete's daughter Shirley Tuber and her husband, Rick Tuber. This is not an "authorized" biography, but when I contacted Shirley online and explained what I was doing, they provided immense help, sharing pictures, videos, documents, and their memories and impressions of Pete. Decades ago, Rick planned to write a biography of Pete and talked to several players who knew him, including Joe Garagiola, Lonny Frey, Carl Warwick, Warren Spahn, and Carl Erskine. He also interviewed Pete and his wife, Pat. The book never got off the ground, but Rick generously shared the tapes of those interviews for this project. Incidentally, he kept writing and has produced three novels, the latest being *Well, I'll Be Damned*, released by Friesen Press in 2020. Best of luck with the writing, Rick. It's fun, isn't it?

I'd be remiss if I didn't thank my crack team of readers who gave me feedback while this work was in progress. One of them happens to be my dad, Will

Joseph, and another happens to be a one-time big league peanut vendor, my father-in-law Jay Lazier. They did see the Brooklyn Dodgers play, usually walloping the woeful 1950s Pirates at Forbes Field. My other readers never had that experience, but I value their input just the same: my wife, Yona, and our sons, Sammy and Elani. They've been very patient with me while I write this, my third book in five years. Am I going to stop writing now? I don't think so. Will I ever stop loving you all? Never.

Introduction

Most don't know it, but millions of current-day baseball fans have seen Pistol Pete Reiser smash a game-changing home run during the World Series.

It happened during Game One of the 2019 series, Astros vs. Nationals. After the Nats went down in the first inning, the TV broadcast switched to a commercial that began with three young children, all in baseball uniforms, running into the living room of a suburban home. A blond boy of about eight turned to a figure sitting on the couch and asked, "Grandpa, what was the best baseball game you ever saw?"

The camera switched to the grandpa, who many viewers undoubtedly recognized as Buzz Aldrin, the second man to walk on the moon.

"Ahh . . . World Series, 1941," Aldrin replied.

The world suddenly turned black-and-white, and viewers saw a young baseball player uncork a sweet left-handed swing. A loud crack and a shot of excited fans rising from their seats told the story: *home run*. The player, a broad number 27 across his back, crossed home plate as a faux 1941 radio announcer exclaimed, "And it's gone! That one went to the moon!"

The joke of the ad was that Aldrin became an astronaut to retrieve the ball from the lunar surface.

The shame of the ad was that it didn't name the player who ostensibly blasted the ball two hundred forty thousand miles to land in a pile of moondust.

That player was Harold Patrick Reiser, better known as Pete.

Reiser didn't possess otherworldly power, but the ad contained a large, rock-solid kernel of truth. Reiser did play in the 1941 World Series, after winning the National League batting title, after leading the league in eight other hitting and fielding categories, and after driving the Brooklyn Dodgers to their first NL pennant in over two decades. And he did slam an eye-popping home run during Game Four of the Series, one that soared over the thirty-five-foot-high scoreboard that served as the right-field wall at the Dodgers' home park,

Ebbets Field. "Boy, that was a wallop!" said the real announcer of the game, Bob Elson, as a sellout crowd roared and buzzed after Reiser's blast, which gave the Dodgers a 4-3 lead.

The Dodgers eventually lost that game on Mickey Owen's infamous two-out, ninth-inning dropped third strike and lost the series too. But that did nothing to tarnish Pete's season or dim his future. He was twenty-two years old, handsome, popular with the fans, played on a championship-caliber team, and possessed one of the most spectacular skill sets in baseball, marked by a keen batting eye, a powerful throwing arm, and speed that whisked him from home plate to first base in three-point-six seconds.

"At that moment, if you had given baseball decision-makers the option to have Ted Williams or Pete Reiser, born seven and half months apart, many would have taken Reiser. And remember that was the same year that Williams hit .400," sportswriter and author Joe Posnanski has written. No question that Williams was the better hitter, but Reiser was superior at everything else—running, fielding, throwing, sliding—and had absolutely no trouble powering an offense, with his penchant for doubles, triples, periodic homers, and timely steals. He was positioned for superstardom, the kind enjoyed by contemporaries like Williams and Bob Feller, maybe even the kind of all-time household name status achieved by only a select few, mostly New York guys with names like DiMaggio, Mays, Mantle, and Ruth.

Then Reiser ran into a wall. More accurately, multiple walls, starting with the concrete center-field barrier at Sportsman's Park in St. Louis in July 1942. He couldn't help it. Pete played baseball with an intensity that the phrase "reckless abandon" doesn't convey. He collided with teammates. He chased after fly balls with no regard for personal safety. He left hospitals too soon, returned to the lineup too soon. He played with torn ligaments, bone chips in his arm, a separated shoulder. He played when he was dizzy. He played with double vision. He batted when he could barely walk, tried to steal bases when he could barely run.

"There are knowing students of baseball who believe Pete Reiser was born to be the greatest player that ever lived," famed sports columnist Red Smith once wrote. "Trouble was, nobody ever built a ballpark big enough to contain his effort. If there was a fly ball to be caught, he went for it. When he was through as a Brooklyn outfielder . . . there was scarcely a bone in Pete's body that hadn't been shattered, a muscle or ligament that hadn't been torn."

Smith was exaggerating, but not by much. Reiser never got through a full season in Brooklyn without making at least one emergency visit to a hospital, nearly all of them triggered by his don't think-just run style of play. During

World War II, he avoided combat but still sustained a serious injury by crashing through a makeshift fence and tumbling down a ditch during an army game. Two years later, back with the Dodgers, Reiser cracked his head against a real outfield wall, another one made of concrete, and was given the last rites of the Catholic church. The prayers turned out to be premature; Pete survived another thirty-four years. And he was back in the lineup within six weeks.

It's hard to document all the incidents, but sportswriters of the time said Reiser was carried off the field eleven times during his career. Some of these carry-offs have inspired legends, which all seem to involve Reiser volunteering to pinch-hit just days after suffering a severe head injury and smashing a blow that gave the Dodgers a walk-off victory. My journalistic soul raised its hand and asked: Are these stories true? Have they been twisted or exaggerated? If they are true, *why* would Reiser push himself to such extremes? What maniacal drive caused him to risk his career, health, and life for a baseball game? Moreover, why would the Dodgers' decision-makers let him even try?

I had to find out. That's the first reason I'm writing this book.

The other reason is that Pete Reiser deserves to be better remembered. In my humble but informed opinion, he is the greatest "what if" player in baseball history. There are certainly other contenders for that title: Pitching star Jose Fernandez, killed at twenty-four in a pre-dawn motorboat crash . . . Slugger Josh Hamilton, his MVP-caliber talents dragged down by drug and alcohol addiction . . . Fireballer J.R. Richard, felled by a stroke just as he was reaching his peak . . . Mark Fidrych, Cecil Travis, Herb Score, Smoky Joe Wood, Charlie Ferguson. There are perhaps dozens of would-be superstars whose careers were cut short by insurmountable injuries or tragic events if one goes back far enough.

Reiser is different. He wasn't just a great young baseball player. He was set to become a central figure in the national pastime. He was in the right place at the right time—New York, baseball and media capital of the world, at the start of the most drama-filled period in the game's long, long history. Even as he struggled to stay upright and in the lineup, Reiser was a key part of the story as the Dodgers became the National League's most popular team, as baseball transitioned in and out of World War II, as Jackie Robinson smashed the color barrier. (The day Robinson debuted, it was Pete, not Jackie, who grabbed the headlines, thanks to a game-winning RBI double.) Had he stayed with the Dodgers through the 1950s, like his pal and contemporary Pee Wee Reese, Reiser would have been there for the renowned *Boys of Summer* era, including the heartbreak of Bobby Thomson's home run, the repeated World Series losses to the Yankees, the euphoria of the 1955 championship, and the team's bittersweet move to Los Angeles—although one wonders if Dodger history might have unfolded differently had a healthy Pete Reiser manned the outfield all those years.

Even in a shortened career, Reiser imprinted himself on baseball's collective memory. Trivia buffs know he still holds the record for most steals of home in a single season (seven in 1946, a mark later tied by Rod Carew) and that he was intentionally walked in a World Series game despite playing on a broken ankle. His style of play inspired a scene in Bernard Malamud's classic baseball novel, *The Natural*. In 1981, baseball historians Lawrence Ritter and Donald Honig included him in their book "The 100 Greatest Baseball Players of All Time," despite Reiser playing only four seasons as a regular. "Of all the careers aborted by injuries, Pete Reiser's may well have been the greatest," they wrote.

That memory has persisted into the twenty-first century, as evidenced by the Aldrin ad, or how sportswriters invoked his name when Bryce Harper briefly acquired the habit of running into outfield walls. While researching this book, I visited the Library of Congress. I was trying to look up a 1947 *New York Herald Tribune* article, and the computer I was using refused to spit out the PDF file. A male staffer I'd estimate to be in his mid-sixties sat down at the adjacent computer to help.

"Is there a keyword you're using?" he asked.

"Reiser," I said, not elaborating.

There was a two-second pause. "Injuries?" he said.

Or consider this. In the final scene of the 2011 Marvel movie "Captain America: The First Avenger," Steve Rogers wakes up to the sound of a Dodgers game emanating from an old-fashioned wooden console radio. As the camera pulls back to show a 1940s-style hospital room, the announcer—a soundalike of the legendary Red Barber—refers to Ebbets Field, letting savvy moviegoers know these Dodgers are from Brooklyn, not L.A.

The savviest know who the announcer refers to when he says: "Soooo, the Dodgers are tied 4-4. And the crowd well knows that with one swing of his bat, this fella's capable of making it a brand-new game again."

That fella is Harold Patrick Reiser, better known as Pete.

I'm giving away the end of the game, not the movie, when I say that Cap hears Pete slash a line drive to right field, drive in three runs, and zoom around the bases for an inside-the-park grand slam. Pete Reiser did that in real life, not just in the movies.

It's possible he would have done it more often had he played with a little restraint. Of course, had he played that way, Pete might have been just another garden variety good outfielder. Restraint was not part of his constitution. God-given ability was, and it's the juxtaposition of those two elements that make him so fascinating, so worthy of further study and re-evaluation.

What if Pete Reiser had stayed healthy and played a full career? There's no way for us to know, but to borrow two words from Red Barber, *ohhh doctor* . . . would it have been something extraordinary.

Daniel Joseph
October 2021

Testimony

"I know what another Ty Cobb means. But if there ever will be another Ty Cobb, his name will be Reiser." —Leo Durocher, 1941

"Reiser isn't just a hard hitter. He's one of the greatest all-around players I have ever seen in the thirty-five years I've been in baseball."
—Red Corriden (coach), 1942

"If he has a batting weakness, I don't know what it is."—Mickey Owen, 1942

"That boy has everything. He can hit. He can run. He can throw. He can field. He can think. He can hustle, and he always does. What more can you ask from a ballplayer?" —Frankie Frisch, 1942

"He has the gift to run and the urge to go." —Branch Rickey, 1942

"Pete Reiser is to the Brooklyns what Joe DiMaggio is to the Yankees; Hank Greenberg is to the Tigers; Ted Williams is to the Red Sox."
—Harry Grayson (sportswriter), 1946

"If he's right, there'll be no better player in the National League."
—Branch Rickey, 1947

"He was always a great ballplayer. But the injuries he suffered would have wrecked a battleship." —Grantland Rice, 1950

"I'll tell you how good he was. He could have been Joe DiMaggio or Stan Musial." —Jimmy Cannon (sportswriter), 1959

"Pete was better than Stan Musial, I think. He could do more things than Stan. He'd run through a brick wall to get a ball—and did try a couple of times." —Pee Wee Reese, 1972

"There wasn't a thing he couldn't do on that ballfield . . . It's just a sin he never became the .340 lifetime hitter he should have been or the base-stealing champion he should have been."
—Tommy Holmes (retired outfielder), early 1970s

"Rose? He was twice as good as Rose." —Danny Ozark (manager), 1981

"Reiser was one of the finest young players I've ever seen, or anyone else ever saw." —Red Barber, 1981

"He could hit, he could run, he could throw, he could catch, and he could do them all superbly at age 18. The only reason he wasn't called another Mickey Mantle is that he came before Mickey Mantle." —Dick Young, 1981

"In his best days, there probably was not a better ball player ever than Pete Reiser. I mean it. He had all the tools." —Carl Erskine, 1989

"He could have been one of the best players of all time, if he hadn't had all those accidents, running into walls." —Billy Herman, 1990

Who was the best hitter you ever worked behind? "I'd have to say, Ted Williams, Musial, and probably if he hadn't gotten hurt early, it'd have been Pete Reiser. What a talent, what a talent." —Al Barlick (retired umpire), 1991

"He was every bit as good as Willie Mays. Might have been better. Pete Reiser just might have been the best baseball player I ever saw." —Leo Durocher, 1975

1

Peak Reiser

Morning dawned the way it always did in Pittsburgh—smoky. The sun was up there somewhere, beaming down the summer heat, but its light had to punch through a thick, dirty haze, the product of dozens of steel mills running seven days a week, twenty-four hours a day, churning out pieces for the nation's war machine. Winning the fight against Germany and Japan was the only thing that really mattered in the United States in 1942. Air quality? Eh. That was an afterthought, a can to be kicked down the road until victory. Many Pittsburghers didn't mind the pollution in a way. It had been like this for generations, ever since steelworks sprouted along the Monongahela, Allegheny, and Ohio riverbanks. People knew the smoke in the air was a sign of good economic times, the kind that produced full-time jobs and fatter paychecks and put dinner on the table. So if the white shirt you wore to work turned gray by noon, or if the bedsheets you hung on the clothesline picked up a fine layer of soot . . . Well, that was just a little nuisance, a price everyone had to pay.

The visiting ballplayers from Brooklyn strolled into Pittsburgh's Forbes Field that June 2nd with a similar point of view. Who cared if a little soot fell on their heads? They'd be wearing their gray road uniforms anyway. Now, if rain fell—*that* would be a cause for concern. This two-game series against the Pirates was a primo opportunity to put notches in the win column, a cause secondary to the war but one damn important to folks in the home borough. The Dodgers were hot, having copped eighteen of their last twenty-four games, many by lopsided margins, seizing first place in the National League and opening a six-game lead over St. Louis. The players were confident, bordering on cocky. "I've always wanted to play on a Yankee-type team. These Dodgers out-Yankee the Yanks," said pitcher Larry French that month – high praise in an era when the Yankees regularly buried their opponents under an avalanche of runs. The team looked so good that Grantland Rice, the country's preeminent sports columnist, told his readers that the NL pennant race might be over in a few weeks unless somebody lit a fire under the Cardinals.

And the Pirates? They were a reeling, hapless bunch, losers of nine in a row and fifteen of their last seventeen. Two days earlier, the Bucs had dropped both ends of a doubleheader to the Reds in Cincinnati, scoring only two runs during a long, disheartening Sunday afternoon. Their manager, Frankie Frisch, seemed utterly at a loss to pinpoint what was wrong with his team. "I know the Pirates aren't as bad as they've been looking," he told a reporter after the losses. "They simply can't be."

The Dodgers in contrast had thoroughly enjoyed their Sunday, sweeping a pair of games in front of twenty-nine thousand raucous fans, nearly a full house at their cozy home ballpark, Ebbets Field. Brooklyn rooters were renowned for being the loudest, loopiest, and most boisterous in the major leagues, and a few got even more out of hand that afternoon, with police being deployed to break up two fights in the stands —"one of the principals being a woman," reported the *New York Daily News*. But most in attendance got sheer pleasure out of watching their Dodgers, their beloved "Bums," dismantle the visiting Boston Braves. Chief dismantler was the team's star center fielder, twenty-three-year-old Pete Reiser. In game one, Pete swatted a single, double, and a two-run homer and scored four times. The home run was a moonshot, sailing over the thirty-five-foot-high scoreboard in right field, newly topped that year with a sign that read, "Buy U.S. War Stamps." In the nightcap, Pete banged out two singles, legged a poke down the left-field line into a triple, and scored what turned out to be the winning run. By day's end, he was hitting .343, the same average he hit for in 1941, when he won the National League batting title. "Reiser Has Big Day," read the headline in one Brooklyn paper, in something of an understatement.

Dodger manager Leo Durocher had to be especially pleased. A year earlier, the brash Durocher—dubbed Leo the Lip for his frequent verbal spats with umpires—had raised eyebrows when he said Reiser could be "another Ty Cobb." Cobb's lifetime batting average of .367 and his four-thousand-plus hits were the highest in baseball history; he was considered one of the game's three greatest players, along with eight-time NL batting champion Honus Wagner and the home run king, Babe Ruth. But in '41, Reiser was simply sensational, leading the league in seemingly everything: runs, doubles, triples, slugging percentage, total bases, putouts, assists, hit-by-pitch, and of course, batting.

Now others were starting to sing tunes akin to Leo's. "Here is a lad who looks like the best Dodger player of all time," wrote veteran sportswriter Tom Meany. Tommy Holmes of Brooklyn's *Daily Eagle* newspaper challenged readers: "If you think he isn't one of the greatest ball players in the game, go on and name a better one in the National League." Gerry Schumacher of the rival *New York Journal American* told readers that Reiser was perhaps the finest natural talent the league had seen in a generation. "We've seen some who were smarter, others more graceful and polished, and three or four batting stylists such as Rogers Hornsby, Bill Terry, and Lefty O'Doul who could outhit him," Schumacher wrote in a piece published the day Pete pummeled the Braves. "But none of them could do all the things that Reiser can. None was a blend of so many playing attributes. Do you remember anybody who could run faster? Could throw harder or more accurately? Or swing a bat with more strength or precision?"

In Brooklyn around this time, a ten-year-old future writer and baseball historian named Donald Honig asked his older brother, "Do you think Reiser is as good as Williams and DiMaggio?" Williams, as in Ted, had hit .406 a year earlier, higher than any player in twenty years; DiMaggio, as in Joe, had put together his legendary fifty-six game hitting streak and was named American League MVP. And yet, Honig's sibling did not consider his kid brother's question out of line. "I think he will be," the older Honig said. "He's only a kid; he's going to keep getting better and better."

More expert opinion came from veteran pitcher Johnny Allen, who joined the Dodgers in 1941 after a decade in the American League. A reporter asked him in '42 to compare Pete to DiMaggio. Allen paused for a second to collect his thoughts, then answered: "Right now, there's little to choose between them. Joe will hit a long ball more consistently than Pete, but Reiser will get more infield hits than Joe. Pete is faster getting down to first base. In fielding, their styles are different. Joe makes his fielding look easy. Pete's fielding lacks the ease that Joe puts into his, but Reiser produces the same results that Joe does."

Pete himself didn't make such comparisons. In fact, he didn't talk much about his abilities and accomplishments at all. Dodger general manager Larry MacPhail—a born chatterbox, showman, and publicity hound—might have preferred more swagger from his star, telling columnist Elsa Maxwell that June, "I just wish he'd make more noise." The fiery Durocher felt the same way, saying, "I sure wish he would holler more." It wasn't that Pete lacked confidence. At his first big-league spring training in 1939, he claimed that he could hit any pitcher who ever lived, and when asked if he felt pressure at the plate, he replied, "Naw,

I just get up there and swing." But in general, boasting wasn't Pete's style. After the '41 season, when the Dodgers won their first National League pennant in twenty-one years, Pete used his World Series check to buy a two-story, ten-room house for his parents and siblings in a suburb of his hometown St. Louis. It was by far the nicest home the family had ever owned, and Pete didn't mind giving a tour to a *Sporting News* reporter who stopped by shortly before Christmas and showing off some of the toys he'd bought, like a pinball machine and baseball-shaped radio. Regarding his on-field performance, though, Pete wouldn't utter a word that could be construed as bragging. When a pal suggested he could hit .400 like Williams, he said, "That Williams can hit. I saw him bust one in the All-Star Game last summer. And that DiMaggio! I wish I could hit like those fellows."

Reiser was also a team guy who meant it when he said Dodger wins mattered more to him than his stats. In 1941, he told a reporter, "I wouldn't mind batting five times and going hitless. If I got up that many times in a game, that would mean somebody on the club was hitting."

"Dad never talked about being better than anyone," says Pete's daughter, Shirley. "He was a very humble man, at least from what I saw and how I was raised to behave."

On the field, however, Pete made more noise than almost anybody. He wasn't a big guy; the Dodgers listed him at five-foot-ten, one hundred eighty pounds, both figures perhaps a tad generous. Williams and DiMaggio were taller and heftier. They hit more home runs. But Reiser had a whip-like swing and muscular forearms that produced plenty of extra-base hits, and he could beat you in additional ways. The two American League superstars didn't have his speed, especially leaving the batter's box. Nor could they drag bunts like him, or match his mastery of baserunning, in particular his "fallaway" slide, a technique that gave infielders just a toe or a hand to tag when Reiser came zooming into a base. No one had his range or throwing arm in center field except DiMaggio and the Cardinals' Terry Moore. And if Pete's long drives tended to bounce off outfield walls instead of soar over them, opponents were highly impressed all the same. The Braves' manager in 1942 was a quotable character and future manager of ten Yankee pennant winners named Casey Stengel. In an interview, Stengel raved about Reiser: "When you lay in for that kid, he's liable to rip your head off [with a line drive]. But just back up a couple of steps, and he'll beat out a bounder every time. What a player!"

Reiser matched up to Ty Cobb in another important way—aggressiveness. He didn't play angry like Cobb, who famously left a long trail of hard slides, fistfights, and enemies over his quarter-century career. What the two did share was an overwhelming will to excel and win. In Pete, that will expressed itself as a laser-beam focus on the tasks before him—getting hits, scoring runs, and catching the ball. Elbie Fletcher, a first baseman for the Pirates in the early 1940s, said Reiser was virtually impossible to distract from his mission. "You know, a lot of times, a fellow would get a base hit, and we'd stand on first and shoot the breeze a little. I was a friendly sort of guy," Fletcher recalled. "But Reiser wouldn't talk. Never would say a word. He'd get on base, and he'd be all concentration. And you just knew what he was thinking about: How am I going to get to second? How am I going to get to third? How am I going to score?"

So intense was this focus that Pete seemed to play with little regard for his own safety much of the time. In April of '41, he crowded the plate against the Phillies' Ike Pearson and took a fastball to his right cheek. That May, he banged against a center field exit gate while chasing a long fly and opened a two-inch-long gash on his back. At least four times that season, he collided in the outfield with teammates. Even in spring training, Pete couldn't restrain himself. In April of '42, the Dodgers played the Yankees in an exhibition game in Norfolk, Virginia. The Yankees scored early and often, and by the sixth inning, the Dodgers trailed by ten runs. Yet when the Yankees' Charlie Keller smashed a long drive to deep center, Pete ran after the ball at full speed and *wham*, charged right into the center-field wall, knocking himself to the ground. After a few seconds, he got up and insisted he could keep playing, but Durocher took no chances and removed him from the game.

The first baseman for the Yankees that day was Buddy Hassett. Hassett had played with the Braves in 1940 and 1941 and felt Pete was destined to be one of the all-time greats. "He was an awful tough man to play against because he could be explosive in any situation, whether it was in the field, at base, on the bases," Hassett recalled. But, Hassett added, "I always felt that he played *too* hard. He was a very intense kid. He suffered those injuries—running into walls, breaking bones—that he might otherwise have avoided. But it was his style of playing, I guess."

In the words of an admirer, *New York Times* sportswriter Arthur Daley: "Pete has such tremendous will to win that he makes every play like his life depended on it."

Pete had started the '42 regular season in a mild slump—nothing horrible, just a few too many hitless games. The U.S. had entered the war when Japan attacked Pearl Harbor the previous December, and some observers thought Pete was distracted by the prospect of being drafted. A few days before the season opener, on April 13th, his Brooklyn draft board said it would classify him as 1-A, meaning he could be called into military service at any time. Reporters kept bugging Pete about it, to the point where Durocher yelled at them to stop: "Why rattle him like this just before Opening Day? Are you trying to rush him off to the Army?" But Pete's bat got going in early May when the Dodgers visited St. Louis for a three-game set against the Cardinals. Playing in front of members of his large family—Pete had seven brothers and sisters—he collected a homer, two doubles, three singles, and three walks in thirteen times up. The Dodgers lost two of three but rebounded immediately, winning ten of their next eleven games, with Reiser frequently racking up two or three hits per day.

His short-term worries about being called up vanished on May 15th when, following an appeal from his parents, the draft board reclassified him as 3-A, deferring his induction on the grounds that it would cause hardship to his dependents. No one in the press objected; as one paper pointed out, Reiser was helping to support a wife, his parents, five of his siblings, and the Dodger offense. He proved the last by slamming three doubles that afternoon against the Pirates in an 8-3 win.

Even when Pete didn't hit, his speed won ball games. On May 17th against the Cubs, Reiser drew a base on balls and advanced to third on a walk and a groundout. A rookie left-hander, Johnny Schmitz, was on the mound for Chicago. Reiser began playing with him, taking long leads off third. "There he was, inching down the line in a half-crouch, watching the pitcher like a famished predator," recalled Honig, who happened to be at Ebbets Field that day. Then, with a roar from the crowd, Reiser bolted down the line and, with a cloud of dust, slid across the plate for an unaided steal of home. The run brought Dodger fans to a state of frenzy, including the team's radio announcer, Red Barber, who got so excited that he yanked his microphone out of its socket, briefly knocking himself off the air. The run was also the difference-maker in the Dodgers' 4-3 victory.

Another Tommy Holmes—this one a ballplayer, not a sportswriter—got his first up-close look at Reiser that spring when he joined the Braves as a rookie outfielder. Holmes was two years older than Reiser but couldn't help but watch his younger counterpart with a sense of awe. "There wasn't a thing he couldn't do on that ballfield," Holmes said years later. "He had already led the league in hitting and was well on his way to doing it again . . . I always admired him, from the first moment I saw him. We were both center fielders, built about the same. But I'll be frank, that's where the resemblance ended. He could hit a ball twice as far as I could; he could run fast as twice as I could."

Holmes was obviously exaggerating. He was an excellent ballplayer who spent a decade with the Braves and even led the National League in hits and home runs in 1945. But his respect for Pete's talents was real and widely shared. "The feeling about him in 1942," Holmes said, "was that he was as great a star as there was in the game."

* * *

Now it was the second day of June, and after an overnight train ride from Brooklyn, the Dodgers prepared to take on the Pirates in Pittsburgh. Even with Pete and the Dodgers tearing up the league, it's safe to say this Tuesday afternoon contest was off the edge of most people's radar. Waves of fresh war news splashed across U.S. newspapers that day. In Europe, hundreds lay dead after Britain carried out "thousand bomber" raids on industrial parts of Germany the previous two nights; one raid leveled an estimated three thousand buildings in Cologne. In Africa, British and German tank forces clashed in the sands of northern Libya, with the British claiming they had the upper hand over the Nazis' famed "Desert Fox," General Edwin Rommel. Across the United States, the war effort was gaining momentum, as reflected in stories about war bond sales, scrap metal drives, victory gardens, and rising arms production. The unions were especially happy: "Factory Workers' Wages Double Boom Year of '29," shouted a headline in that day's *Pittsburgh Press*.

The good news was tempered by the sinking of tankers and freighters by German submarines prowling the eastern seaboard. More than one hundred twenty U.S. and Allied ships had gone down off the Atlantic coast since mid-January, taking the lives of over a thousand merchant seamen, with many more rescued from the freezing cold waters. On Monday night, as the Dodgers' train chugged toward Pittsburgh, German sub *U-404* claimed its second vessel in three days, shelling and sinking the merchant ship *West Notus* three hundred twenty miles off the coast of Cape Hatteras, North Carolina. The loss would not be reported for half a week until other ships picked up the survivors from lifeboats and ferried them to New York.

More than five thousand miles to the west, events of even greater significance were starting to unfold. An armada of Japanese warships, led by four aircraft carriers, was steaming toward Midway Island, a lonely but strategically important U.S. outpost in the central Pacific. The Imperial Japanese Navy planned to bomb and invade the island in an attempt to lure the U.S. fleet, already weakened by the bombing at Pearl Harbor, into a destructive battle that would clear the way for further Japanese conquests in the Pacific. The sailors of the IJN had no clue that American intelligence had cracked their messaging codes and knew the attack was coming. Two days later, U.S. forces—at a loss of more than one hundred fifty planes and three hundred men—would send all four carriers to the bottom of the ocean. The American victory in the Battle of Midway dealt a crippling blow to Japanese capabilities and ultimately turned the tide of the war in the Pacific.

In Pittsburgh, probably none of this was on the mind of Frankie Frisch. Frisch was a baseball lifer, a future Hall of Fame second baseman who had played on eight pennant winners and four world champions for the Cardinals and the New York Giants. Now stuck managing the more modestly talented Pirates, he just wanted to light a spark under his sagging team. His best starters had been getting hammered lately, so he decided to pitch a second-year swingman, Lefty Wilkie, who had managed to beat the Dodgers in a shaky, twelve-hit complete game a month earlier. Frisch's real concern was his offense, which had been weakened by the offseason trade of hard-hitting Arky Vaughn to the Dodgers for a quartet of forgettable players. In recent days, the Pirates had been lucky to scratch out two runs per game. The situation was so bad that Frisch had taken to comically asking waiters, autograph seekers, and other random folks, "Hey, can YOU hit?"

There weren't too many people around to ask, though. When the gates of Forbes Field opened that afternoon, fewer than thirty-three hundred diehard fans pushed through the turnstiles to see if the Pirates could snap their losing skid.

As it turned out, they couldn't. However, those in attendance got to see a world-class bombardment by the USS Reiser.

His first time up, Pete doubled down the left-field line to score Vaughn. In his second at-bat, he blasted a Wilkie pitch into the upper deck of the right-field stands. The third time up, he singled, zipped to third on a Joe Medwick hit, and scored on a groundout. At-bat number four resulted in an RBI double off the right-field wall. Fifth time up: another double off the same wall. "Every blow was a solid line drive save the first, which was a hot grounder just inside third base," reported the *New York Times*.

Reiser's teammates were pounding the ball as well, and by the top of the seventh inning, Brooklyn had built a 14-2 lead. Durocher removed several regulars to give them a rest, but not Reiser, who characteristically kept playing, and playing at full intensity. After his second double of the day, he scampered to third on a sacrifice fly. And when Frenchy Bordagaray tapped a roller toward third baseman Bob Elliott, Pete didn't hesitate—he broke for home like it was the ninth inning of the seventh game of the World Series, and irate fans would shoot him if he didn't score.

Elliott scooped up the ball and whipped it to catcher Al Lopez, who tossed aside his mask, caught the throw, and tagged out the sliding Reiser. During the slide, Pete's left foot made what McGowen described as "violent contact" with the discarded mask. Visions of his star snapping an ankle must have flashed through Durocher's mind. But Pete's luck held; he emerged from the play hobbling but able to walk. Just a bruised instep, it turned out.

The injury gave Durocher a good excuse to remove Pete from the game. He had done his work: five hits in five times up, three runs scored, three RBI, and eleven total bases on the day. The Dodgers won 17-2. It was the most runs scored by any team in a National League game that season.

Pete made headlines on sports pages across the nation the next morning. Some of the most colorful: "Pete Reiser Stars as Frisch Growls" . . . "Dodgers Playing Like Yankees in National; Pete Reiser is Hero" . . . "Reiser's Murderous Bat Produces Five for Five" . . . "Reiser Grabs a Perfect Day." This was nothing new. Pete's name had been helping to fill newspaper columns since he burst on the scene in spring training 1939, an unheralded minor leaguer who got a chance to play and proceeded to get on base his first eleven times at-bat, with three walks, five singles, and a trio of home runs. But now, because of performances like this, he was on the road to celebrity. He was starting to get endorsement deals—for Wheaties, for Spalding bats, for a Reiser-branded baseball glove—and had made a handful of appearances on the nighttime network radio shows, like CBS's "Vox Pop" and NBC's "Your Happy Birthday." The national magazines were paying attention too. Late in the '41 season, *Collier's* recapped his young life for its approximately two-point-five million readers. Tom Meany was beginning to write a more in-depth piece for the *Saturday Evening Post* and its even bigger circulation of three million-plus. A new periodical called *Baseball Digest* would shortly prepare a cover story on Pistol Pete. And the venerable Street & Smith publishing company was getting ready to tell his tale in comic book form as part of its *True Sport* series.

The Dodgers hoped to renew their assault on the Pirates pitching staff on Wednesday, but the game was rained out. The postponement allowed reporters traveling with the team to chat up the players about the superstar in their midst. Pete's teammates didn't mind pouring on the praise. "Pete is hitting the ball like the champion he is," said first baseman Dolph Camilli, the Dodgers' top home run hitter, and the reigning National League MVP. "Yes, and he's getting his hits on real good pitches, no soft stuff," chimed in Joe Medwick, another past MVP.

Catcher Mickey Owen went further: "He's so far ahead of all the other hitters in our league it's no contest. He'll win the batting championship again this year, and I look for him to finish on top with a much higher batting average than he had when he won last season. If he has a batting weakness, I don't know what it is. Pitch the ball to him inside, outside, high or low, and he'll hit it. I've seen him get base hits on every kind of pitch."

The strongest acclaim of all came from the Dodgers' first base coach, John "Red" Corriden. Corriden was a veteran of over three decades in pro ball. As a young man in the 1910s, he had played with or against all-time greats like Cobb, Wagner, Walter Johnson, and Shoeless Joe Jackson. He was not known for giving excessive praise to modern-day players, noted *Daily News* writer Hy Turkin. But after seeing Reiser's dismantling of the Pirates, Corriden couldn't hold back. "Reiser isn't just a hard hitter. He's one of the greatest all-around players I have ever seen in the thirty-five years I've been in baseball," he told Turkin. "He can hit, run, catch and throw with the best, and he has the calm aggressiveness that would make even a mediocre player good."

Corriden liked Reiser's attitude just as much as his talents: "The boy has a great disposition. He started the year poorly but never let the slump affect his hustle. He doesn't talk much, and he's no 'I' guy. No matter what the score, he only plays one way—hard! But he's a stocky, sturdy athlete, the kind that will never be sidelined for long by any injury."

The old coach's description of Reiser was bull's eye perfect. As for the last comment, it was true in ways Corriden could not have known.

In later years, Reiser spoke of a streak in '42 where he got an incredible nineteen hits in twenty-one at-bats. That never happened. But his memory wasn't all that far off. Including the doubleheader against the Braves, Pete had now racked up eleven hits in his last thirteen times up, hoisting his batting average to a league-leading .366. Over his previous twenty games, he had averaged an eye-popping .461, with half of his hits going for extra bases. Given this run of near-perfection, Pete can't be faulted for putting aside modesty as an older man and making some retrospective boasts. "[I was] just starting to get warm," he said in the 1970s to Donald Honig, by then an established baseball historian. "Just starting to get the bead on everybody. I could've hit .400 that year. No doubt in my mind about that." Neither Honig nor other writers who heard Reiser make that claim offered a rebuttal; given Reiser's talents and drive, .400 was within the realm of possibility.

It was no surprise when National League managers unanimously picked Pete for the '42 All-Star Game and named him the NL's starting center fielder for the second straight year. Reiser did nothing special in the contest at the Polo Grounds, managing a single in three at-bats. But two moments demonstrated his growing stature. One came when he posed with Ted Williams for the newsreel cameras. Pete showed Ted his batting grip, and the film caught Ted looking down at Pete's hands—indicating that maybe, the greatest hitter of all time thought he could learn something from the NL batting champ. The other was a pre-game photo of Reiser with the game's heaviest hitters—Williams, DiMaggio, Medwick, and the Yankees' Joe Gordon. One year earlier, the photographer would have saved the center spot for DiMaggio, whose batting streak had turned him into a national idol. Or he might have arranged the men around Williams, easily the tallest of the group and unquestionably the best hitter.

But on this day, DiMaggio and Williams were pushed to the side. In the center of the photo, surrounded by four future residents of Cooperstown, two of them among the greatest players of all time, stood Pistol Pete Reiser.

He was the smallest of the five, and to current-day fans he is probably the least well-known. But it's hard to miss the muscular right forearm holding his bat or the confident gleam in his eyes. He had no doubt he belonged in this circle. And given his place of honor in the shot, a casual observer might conclude that in July 1942, less than two years after he arrived in the major leagues, Pete Reiser reigned as the very best player in all of baseball.

2
Like Father, Like Son

In an alternate universe—one without hard, unforgiving outfield walls—the home at 3018 North Taylor Avenue in St. Louis, Missouri, might be known as the Pete Reiser House. There, it would be the site of a museum, or at least a large bronze plaque, extolling the greatness of the wonder boy athlete who once ran through its hallways and burst out the front door on many a summer morning, running to join his friends for marathon games of baseball, in preparation for the career that made him the idol of millions and one of the greatest players in major league baseball history.

This is not that universe, and the house, as of this writing, is not home to anything except rats or squatters. In fact, 3018 North Taylor looks as though no one has lived there for decades. Judging from the photos available online, its red brick façade is in decent shape; give it a little scrubbing and patching, and a real estate agent could pass it off as attractively retro. But most potential homebuyers would still be turned off by the boarded-up windows, gutted interior, peeling paint, weed-choked lawn, and overgrown, gnarled trees, which when stripped of their leaves in the winter loom over the property like towers of tangled barbed wire. Several other homes on the block are in the same condition, or worse.

The Reiser home is currently owned by St. Louis Land Reutilization Authority (LRA), a government agency tasked with managing city properties abandoned by their owners. As of 2021, anyone could purchase the aged house for a mere one thousand dollars—far less than its estimated value even in the 1930s, in the depths of the Great Depression. The LRA controls more than twelve thousand similar properties around the city, a testament to St. Louis' steep population decline since the mid-20th century. The phenomenon is especially pronounced in the Reisers' old neighborhood, known as the Greater Ville, littered with empty, crumbling homes and vacant lots where such homes were recently demolished. Some civic-minded groups and individuals are trying to revive the area by rebuilding some old houses and tearing down others on the verge of collapse. But violent crime has so far undercut their efforts. Since the mid-2010s, the Greater Ville has been the site of ten to twenty murders per year, a shockingly high number for an area with just a few thousand people, nearly all poor and Black. A website focused on gun violence, The Trace, noted in 2016 that the murder rate there was three times higher than in Honduras, which news outlets have often labeled "the murder capital of the world."

So, to execute a proper dive into the Pete Reiser story, one must put aside the grim statistics and scarred avenues of the current-day Greater Ville and envision a world that has vanished. For there was a time, not all that long ago, before urban decay and suburban growth and white flight hollowed out St. Louis when the Greater Ville and neighborhoods nearby housed tens of thousands of families. Most of them were middle class or working class, trying to get ahead in a city humming with industry, trade, and jobs. And one of those families was headed by a man named George John Reiser.

George had grown up poor in DeSoto, Missouri, a tiny, railroad-centered town about fifty miles southwest of St. Louis. His father, John Reiser, was a German immigrant from Bavaria who spent decades bouncing around Missouri, working on farms, roads, quarries—any type of place that needed an able pair of hands. John married and raised one family, and when his first wife died, he married again and started another one. By the time George was born in 1883, John was fifty-eight, and his earning power was limited by the loss of his left eye, which had been pierced by a flying chip of stone during a house-building project, and the lasting pain from a Civil War injury, when he was thrown from a horse at a Union base in St. Louis, breaking three ribs on his left side. John's infirmities forced his second wife Antonia—herself an immigrant from Bohemia, in what is now the Czech Republic—to take in neighbors' laundry to supplement John's war pension and whatever money he picked up doing odd jobs. No doubt trying to escape this life of scraping by, George moved to St. Louis a few years after his dad died in 1900. In his twenties, he joined a large commercial printing firm, Woodward & Tiernan, and became the very definition of a company man, starting with W&T in 1910 as a stock clerk, rising to warehouse foreman, and holding that post for decades until he retired in 1952.

But ultimately, the warehouse job was to pay the bills. Like many Americans back then and now, George's passion was baseball.

A stocky, five-foot-ten right-handed pitcher, George had some talent for the game. In the spring of 1907, at age twenty-three, he joined the Repples, a squad in the Trolley League, St. Louis's highly competitive semipro circuit. The Repples finished seventh in an eight-team league, undone by weak hitting and even weaker glove work; the team finished with a sub-.900 fielding percentage. But young George gained good press notices. A *St. Louis Globe-Democrat* story called him and a teammate "two of the best twirlers in the league," and on the final Sunday of the season, he mowed down his opponents for a 4-0 shutout. "Reiser pitched great ball for the winners, allowing but one hit, which was of the scratch variety," reported the *Globe-Democrat*. His final record was 4-13, but his ninety-nine strikeouts ranked third in the league.

The following April, George left home to take a fling at professional ball. The Winnipeg Maroons, a team in the Northern League—class-D ball, the lowest rung of the minors—had offered him a tryout. He joined the squad at spring training in Quincy, Illinois, and stayed with them as they barnstormed north through Minnesota. The sketchy press reports that survive suggest it didn't go well:

> *April 30*: "Reiser, the pitcher, who was holding down right field, contributed a dumb play, holding the ball on a hit to his territory, and allowing two runners to score."
>
> *May 9*: "Reiser was on the mound for the Maroons, and the collegians found him for seven hits, three of which were two-baggers. His support was off-color at times, and the men showed lack of experience together."
>
> *May 12*: "Reiser was let go in Minneapolis . . ."

George made his way back to St. Louis and rejoined the Repples. But in August, he was off again, this time for a stint with the Argenta Shamrocks, a team in the class D Arkansas State League. Newspaper reports indicate that again, George's experience was brutal and short:

> *August 9*: "The Vaporites won the third game of the series from the Shamrocks this afternoon, batting Reiser the Trolley League pitcher from the box."
>
> *August 12*: "Bevans for the visitors and Reiser for the locals started the game, but neither was effective . . . Reiser lasted nearly four innings when ex-manager Reese assumed the responsibilities of the hurling hill."
>
> *August 13*: "Pitcher Reiser of the Argenta club was released last night . . ."

George trudged home to St. Louis a second time, his dreams of a professional baseball career laid to rest. He pitched a few more games for the Repples but his 1908 Trolley League stats—zero wins, eight losses, and a nearly one-to-one ratio of walks to strikeouts—suggest that any magic which might have coursed through his pitching arm had dried up.

Instead, George settled into family life. Between his trips to Quincy and Argenta, he had applied for a St. Louis marriage license in July and tied the knot with 22-year-old Stella Boody. The two probably knew each other from childhood; "The families were friends-slash-neighbors in DeSoto," says Gerry Meier, a cousin of Reiser's who has done extensive genealogical research on the family. The following January, Stella gave birth to the couple's first son, Ralph, followed by a flock of eleven more children over the next two decades. Three of the kids died in infancy, but arrival number seven was a healthy male child, born on St. Patrick's Day, March 17th, 1919, and thus christened Harold Patrick Reiser.

The name underwent some early alterations. By the time he was in grade school, "Harold" had fallen away, replaced by the more athletic-sounding "Pete." Sportswriter Tom Meany wrote that Reiser got his nickname from a Western movie serial, "the central figure of which was a virile son of the saddle named Pistol Pete." Stella remembered it a bit differently: "I think the Pete came from the fact that he used to play cowboy a lot when he was a youngster. He was Two-Gun Pete to the boys." The name "Two-Gun Pete" was a moniker often bestowed on characters in Western stories and movies. It gained wider currency the year before Reiser's birth when a stagecoach bandit using that name in Arizona was disarmed and arrested by—in a novelty for the times—a female deputy sheriff.

Pete's surname never changed, but the sound of it did. Reiser is a German name, and its spelling and origins indicate it should be pronounced with an "eye" sound, like "Riser." But at some undetermined point, George and other family members began to verbalize it with an "ee" instead. "George . . . insists that the name is pronounced 'Reeser,'" noted a 1941 *St. Louis Post-Dispatch* article. The change could have been prompted by the strong wave of anti-German sentiment that swept the U.S. during World War I. Or maybe George and his relatives just thought the "ee" sound had a better ring.

From an early age, Pete demonstrated a fighting spirit. Donald Honig, a lifelong, passionate Reiser fan, once asked his idol what he was like as a child. "Ornery, mean, nice. A mean nice kid. I had a bad temper," Reiser explained, none too clearly. The family had his grandfather's cavalry sword around the house, he recalled. "I'd get mad once in a while and chase my sisters and anybody else who was in the way with that sword. Just to scare 'em," he said. Not that Pete was interested in hurting anyone; he just wanted always to prevail, as he explained in his talk with son-in-law Rick Tuber: "I was born in a rough neighborhood. And we used to fight. We knocked guys on their rear ends in every sport. We were mean. I say mean—we wanted to win. And wanting to win makes you mean a little bit. Even coaches today say, 'He's not mean enough to win.' They don't mean he's a killer."

Outside baseball, his life was centered around church. The Reisers were a strongly Catholic family who sent their kids to parochial schools and attended services every Sunday, as a Brooklyn Catholic weekly, *The Tablet*, noted approvingly during Pete's breakout season of 1941. "Harold Patrick was an altar boy at Holy Ghost Church. He served Mass for eight years and still knows how to serve," the paper said. Pete's daughter Shirley confirms the family's strong Catholicism. "Yes, yes—double yes," she says with a laugh. "Went to church every Sunday, didn't eat meat on Friday when that was the rule. Couple of my aunts, you'd walk in, and there's a statue of the Blessed Virgin and crosses hanging. It was very much a part of who they were, and how they were raised, and how I was raised."

However, it's safe to say that baseball was of equal if not greater importance in George Reiser's worldview. "As soon as you were old enough, he put a ball in your hand," Pete once said. His older sister Julie concurred. "We were a baseball-playing family," she told author Sidney Jacobson. "All of us kids played ball, but Pete had it in his blood. That's all he wanted to do." George was happy to oblige his son, starting with games of catch in the backyard and graduating to hours of batting and fielding practice, usually at one of two nearby locales: Sherman Park or the Fairgrounds, the site of the 1904 St. Louis World's Fair. This was the era before Little League, but Pete got plenty of game action through pickup games with his buddies at the Holy Ghost Parochial School and a neighborhood club, the Phantoms. "He was the dirtiest kid in the neighborhood, always coming home with his baseball uniform, socks, and shoes full of mud," remembered his mother. "I think he did a lot of sliding just to get dirty."

The whole city was somewhat baseball-mad. Each weekend, ballfields around the city were jammed with boys and young men, playing for every manner of church, school, union, factory, business, fraternity, and YMCA team found under the St. Louis sun. A single page of the Sunday *Post-Dispatch* might contain up to thirty-five box scores from the previous day's "Municipal League" action. Not surprisingly, the city turned into a gusher of top baseball talent. Over 300 major leaguers have been born or raised in "The Lou," including 21st-century notables like three-time Cy Young award winner Max Scherzer and 2006 National League MVP Ryan Howard. Reiser's high school, the now-shuttered William Beaumont, produced thirteen major league players alone, including 1957 American League home run champ Roy Sievers, 1960s ace relief pitcher Bob Miller, early Los Angeles Angels slugger Lee Thomas, and combative Hall of Fame manager Earl Weaver. From another neighborhood a few blocks south, the Hill—sometimes called "Dago Hill" for its large population of Italian immigrants—came the city's most famous baseball products: catcher-turned-broadcaster Joe Garagiola and his childhood buddy, Yogi Berra, a three-time American League MVP and the backbone of fourteen Yankee pennant winners. Berra is still considered one of the five best backstops in baseball history. Garagiola, a nine-year National League journeyman before launching his long TV career, used to joke: "Not only was I not the best catcher in the major leagues, I wasn't even the best catcher on my street!"

Reiser often played catcher as a kid and later said his "secret regret" was that he never got to play the position in the big leagues. ("He was a good one too," said his father. "As agile as a cat, and he could throw harder than the pitchers he caught.") But squatting behind home plate would be a misuse of his talents. From an early age, three things about Pete were obvious: he was strong, extremely well-coordinated, and born to run. He soon found these skills propelled him ahead of his peers in just about any sport he tried. "Sure, I wanted to be a ballplayer when I was a kid, but it wasn't my first love. Football was," he told Honig. "My ambition was to be the greatest football player Notre Dame ever had. When I was ten, I was competing in football against fifteen-year-olds, running right over them." Pete told another writer that he ran dashes and relays for his high school freshman track squad and was set to be the team's number one-sprinter but was declared ineligible by school officials. His violation? Accepting fifty dollars to play in local soccer games against adults, under the name of Murphy. It was a "sucker" thing to do, he said, but how could he resist the money? His dad was making just twenty-five dollars per week at the printing plant. "I was a hell of a soccer player, too," Pete boasted.

But the other sports were ultimately infatuations. Baseball was Reiser's true love. He was carried along in this not only by his father but also by one of his brothers. George Michael Reiser, born in May 1914 and known to all as Mike, scampered onto the St. Louis ballfields a few years earlier than Pete and demonstrated an equal or greater level of skill, at least in Pete's estimation. "I was always a pretty good ballplayer, but the real ballplayer in my family was my older brother Mike. Mike could do everything, and then some . . . he was my hero," Pete told Honig.

Pete's daughter Shirley heard the same scouting report. "My dad idolized Mike," she says. "I'm pretty sure if Mike was that much older, my dad kind of followed him around. He always, always mentioned him and said he was a better ballplayer than himself." There's at least one surviving photo of Mike in a mid-1920s, black-and-white portrait of the Reiser family dressed in their Sunday finest. Mike stands at the top center, dressed in a suit and tie, reddish-looking hair parted down the middle, smiling genially for the camera. The shot reveals nothing about his baseball skills other than to suggest he would be tall and had a lot of confidence in his eyes, not unlike his younger brother.

Mike was responsible for one of Pete's most unique if overhyped talents. Pete was a natural righty, but he sometimes surprised spectators and teammates by firing hard throws with his left hand during pre-game warmups. He said he learned the trick from Mike. "My brother was really good at it," he explained. "He could throw either hand from any position. I picked it up from him and was surprising how quickly it could be acquired. It is not at all difficult." That's not to say Pete threw as well with his left hand as he did with his right. Reporters who saw his southpaw throws said they had plenty of oomph but lacked something in accuracy. That's probably why there's no known record of him throwing lefty during a game, despite his claims to have done so, if only in the minors or spring training.

Mike had one other lasting effect on his younger brother by stoking his already brightly burning competitive fires. Sometimes, Mike would bring him along to play against fifteen and sixteen-year-olds, several years older than Pete. "The other guys would say, 'What's this kid doing here?' My brother said, 'He'll show you,'" Pete recalled. Pete did not want to disappoint his hero and strained to keep up with the older kids. Later, he traced his famed on-field intensity to those afternoons. "So maybe it started there," he said, "having to try hard, hard and harder, to prove to him, to live up to the expectations of somebody who you admired the hell out of, and to keep on proving it."

Tellingly, he added: "And I always felt I could do better than I was doing. There was no limit. I couldn't wait from one day to another to get out there and prove it."

In Pete's view, there should have been two Reisers in the major leagues. According to Pete, Mike signed a contract with the Yankees in 1930, when he was just sixteen years old, and planned to report to spring training with a Yankee minor league club in 1931. The story appears impossible to verify but is plausible. The name Reiser turns up in numerous box scores for St. Louis Municipal League games between 1928 and 1930 when Mike was in his mid-teens. Yankee scouts might have watched him play and liked what they saw. "Back then, the scouts were roaming around those St. Louis neighborhoods, and it didn't matter how old you were," says Shirley. The Yankees were just establishing their farm system, having bought a class-D team in Chambersburg, Pennsylvania, before the '29 season. Even before then, they had working agreements with other minor-league clubs to train and develop young players.

However, Mike never got a chance to launch a career. In January 1931, he came down with scarlet fever, a severe illness often life-threatening in the days before antibiotics. Pete said he caught scarlet fever, too, after disregarding orders to stay out of the room where Mike was resting. He said both of them ended up with throat infections and that a doctor lanced their throats to remove a build-up of pus. "Operated on both of us right in the house," Pete told Honig.

What follows is Pete's dramatic telling of what happened next, in the wee hours of a St. Louis winter morning.

> "The doctor was more concerned about my condition than Mike's, and he told my parents to watch me, that I could have a rough night. So, I was the one everybody was worried about. About two o'clock in the morning, my brother asked me how I was. I told him all right. 'Well,' he said, 'I've got something in my throat. I've got to get a drink.' And then he coughed, and the blood just came rushing out. I screamed for my mother, and she came running in. It was terrible. She yelled for somebody to get a priest. I ran out of the house in my bare feet. It was snowing out. I ran for twelve blocks. I got to the door of the rectory and pounded on it. When they opened the door, I said, 'My brother is dying.' Then I collapsed."
>
> "I woke up the next morning in the hospital, not a damn thing wrong with me. My throat was almost healed. Perfect health. It was a miracle. It had to be. I was the one who was supposed to have the hemorrhage, not him. That's what the doctor said. We both should have been in the hospital, but there was no money for that. He was some kind of ballplayer, my brother Mike. But I guess it just wasn't meant to be."

By the phrase "wasn't meant to be," Pete meant that Mike had passed away. He was buried two days later at Cavalry Cemetery in St. Louis, where he rests today next to his parents.

Let's pause for a second, for this is another point in the Reiser saga that my journalistic soul spoke up and said, "Take a closer look." Pete's story is packed with theatrical details: an at-home operation, a sudden hemorrhage, a cry for help, a frantic nighttime run through the snow, a miracle recovery for one brother while the other boy dies. It sounds like a scene in a movie, not unlike some other tales that Reiser liked to tell about himself, especially when he chatted with admiring sportswriters. More than one reporter noted that he had a gift for gab and knack for storytelling; Honig said his 1974 interview with Reiser partially fueled with whiskey stretched on for nearly eight hours, as Pete spun out one anecdote after another. And as anyone who has done oral history interviews can attest, some storytellers like to embellish their tales, throwing in sudden turns and colorful twists to hold the listener's interest. If any details might bog down or complicate the story, they often get shooed away, like a pesky fly.

That said, the basic facts behind this particular story turn out to be true. Mike Reiser's official Missouri death certificate says he died at 2:30 A.M. at his parents' home on the morning of January 30, 1931. The cause of death was listed as "post tonsillar abscess," meaning complications from an infection that had started in Mike's tonsils, then spread to his throat and beyond. Scarlet fever was listed as a contributing cause.

As for Pete's account of running barefoot through the snow to get a priest, then waking up in the hospital—who's to know? There are no contemporary or near-contemporary accounts to confirm the details, only Pete's recollections more than forty years later. All one can say is that it's not hard to picture a young Pete Reiser racing through the streets of St. Louis, and not hard to see him bouncing back quickly from illness or injury, even one that threatened his life.

* * *

"Behind the three-hit pitching of Harold Reiser, the Holy Ghost nine trimmed the St. Rose team 3 to 2. Reiser struck out 14 and walked only one man." —St. Louis Post-Dispatch, *June 4, 1933*

Mike's death did nothing to derail Pete's athletic career. If anything, Pete threw himself more deeply into sports, especially baseball. In the fall of 1933, he left Holy Ghost parochial school and entered Beaumont High. But he showed no particular interest in academics and clubs. His daily routine in the summer after ninth grade illustrates his priorities. "All morning and early afternoon," he said, "I'd play ball at the Fairgrounds or Sherman Park. At 2:30, I'd head for the big-league game. I was a member of the Knothole Gang [for kids] and didn't have to pay to get in. That is, except on Saturdays and Sundays. Those days I'd play ball all day."

Pete could maintain this all-baseball, all-the-time schedule because St. Louis then had two major league franchises: the Browns in the American League and the Cardinals in the National. Almost every day from mid-April to late September, one team or the other played at the stadium they shared, Sportsman's Park, located about a mile and a quarter east of the Reisers' home, an easy walk or bike ride for an energetic fifteen-year-old like Pete. Sportsman's Park was not the greatest place to watch a ballgame; the non-stop use left the playing field torn up and brown, and in that era before night baseball, fans had to endure St. Louis's mid-day summer heat and oppressive humidity. But Pete picked the perfect year to hang out at the ballpark, for 1934 was the year of the Cardinals' legendary "Gas House Gang." All summer long, sitting in the bleachers, Pete and pals watched the Cards scratch and claw their way to a National League pennant, often utilizing hard slides, brushback pitches, and rough-edged trash talk to unsettle their opponents before beating them with timely hits and shutdown pitching. Dizzy Dean was the tobacco-chewing, wisecracking, fireballing ace of the pitching staff, and freely bragged that he and his brother ("Me n' Paul") would pitch the Cardinals into the World Series—which they did, on the strength of forty-nine victories between them, more than half the team's win total. The pair then accounted for all four wins as the Cardinals beat the Detroit Tigers in an exciting seven-game World Series.

However, Pete's favorite Cardinal was the left fielder, Joe "Ducky" Medwick, who hit .319 with eighteen homers and a league-leading eighteen triples that season. Ducky was a deceptive nickname; in reality, Medwick could be sullen and short-tempered; his other nickname was "Muscles." In the seventh game of the World Series in Detroit, with the Cardinals leading 9-0, he slid hard into Tiger third baseman Marv Owen, and the two exchanged punches. When Medwick went out to his spot in left field the next inning, Tiger fans showered him with fruit, pop bottles, and trash and refused to stop despite appeals from Tigers officials and players. Over the Cardinals' protests, baseball commissioner Judge Kenesaw Mountain Landis finally ordered Medwick to be removed from the game for his own safety. Medwick complied but hurled his glove into the dugout in a show of disgust.

Pete didn't care about incidents like that. He admired Medwick's prodigious slugging. In '35, Medwick lifted his average to .353, and two years hence he'd capture the National League triple crown, leading the league in batting average (.374), homers (31), and runs batted in (154). "I used to sit out there with the Knothole Gang on those hot St. Louis afternoons and watch Joe go to town," Pete recalled. "I kept track of everything he did in those days. He was my hero. I wanted to become a player like him." Little did Pete know that in a few years, he would be Medwick's teammate.

The '34 season marked the Cardinals' fifth pennant and third World Series title in nine years. Most observers agreed on the reason for the Cards' success: their minor league network, universally called the farm system, pioneered by the team's general manager, Branch Rickey. Over the previous fifteen years, the Cardinals had built up an unmatched organization of scouts and coaches to find and train the best young ballplayers in America. Before Rickey's brainstorm, major league teams employed scouts but discovered many of their players by keeping tabs on the prominent high school and college teams and getting tips from fans and associates around the country. If a young player drew a lot of attention, a bidding war for his services would inevitably erupt, which the Cardinals, one of the National League's financially weaker operations, usually lost to richer teams, like the Giants, Yankees, and Cubs.

Rickey's groundbreaking idea was to sidestep that process by casting a vast, nationwide net for good ballplayers, signing them up as teenagers for small salaries, and developing them on minor league squads that the Cardinals either owned or controlled. Famed baseball announcer Red Barber, who later worked for Rickey in Brooklyn, summed up his boss's thinking this way: "He said, 'I can't compete financially with these other people, I don't have the money. There must be some way I can compete.' [He decided,] "I can be patient, I can create a core of scouts, I can send them around the country. I can have training camps, I can select the best of these young players, I can have a lot of minor league teams, and I can have my managers as teachers, and their job is not so much to win a game or a pennant but to train these players to play the way I want them to play."

Not everyone liked Rickey's concept. Critics, the most notable of whom was Commissioner Landis, said the Cardinals were running a "chain gang" that hurt competitive balance at both the major and minor league levels and kept good players stuck in the minors earning peanuts. Landis in particular thought major league ownership made minor league teams less interesting to their local fans. "How can you expect a man to go out and throw his hat into the air and root for a team when he knows that the team is owned by someone a thousand miles away and that he is cheering and backing their interests, and not those of his own community?" Landis said at a December 1929 banquet. "We ought to get back to a situation where a man can think about the town's club as his own, and there is old-time traditional rivalry between the neighboring towns." But Rickey's critics were outnumbered by Rickey's admirers, who sometimes termed him a genius—though Rickey himself said the farm system was created out of "stark necessity," to give the Cardinals an affordable supply of able ballplayers.

The system worked because Rickey hired top-notch scouts. His chief talent-hunter—"ivory hunter" in the jargon of the day—was Charley Barrett, a bespectacled, usually smiling former minor league journeyman who joined the Cards in 1919 after a decade scouting for the Browns and Detroit Tigers. Barrett's nickname was "King of the Weeds." He earned it by spending some thirty years on the backroads of America, passing through nearly every town and village, visiting every type of sandlot and old-time wooden ballpark the country had to offer, in a search for players who might make the major league grade. "He knows the Midwest so well that he can identify every barn within a one hundred miles radius of the Mississippi River," joked one sportswriter in a 1931 profile of the scout. More importantly, Barrett could identify good ballplayers who lived near those barns and was adept at convincing them to sign with the Cardinals. The team's first World Series champion, in 1926, featured four regulars signed by Barrett, including a future Hall of Famer in first baseman Jim Bottomley. Another Barrett discovery, Pepper Martin, sparked the Cards to an upset victory in the 1931 Series, scorching the two-time champion Philadelphia A's for a dozen hits and five stolen bases. Martin thanked Charley publicly after the series and did so regularly for years thereafter.

A few times per year, Barrett would come off the road to help run a mass tryout for aspiring ballplayers. The Cardinals held such events periodically in St. Louis and nearby cities, hoping to pluck rough diamonds from the rich baseball fields of the Midwest. Word of the affair would appear in the local papers: "Boys wishing tryouts . . . should present themselves at nine o'clock tomorrow morning, bringing their baseball shoes, gloves and uniforms," read a typical announcement. No registration was needed, no fee was charged. Not surprisingly, hundreds of boys might show up, far too many for the Cards to give each one a thorough look. Instead, scouts would reduce the tryout to a few basic drills—a sixty-yard dash, a few throws from the infield or outfield, maybe three swings at the plate –to separate the might-bes from the never-wills. Under the circumstances, a player had to show genuine talent instantly or get lost in the crowd.

One day, when Pete was in his mid-teens, George Reiser saw a notice for a Cardinal tryout and suggested that his son give it a shot. Pete's formal education had ended by then. He later told a reporter he quit school in the spring of 1935, his sophomore year after a throat infection kept him home for three weeks; when he got better, he simply didn't go back. If he had plans to while away another summer at Sportsman's Park, George derailed them, making him get a job at Woodward & Tiernan. The teenage Pete became a five-day, forty-hours-per-week factory worker, taking masses of paper products and wiring them into bundles. His pay was sixteen dollars per week. It was useful money for a big family like the Reisers during the Depression. But both he and George knew that his future was not inside a printing plant.

Pete showed up for the tryout at Public Schools Stadium, a football and track facility on Kings Highway Boulevard that the St. Louis high schools shared. As usual, several hundred would-be Cardinals had turned out, hoping to pursue their big-league dreams. Pete could tell he was one of the youngest boys there but plunged ahead. He ran the dash, made his throws, got his swings. And then . . .

And then Pete told different stories about what happened next. In one version, Charley Barrett walked up to Pete after watching him field a single grounder and fire a bullet to first base. "Do you want to want to play pro baseball?" the old scout asked. When Pete stammered yes, Barrett allegedly pulled a blank contract out of his pocket, pressed it into Pete's hands, and told him to get permission from his dad.

In another version, Barrett offered the contract after seeing Pete's *second* throw.

In still another, more dramatic version, the Cardinals sent Pete home after a few hours at the tryout. Pete assumed it was because the scouts were unimpressed. "I told my father, 'Well, I guess I'm not as good as I thought I was.' 'Don't worry about it,' he said. 'You're only fifteen years old.'" But a couple of days later, according to Pete, a big Buick pulled up in front of the Reisers' home on North Taylor. Out stepped Charley Barrett, who knocked on the front door, introduced himself, and said he wanted to talk with George about his son.

Pete picked up the story:

> "'Well, I want to talk to you too,' Dad says. 'Why'd you cut him [at the tryout]?'
> 'We didn't want anyone else to see him,' Charley says. 'That's why we didn't ask him to come back. We know who he is.'
> It turned out they'd been watching me play ball since grade school. They never said anything because they didn't want anyone else to know they were interested until they could sign me. You see, in those days, if the Cardinals showed any interest in a kid, the other clubs would rush in and try to sign him, simply on the basis of the Cardinals' interest."

All of the stories sound a bit like baseball fairy tales but, in the end, are perfectly possible, given the level of Pete's talent and the astuteness of the Cardinals' scouting operation. Barrett and George Reiser turned out to be old acquaintances from the Trolley League days and settled down for a long chat. "The two of them proceeded to ignore me so completely that I began to wonder whether Charlie came to sign me or my dad," Pete joked. But after a few hours, George affixed his signature on the contract for his son, who was legally still a minor. His dad was ecstatic, and Pete was too. The team would pay him just fifty dollars per month, less than what he made at the printing plant. There was no signing bonus. George likely could have demanded more. But the new Cardinal farmhand didn't care.

"You know, when Pete got that contract, he ran out the front door and down the street showing it to everybody," Stella recalled a few years later. "He always has been just crazy to play ball."

Crazy committed . . . and crazy good, as the baseball world would soon learn.

3

Gentleman's Agreement

It's Saturday morning in the San Fernando Valley, and Pete Reiser is having a drink: a pre-lunch Bloody Mary, whipped up by his son-in-law Rick Tuber. Rick, who is enjoying a cocktail himself, has turned on a tape recorder which captures all the sounds echoing around his Van Nuys house: the chime of a grandfather clock, Pete's wife and daughters chatting in the kitchen, a TV blaring out a Vegas-style tune from Anthony Newley—"your favorite singer!" one of the women says to Pete in jest—and the men sipping and stirring their drinks, the ice cubes inside making a telltale *clink*.

Still, it's Pete's low, frayed smoker's voice that cuts through the audio clutter. The vodka has unlocked the vault of his memory, and at Rick's urging, he's telling stories of his early days in baseball, events that happened forty years earlier or more, during the Depression, before World War II. The pace is slow, the mood is relaxed, and Pete's words are coming out ever so slightly slurred—station becomes *sh*tation, to give one example. But there's a serious intent in his voice. There are things he's in the mood to talk about, things that shaped the course of his life and career, and since Rick is asking questions . . . Well, this is as good a time as any to put them down for the record.

"I wanted to be a Cardinal," he says, matter of factly. He remembers explaining this to Judge Kenesaw Mountain Landis, the white-maned, stern-faced, czar-like commissioner of baseball. "He said, 'You like the Cardinal organization?' I said, 'That's the only ballclub I'd play for.' [He said] 'Why?' [I said] 'I was born and raised in St. Louis; I've been a Cardinal fan.'" He doesn't bring it up, but for proof, Pete could refer to the baseball scrapbook that he and his sisters kept at the start of his career. Page one features a mid-1930s rendering of the team's familiar logo, a bright red Cardinal perched atop a baseball bat. The caption below says Pete got the emblem from the scout who signed him, Charley Barrett. One page over, there's a photo that would stun old-time Brooklyn fans: a beaming Pete Reiser in a white Cardinals uniform, flanked by his teammates on a St. Louis farm team in tiny Newport, Arkansas. The uniforms they sport are exactly what the big club wore at home in those years, complete with parallel lines of red piping down the front of the shirt. Replace the white 'N' on his cap with an interlocking 'STL', and Pete would be outfitted to play with any Cardinal team from the '30s or '40s, alongside stars like Musial, Medwick, and Dean.

But history tells us that upon reaching the majors, Pete Reiser starred for the Brooklyn Dodgers, not the St. Louis Cardinals. A curious Rick asks: how did you end up with the Dodgers? "Well, the best, ah . . ." Pete says, before pausing for another sip of his drink. He doesn't say it, but there's not a short answer here. He wasn't traded exactly—though he was. He wasn't released per se—though he was. He was declared a free agent, but he wasn't really free. There were other forces at play, beyond his control and largely beyond his knowledge, which tore him away and kept him away from the team he preferred. For a time, the same forces also blocked his advancement to the major leagues.

He keeps coming back to the phrase "gentleman's agreement," the term for an unwritten pact between two or more parties, enforced by honor instead of a legal contract. Such agreements were once common throughout American life, and they were used primarily for two things: price-fixing and racial discrimination. Regarding baseball, the words usually evoke the color line that stood for sixty-plus years until the Dodgers signed Jackie Robinson in the autumn of 1945. Blacks were not banned from the White major or minor leagues by a written rule; teams simply refused to hire them, a practice that Judge Landis consistently upheld.

But Pete is talking about a different type of agreement, a deal unique to him. The pact was unknown to the public for decades, coming to light only when Pete mentioned it in his interviews with Donald Honig. The story was confirmed by former sportswriter and Brooklyn's one-time traveling secretary, Harold Parrott, who wrote a tell-all expose about the Dodgers of the 1940s and '50s entitled *The Lords of Baseball*. According to Parrott, the agreement was the work of Dodger general manager Larry MacPhail and his Cardinal counterpart Branch Rickey. "MacPhail and Rickey cooked up a cover-up deal that could have had them both thrown out of baseball had Commissioner Landis gotten wind of it—thrown out for life!" he wrote, perhaps a touch hyperbolically. Parrott's 1976 book won good if not glowing reviews but never found a wide audience, and Parrott went to his grave believing that longtime Dodgers owner Walter O'Malley, who Parrott depicted as a greedy, Machiavelli-like betrayer of all who surrounded him, secretly bought most of the copies, denying the public a chance to read his work.

Talking to Rick, Pete makes no mention of Parrott's book; he says he was told about the gentleman's agreement early in his career, and looking back, he seems to have accepted it and the impact it had on his life. "Who can I sue?" he says with an air of resignation. However, his daughter Shirley says he may have kept some stronger feelings bottled up. "When my parents sold their house in Woodland Hills [California] and moved to the desert in Palm Springs, they were cleaning out the house," she recalls. "They had all the scrapbooks. My dad was, 'Eh, just toss 'em.' I said, "No, no!" And I actually had to physically rescue them and keep them, cause he was 'Ahh, you know, cleaning out stuff, we're moving, I don't need those." I rescued them. Maybe he was like, 'I don't want to deal with the past.'"

* * *

From the beginning, Charley Barrett knew he had a jewel on his hands. Long before Reiser made the majors, before he even played in a big-league exhibition game, Barrett told J. Roy Stockton of the *St. Louis Post-Dispatch*, "There's a boy that's going to go places. That kid is going to be a star." He liked Pete too—"took a shine to him," as the old scout said in his folksy way. After signing such a talent, Barrett wasn't going to pack him off to just any team in the Cardinals' minor league system. No, this youngster had to be put in a good situation, with a manager that didn't try to change him or stifle him, one who would let him play every day and learn the fundamentals of the game, so that when the Cardinals called him up in a few years, he'd play ball in the smart, aggressive way that had become the organization's hallmark. The search for that just-right situation took Barrett longer than expected and gave Pete an experience—an apprenticeship, really—like few if any other players in the history of the game.

It started with the driving. By the time he signed Pete, the unmarried Barrett was in his mid-sixties and had been on the road for more than a quarter-century, covering what one sportswriter estimated to be a half-million miles. Most of his travel in recent years had been by car, and it wasn't getting easier. In March 1936, he endured a true Murphy's Law of road trips. Ahead of the trip, he had purchased a new vehicle, a supposed top-of-the-line model known as the Lincoln Zephyr. However, the car lacked a heater—still a newfangled thing in 1936 cars—and

Charley shivered fearfully as he drove through a blizzard in central Missouri. After driving for a few days, he reached Arizona, and the weather warmed up considerably. But as he approached Tucson, he encountered a stray cow standing in the middle of the road. Barrett, who possessed a streak of stubbornness found in many scouts, revved the engine and drove toward the bovine at top speed in hopes of making it move. The cow, alas, didn't budge. Charley could not stop in time, and a local reporter said Barrett's Lincoln was so banged up in the resulting collision that it was reduced to a Model T.

To ease the burden—and conceivably to help him make better decisions—the Cardinals approved Barrett hiring a part-time driver. They may not have envisioned that driver being a teenager who was barely old enough to drive or shave. But sometime after the Arizona trip, Barrett offered his prize prospect a job as a chauffeur. Pete grabbed it; heck, he wasn't doing much at home except playing nights and weekends and working at the plant, and his parents apparently had no objection to leaving him in Barrett's hands, despite his status as a minor.

How *much* of a minor Pete was at this stage is a little fuzzy. Pete sometimes said the Cardinals signed him when he was fifteen years old. Other times he said it was sixteen. Barrett said in 1939 that Pete was seventeen when the Cardinals "picked him up" at a tryout. In all likelihood, the Cardinals signed him before age seventeen but waited a year or two to file the paperwork—a not-uncommon legal maneuver for Branch Rickey's team as it tried to vacuum up every young prospect in the land. For example, in the fall of 1937, a Cardinal scout got a promising sixteen-year-old player in Western Pennsylvania to sign a contract. Stanley Frank Musial was still attending high school in his hometown of Donora and wanted to play for the school's basketball team that winter. So, to protect his amateur status, the Cards did not file the contract with the commissioner's office until the following June, at which time Musial joined a minor-league club in tiny Williamson, West Virginia, the starting point for his twenty-two-year Hall of Fame career.

Whatever his contract status, Pete effectively began his career in professional baseball as Charley Barrett's traveling buddy. The two traveled in the same Lincoln Zephyr that the scout nearly wrecked that spring, adorned with red Cardinal logos on the front and back and Barrett's name on the door so everyone would know who he was. Being so young, Pete didn't drive the bulky car much at first, but Barrett let him take the wheel on open roads to gain experience and gradually assumed more of the duties. They spent several months—Pete said it was the summer of 1936—crisscrossing rural, small-town

America, checking out players in the Cardinals farm system. And the Cardinals had a huge number of players, more than five hundred in all that season, scattered across twenty-four clubs at every level of professional baseball, from class-D squads in towns like Mitchell, Nebraska (population 2,058) and Ozark, Alabama (population 3,103), to the AA teams, one step below the majors, in budding metropolises like Houston, Sacramento, and Columbus. Barrett and his young assistant didn't visit every team in the system but probably got to at least a dozen, mostly low-level teams across the southeast, in Georgia, Arkansas, Alabama, Louisiana, Tennessee, and of course, Missouri.

What did Pete experience on Barrett's expedition for baseball gold? The traveling itself was an endless stream of two- and four-lane roads, family-run diners, and small hotels; big interstate highways and motel/restaurant chains like Howard Johnson's were still some ways in the future. If they ventured far enough west, into the Plains, they also saw farm fields laid bare by years of drought, the topsoil blown away by the region's high winds in conditions forever more known as the Dust Bowl. Their actual destinations were mostly little-town ballparks that seated three or four thousand people on wooden benches and usually had no lights for nighttime games. Nighttime ball would have been much appreciated, for the summer of 1936 was searingly hot, one of the most sizzling of the century, with large parts of the country wilting under weeks of dry skies and hundred-degree temperatures. Like everyone else, Pete and Charley had to sweat it out; their car wasn't air-conditioned, and neither were most of the buildings they entered except for movie theaters.

At the ballparks, Pete came face-to-face with eighteen and nineteen-year-olds very much like himself—White, American-born, working-class boys, nearly all without college educations, many of them hoping to escape lives of drudgery on small-town farms or in big-city factories. Despite his comparative youth, Pete showed he could take the field with them. "Whenever we went into a town, I'd work out with the club, take infield [and] batting practice. Then, when the game started, I'd have to get out of uniform," he recalled. More than once, according to Pete, managers asked Barrett to "leave the kid here" so he could join the team. Barrett demurred, saying Reiser was too young. The managers pressed their case: we'll change his name, no one will ever know, they argued. Barrett still said no, and when the old scout was finished checking out the local talent, he and his driver-slash-prospect would move on to the next town.

At that point, the Cardinals' farm system was by far the largest in baseball, more than twice as big as any other franchise's, and Barrett viewed it as his pride and joy. "Don't let anybody tell you that player sources are dried out. We got more high-grade prospects this year than ever before in the history of the chain store system," he told a reporter that May. He wasn't kidding. That spring, the Cardinals promoted a youngster from their class AA club in Rochester, New York, and installed him at first base; Johnny Mize would hit .329 with nineteen homers in his rookie year, the start of a career marked by four home run titles, five World Series rings (with the Yankees) and a spot in the Hall of Fame. The farm teams below were studded with future stars who'd carry the great Cardinals teams of the 1940s: Marty Marion, brothers Mort and Walker Cooper, Whitey Kurowski, Howie Krist, and another Hall of Famer, Enos Slaughter. Other players in the system like Mickey Owen, Nelson Potter, Bob Klinger, Johnny Rizzo, and Don Gutteridge would enjoy success at the major league level with other clubs, often after Rickey sold them off for significant sums of cash, for which he was contractually entitled to a ten percent cut.

The Cardinals could pile up so much talent due to the backwardness of other teams, some of which still had only one or two minor league affiliates, and the deep nationwide business depression that had begun in 1929 and continued until World War II. With unemployment usually bouncing between fifteen and twenty percent, young players jumped at the chance to pursue their major league dreams, even in a minor league system already well-known for low salaries and fierce competition. "The boys are there, begging for jobs, begging to be developed, begging to play baseball," said Barrett that spring. Pete acknowledged that prospects like himself essentially had no negotiating power. "Bonuses? We couldn't even spell bonus," he joked to his son-in-law. "It's like, 'you wanna play baseball, or you don't wanna play baseball?' They'd give you $50 a month, and your dad is making only so much . . . Today, talking about free agents, they play out their options. Our only option years ago was don't miss the bus!"

In the eyes of sportswriter and author Robert Creamer, the rough conditions showed on the faces of the Cardinal players. St. Louis, he noted, was the westernmost city in the majors then, the one closest to the Dust Bowl. "The Cardinals seemed to represent that area of Depression America," Creamer wrote. "Henry Fonda as the undefeatable Tom Joad in the film version of John Steinbeck's *The Grapes of Wrath* looked like a St. Louis Cardinal: lean, bony; hard; grim, tight smile; defiance in adversity; spirit. The St. Louis Browns were also in existence then, but except for one flukey war year, the Browns lost *all* the time. The Cardinals didn't. Like the Joads, they were resilient. They came back from defeat. They were country tough."

Pete finally entered the Cardinal farm system for real in April of '37. He started at a Cardinal training camp for class C and D level players in Springfield, Missouri, a few hours northwest of St. Louis. There, Barrett and a coterie of fellow scouts and minor-league managers evaluated and trained more than two hundred prospects, sending home the unqualified, divvying up those deemed good enough for minor league roster spots. When the camp was over, Pete was assigned to the Springfield club, playing in the class C Western Association. The manager of the squad was Clay Hopper, best known today as Jackie Robinson's first-minor league manager in Montreal in 1946. According to his scrapbook, Pete stayed with the club three weeks, riding buses to places like Muskogee, Oklahoma, and Hutchinson, Kansas, no doubt getting an eyeful of Dust Bowl conditions along the way. But there is no record of him getting into any games, and within a short time, the Cardinals pulled him off the squad, looking for a team that would give him playing time. This proved surprisingly difficult, and for the next two months, he was shunted around the farm system like an unwanted problem child, traveling up and down the spine of America, watching the countryside roll by through windows of a Greyhound.

Pete later summarized the entire odyssey: "I was assigned by the Cardinals to their Cedar Rapids [Iowa] team in the Three-I League, but the club had so many players I never got a chance to play, and I was shipped to New Iberia [Louisiana] in the Evangeline League," he said. "I got to play seven games before I was sent to Union Springs in the Alabama State League, and after riding the bench a couple of weeks, I found myself with Monett, an Arkansas-Missouri League club in Class D. I didn't play there either and finished the year with Newport in the Northeast Arkansas League. Generally, I kept about three hundred miles ahead of my laundry during all that jumping around."

He added: "Every time I was shifted, I'd be recalled to St. Louis for a talk with Mr. Rickey before joining my new club. He'd ask me about different players I'd seen, and I thought he was figuring on making a scout out of me. Hell, he never asked me what I'd been doing, but I guess he knew all right."

Pete sometimes told tall tales about his career, but most of this story checks out. Baseball-reference.com shows him playing with New Iberia and Newport, and various newspaper articles confirm he spent time with the Springfield and Monett teams and played in at least one game with Union Springs. The most consequential of his assignments would be Cedar Rapids. Pete had not a single at-bat for them, but the fact he was affiliated with them, even briefly, would have a massive impact on his career.

The team where Pete finally landed was the epitome of class-D baseball circa 1937. Newport was a farming community of about forty-five hundred people, the smallest of six small locales represented in the Northeast Arkansas League. The team played its games on the local high school grounds, at no-frills Mann Field, a ballpark constructed by the Depression-era Works Progress Administration. Sometimes, when the club wasn't playing, the park was used for horse shows. Most of the players, like Reiser, were newbies to the professional ranks, earning around fifty bucks per month, less than half the salary of the average American worker at the time. They stayed in local rooming houses and took most of their meals at the red-brick Hazel Hotel, where the proprietor, a Mrs. Rush, gave ballplayers an "all you can eat" deal for five dollars a week. ("We couldn't live without her, couldn't survive," Pete told Rick.) Crowds for the games were small, usually no more than a few hundred, but the fans took the outcome seriously, Pete recalled. "If you got beat and had a bad day, you didn't go into town," he said. "Those farmers used to bet on the ball games, and I don't care if it was a quarter or fifty cents, boy could they make life rough for you."

Pete made life rough for the fans, too, if they sat within range of his powerful throwing arm. "I can remember nobody used to sit behind first base when I played shortstop. I had a good arm but wasn't too accurate in those days," he joked. The official stats bear him out; Pete committed thirty-three errors in just sixty-eight games at short. He stayed on the team by virtue of his bat, cracking out a solid .285 average with six homers, nine triples, and a team-high slugging percentage of .444 in seventy games. His best day came on July 15th, a 2-1 Newport victory against the Caruthersville Pilots. Caruthersville's star, Whitey Kurowski, scored the only Pilots' only run, but Reiser homered in the fourth and seventh innings "to win the ballgame alone," reported a local paper.

The Cardinals and Charley Barrett were pleased with Pete's '37 performance and invited him to attend the team's "School of Baseball," an instructional camp for prospects, held in February 1938 in Winter Haven, Florida. Barrett personally paid his protégé's expenses to attend the camp and said Pete impressed everyone with his ability. According to Barrett, Ray Blades, manager of the Cardinals' top farm team in Rochester, wanted the Pistol-in-training on his roster. The boy would have to make a massive leap from class D to class AA ball. But Blades was a ten-year big-league veteran and a future manager of the Cards. He wouldn't ask for Pete unless he thought the youngster could hack it one notch below the majors.

In the end, though, Pete wouldn't be assigned to any Rochester or any other Cardinal farm team. A higher power, one of the few men in baseball with more influence and authority than Branch Rickey, had decided that a separation was in order.

* * *

Mar. 30, 1938

Mr. Harold Reiser
3018 N. Taylor
St. Louis, Mo.

Dear Sir:
You are advised that, in accordance with the Commissioner's ruling of Mar. 22nd in the St. Louis-Cedar Rapids matter, you have been declared a free agent.

Very truly yours,
K.M. Landis
Commissioner

The letter from Landis was not exactly a bolt out of the blue. As early as November 1937, newspaper reports said Landis was investigating the Cardinals for suspicious arrangements with minor league clubs. The details of these arrangements were hazy, complex, and contested, and Branch Rickey always insisted he and his colleagues did nothing wrong. Suffice to say, Landis—a longtime opponent of farm systems in principle and of the Cardinals' vast system in particular—believed the Cards were using handshake deals, phony sales, and other sly methods to keep or gain control over players to which the team technically had no rights. Central to the scheme was the friendship between Rickey and the owner of the Cedar Rapids Raiders, a team in the "Three-I" (Illinois-Indiana-Iowa) League. In the commissioner's view, the Cardinals were using the class-C Raiders as a front to build *de facto* affiliations with class-D teams, giving the Cards control of more than one club in several leagues. These included the Northeast Arkansas League, where the Cards allegedly ran both Pete's team in Newport and the one in nearby Caruthersville, where Whitey Kurowski played.

Landis found that to be a violation of baseball laws aimed at maintaining genuine competition in minor league circuits. And rather than suspend Rickey or levy a big fine against the club, the commissioner stripped the Cardinals of what they really wanted: players. Ninety-one of them, including Pete Reiser, were declared free agents. Most, including Pete, were barred from re-signing with the franchise for three years.

For the record, Pete had no problem with Rickey's dealings, which he thought helped many a minor league team weather the Depression. "He kept leagues alive, maybe not honestly, but it had to be done," Pete told his son-in-law. "He wanted it [minor league ball] to survive. In a lot of leagues, he supplied more than one club with players, uniforms, bats, balls, expenses, paid their salaries. It wasn't a whole lot, but he paid 'em."

Regardless of his opinion, Reiser was looking at a future with no pay at all when Landis announced his edict on March 22, 1938. At that moment, he was just a kid who had spent one year in class D ball without making a real splash. He was nineteen years old, a thousand miles from home in Florida, had almost no money and was losing his contract to play pro ball. He was, he later admitted, scared. So, he must have been relieved the next day when a scout for the Brooklyn Dodgers, Ted McGrew, called him and asked for a meeting in Winter Haven.

More than twenty years later, McGrew discussed the circumstances that led him to Pete with newspaper columnist Joe Williams. "Charley Barrett had been tipped off to Landis' action. He told me where to find Reiser. He didn't have to tell me anything else. I already had a good book on the kid," he said. Williams expressed surprise that Barrett would help a competitor reel in a prized prospect. McGrew said Barrett was simply returning a favor. "I touted him off on a bad ballplayer Rickey was high on," he said. "The biggest favor one scout can do another is tout him off a clinker."

Maybe so, but . . . it would be against character for Barrett, or Rickey, or the vast majority of major league scouts and executives, both then and now, to let a player with such a high ceiling simply walk away. What seems likely, given later events, is that instead of simply handing Reiser to the Dodgers, Barrett asked the Brooklyn franchise to sign the young prospect and bury him in the minors until the Cardinals could reacquire him.

"Charley Barrett was a good friend of Ted McGrew, and vice versa," Pete told his son-in-law. "They made some kind of gentleman's agreement—you sign him, and you play him for a couple of years in the Dodger organization, and then we'll make a deal to get him back. I didn't know this at the time, but this was the agreement." It was exactly the type of deal that had put the Cardinals in hot water with Judge Landis. But Barrett, undoubtedly acting with Rickey's approval, and McGrew, presumably acting with Larry MacPhail's, pressed ahead. McGrew met Pete and offered him a job with the Dodgers' organization. Pete accepted and signed a piece of paper, dated March 24th, that read, "In the event I am declared a free agent I agree to sign a contract with the Dayton club of the Middle Atlantic league at One Hundred Dollars per month, providing

I am paid a bonus of One Hundred Dollars for signing said contract." Pete's daughter Shirley still has the wrinkled paper, as well as the letter from Landis that declared her father a free agent.

In later years, Reiser would look back and wonder if he got robbed. "If I was a kid breaking in today, sure I'd laugh at a hundred bucks," he said in 1956. "But . . . in the late '30s, a hundred dollars looked like a lot of money to the Reiser family. I took it because I was half afraid nobody would sign me." At other times, he questioned whether his agreement with the Dodgers was even legal, given that he signed it before getting official word of his free agency from the commissioner. "I could have hollered to Landis, after I had come to realize what a financial boner I had committed and got my freedom and maybe got myself ten grand, or even more, from some other team, the Yankees probably . . . Sometimes the fact that I ignored my chance to get important money out of all that gets me all roiled up," he said.

In 1938 however, Pete chose not to holler and became a Dodger farmhand. In mid-April, he reported to the team's class-C Dayton, Ohio squad and was installed at shortstop for two exhibition games. He homered in the first game and went hitless in the second. Then, amid a pre-season shuffling of players, he was released by manager Ducky Holmes. Pete said the Dodgers next sent him to their team in Winston-Salem, North Carolina, where he was again given a brief tryout and again released. "Each time, McGrew almost had a heart attack, not just because the Dodgers released me, but because they had this agreement with the Cardinals," Pete recalled. He said the Winston-Salem team actually gave him a release paper. He said upon learning of this, a horrified McGrew hustled to Winston-Salem, tore up the paper, and put Pete on a bus bound for Superior, Wisconsin, twelve hundred miles to the north, with a meal allowance of fifty cents per day.

After this second spring of mind-numbing travel, Pete finally found a place to play with the Superior Blues of the class-D Northern League. On opening day, he cracked three hits, including a two-run homer, and the next day sparked a game-winning rally with a triple. The local sportswriters had trouble getting his name right; one game summary referred to him as Johnny, and another called him Al. But by mid-June, Blues manager George Treadwell was calling him the best shortstop in the league. When the campaign ended, Superior had captured a division title, and Pete ranked among the league's top hitters with a .302 batting average and a team-high slugging percentage of .563. In ninety-five games, he racked up twenty-one steals, twenty-seven doubles, ten triples, and eighteen home runs.

A promotion was clearly in order, and that fall, the Dodgers informed Pete that he'd move up to their class-A team in Elmira, New York, the following spring. But Pete nurtured bigger dreams. Since Elmira wouldn't start spring training until the end of March, he asked the Dodgers if he could go to the major league camp in Clearwater, Florida, to get a head start on the 1939 season. Charley Barrett, still working for the Cardinals but still Pete's friend and mentor, put in a word with Brooklyn's new player-manager, who happened to be the Cardinals' old shortstop, Leo Durocher. Durocher said sure, and Pete went south in late February, officially assigned to the training camp of Brooklyn's double-A team, the Montreal Royals.

From the minute he arrived, Pete put his hustle and skills on full display. Brooklyn had an older club, with many players over thirty who were slow to get going in the spring. "These guys were old and fat and couldn't run and couldn't throw. I thought, 'I can outplay anybody on this ballclub.' I was that cocky," Pete recalled. "And every chance the batting cage was open, I'd jump in. Everybody was going, 'Who is this guy?'" More importantly, when Pete took his stolen swings, he hit the ball. When the players held footraces, he'd win, and when the players had to run laps around the ballpark, Pete would finish a full lap ahead. Durocher, who liked cockiness when it was backed up with talent, took notice. By the second week in March, Pete had been transferred from the minor league camp to the major league one, and the new Dodger manager began to drop his name to reporters. There was still confusion over that name—some stories referred to him as "Hal" Reiser—but no one missed the meaning when Durocher compared him to Red Sox shortstop Joe Cronin, a future Hall of Famer who hit .325 the previous year and topped the majors in doubles with fifty-one.

Thus, the press corps was primed for a story when Durocher decided to let the youngster take his place at shortstop the afternoon of March 22, 1939, for a game in St. Petersburg against the Cardinals. On paper, Durocher was throwing Pete in over his head. The starting pitcher was the Cards' top pitching prospect, Ken Raffensberger, a six-foot-two lefty with a sidearm delivery and a live fastball who had won fifteen games the previous year in double-A, with an excellent 2.91 ERA. But Pete showed no jitters when he came to bat with two out and two on in the first inning. Batting righty, Reiser swung hard at Raffensberger's first pitch and slammed a long, high fly down the right-field line. Durocher bellowed, "Stay fair! Stay fair!" The ball heard his plea and landed just inside the foul pole: home run. Reiser, no doubt a little overwhelmed, trotted uncertainly to second base and stopped before he was shooed home. By day's end, he had also walked and hit two line-drive singles, both as a lefty. His homer was the margin of victory in the Dodgers' 6-4 win.

Reporters took due notice of his performance, and the game story in the next morning's *New York Times* was headlined, "Dodgers Subdue Cardinals on Reiser's Home Run in the First." For some players, that would have been the highlight of their career. But for Pete, it was just the warm-up. The next day against the Reds, he singled, homered to right-center, beat out an infield hit, and homered a second time, this one traveling an estimated four hundred feet. The press corps snapped to full attention:

- "The kid has now faced six pitchers since climbing into a major league uniform yesterday, and not one has succeeded in getting him out!"—Hy Turkin, *New York Daily News*.
- "Nobody is talking about anything else but Harold (Pete) Reiser, the most spectacular class D kid ever to bust unexpectedly into a big-league camp." —Tommy Holmes, *Brooklyn Daily Eagle*
- "The amazing adolescent, six months out of a class D league, the deepest bush, is the damndest wonder worker since the Middle Ages, at least." —Stanley Frank, *New York Post*

Roscoe McGowen of the more reserved *New York Times* laid off the superlatives but noted that when Reiser caught the final out of the game, he was immediately surrounded by photographers who kept him posing for fifteen minutes.

The following day against the Tigers, Pete batted in the second inning against highly touted rookie Fred Hutchinson. Reporters took note of their respective price tags: Detroit had paid fifty thousand to acquire "Hutch" from the Pacific Coast League while Brooklyn had obtained Pete's signature for a hundred bucks. In this case, Dodger thriftiness prevailed, as Pete lined an RBI single to center. Two batters later, he scored on a double but strained a leg muscle coming around third. Durocher pulled him from the game as a precaution. The move preserved Pete's perfect batting line: eight hits in eight times at bat, plus one walk, for a batting average and on-base percentage of 1.000. He had also driven in eight runs and scored five.

The reporters kept gushing. The next day, Turkin wrote: "The latest headline hero has a rifle arm, the speed and grace of a frightened faun, keen competitive spirit, the swing of a piledriver and even temperament—a born ballplayer!" Frank chimed in: "Our incredible infant has yet to be troubled by an actual or alleged pitcher."

The on-base streak finally ended against the Yankees on March 27th when, after drawing two walks, Pete lined out to right fielder Tommy Henrich. He was held hitless the rest of the game but helped manufacture the winning run; in the sixth inning, he reached first on a force play, dashed to third on an infield hit by Gene Moore, and scored on a groundout. After the game, Yankee pitcher Lefty Gomez, who issued the two walks, said, "I'll say one thing for him. He won't swing at anything that isn't a strike."

Watching Pete wow players and press alike that day was a man whose fortunes were sinking as fast as Pete's were on the rise: Lou Gehrig, the Iron Horse. Moore's infield hit in the sixth was actually a grounder that bounced off Gehrig's glove. Such mistakes had become embarrassingly common for the thirty-five-year-old Gehrig that spring, as he tried to cope with the sudden, mysterious disappearance of his legendary batting power and always capable reflexes. No one knew yet that Larrupin' Lou was suffering from amyotrophic lateral sclerosis, ALS, the paralyzing disease that would force him to retire that May and take his life just two years later. For the moment, Gehrig brushed aside talk of his decline. "They've been burying me all spring, but no one has sent me lilies yet," he said. But the following day, Yankee manager Joe McCarthy offered a harsh assessment of his first baseman: "He's definitely lost his speed. He'll never get it back. They never do."

In contrast, McCarthy praised Reiser, saying, "He's a natural hitter and can run like a rabbit." Those weren't empty words for the press; McCarthy told Pete the Yankees were trying to trade for him. "The Dodgers needed ballplayers, and McCarthy wanted me real bad," Pete said to his son-in-law. "In fact, he told me, 'We've got the deal almost made. We're giving up quite a bit to get you, but the deal is going to be made.'" Of course, no such deal materialized; MacPhail's secret agreement with Rickey prevented him from trading the prize prospect.

Reiser continued to impress as spring training rolled on, smashing a homer against the Yankees, getting on base five times against Detroit, keeping his batting average in the .500 range. By this time, McCarthy wasn't the only manager who wanted Reiser in a big-league uniform. Durocher was blown away by the Pistol's performance and started to think that the twenty-year-old, despite his inexperience, belonged in the big leagues. In his 1975 autobiography, *Nice Guys Finish Last*, Leo recalled, "I just kept staring at him, wondering if it was all a dream. Holy cats, I'm thinking. What have I stumbled upon here? This is a diamond, Leo. All you have to do is polish him. Sit down and let the boy play. And I'm thinking, MacPhail must be flipping. They'll break down the gates at Ebbets Field just to see what this kid looks like."

Larry MacPhail was indeed flipping, but not for the reason Durocher imagined. The attention Pete was getting left the Dodger general manager aghast, for it complicated his plan to send the phenom down to the minors and, in time, back to the Cardinals. At first, MacPhail played it cool, expressing admiration for Pete's skills ("as natural a hitter as you ever laid eyes on") but emphasizing to reporters that he would be farmed out for more seasoning, probably with Elmira. However, the cool gradually evaporated as the Durocher kept flapping his mouth to the press. Reiser might be the twenty-fifth man on the Dodgers' roster, Leo said. Hell, he said, Reiser might be the Dodgers' second baseman—statements that undoubtedly alarmed Branch Rickey and brought MacPhail to a boil.

Even under the best of circumstances, MacPhail had something of a low boiling point. Forty-nine years old in 1939, Leland Stanford MacPhail was widely regarded as one of the sharpest minds and greatest innovators in baseball. After turning around a moribund minor league franchise in Columbus, Ohio, in the early 1930s, he rescued the Cincinnati Reds from bankruptcy by installing the major leagues' first lights for nighttime ball, hiring talented young Red Barber for radio broadcasts, and gradually acquiring the players who would win back-to-back pennants for the Reds in 1939 and 1940. Ahead of the 1938 season, he brought his talents to Brooklyn, where he improved the struggling team by fixing up the rundown ballpark, installing lights, bringing in Barber, briefly hiring Babe Ruth as coach-slash-gate attraction, and spending freely to raise the team's talent level, starting with a fifty-thousand-dollar layout for Phillies' slugger Dolph Camilli.

But with the successful methods came a kind of madness. Sportswriter Harold Parrott called MacPhail unpredictable as a gust of wind—able to charm a cobra one minute, prone to explode into rage the next. He was fired from the Reds for allegedly punching the team's owner, radio magnate Powell Crosley, as well as a Cincinnati police detective. Later on, he punched Parrott. A *New Yorker* profile of MacPhail, complimentary of his abilities in many ways, also described him as bellicose and clownish, with a voice akin to that of an adult male moose. "On mornings after the Dodgers have lost a game, MacPhail sits in his office and brays with such effect that small crowds gather on the sidewalk three stories below," said the writer. Not for nothing was MacPhail's nickname the Roaring Redhead. The mood swings were made worse by alcohol, several bottles of which the GM usually kept in his desk. "MacPhail, man, he would go wild," recalled Barber. "In the press room after a ballgame in Brooklyn, when I saw MacPhail have a drink, I was already late for my next appointment. I never stayed. That's one reason I never got in trouble with him."

Durocher, in contrast, didn't mind getting in trouble with MacPhail or anyone, and the situation with Reiser boiled over the first week in April, as the Dodgers barnstormed through the South ahead of opening day. MacPhail sent his manager a no-nonsense telegram: "DO NOT PLAY REISER AGAIN." Durocher, who was not privy to the gentleman's agreement with St. Louis, ignored the warning and kept inserting Pete into games. MacPhail finally got fed up with his manager and hopped on a plane. He caught up with Durocher in a Macon, Georgia hotel room as the Dodgers played exhibition games at a nearby army base. In a somewhat legendary confrontation, recounted in several memoirs, an inebriated Roaring Redhead launched into a top-volume tirade at Leo the Lip, calling him, according to Leo's account, "every filthy name I had ever heard," including dirty son-of-a-bitch. Leo, true to form, yelled right back. An incensed MacPhail then fired his rookie manager on the spot and ordered the team's traveling secretary, John McDonald, to get on his typewriter and whip up a press release to that effect. When McDonald tried to stall by making repeated typos and rolling in fresh pieces of paper, hoping MacPhail would calm down and change his mind, MacPhail told McDonald that *he* was fired—but ordered him to finish the press release before packing up.

MacPhail rehired both men within a few minutes, marking the first of the many, many, many times the tempestuous Dodger GM would sack and bring back Durocher in the span of a day. A quarter-century later, MacPhail characterized the incident in Macon as a disagreement instead of a screaming match and insisted that he simply wanted to keep Reiser in the minors for more training. "Reiser was just a kid. My idea was to play him at Elmira a half-season, then move him to Montreal and then bring him to Brooklyn to finish out the year," he said. "But Durocher kept playing Reiser, and the kid was winning game after game in the exhibitions. This was going to make it hard when we tried to send him out for the seasoning he needed, and I told Leo this."

Despite the MacPhail-Durocher rhubarb, Pete remained with the Dodgers as opening day approached, and the press kept suggesting he might make the final roster. "Twenty-fifth man on the squad will be either Pete Reiser, infielder, or Oris Hockett, outfielder. Both are savage swingers and serve as offensive reserve," reported the *Daily News* three days before the first regular-season game. That afternoon, Pete was in the lineup for an exhibition against the Yankees at Ebbets Field, playing the whole game at shortstop, handling five chances without an error, and drawing a pair of walks. He finished the spring with a .417 batting average, the best on the club.

So, Pete was utterly blindsided the afternoon of April 18th when, less than a half-hour before the first pitch, with Ebbets Field filled to near capacity, the Dodgers announced their spring training sensation was being optioned to Elmira. Pete said MacPhail gave him the news during pre-game warmups. "Imagine, I had just taken infield practice," he said. The twenty-year-old Pistol, unaware of the secret deal blocking his progress, was so upset that he refused to accept the demotion—and jumped the team.

"When they sent me back in '39, I didn't understand it," Pete told Rick as they sipped their Bloody Marys. "I was hurt. It was five minutes before opening day I was sent back . . . Of course, I was a young kid, I thought I knew quite a bit about baseball, and I had quite a spring training. So instead of going right to Elmira, I got on a train, went to St. Louis. My dad met me at the station, and to give him credit, most fathers probably would have said I was right. [He said,] 'What the hell you doing here?' [I said,] 'I think I belong in the big leagues.' 'Well,' he says, 'until you're a general manager and know as much as Mr. MacPhail, get your butt back to Elmira and play baseball.' Uggh. Dad was German and French [heritage], and you didn't argue with him. So, I got back on the train and went to Elmira."

Rick suggested that Pete, with only two seasons in class D ball, was being a little impatient with the Dodgers. Pete batted away the idea. "I wasn't impatient; I was good," he said.

Pete finally reported to Elmira on April 25th for what would turn into a difficult season. He made a strong impression in his first game, beating out an infield dribbler with his speed and hitting a triple to deep center. "Reiser is fast and loose on the bases and afield . . . He has the confidence and poise usually rare for a 19-year-old breaking into class A company," noted the local *Elmira Star-Gazette*. But less than two weeks into the season, Pete injured his throwing arm. It happened, most unusually, on a swing; Pete took one of his characteristically hard cuts during a game against Scranton and suddenly felt a sharp pain in his elbow.

The initial diagnosis was a pulled muscle, and he missed a dozen games. When he returned, manager Clyde Sukeforth moved Pete to the outfield—and he showed he could dominate the league. In one 11-10 victory, Reiser banged out three hits and stole home for the winning run. Two days later, he blasted a four-hundred-foot homer. Two days after that, he got four hits, including a triple and another round-tripper. On June 5th, he hit still another homer, this time an inside-the-park job. He was also regularly taking extra bases if opponents made the slightest mistake in the field. "Everyone was commenting on the exceptional speed of Pete Reiser," noted a Wilkes-Barre, Pennsylvania paper after the Pioneers beat the local team 10-2, with Reiser scoring twice from second base on singles.

However, the pain in his right elbow was mounting, and in late June, doctors correctly diagnosed the problem: bone chips. Pete said he could throw left-handed, but contrary to his later claims that he played as a lefty, the *Star-Gazette* reported he "isn't a good enough southpaw to use in the outfield." The Dodgers sent him to Johns Hopkins University Hospital in Baltimore for the operation. For reasons that were never explained, doctors there gave him a two-for-one on the surgery. Pete told W.C. Heinz: "When I came to after the operation, my throat was sore, and there was an ice pack on it. I said, 'What happened? Your knife slip?' They said, 'we took your tonsils out while were operating on your arm.'" Pete came back for a few games at the beginning of August, only to be shut down for the season when the elbow flared up again. Contemporary stats put his final batting average for the season at .314, though baseball-reference.com lists him at .301.

By early October, Pete reported himself to be back at full health. "My arm has completely healed. I've been whipping the ball in the past two weeks, and my arm is as strong as ever," he said. He wasn't done with the operating room, however. In mid-November, he suffered an attack of appendicitis and had his appendix removed at St. John's Hospital in St. Louis. The operation was performed by Robert Hyland, the official team surgeon for the Cardinals and the Browns. It was the first of many times Pete would receive treatment from the good doctor, whom he would praise as a "friend to all ballplayers." Pete would see the doctor so often, especially in the latter part of his career, it was as though he regarded Hyland as his magic talisman. At a minimum, he valued Hyland as a good resource and a person he could trust—the type of person he was not encountering with great frequency in the world of professional baseball.

* * *

In February 1940, Pete went to Clearwater for training camp and quickly realized he would not be this year's spring sensation. The writers were now focused on another shortstop with the initials H.R.—Harold Reese, better known by his nickname, Pee Wee. The Dodgers had purchased Reese from the Red Sox organization the previous year for the reported sum of seventy-five thousand dollars, after Joe Cronin, who was Boston's manager in addition to its shortstop, allegedly decided he didn't want a young rival threatening his job. On the first day of camp in Clearwater, Durocher organized a fielding drill with Reese at shortstop and Reiser at second, and Reese promptly grabbed the spotlight. "No fungoed grounder passed him. He displayed the speed of an [Jesse] Owens, the sure-grabbing fingers of a monkey, and the fast, accurate throw of a rifle. He ranged over territory like a pointer dog, close to the ground while traveling at top speed," said an unbylined article in the *Daily News*. The Dodgers' shortstop of the future had arrived. It was likely no coincidence that the very next day, an AP report said the Dodgers planned to move Reiser full-time into the outfield.

If Pete harbored hopes of making the big club that spring, they were dashed early, as he played little in the Dodgers' exhibition games, and by mid-March, he was assigned to the Montreal camp. However, he didn't object—he'd still be moving up a step to double-A ball, which was then one rung below the majors. In the Royals' final exhibition games, Reiser went on a Babe Ruth-like tear: twelve hits in twenty-five times at-bat, including two doubles, a triple, and five home runs. In Montreal's lineup on opening day, he knocked out three hits in his International League debut, as the Royals romped over Jersey City 12-1. "I say, no way I can't play now, with the spring I had," Pete recalled.

So, he was naturally puzzled when he was benched three games into the season, as Montreal played at Baltimore. He told Rick that the same day, he learned the Dodgers were sending several players down to the Royals. "I think, 'What the hell's going on here?' So, I go back to the hotel. I'm up in my room, the phone rings. A man says, 'Pete, this is Larry MacPhail.' I think he's calling me into the big leagues. He says, 'Your contract has been reassigned to Elmira.' I think, 'oh, you lousy no-good so-and-so.'"

Most certainly, "so-and-so" was not the phrase that ran through Pete's head. He also must have wondered: what the hell do I have to do for this outfit to get past class A?

This time, a dejected Pete didn't hop a train to St. Louis. "I thought, no sense in going home, Dad is going to send me right back to Elmira," he told Rick. But by now, it had dawned him that something odd was going on, and he decided to share his feeling with Elmira's new manager, Bill Killefer. Killefer was a thirty-five-year veteran of baseball, his main claim to fame being the ten years he spent as the catcher for Hall of Fame pitcher Grover Cleveland Alexander, still the National League's all-time wins leader with three hundred seventy-three. As a Dodger coach, Killefer had seen Pete pulverize big-league pitchers during spring training the previous year. "He really liked me," Pete told Rick. "So, Bill met me at the [train] station. I used to call him Fibber McGee, like 'Fibber McGee and Molly' on the radio. I said, 'Fibber, somebody's out to get me.'"

According to Pete, Killefer not only sympathized but also promised to take action. "He says, 'I am now the boss. I'm not only the manager; I'm also the general manager. I promise you that if you're going good before June 15th, do what I think you can do, if the Dodgers don't bring you up, you'll be sold to the highest bidder.' I said, 'Bill, you'll get fired.' He said, 'I don't care cause I'm retiring anyway.'"

Pete upheld his part of the deal, hammering away at Eastern League pitching from day one of his return. In his first game, he hit a single, double and triple. Two days later, he topped that with a double, triple, and home run. By the second week in May, he sat atop the league batting leaders at .429. When MacPhail made a one-day stop in Elmira on May 12th, he said nothing about Pete to the press, but the Dodger GM had to notice what was happening. In one late May game against Hartford, Pete went four-for-four, stole two bases, and threw out a runner at the plate from right field. A week later, against Scranton, he scored from first base on a bunt after prompting a wild throw across the infield. "To make a long story short, I tore the league up," Pete said.

As the middle of June approached, Pete said he talked to Killefer again: "'Bill, remember the talk we had?' He said, 'Give me a couple of days. I think something's cooking.'" And it was. On June 12, 1940, the Dodgers and Cardinals announced a monumental trade. The Cardinals sent star slugger Joe Medwick and starting pitcher Curt Davis to Brooklyn for outfielder Ernie Koy and three backup players. For baseball fans, the trading of Medwick, the 1937 Triple Crown winner, and a three-time National League RBI leader, was earthshaking news. In both Brooklyn and St. Louis, the trade made the front page of the newspapers, right next to stories about the German army's *blitzkrieg* through France.

But of equal note was the price tag. Along with the players, the Dodgers had forked over an amount variously reported to be one hundred twenty-five, one hundred fifty, or two hundred fifty thousand dollars. It was one of the largest sums paid for talent in baseball history. And to some observers, it seemed excessive. Medwick was still a good hitter, but his performance had gradually declined since his '37 MVP season. He was also a temperamental, me-first player who sometimes played indifferent defense and clashed with his Cardinal teammates and coaches, though in fairness, Durocher was an old pal and had pushed for the trade.

More than three decades later, Harold Parrott connected the dots in *The Lords of Baseball*. He said the six-figure payment was partly to compensate Rickey and the Cardinals for the loss of Reiser because MacPhail had decided to break their secret deal.

"[The writers] had gotten another glimpse at Reiser in 1940, after his exile to Elmira, and they had fallen in love with him all over again. They were starting to ask embarrassing questions: When was Pistol Pete going to get his chance? Wasn't he better than some of the relics in the Brooklyn outfield, like Old Joe Vosmik, who had to wear a corset to keep his back together and couldn't bend over to pick up a rolling ball?" Parrott wrote. "MacPhail realized by then he had to renege on returning Pistol Pete. He called Rickey, pleading, almost in tears. 'Branch, they'd lynch me here if I trade Reiser away for Medwick right now, even up. Durocher has talked too much, and the reporters have written every word. The fans here are so excited there would be a scandal. I just can't give him back to you.' Naturally, Rickey was in no position to complain, being a co-conspirator. But the Old Man would have to get cash, lots of cash instead of the superbaby."

Parrott put the Dodger payout to the Cardinals at one hundred thirty-two thousand dollars, the equivalent of nearly two and a half million dollars today. The recent release of 1940 Dodger financial records online confirmed that was indeed the amount.

Pete told the story from a slightly different angle. In his recollection, the Medwick deal included a player to be named later, given by St. Louis to Brooklyn. He said he learned this three days after the trade when Killefer called him in for a meeting. "I can't prove that I'm the player," Pete told Rick, "But Killefer knew the deal, and he told me, '*You* are the player to be named. All this time, you have been a Cardinal ballplayer. He says they have no papers to prove it. It was a gentlemen's agreement; between MacPhail and Rickey and McGrew and Charley Barrett, the deal was all set up." According to Pete, Killefer said that if he wanted to protest to Commissioner Landis, he could still be declared a free agent. Pete said he declined because Killefer told him he'd shortly be going up to the majors with Brooklyn.

For the record, newspaper stories on the Medwick trade did not mention a player to be named later, and neither Rickey, MacPhail, or McGrew ever confirmed Pistol Pete was part of the exchange. But this would hardly be a surprise, given the nature of their agreement on Reiser and the three men's desire to avoid punishment from Landis. By this time, Pete couldn't ask Charley Barrett what was going on; Charley had died of a heart attack in July 1939.

If Pete expected to go to the majors the day after the Medwick trade, he was disappointed again. The Dodgers were tied for first place at the time, and with the acquisition of Medwick and Davis, MacPhail decided they didn't need further help. In any case, Pete suffered a groin pull that forced him to the bench for two weeks. He renewed his assault on Eastern League pitching when he returned, keeping his batting average in the .370 range. By early July, it was clear he had outgrown the competition. In a three-game series against the Scranton Miners, he went seven-for-eleven and threw out two runners trying to score. "Pete Reiser looked so well against our Miners they can't understand what he's doing in this league," wrote a *Scranton Tribune* reporter. In an exhibition game against the Dodgers the following day, Pete got two hits off major-league pitchers and cut down yet another runner at the plate.

Two weeks later, with Pete batting .378 and the Dodgers slowly sinking behind the Reds in the National League pennant race, MacPhail finally bowed to the inevitable, calling up Pete from Elmira. "A team five games out of first place can't afford to stand pat," the Dodger GM explained to the press. It was apparently a last-minute decision. On the night of July 22nd, the Dodgers decided they needed Reiser the next day for a doubleheader against Cincinnati at Ebbets Field. The Pioneers' business manager was told to send Pete to New York immediately. But the one train that would deliver him to Brooklyn in time was passing through Elmira at three A.M. Pete first had to stay up to catch the train, then had to sit in coach during the eight-hour ride to Brooklyn. Not that he cared. "Couldn't sleep a wink; I was so excited," he recalled.

Maybe the lack of sleep explains his struggles during his long-delayed debut. In his first at-bat, he grounded out with two runners on. In his second at-bat, he flied out with two runners on. The third time up, he grounded into a double play and slightly pulled a leg muscle running down to first, prompting Durocher to remove him from the game. In the nightcap, Pete appeared again—this time as a pinch-hitter—and flied out with two runners on. The *Daily Eagle* spared no punches in an article on Reiser's debut the next day: "Everything Goes Wrong with Rookie Outfielder Recalled from Elmira Farm," read the subhead.

Yet within two weeks, Reiser was playing regularly. Durocher initially inserted him at different spots—pinch hitter, right field, shortstop—before installing him as the regular third baseman when Cookie Lavagetto went down in late August with severe appendicitis. The Dodgers failed to catch the Reds, and by no means was Pete an instant star. He struck out more than twice as often as he walked, rarely tried to steal, and managed just three homers in more than two hundred forty times at-bat. But after a slow start, he began knocking out singles and doubles, and Durocher made him the Dodgers' leadoff hitter. Playing every day from August 20th onward, Pete hit a more-than-acceptable .319. Over the final two weeks, he batted an even .400. In mid-September, Durocher announced Pete had clinched a starting spot for '41. "When we start training next spring Reiser will be my right fielder," he said. "He's fitted for the job, and I know he'll solve a lot of my problems."

Leo, for once, was underestimating his star prospect. When the next season rolled around, Pete would drive the Dodgers to new heights—and finally, no so-called gentlemen were standing in his way.

4
"Some Kind of Year, '41"

The 1941 season was exactly eight days old, and Dodger management feared it might already be over.

Pete Reiser, the new kick in the Brooklyn offense, the new lead dog on the Dodger sled, was curled up on the ground next to home plate, clutching his head, writhing in agony from the Ike Pearson fastball that had just crashed into his right cheekbone. Assorted Dodgers, Phillies, and ballpark staff rushed in as soon as Pete went down; the pitch striking his face made a sound loud as a gunshot, "and couldn't have dropped him any faster if it really were one," according to an observer in the press box. The crowd, which had reacted with a loud "OOOOH" when Pete was hit, watched in silence as stadium attendants placed him on a stretcher and carried him to the Ebbets Field clubhouse.

When he got there, Larry MacPhail was waiting. "I was so scared I was sick. I could not get back to the clubhouse fast enough," the Dodger GM told reporters after the game. Leo Durocher chimed in: "You weren't any more scared than I was. He dropped like a bullet [had hit him] and stayed so still."

MacPhail and Durocher's grim concern was more than justified. There was no such thing as batting helmets in 1941, and a single "beanball" to the head could end a player's career—in the worst cases, his life. Just two decades earlier, Cleveland shortstop Ray Chapman, another fine "what if" player, had died of brain injuries after a pitch from the Yankees' Carl Mays severely fractured his skull. Chapman remains, to date, the only player killed by an injury sustained during a major league game. But several minor leaguers had also died of beanings. Pete played against the most recent victim, Linus Ebnet of the Northern League's Winnipeg Maroons, who passed away four days after being struck in the head by a fastball in a July 1938 game. Pete's team that '38 season, the

Superior Blues, suffered their own player death two years earlier when infielder George Tkach was hit in the upper left jaw by a pitch and suffered fatal brain swelling.

Less than a year before Reiser was felled, Durocher and MacPhail got an up-close look at another scary beaning. The Dodgers, as noted, paid more than one hundred thirty thousand dollars to the Cardinals in June 1940 to acquire former MVP Joe Medwick—and, quite possibly, to compensate the Redbirds for the loss of Reiser. On June 18th, Medwick came to bat against his former team for the first time. On the very first pitch, Cardinal starter Bob Bowman fired a high, inside fastball that smashed into the left side of Medwick's face, leaving him unconscious and spread-eagled on his back next to the plate. In that instance, as doctors attended to Medwick on the field, a bellowing, out-of-control MacPhail stomped out of the Brooklyn dugout, over to the Cardinal bench, and challenged several players to fight. Dodger coaches pulled him away, but that night, MacPhail went further, publicly accusing Bowman of attempted murder. His "evidence" was a testy pre-game conversation at the Hotel New Yorker between Durocher, Medwick, and Bowman in which the latter vowed to "take care of" the new Dodger slugger.

At MacPhail's request, the Brooklyn district attorney's office conducted an investigation, questioning several players. Ultimately, the D.A. declined to press charges, MacPhail calmed down, and the matter was dropped. As for Medwick, he was diagnosed with a concussion. In the grit-it-out fashion of many elite athletes, he returned to the Dodger lineup just five days later. However, the beaning left its mark; many observers felt that afterward, Medwick was gun-shy at the plate—afraid of inside pitches—and was never again the same hitter.

MacPhail refrained from screaming bloody murder after the Reiser beaning, as no one seemed to think Ike Pearson had hit Pete intentionally. The pitch still could have been deadly. Fortunately, Pete had some protection. Before the '41 season, MacPhail, a man of both talk and action, had ordered the Dodgers to wear specially-designed plastic inserts in their caps when hitting. The inserts were flimsy compared to the hard-shell batting helmets invented in the 1950s but offered a defense of sorts against the knockdown pitches that were a standard and largely accepted part of pitchers' repertoires in this era. Pete used the insert as instructed and was wearing it on April 23rd when the pitch from Pearson slammed into his cheekbone, an inch or so away from his right temple.

Doctors who X-rayed him afterward at Brooklyn's Caledonian Hospital said the plastic had possibly saved his life. "He's a very lucky boy because he certainly would have had a fractured skull but for his 'helmet,' which absorbed part of the shock," Dr. D.A. McAteer told reporters. Instead, the doctor said, Pete got off lightly with a concussion and a "very sore face."

The Dodgers breathed a collective sigh of relief for their brilliant young centerfielder, who had singled and scored in his only other at-bat that day. Meanwhile, the impact left Pete a little foggy. "I don't know what just happened. I saw the ball come up to me, and I pulled back. I don't know whether I lost it or whether it sailed," he told reporters at the hospital. Then he went to sleep.

* * *

The haze cleared up as Pete spent the next three days at Caledonian, following orders to stay in bed and stay away from exercise. It was his first extended rest in some time. The Dodgers had started spring training early that year; for a change of pace, MacPhail arranged for them to train in Havana, Cuba, and flew them to the island in mid-February, more than two months before the season opener. An eager Pete, who had never left the United States before, was with them all the way. He had signed his 1941 contract without hassle that winter, accepting MacPhail's offer of four thousand five hundred dollars. "Pete is more than satisfied with the salary terms," his father told a St. Louis paper. Pete had to be equally happy with Durocher's projection that he would be the Dodgers' starting right fielder.

Pete certainly got a kick out of the whole Cuban experience, filling his scrapbook with black-and-white snapshots of friends and teammates relaxing on the beach, standing under the palm trees, basking in the warm Havana sun. But as always, he was mainly focused on baseball—that and meeting the Dodgers' high expectations. In the first week of camp, he had to fend off a challenge for the right-field job from thirty-seven-year-old Paul Waner, a future Hall of Famer and lifetime .333 hitter trying to extend his career. Once that was accomplished, the Dodgers presented him with a new task: be our center fielder. Dixie Walker had covered the position in 1940 but evidently not to Durocher's satisfaction. The manager thought Pete, with his speed and strong throwing arm, would be a better fit. He assigned coach Red Corriden to teach Pete the basics. "I told Corriden to specialize in cracking out those sinking liners because Pete is going to be seeing a lot of them in his new job," he said.

There were moments when the experiment stood on shaky ground. Against a team of Cuban all-stars in mid-March, Pete charged too fast on a pair of singles and let them skip by, turning the first into a triple, the other into a home run. But by early April, he had shown he could handle the job. And the stress of learning center field did nothing to his bat. Playing in nearly every exhibition game, his batting average for the spring was .382. The only thing that stopped his progress was an awkward swing in an exhibition game six days before the April 15th opener; Pete whipped the bat so hard that he pulled a back muscle. An unusually cautious Durocher planted him on the bench for a week and played Walker in center field on opening day so Pete could fully recover.

Once he got going, he was almost unstoppable. In his first thirty-eight plate appearances, Pete got on base twenty-two times: eleven times through hits and another eleven through walks, hit by pitch, fielder's choice or errors, the latter two caused in part by infielders hurrying plays as Pete sprinted down to first. In the two games he missed, the Dodgers scored a total of five runs and dropped both contests. In the ones he played, the club averaged seven runs per game and won six of eight. The highlight had been a Sunday afternoon thriller against the Giants. In front of fifty-six thousand fans, one of the biggest crowds in Polo Grounds history, Pete singled in the sixth, doubled in the seventh, and doubled again in the eighth, fueling rallies that enabled the Dodgers to pull out a come-from-behind 10-9 win.

"Ever since Pete Reiser got back in the lineup, the Dodgers have looked like a different team," wrote beat reporter Lee Scott in the next day's *Brooklyn Citizen*. "Once his potent bludgeon went into action, the Dodgers began to click."

To MacPhail's relief, the Dodgers kept clicking even with Reiser sidelined, winning six in a row to seize first place. Pistol Pete was hardly the only gun in Durocher's arsenal. The team he joined in 1940 already had several potent bats: the still-dangerous Medwick; stocky first baseman Dolph Camilli, good for twenty-five homers and a hundred RBI per year; and lanky Dixie Walker, a steady .300 hitter who had emerged as the Brooklyn fans' favorite, nicknamed the "People's Choice" (rendered in the Brooklyn accent as the "Peepul's *Cherce*.") Behind them, Pee Wee Reese provided speed and solid defense at shortstop, Cookie Lavagetto had a strong handle on third, and a somewhat older pitching staff led by Whitlow Wyatt, Freddie Fitzsimmons and Hugh Casey provided capable if not dominating mound support. The 1940 team's eighty-eight wins were the most by any Brooklyn squad since 1924.

But MacPhail was not satisfied, and he spent freely ahead of the '41 season to address the team's weak spots. In November, he parted with three players and one hundred thousand dollars to acquire the Phillies' top pitcher, Kirby Higbe. In December, he forked over sixty-five thousand dollars to get the Cardinals' starting catcher, Mickey Owen. Higbe, excited to be away from the basement-dwelling Phillies, said later that the players smelled pennant before the '41 season began. "We knew in spring training we had a shot at it," he remembered.

Durocher, of course, radiated pure confidence. "Everyone is asking me what our chances are for the flag. Well, I think this is our year," he said that March. Three weeks into the season, MacPhail further strengthened the roster by acquiring the Cubs' all-star second baseman Billy Herman, this time for the price of two players and another sixty-five thousand dollars.

This was decades before critics derided George Steinbrenner's Yankees as "The Best Team Money Could Buy." After the Herman purchase, Whitey Martin of the Associated Press wrote, "MacPhail has just bought the best pumpkins and entered them in the county fair as his own. Maybe he doesn't deserve the credit for developing his club, but you've got to admire his enterprise."

With Brooklyn's hopes running so high, Pete returned to action soon as he could after the Pearson beaning. In his famous magazine piece "The Rocky Road of Pistol Pete," W.C. Heinz reported that a still-groggy Reiser came off the bench just one day later, woozily pinch-hit with the bases loaded and somehow blasted a grand slam homer into the center-field stands. That was fiction. In reality, Pete was out for a full week until April 30th and didn't even get a chance to hit his first game back. He did score the winning run, though; Durocher inserted him in the ninth to run for Owen, who had just doubled, and two batters later, Reese smoked his own double to left-center to drive in Pete and give the Dodgers a 4-3 win. "The nearly apoplectic crowd ... poured onto the field to do snake-dances of victory," reported the *Daily News* the next day. The triumph was the Dodgers' ninth in a row.

The following day, Reiser was back on full-time duty and hit safely in the next five games, mostly in situations classified as "clutch." May 3rd against the Cubs, he doubled in the eighth inning and scored on Medwick's single for what turned out to be the winning run. The next day he crashed a two-run homer in the ninth as the Dodgers tried to come back against the Pirates, although the rally fell short. Against the Cardinals on May 7th, he saved a run in the fifth by throwing out Walker Cooper at home, then banged out a key RBI single in the eighth as the Dodgers overcame a two-run deficit to win 4-3.

Pete wasn't blessed with clear sailing just yet. On May 8th, thirty-two thousand fans (including eleven thousand "Ladies Day" customers) crowded into Ebbets Field to see another matchup with the Cardinals. The Dodgers were ahead 2-0 in the second inning when the Cards' Enos Slaughter hammered a pitch toward the deepest part of the ballpark, the center field notch. The notch was one of the oddities of Brooklyn's little stadium, a hexagonal-shaped feature where the right-field fence met the center field stands. It also housed an iron gate that allowed fans leaving the game to exit onto Bedford

Avenue. Reiser, wearing sunglasses, his eyes focused solely on Slaughter's drive, paid no heed to the gate or the walls around it as he raced back. A few steps into the notch, he made a running, leaping stab at the ball—and caught it, robbing Slaughter of extra bases. He didn't quite stick the landing, though, and fell back-first into the gate. A piece of metal dug through his jersey and into his skin, opening a two-inch long gash in the lower part of his back.

Ignoring the pain, Pete flipped the ball to Dixie Walker, who fired it back in and stopped baserunner Johnny Mize from advancing to second. Then the Dodgers attended to Pete, who was dazed and bleeding through his uniform. He was able to walk off the field on his power, but for the second time in two weeks, he was transported to Caledonian Hospital, where doctors stitched up the cut and, a day later, as a precaution, gave him a tetanus shot.

It was Pete's first major collision with an outfield wall. Compared with the ones to come, he got off easy.

Again, Durocher kept Pete on the bench for several games to heal, with backup Jimmy Wasdell taking his place. While Pete recuperated, Boston manager Casey Stengel made an astute observation about Brooklyn's young center fielder. "I believe that boy has really arrived," Stengel said. "I always suspected him of having it—and this season, he's clinched it. He's there. He's a star player right now—if he stands up. He's been hurt a couple of times. Maybe he's fragile. You know a star can't deliver unless he stands up."

Pete returned to action May 18th in Chicago and proceeded to both stand up and stand out, batting .397 for the balance of the month. His peak came during a Dodger five-game sweep of the Phillies, during which he lashed out eleven hits in twenty-three at-bats. Pete did significant damage in all five games, but the May 25th contest made heads turn. Brooklyn was losing 4-3 in the sixth when long-suffering Philly manager Doc Prothro, dragging himself through a third consecutive year of last-place, hundred-loss baseball, removed starter Lee Grissom from the game after he gave up one too many walks. Grissom's replacement? None other than Ike Pearson, who'd gotten himself demoted to relief pitching after getting bombed in several early-season outings. Pearson wasn't awful on this day, but the Dodgers managed to tie the game without a hit, using an infield error, a sacrifice, an intentional pass, and a groundout to score a run. Pearson then walked Billy Herman to load the bases.

Next batter: Pete Reiser, facing Pearson for the first time since the beaning. With the bases full and the score knotted 4-4, the situation "couldn't have been more dramatic if it were part of a Hollywood scenario," wrote *Times* reporter Louis Effrat. Another beaning wasn't out of the question. Pearson topped

National League pitchers in hit batters that season with eight, and Reiser would be plunked a league-leading eleven times by year's end. But there were no brushback pitches as Pete worked the count to three balls, one strike. Pearson came in next with a fastball, a little outside. It could have been ball four. However, Pete made what one writer described as a mad lunge for the pitch and connected.

The ball soared toward the center-field wall on the fly. Philly center fielder Joe Marty raced back but had no chance for a catch; the ball cracked off the top of the wall and ricocheted away from him. While he chased after it, all three Dodger runners galloped around the bases and scored. The only question was whether Pete would come in behind them. With most players, there would be a close play at the plate. But most players didn't have Pete's fleet feet. By the time Marty got his hands on the ball, Reiser had reached third base. And by the time Marty's throw reached the catcher, Pete had already crossed the plate standing up, greeted by Medwick and Herman and Walker, all giving him hard atta-boy slaps on the back as he trotted back to the dugout in triumph.

Pete had hit an inside-the-park grand slam, a rare feat in the 1940s and one that has almost vanished from the game today. As of this writing, the last one was accomplished by the Nationals' Michael Taylor in 2017.

The Dodgers won the game 8-4. The next day, Reiser's homer was headline news on all the New York sports pages. "His Grand Slam a Wow," proclaimed the *Brooklyn Citizen* above a half-page photo of Pete. And in the long run, Effrat wasn't the only one who found the moment worthy of Hollywood. In 2010, while scripting the movie *Captain America: The First Avenger*, screenwriters Christopher Markus and Stephen McFeely decided to have a baseball game playing on the radio when S.H.I.E.L.D.—the chief good guy organization in the Marvel universe—tried to convince Steve Rogers it was still the 1940s as he woke from a seventy-year nap.

The original script had Rogers opening his eyes to the sound of an unidentifiable game where a highly obscure Brooklyn pitcher, Bob Chipman, was pitching to a mostly forgotten Boston Braves outfielder, Chuck Workman.

As they revised the script, Markus and McFeely rightly chose to focus on a more memorable contest and picked the one decided by Pete's round-tripper. The final version had Rogers rising from bed as a Red Barber-soundalike described the action:

> . . . *Just an absolutely gorgeous day here at Ebbets Field. The Phillies have managed to tie it up at 4 to 4. But the Dodgers have three men on. Pearson beaned Reiser in Philadelphia last month. Wouldn't the youngster*

like a hit here to return the favor? Pete leans in. Here's the pitch. Swung on. A line to the right. And it gets past Rizzo! Three runs will score. Reiser heads to third. Durocher's going to wave him in. Here comes the relay, but they won't get him. Pete Reiser with an inside-the-park grand slam! . . . The Dodgers take the lead 8 to 4. Ohh, doctor!

The only thing that marred Pete's brush with Marvel movie fame was the pronunciation of his name. The actor repeatedly said it with a long "i" sound, making it rhyme with wiser or geyser. Such is the difference between being one of baseball's all-time greats and being the sport's greatest "what if."

* * *

Pete finally stayed healthy for an entire month that June, getting enough at-bats to qualify for the NL batting race while the Dodgers bounced in and out of first, wrestling with the Cardinals for the league lead. Brooklynites smelled pennant in the air and flocked to Ebbets Field in record numbers. You could say the borough of two-point-five million people had a pent-up demand for winning baseball. Their team was one of only three that had never won a World Series; the others were the lowly Phillies and St. Louis Browns. The Dodgers hadn't even reached the Fall Classic since 1920, and the bulk of the intervening years were losing ones. The team had become so downtrodden that in the spring of 1934, when a sportswriter asked Giants manager Bill Terry where he thought Brooklyn would finish that season, Terry replied, "Brooklyn? Is Brooklyn still in the league?" The Dodgers made Terry eat those words on the final weekend of the season, downing the Giants twice in a row at the Polo Grounds to deny them a second straight pennant and allowing Pete's favored Cardinals to claim the NL flag. But Terry's sarcastic jibe wasn't without foundation: the Dodgers limped through the 1930s with a string of sixth- and seventh-place finishes which in tandem with the Depression led to falling attendance and rising debt for the club's owners.

Not that the club was *boring,* mind you. By the mid-'30s, the Dodgers had earned a reputation for bizarre happenings. Club mainstay Wilbert Robinson, who managed the club for eighteen years, was at the center of many of them. One time "Uncle Robbie" let the players pick the starting lineup out of a hat; the Dodgers won. On another occasion, Robinson created a Bonehead Club to discourage mental errors, then gave the umpire a lineup card with his players in the wrong order. Another time, he agreed to try to catch a baseball dropped from a low-flying plane. The pilot dropped a grapefruit instead, which exploded upon hitting Robinson's glove. Liquid splattered everywhere, and for a terrifying second, Robinson thought he was covered in his own blood. Then he realized the warm ooze was grapefruit juice.

This era's quintessential moment occurred in a 1926 game against Boston at Ebbets Field. Batting with the bases loaded, rookie outfielder Babe Herman smashed a line drive off the right-field fence. The runner on third base, Hank DeBerry, scored. The runner on second, Dazzy Vance, rounded third but came back to the bag because of a quick throw-in from the outfield. That would have been fine, except that the runner on first base, Chick Fewster, failed to notice Vance retreating and charged into third as well. Herman, evidently running with his head down and his ears stuffed with cotton, also kept motoring ahead and soon stood face to face with his teammates. The Dodgers had accomplished a baseball first: three men on third base. A confused Braves infielder tagged Vance, Fewster, Herman, the third base coach, and everybody else in sight until the umps sorted out the mess, declaring that Vance was entitled to the bag and that Fewster and Herman were out.

In stories about the game, Herman often got credit for tripling into a triple play. That was unfair—he had doubled into a double play. But incidents like this prompted columnist Westbrook Pegler to dub the Dodgers "the Daffiness Boys" and for Brooklyn fans to start calling them "dem Bums"—a name that could be used as a term of derision or endearment, depending on the user's mood.

The bizarreness extended off the field. In 1925, club co-owner Charles Ebbets, who owned half the stock, died of heart failure. The other half-owner, Ed McKeever, caught pneumonia standing in the rain at Ebbets' funeral and died just eleven days later. The two men's heirs spent the next dozen years feuding about money and power, allowing the team to fall into its bedraggled state. Fortunately, the Dodgers had a base of hearty fans. Actually, *fanatics* would be a better word. No other team in baseball had supporters who rooted so loudly, vociferously, and theatrically for their heroes. Eddie Battan marched around in a white safari helmet and blew a high-pitched whistle. Jack Pierce popped balloons and cheered non-stop for his favorite player, Cookie Lavagetto. ("COOOOOKIIEEEEE!") The Dodger Sym-phony (emphasis on the word *phony*) played an array of drums, trumpets, and trombones with little talent but at inescapable volume, taunting umpires with their rendition of "Three Blind Mice." And planted in the center field bleachers, right where Pete could hear her, was Hilda Chester, a middle-aged woman armed with powerful lungs, a loud bell, and undying devotion to her team. "She never missed a game, it seemed," Pete remembered. "She'd sit out in the bleachers yelling in a foghorn voice and ringing this big cowbell she always carried . . . I hear that voice: 'Hey Reiser!' There could be thirty thousand people yelling at once, and Hilda's the one you'd hear."

Brooklyn's ballpark itself encouraged such intimacy. Constructed in 1913, Ebbets Field was originally built to hold only eighteen thousand people. The club expanded the seating capacity over the years, but not the stadium's footprint; the added seats merely brought fans closer to the action. According to Red Barber, the effect made Ebbets Field the most intimate ballpark in the majors. "You weren't back in the stands; you were in the ballgame," he recalled. "You were close enough to hear the players breathe and grunt, and you could see whether they had a pimple on the back of their neck or not. You could hear what they said to each other, and they could hear what you said to them. And you, in turn, could hear what they said back to you."

The Dodgers' board of directors hired MacPhail in 1938 to turn around the floundering franchise, which had drawn barely half the attendance of the pennant-winning Yankees and Giants the previous year. The club was more than a half-million dollars in debt to its bank, the Brooklyn Trust Company. Still, the driven MacPhail demanded and received more money from the bank to build up the farm system, to fix up rundown Ebbets Field ("a mess of broken seats, begging for a coat of paint," in the words of sportswriter Harold Parrott) and to buy quality ballplayers.

His most astute move may have been hiring Leo Durocher as manager before the '39 season. Not everyone liked Leo. In fact, many people outright hated him. Bad guy, vicious, ill-tempered, amoral—these were just some of the labels that Durocher's detractors stuck on him during his fifty-year baseball career, first as a speedy, slick-fielding shortstop for four major league teams and then as a manager, primarily for the Dodgers, Giants, and Cubs. Off the field, he was accused at various times of stealing Babe Ruth's watch, passing bad checks, cheating on his wives (there were four), punching a fan, and hanging out with mob associates like actor George Raft and at least one outright mobster, Bugsy Siegel. On the field, he was known for sliding with spikes high, calling for knockdown pitches ("Stick in his f---ing ear!"), freely taunting the opposition and endless, blistering arguments with umpires. Wherever Durocher went, tempers were likely to flare, and one of his employers, Branch Rickey, often described Durocher as a man with "a fertile talent for taking a bad situation and making it immediately worse."

But, Rickey added, "I would take him to manage any club." His supporters said he ran a game like a card shark, or a pool hustler, thinking two or three moves ahead of the other team. The on-field rowdiness was meant to unsettle opponents and get them mentally unfocused. Then they'd be more vulnerable to some of the aggressive tactics Leo favored, like double steals, the hit-and-run, and surprise squeeze bunts. Even his critics had to admit Leo was good at making his personnel play harder and smarter and getting more wins out of a team than might be expected. It helped that he was a fairly advanced baseball thinker for his time, one who embraced innovations such as frequent use of relief pitchers and playing righty-lefty percentages. He also had a charming side, sometimes funny, that took the edge off his intensity. Monte Irvin, who played for Durocher with the Giants, recalled a game in Cincinnati where he dropped a fly ball to cost the team a victory. "When I came in, he said, 'Monte, if I had a gun, I'd shoot you.' I said, 'No, let me do it; I'll shoot myself.' He said, 'Well, if you did, you'd miss.' You know, made a little joke out of it. He was tough, but I guess everybody appreciated a manager of that type, who was tough but fair."

Like Leo, Pete cared about winning more than anything else and was one of the manager's biggest fans. "I've heard a lot of guys knock Leo for a lot of things," he said after his playing career was over. "But I've always said this about him: If you didn't know him, you'd hate his guts. But if you knew him, you'd love him. He was the best. He was aggressive, and he fought for you."

But in the end, it wasn't the manager, the owner, the ballpark, or the fans that made the '41 Dodgers special. The players were the ones driving the team to the top. Whitlow Wyatt, just a fair-to-middling pitcher to that point in his career, suddenly emerged as the staff's ace, winning nine of his first twelve starts, all nine by complete games, four of them by shutout. All of the regulars were hitting well, especially Billy Herman, who batted a scorching .369 in his first thirty games after coming over from the Cubs, and to everyone's surprise, Lavagetto, who finished the first month of the season hitting .340, about seventy points above his lifetime average. Gradually, it dawned on everyone that the Dodgers' strong start was no illusion. When the red-hot Cardinals came to town in early June, manager Billy Southworth started his best young pitchers: Max Lanier, Ernie White, and Mort Cooper. Durocher's men dropped them two out of three, pulling into a tie for first place. The defending champion Reds came into town that weekend and stopped Brooklyn cold, sweeping a three-game series. But the Dodgers rebounded on a western road trip, taking ten of fourteen.

And as often as not, it was Pete powering the offense. In a 6-0 win against the Cardinals, he banged a two-run homer in the first inning and singled to start a three-run fifth. The next day the Dodgers lost one to the Reds but not because of Pete, who singled, doubled, and homered. In St. Louis on June 14th, Brooklyn was down 4-0 when Pete got to work: RBI single in the sixth, single and run scored in the seventh, home run in the eighth. The Bums roared back to win 12-5. Three days later in Chicago, the Dodgers trailed 4-2 in the eighth when Pete hit an RBI double, scored minutes later on another double, then singled in the tenth to spark the game-winning rally.

At times that month, Pete's batting average crossed the .370 line. "I don't know anybody with a better chance to lead the league," said Camilli, who was leading the NL in home runs. "It's a potential hit every time his bat meets the ball."

The road trip climaxed with a June 22nd doubleheader in Cincinnati. In the opener, Wyatt and the Reds' Paul Derringer, laboring in muggy, hundred-degree heat, each pitched ten scoreless innings. In the top of the eleventh, Wyatt, a good hitter for a pitcher, broke the tie by cracking a homer into the lower left-field stands. Then he had to leave the game; he had accidentally swallowed a large swig of mouthwash instead of water and threw up in the dugout. Hugh Casey, sent out with little warm-up, allowed four hits and the tying run. The Reds would have enjoyed a walk-off win if not for Pete, who threw out Lonny Frey at third as he tried to extend a sure two-bagger into a triple.

Derringer was doggedly still pitching when Pete led off the top of the sixteenth. Six times that day, the Reds' ace had set him down, not permitting one ball to leave the infield. Third base coach Charley Dressen gave Pete some quick advice: "Derringer's stopping you by placing the ball close to your knuckles. Step back six inches when I give the curve sign, then swing." Pete listened and connected, lashing a single to center. The next batter, Lew Riggs, laid down a sacrifice bunt that the Reds mishandled, allowing Pete to race all the way to third. For only the second time all day, the Dodgers had a man ninety feet from home. Durocher ordered a suicide squeeze. Pete rushed the plate as Dixie Walker laid down a bunt. Reds' first baseman Frank McCormick charged, scooped up the ball, and tossed it home—but not in time to catch Pete, who tapped the plate with his left hand as he executed a fadeaway slide to the right.

Minutes later, Casey set down the Reds to seal the 2-1 victory. Then the teams played the second game, rushing to complete it before darkness set in. Pete helped slay the Reds in that one, too, singling in Billy Herman with what turned out to be the winning score.

While the Dodgers and Reds tangled in Cincinnati, a more titanic clash was unfolding five thousand miles to the east, where more than one million soldiers, backed by massive fleets of tanks and warplanes, were storming east on day one of Germany's epic, Adolf Hitler-masterminded invasion of the Soviet Union. Even in baseball-crazy New York, the invasion was enough to push news of the Dodgers' triumphs or Joe DiMaggio's growing hitting streak (now at thirty-five games) off the front pages. The back page of the *Daily News*, which was often devoted to baseball photos, was also covered in pics from Berlin and the war front. Nevertheless, the headline above the shots read, "Yanks Win, Set HR Mark; Dodgers, Giants Win Two." Even with history's biggest war expanding by the day, the paper had its priorities.

* * *

As the Dodgers hung in the race, never slipping more than four games behind the Cardinals, never climbing more than four ahead, insiders began to heap praise on Reiser, who was now delivering a key hit, running play, catch or throw on an almost daily basis. Durocher naturally led the way, predicting in May that Pete would win the batting title and turn into a superstar. "This is no early-season streak he's having. He's a great natural hitter, one of the greatest in recent years," said Leo.

Some might have been tempted to dismiss Leo's words as hype, but other skippers were chiming in. Stengel had proclaimed Pete a star. Reds manager Bill McKechnie said, "I'm nuts about that kid center fielder, Reiser. He's a whale of a ballplayer." Pirates' manager Frankie Frisch spoke up after a game in which Pete stole two bases and scored twice, the second run coming when his dancing off third base caused pitcher Lefty Wilkie to commit a balk. "That Reiser is the best to come along in several years, isn't he?" Frisch said. "Is there anything he can't do? I see no weakness in him at all. What a guy he's going to be as the years go by."

The beat reporters were raving too:

- "There wouldn't be any pennant race if Pete Reiser, the flash of Flatbush, was a St. Louis Cardinal instead of a dashing Dodger . . . Maybe it is just as well that Landis intervened." —Gerry Schumacher, *New York Journal-American.*

- "On every bench in (NL president) Ford Frick's domain, they're talking about Reiser. Rival players watch him take his cut during batting practice, announce when he's going to make a throw to the plate or third base during the outfielding drill and just whistle their amazement when he scoots down the first base line on an infield dribbler or a well-placed bunt." —Arthur Patterson, *New York Herald Tribune*.

- "His average has remained far in advance of the rest of the league. He's shown them more than great batting ability, however. He's stunned them with his speed, thrilled them with his outfielding, and made them marvel at his rifle-like throws. They all realize now that they're watching a youngster who's going to be one of baseball's outstanding players for a long time to come." —Jerry Mitchell, *New York Post*.

On July 2nd, the celebration of Reiser's talents went coast to coast when Grantland Rice chose to focus his column on the phenomenon of Pistol Pete. "Granny" Rice had a well-deserved reputation for turning sports figures into heroes and legends. In the 1920s, his stories helped build a select group of athletes into national idols, including boxer Jack Dempsey, golfer Bobby Jones, footballer Red Grange, tennis star Bill Tilden and naturally, baseball's supernova, Babe Ruth. Rice's writing occasionally veered into the hyper-dramatic; he sometimes invested in athletic contests with importance usually reserved for great military battles and didn't mind comparing the athletes to figures from literature, ancient history, or the Bible. His most famous story concerned the backfield of the 1924 Notre Dame football team. The Fighting Irish had pulled off an upset over Army, beating them 13-7 in front of fifty-five thousand at the Polo Grounds. Rice, looking for a striking way to describe the Notre Dame backs, was somehow reminded of the Four Horsemen of the Apocalypse in the New Testament's Book of Revelation. He fashioned the allusion into the most famous sports lead of its time: "Outlined against a blue-gray October sky, the Four Horsemen rode again. In dramatic lore, they are known as famine, pestilence, destruction, and death. These are only aliases. Their real names are Stuhldreher, Miller, Crowley, and Layden."

In July 1941, Rice steered away from Christian mythology when writing about Pete Reiser. In fact, it could be said he didn't write the column at all. The piece was mostly a monologue by Durocher, a pal to Rice and sportswriters everywhere, for his tendency to talk freely and at length about almost any baseball-related subject. But Rice did Leo the favor of letting him compare Reiser to a legendary, imposing figure from baseball's past.

"I know what another Ty Cobb means. But if there ever will be another Ty Cobb, his name will be Reiser," Durocher proclaimed. "He weighs about one hundred eighty-five pounds, about Cobb's ballplaying weight, and like Cobb, he is strong and rugged. He is a little faster than Ty was at his best. To my mind, I'll take Reiser for speed against anyone in baseball today from either league. Yes, Johnny Rucker of the Giants is fast, but not as fast down to first as Reiser is."

"That isn't all," Leo went on. "Pete is a natural hitter. He has no weakness that I've ever seen or that any pitcher has yet found. When he learns a little more through experience, he may easily move into the .400 class. That still isn't all. Reiser has a fine arm, better than most. He sizes up the play in a flash and starts in a flash." Durocher also extolled Pete's versatility ("He can play any position on the club and look good in them all,") his work ethic ("Pete is always anxious to learn,") and his gung-ho attitude ("I don't think I ever saw anybody who loved baseball more.")

At least one paper, *The Daily Oklahoman*, made light of Leo's fawning. The caption under Reiser's photo and name read dryly: "Durocher is high on him." But tellingly, no one in the baseball or newspaper worlds felt the need to correct Leo or admonish Rice for allowing a comparison between the Pistol and the great Georgia Peach. There was a likeness that couldn't be denied.

The day before Rice's column appeared, it was announced that Reiser, in his first full season in the big leagues, had been named to the National League's roster for the All-Star Game July 8th in Detroit. At twenty-two, he was the youngest player ever chosen for the NL squad. A few days later, the honor was doubled when NL manager Bill McKechnie said Pete would be his starting center fielder. On the last day before the all-star break, Pete proved himself worthy by bashing three hits against the Braves, including a two-run homer, pushing his batting average up to a league-leading .360. More importantly, the Dodgers ended the first half in first place, three games ahead of St. Louis.

Two days later, he was standing on the field at Detroit's Briggs Stadium, mingling with the very best in his profession. The rosters were sprinkled with future Hall of Famers: Mel Ott, Enos Slaughter, and Johnny Mize on the National League squad, Joe DiMaggio, Bob Feller, Ted Williams, and Jimmie Foxx, among others on the American League side. Pete was starstruck. "I'll never forget the All-Star Game," he later recalled. "I started in center field, and every once in a while, I'd reach down and pinch myself. 'Is this real, or is this a dream?' I'd ask. 'Am I really playing with all these great players I'd read about and admired?'" So intense was this feeling that for the first time, maybe the only time in his baseball career, Pete seemed a touch distracted on the field. At the plate, he failed to get a hit in four times up, striking out twice and hitting into a double play. In the field, he misplayed two singles, both by Cleveland's Lou

Boudreau, and was charged with a pair of errors. The *Daily Eagle* blamed the slip-ups on "stage fright."

Going into the bottom of the ninth, the National League led 5-3. But DiMaggio knocked in one run on a groundout, and with two men on and two out, Williams walloped a Claude Passeau pitch into the upper deck of the right-field stands. As he rounded the bases, the usually undemonstrative Splendid Splinter skipped and clapped and smiled like a miner who'd just struck gold. His homer gave the American League a 7-5 win and gave Ted one of the signature moments of his career.

The one big name missing from the lineups that day was the Tigers' Hank Greenberg, winner of the previous year's AL MVP award. Hammerin' Hank was at the game all right, watching unobtrusively from the stands, but only because his superiors permitted him. Two months before, the thirty-year-old Greenberg had been inducted into the U.S. Army, one of the first major leaguers drafted under the 1940 Selective Training and Service Act, which required one year of military service for draftees. Overnight, he went from a sports star making fifty-five thousand dollars a year to an army private making twenty-one bucks per month.

Greenberg was less than thrilled to be giving up baseball—"It's a pretty tough thing to give up. It's almost the only thing I've thought about all my life," he told teammates. But he went along with it; like many Americans, he believed the U.S. had to get ready for entry into the spreading world war. Brooklyn had also lost a player to the army, reserve outfielder Joe Gallagher, while the Phillies lost their best hurler, Hugh Mulcahy. Other players who'd been called to service, such as Chicago White Sox pitcher Johnny Rigney and the Washington Senators' hard-hitting shortstop, Cecil Travis, were trying to get deferments that would let them finish the season before starting their hitch.

The military hadn't come calling for Pete just yet, but he knew it might only be a matter of time. After Congress passed the Service Act the previous year, he registered with his Brooklyn draft board, listing his place of employment as "215 Montague Street," the Dodgers' home office address. Being just twenty-two, athletic and unmarried, he was prime draft material. The one thing that might delay induction was that he helped support his parents and siblings back in St. Louis. They were dependents, in a way. They'd face hardship if he couldn't play ball.

For the moment, he put the whole matter to the side. America was not yet at war. No one had said his call-up was imminent. And there was still a pennant to win.

* * *

Brooklyn, as a whole, was going gaga over that possibility. The first Sunday after the all-star break, more than thirty-five thousand fans stuffed Ebbets Field—an impressive feat for a ballpark that officially held only thirty-four. Home games weren't enough for the most ardent rooters. A new organization calling itself the "Brooklyn Dodgers Victory Committee" had begun organizing trips to out-of-town games. In late June, several hundred caught a steamship to Boston to watch their heroes play (and split) a Sunday doubleheader against the Braves. In May, some two thousand went by bus to see their beloved Bums play (and win) a night game in Philadelphia. The organizers gave themselves a share of credit for the victories. The committee "firmly believes that the vocal support of the faithful is a strong factor in swinging the decision at many games," explained an item in the *Citizen*.

The fans' ardor was especially strong for certain players, in particular Dixie Walker, who cruised to victory in a popularity poll of Dodger players conducted by the Victory Committee and the *Daily Eagle* that September. (Camilli finished second, Pete a strong third.) But a certain segment of the fans focused on the two youngsters in the lineup. Early in the season, a group of female fans hung a sign on a railing that read, in capital letters, "PETE REISER—PEE WEE REESE." It tended to reappear when the team held one of its periodic Ladies Day promotions. Before one such game in July, Walker was sitting on the dugout steps when an attractive young woman leaned over the roof and dropped a note into his lap. The outfielder, who was coming up on his thirty-first birthday, proudly held up the paper and waved it in front of some teammates. "So, you thought Dixie was getting too old, did you?" he boasted.

Then he opened the note. It read: "Dear Mr. Walker, will you please give this note to Pete Reiser and tell him several of his fans will phone him at his hotel tonight at nine o'clock?"

Walker sighed: "Well, I'll be—I'm just an intermediary!"

Cookie Lavagetto consoled him: "Don't feel bad, Dixie, you could probably go along—maybe as a chaperone."

The result of the phone call is lost to history. Pete was more focused on baseball than his social life, anyway. Usually, when he ventured out at night, it was to a movie or on a double date with Reese, his closest pal on the team. "If you see one, you know the other isn't far away," read a *Daily Eagle* caption below a shot of Pete and Pee Wee chatting during a train ride. The Dodgers had put them together as roommates during spring training, and the two decided to keep the arrangement going during the regular season, both on road trips and at an apartment in Brooklyn, in the Hotel St. George, the in-season residence for several Dodgers players. "We just clicked," Reese explained. In many ways, they were natural buds. They shared the same first name, Harold. They were both in their early twenties, both bachelors, both friendly guys, and both serious about sticking to curfew and training rules, a trait that set them apart from some older, hard-drinking teammates, like Higbe and Casey. The press dubbed them the Gold Dust Twins, a moniker that referred to their talent, similarities, and presumably lucrative futures.

Pee Wee was more naturally outgoing of the pair and got the lion's share of female attention, even though he had a steady girlfriend back in his native Louisville. "How do they all find out where you live?" he mock-complained to a visiting *Sporting News* reporter that summer. "That phone is ringing all day. 'Can I bake you a cake, Pee Wee?' 'Do you like spaghetti, Pee Wee?'" Reese acknowledged that Pete didn't have a girl at that moment, but not because of any lack of personality. "It gives me a laugh when I read in the papers that I'm the lively guy, and Pete's the deadpan," he said. The girls would focus more on Pete, he added, "if they only knew what a funny guy he is."

The reporter caught a bit of the good-natured banter between the pals when Reese loudly remarked that Pete "gets all the base hits in the room. Those .350 hitters are greedy." Reiser shouted out from his bedroom: "You're not fit to live with when you're not hitting!"

The retort contained a kernel of truth: Reese was struggling at the plate that season. He had done well in his rookie year, 1940, batting .272 in eighty-four games before a broken heel bone ended his season. His play at shortstop was so good that Durocher, the Dodgers' regular at the position in '39, demoted himself to backup. But in 1941, Reese had difficulties both at bat and in the field. Somehow, he made ten errors in the first fourteen games of the season and was never sure-handed all year long. Hitting-wise, his batting average stayed in the .230 range, with precious little power. Durocher stubbornly kept him in the lineup, batting him leadoff most of the time. "Pee Wee was a young kid, and he'd get a little flighty, a little erratic, and Durocher would take him out for a game or two, and he'd play and then put Pee Wee back in there," remembered Billy Herman. MacPhail occasionally voiced a wish to see Durocher take the field more often but, in the end, didn't complain about Reese's presence—with him as the shortstop, after all, the Dodgers were in first place.

The team came charging out of the all-star break, winning six of eight. Then the bottom fell out: ten losses in thirteen games, with a worthless tie thrown in.

The lead over the Cardinals evaporated, turned into a three-game deficit. Some of the regulars, especially Medwick and Camilli, were mired in slumps. The pitching stars, Whit Wyatt and Kirby Higbe, were suddenly very hittable. (One smart alec said if Wyatt kept losing, Durocher would be at his "Whit's end.") And it seemed like the team just couldn't catch a break. One day in Cincinnati, Casey tried to protect a 4-1 lead with the bases loaded in the ninth and threw a brushback pitch to pinch-hitter Chuck Aleno. Aleno ducked, but the ball accidentally hit his bat and looped over Camilli's head at first, landing on the right-field foul line and bouncing away from Walker. Three runs scored, and Aleno sped all the way to third. Bucky Walters then hit a sacrifice fly for the game-winner. An incredulous Durocher said the loss made him "want to throw the furniture out the window."

Pete wasn't responsible for the slide. His batting average stayed north of .330. In one loss to the Pirates, he banged out four hits, including a double, but none of his teammates could bring him around to score. Three days later, the Dodgers were in St. Louis. In the eighth inning, Pete came to bat with one man on and the Cardinals ahead by a run. The pitcher, Ernie White, tended to dominate Pete, usually made him look "as though he were waving a stick of macaroni," in the words of *Eagle* sportswriter Harold Burr. On this day, Pete got the upper hand, launching a three-two pitch entirely out of Sportsman's Park, onto Grand Avenue behind the stadium. The blast put the Dodgers ahead 4-3. But relievers Mace Brown and Casey maddeningly gave up three runs in the bottom half of the inning, sealing another Dodger loss.

Whitney Martin declared the Dodgers all but dead and blamed it on the team's early spring training in Havana. The Brooklyn players, he wrote, were oh so tired. "They're plumb fed up on baseball for a while and anxious to get started on their off-season loafing," he added.

Obviously, Martin was not familiar with Reiser's drive or Durocher's powers of motivation. The next day, the Cardinals knocked out Wyatt in the third inning, but his teammates came roaring back. Pete broke a 3-3 tie with an RBI double in the fourth, and the Dodgers pressed on to a 9-5 win. It was the start of a seven-game winning streak that pushed the team back into a tie for first.

The injury bug was still circling, waiting for more chances to bite. Pete was sidelined for the fourth time that season on August 4th by an attack of sciatica, pain that radiated from his lower back down his legs. MacPhail put him in a cab and sent him to New York Hospital, where he underwent diathermy treatments. This time he missed only three games. He returned to the starting lineup on the 10th for a doubleheader sweep of the Braves. Boston put a wild righthander, Dick Errickson, on the mound in game one. In the span of two innings, Errickson plunked Medwick on the elbow, Camilli on the top of the head, and Reiser on the back of his head. Somehow, none of them were seriously hurt. In later years, Pete would mischaracterize this incident; he said he was hit in the head by a Cubs pitcher, *Paul* Erickson, and crafted a story about being sent to the hospital and getting a bedside visit from Judge Landis, investigating whether the beaning was deliberate. In actuality, he went right to first base after getting hit and played the rest of the game, a 14-4 Dodgers victory. He played the next day, too, banging out a double and a triple and throwing out a runner at the plate in a 15-7 win.

After an oh-fer-doubleheader against the Giants, Durocher gave Pete a one-day breather, then threw him back in action. The pennant race was too hot to give anyone a real rest. In the thirty-one days of August, the Dodgers and Cardinals spent nine days tied for first place and the rest no more than two games apart. "I can't recall any two teams that have moved head and head, nose and nose, for so many ball games," wrote Grantland Rice, using a horse race analogy. He refused to venture a guess on which squad was superior. "What would be your answer when two teams have remained practically deadlocked, eyelash against eyelash, after playing about one hundred twenty games for more than four months? I can't see enough difference to start a debate."

If there was any difference-maker between the teams, it was Pete, who continued to thrill and excel. After a weekend trip to Boston, the Dodgers began a crucial eleven-game homestand on Monday, August 18th. The first game against the Pirates was a ghastly affair for the Brooklyn infield, which committed six errors, giving the Pirates five free runs. But Pete bailed them out. With the score tied 5-5, he led off the bottom of the ninth. Durocher told him to get a rally started: walk, slap a single, just get on base. Pitcher Max Butcher hurled a fastball. Pete ripped the air around home plate with a mighty swing. Strike one. Durocher started yelling at him: just meet the ball, get a hit, get yourself to first. Butcher came back with a changeup. Pete took another Ruthian cut. This time, bat met ball and propelled it over the right-field fence for a walk-off homer and a 6-5 victory. Dozens of delirious fans charged on the field to greet Pete at home plate. In the clubhouse, Durocher joked: "I don't know whether to fine the kid fifty or recommend a bonus."

If Leo imposed the fine, he surely returned it by the end of the week. On Tuesday, Pete's two-out, two-run double in the eighth gave the Dodgers the lead en route to a 6-2 victory. On Wednesday, he pounded a seventh-inning homer off Rip Sewell to tie the game 6-6 and walked during the ninth-inning rally that scored the winning run. On Friday, he racked up three hits and two RBI and made a diving, rolling catch of a fly to short right-center to close out an 8-5 triumph over Chicago. After that win, Pete got a bonus of a different kind. "As Reiser ran in, a young woman dashed out of the lower stands near first base and kissed Pete. The crowd roared and shrieked its approval of the tribute," reported the *Times*.

Pete was still a near-rookie, only twenty-two years old, and sometimes, his enthusiasm for the game got the better of him. That July, after the All-Star game, he told reporters he had developed a simple theory on hitting: "Anything I think I can get my bat on, I swing for." He certainly wasn't taking many pitches; he walked only twice during the eleven games at home. Many days, this worked out fine, but mid-homestand, he suddenly hit a slump, going fifteen at-bats without a hit. His batting average drifted down to the low .320s, and he lost his place atop the league leaders. Durocher watched him flail for a few days, then publicly groused about his young star's overswinging after an August 26th loss to the Cardinals. In the fourth inning of that game, Pete had come to bat against Mort Cooper with the game scoreless and the bases full. "I begged him not to try to murder the ball—that's been some of his trouble lately," Leo said. "But what does he do? He breaks his back swinging, gets only a piece of the ball, and pops up to short."

Pete must have been listening. He was reported crying in the clubhouse after the game.

By the time the Dodgers visited the Polo Grounds for four games at the end of August, Pete had fixed his batting stroke and slammed out seven hits in sixteen times at-bat, in addition to accepting three walks. His average began to inch back up. For Durocher, it couldn't happen at a better time. September was here, the season had four weeks to run, and the Dodgers and Cardinals were separated by exactly two percentage points in the standings—about the width of a love note dropped from the stands.

* * *

The final month began with the Braves coming in for a Labor Day doubleheader. Durocher's men needed fifteen innings to win the opener, 6-5, pushing game two to a late afternoon start. Entering the bottom of the sixth, the Dodgers trailed 2-1 with darkness falling. They needed a run immediately, as National League rules in 1941 prohibited teams from turning on stadium lights to finish a day game. Pete came through, blasting a leadoff triple. At Stengel's direction, the Braves began dawdling between pitches, holding unneeded conferences, letting more daylight slip away, trying to make the umpires call the game. Wise to Casey's scheme, the umps kept things going long enough for the Dodgers to pull a suicide squeeze, Lavagetto bunting so Pete could race home to make the score 2-2. The game ended in a tie, which counted for nothing in the standings, but the Dodgers converted it to a win with a 9-2 romp in the makeup match the next day.

After splitting a doubleheader in Philly, the Dodgers came home for a critical series against the Giants. Reporters asked Durocher for a comment on his struggling fifth-place opponents. Leo remembered Bill Terry's putdown of the Dodgers in 1934 and didn't bite. "You know what would happen if I came out with some wisecrack about Terry or the Giants," he said. "They'd play harder than they've played all season and be three times harder to beat." The Lip was wise to clam up. It was the Dodgers who came out inspired. In the first game, Pete doubled and tripled, Curt Davis went the distance, and Brooklyn won 4-1. In game two, the Dodgers chased Carl Hubbell after four innings and racked up fourteen hits, including two home runs by Camilli, in a 13-1 cakewalk.

Game three? That was an only-in-Ebbets Field classic. In the fifth inning, umpire Tom Dunn ejected Durocher for his ear-rattling, dust-kicking, profanity-spewing protest of a strikeout call. The heave-ho triggered a tsunami of boos from the crowd, and several beer bottles came flying out of the stands toward Dunn; one missed him by only a foot. Things calmed down until the bottom of the ninth when the Dodgers came to bat trailing 3-1. Billy Herman led off with a single. Pete hit a bounder at second baseman Odell Hale, a potential double-play ball. But Hale, worried about Pete's speed, charged too fast and let the ball squirt by, enabling Pete to race to second and Herman to third. Now it was Medwick's turn, and Joe lined a single to right that drove in both Herman and Reiser, tying up the score. The thirty-four thousand fans erupted in deafening cheers—and more oddly, erupted in paper, showering the field with confetti from torn-up scorecards, newspapers, and the like. The purpose of the display was unclear unless it was a pointed "Take that!" directed at the Giants and the umpires, or this being Brooklyn, an emphatic "Up yours!"

After a ten-minute delay to clean up the mess, Giants' pitcher Cliff Melton retired the side. But Melton got in trouble an inning later, allowing Owen to reach second with two out. Pete came up again and worked Melton to a 3-2 count. Dressen, the expert sign stealer, signaled the next pitch would be a curve. Pete waited an extra fraction of a second on his swing and slammed the ball into left for a single that scored Owen and won the game. Hundreds of ecstatic fans poured onto the field to celebrate, among them trumpet-bearing members of the Dodger Sym-Phony, who lined up in front of the third-base dugout and serenaded the Giants with the grave, familiar tones of Frederic Chopin's death march.

There could be no purer display of the Dodger faithful's spirit circa 1941. There could also be no better example of the clutch hitting Pete was now providing. Over the previous twelve games, he had batted .440, with twenty-two hits in fifty at-bats, and had reclaimed the top spot in the National League batting race. An exuberant Reese praised his teammate after the game. "He can hit for my money," Pee Wee said. "My roomie can hit with a broomstick."

While the Dodgers swept the Giants, the Cardinals dropped two out of three to Cincinnati. Durocher's men now had a three-game lead, their biggest since mid-July. They'd have to hold onto it during a grinding six-city, seventeen-game road trip that began September 10th. From Brooklyn, the team would travel to Chicago, St. Louis, Cincinnati, Pittsburgh, Philadelphia, and Boston—well over two thousand miles, all of it by train. MacPhail put the players in private luxury cars on the first leg west, hoping to keep them fresh and relaxed. The move seemed to backfire in Chicago, where the Dodgers lost both ends of a doubleheader. But they regained momentum in St. Louis, defeating the Cardinals two out of three. Then it was on to Cincinnati, where they beat Bucky Walters with a ninth-inning rally that featured an RBI double by Reese and a home run by Herman. The win mathematically eliminated the defending champion Reds from the pennant race.

Maybe that's why only six thousand souls filed into Crosley Field for the next day's game. Those present got a virtual replay of the June 22nd marathon. Again, Paul Derringer pitched for the Reds, and again he mowed down the Dodgers inning after inning—sixteen of them, allowing plenty of singles but no runs. Again, his Dodger mound opponent—Johnny Allen this time—was equally stingy, holding the Reds scoreless for fifteen innings before Casey took over. By the end of the sixteenth inning, the sun was dipping below the horizon, and the umpires conferenced on whether to call the game on account of darkness. They decided to go for one more inning over the objection of Reds' manager Bill McKechnie.

McKechnie sent Derringer out for the seventeenth. Pete came to bat. He took the first pitch for a ball. On the next pitch, he swung; the ball leaped off his bat and zoomed an estimated four hundred feet over the center-field wall. "With the suddenness of a slap in the face," wrote one reporter, the tie was broken. Dodgers 1, Reds 0.

Like the Braves on Labor Day, the Reds went into stall mode, changing pitchers twice, deliberately misplaying grounders and pop-ups, trying to make the umps call the game before it could be completed. The Reds virtually *gave* the Dodgers four extra runs before the Dodgers stooped to the same level, with Herman striking out on purpose to end the inning. In the bottom of the seventeenth, with fans lighting trashcan bonfires in the stands so they could see, Casey struggled to throw strikes but set down the Reds for a 5-1 victory. The elongated win put the Dodgers up by two games with twelve to play.

Next, it was onto Pittsburgh and another nerve-wracker. The Pirates started one of their better pitchers, Ken Heintzelman. He stifled the Brooklyn bats for eight innings, and the Bucs built a 3-1 lead. The Dodgers came to life in the ninth, opening with three straight hits, cutting their deficit to one. Up came the National League's leading hitter. Heintzelman got two quick strikes, making Pete miss badly on the second pitch with an outside curve. Next pitch, Heintzelman tried the curve again. Pete adjusted and slammed a liner to right-center that bounced past Joe DiMaggio's brother Vince. By the time DiMaggio threw in the ball, "Bad News Reiser," as one of the Pittsburgh papers dubbed him, was standing on third with a go-ahead, two-RBI triple. The Dodgers went on to win 6-4.

After the game, the Pirates' Rip Sewell said he'd pick Camilli, the league leader in home runs, as National League MVP. His mound colleague Max Butcher disagreed. "I don't see how they can keep the prize away from Pete Reiser," he said. "He has caused us more trouble than any player in the league."

Tom Meany, traveling with the team, noted how well Pete and his roomie were holding up under the late-season pressure. "Baseball still was a game to them until a couple of weeks ago," he wrote. "Now Reese and Reiser are hard-boiled grim-lipped guys. The metamorphosis must be much the same as the time U.S. Grant took an army of boys into the Battle of the Wilderness and came out with a bunch of professional soldiers, hard-bitten, battle-scarred warriors."

A Dodger loss the next day kept the race tight, and the Cardinals weren't giving up. On the 17th, manager Billy Southworth decided to play a newcomer, just recalled from double-A ball. Stan Musial singled, doubled, and drove in two runs in his major league debut, helping the Cards beat Boston, 3-2. Stan, not yet quite a man, would bat .426 in the final two weeks of action and give the Redbirds a mightier offense down the stretch.

However, the Dodgers had something even better than a superpowered rookie working in their favor—five games against the dreadful Phillies, limping to the end of a season where they lost one hundred eleven times, still the franchise record some eight decades later. Rabid Dodger fans didn't want to miss a pitch, and at least fifteen thousand trekked down to Philadelphia by bus, train, and plane to take in some or all of the games. The Phillies, used to crowds of about fifteen hundred, lacked the staff to control the high-spirited Brooklynites and hundreds wandered onto the field during batting practice before a Sunday doubleheader. Some spread picnics on the outfield grass. Others hounded the players for autographs, using balls pilfered from the Dodgers' own supply. The field was eventually cleared, but the Phils could exert no better control over the Brooklyn players, who swept the twin bill and took four of the five games. Pete battered the Philly pitching staff at will, knocking out eight hits in sixteen at-bats, scoring six runs, driving in another six. Including walks, his on-base percentage for the series was .636.

On to Braves Field in Boston. On September 24th, Durocher's gang beat the Braves 4-2, with Dixie Walker striking the big blow, a three-RBI triple. The 25th dawned with the Bums needing a win coupled with a Cardinal loss to clinch the pennant. Medwick, Walker, and Lavagetto drove in runs to give Whit Wyatt an early lead. The score was still a tight 3-0 when Pete came to bat in the seventh with one man on and two outs. Pete usually struggled against the pitcher, righty Tom Earley, but not on this day; he cracked Earley's second pitch into the right-field stands. The homer, his fourteenth and final of the year, iced the ballgame and put an exclamation point on his wonder of a season.

Pete was up again in the ninth when a telegraph operator in the press box, keeping track of the out-of-town scores, made a casual announcement: "It's over." The Cardinals had just lost to Pittsburgh. The newspapermen traveling with the Dodgers frantically waved toward the Brooklyn dugout. The players began to whoop; they knew what the signal meant. Durocher somehow kept everyone focused on the business at hand. In the bottom of the ninth, Wyatt bore down and retired the Braves on nine pitches, the last of which turned into an infield bouncer that Lavagetto gloved at third and fired across the infield to Camilli for the final out.

After twenty-one years, the Dodgers were National League champions. And the borough of Brooklyn, listening to Red Barber's radio broadcast, erupted in ecstatic, euphoric, delirious joy.

For those who have never seen it, I suggest going online and watching newsreel footage of the Dodgers' 1941 victory parade, held the Monday after the end of the regular season. Hundreds of thousands, very possibly a million, souls pack the streets along the parade route, pushing against the police to get at their heroes, who are being transported to a ceremony at Brooklyn Borough Hall in open-top convertibles. The overwhelmed officers use horses, motorcycles, batons, and plain old muscle in a valiant effort to hold back the masses. But it's no use. Teenage boys run alongside the vehicles with excited glee. Several happy folks climb on the back of the car transporting MacPhail and Durocher, ignoring Leo's request to get the hell off. It's as if the players had captured Hitler and landed on the moon. They are idols; they are icons. They're not quite Beatles—no one is trying to pull on Durocher's hair, in part because he has none. But the jubilation is palpable. One guy carries a giant sign that reads, "Lippy for Mayor." A fellow celebrant's sign proclaims, "Yes Mr. Terry We're Still in the League." Nearby, a dark-haired youngster holds up a sign with no words, just pictures of Pistol Pete and the number .343, representing Pete's final batting average, best in the National League.

Pete had lifted his average with a torrid September, batting .408 for the month with an OPS of 1.135, both team-best figures during the Dodgers' stretch drive. Given the number of games where he delivered clutch, late-inning hits, it's a bit of a head-scratcher why the baseball writers association, after the season, did not elect him National League MVP. Instead, they gave the award to Dolph Camilli. Camilli wasn't a horrible choice. He led the league in homers (34) and RBI (120). Unlike Pete, he was rarely out of the lineup, and he was one of only three players to walk at least a hundred times. But Reiser would have been the superior pick. Among categories counted at the time, Pete led the league in runs scored (117), doubles (39), triples (17), slugging percentage (.558), total bases (299), hit-by-pitch (11), in addition to winning the batting title. Fielding-wise, he topped all NL outfielders in putouts (355) and assists (14). The advanced metrics of the twenty-first century show these stats were no illusion. Pete paced the league in OPS (.964), adjusted OPS (164), wins above replacement (8.0), and range factor in center field (2.77).

The only ordinary parts of Pete's stat line were his homers and RBI. Pete was never a true longball hitter, and the fourteen homers he hit in 1941 would be a career-high. He also drove in only seventy-six runs while hitting third for a team that led the league in runs scored. One may ask: did he fail to hit in RBI situations? The answer is no. Pete hit .318 with men on base and .327 with runners in scoring position. There simply weren't many runners to drive in when he came to bat. For most of the season, from April until mid-August, Durocher stuck with Reese as his leadoff hitter. After the war, Pee Wee would emerge as one of the best hitting shortstops in baseball. His final average for 1941, however, was an anemic .229. In the second spot, Durocher usually put Billy Herman. Herman hit a solid .291 for the Dodgers but slumped to .214 in September when Pete was at his hottest. More often than not, Pete was a rally starter rather than a finisher in 1941.

Reiser never complained about the MVP voting or anything regarding the 1941 season. "Some kind of year, '41. Everything happened," he told Donald Honig years later, in a serious bit of understatement. After the war, Arthur Daley of the *Times* asked Pete to choose the favorite game of his career. Pete answered, "Every one I played in during 1941. I won the batting championship in my first full year. I played in the All-Star Game, and I played in the World Series. What more could a twenty-two-year-old kid ask?"

* * *

Well before the first pitch, it was clear the intensity the Brooklyn fans was going to make this World Series special. As the Yankees rampaged to four straight championships in the late 1930s, winning four straight Series in lopsided fashion, interest in the games had dipped, and so had the crowds. Game Three at Yankee Stadium in the '38 series was played to almost twenty thousand empty seats. In Game Four, played to only ten thousand empty seats, fans began rhythmically clapping for the Cubs during a rally, hoping they would make a fight of it. But in 1941, reserved seats for the games sold out instantly, and on the morning of Game One, long lines snaked around Yankee Stadium as fans tried to get tickets for the unreserved bleachers and grandstand. "I don't see a vacant seat right now, and to all appearances, unless the eye is very deceiving, this is beyond a doubt the greatest crowd ever to see a World Series ballgame," Red Barber told radio listeners fifteen minutes before the one-thirty P.M. start time. The Ol' Redhead was correct. The attendance of over sixty-eight thousand would set a new record, as would the single-game receipts of two hundred sixty-five thousand dollars.

The infant television industry wasn't ready to air the Series yet, but the radio audience was expected to be equally impressive. The Gillette Safety Razor Company had paid one hundred thousand dollars to sponsor the broadcasts, aired on three hundred affiliates of the Mutual network in the U.S., the Canadian Broadcasting Corporation to the north and Cuba through a Spanish-language feed. The Muzak company set aside its usual fare of soothing background music and piped the games into commercial establishments like restaurants and doctor's offices. For anyone without access to a radio, the New York Telephone Company offered a number to call for the latest score. And New Yorkers who wanted post-game analysis could tune in to Mutual flagship station WOR each night. At five-fifteen P.M., Yankee pitcher Lefty Gomez shared his impressions of the day's action; at seven-thirty, the Dodgers were represented by none other than Pete Reiser. The station paid Pete four hundred dollars for his work, another sign that his profile and popularity were rising.

For all the public's passion, few expected a Dodger victory. The Bronx Bombers had appeared in seven World Series since 1927 and won them all, sweeping five of the matchups in four games straight. Bettors made them twelve-to-five favorites, and most of the newspaper prognosticators picked them to win in six games, tops. Outside first base, where they fielded weak-hitting rookie Johnny Sturm, the Yanks were seen as superior at nearly every position—including center field. "Reiser, the golden boy, is just a boy in comparison to the great DiMaggio," wrote Stanley Frank in the *New York Post*. John Drebinger of the *Times* opined that "Pete Reiser isn't quite a DiMaggio, especially in the matter of sheer power," though he added that Reiser "has stamped himself as a high-grade hitter" and did an "amazing" job covering ground in the outfield. A writer for the communist *Daily Worker* did a point-by-point breakdown that acknowledged Pete "hit like no other batter in the National League" but gave Joltin' Joe the edge in hitting, fielding, and throwing.

Given that DiMaggio had reeled off his fifty-six-game hitting streak that summer, batted .357, led both major leagues in RBI, and somehow averaged just one strikeout per forty-eight times at-bat, it's hard to argue with the analysts' conclusions. But at least one, *Times* columnist John Kieran, aired the view that Reiser would soon close the gap. Kieran quoted an unnamed Brooklyn supporter who said, "I call Pete Reiser a young Joe DiMaggio. He's wonderful, but he isn't a Joe DiMaggio yet. Next year, maybe. Two years, certainly."

Naturally, Durocher conceded nothing in pre-series interviews, though he also declined to predict the winner. Asked whether he thought the Gold Dust Twins would be nervous in their first World Series, he said at first he wouldn't be surprised, then reversed course: "Do I think Reiser and Reese will be nervous? Not on your life. If they were not nervous on that stretch drive, where there was more money at stake, believe it or not, they won't be in the series. Remember, the heat was on our club since April 26th and Reiser and Reese stood up under all kinds of pressure." During the Game One pre-game show, analyst Bill Corum concurred with Leo's opinion on Reiser. "You might not think it from the All-Star Game, but I don't think anything bothers that fellow," said the gravelly-voiced Corum. "Red and I were talking yesterday about him, and he hardly seems to care whether the fella is a righty or left-handed pitcher. As Red says, he just takes the lumber up there and wears pitchers out."

Once the game started, however, Pete's lumber fell strangely quiet. Batting against Yankee ace Red Ruffing, a veteran of five previous World Series, he flied out, struck out, and harmlessly walked his first three times at-bat. Batting in the eighth with the Dodgers down by one run, he finally cracked a sharp line drive, but right at Yankee shortstop Phil Rizzuto. "And he takes a base hit away from Reiser!" Barber exclaimed in the broadcast booth. The Dodgers got two hits in the ninth, but Joe Gordon and Rizzuto turned a double play to seal a 3-2 Yankee victory. The Bronx Bombers had now won twenty-eight of their last thirty-one World Series contests, a streak of postseason dominance unmatched to this day.

Pete continued to struggle in Game Two, going hitless in four at-bats, although he made a key defensive contribution. In the fourth inning, with the Dodgers losing 2-0, Yankee pitcher Spud Chandler, a fast runner and a former halfback for the University of Georgia Bulldogs, tried to advance from first to third on a Texas Leaguer to center. Reiser charged the ball, made a clean grab, and fired a bullet to Lavagetto to throw out Chandler and end the inning. The Dodgers tied it up an inning later on RBIs from Reese and Owen. In the sixth, Pete struck out with two runners on, but Camilli swatted a single to score what turned out to be the winning run in the Dodgers' 3-2 victory, evening up the series.

Back at the Ebbets Field madhouse for Game Three, Pete's hitless streak stretched to eleven at-bats with an infield groundout and a liner straight at Gordon. In the seventh, he finally broke through, smashing a double off the right-field fence, missing a home run by about five feet. However, his teammates couldn't bring him around, and with the Dodgers looking for the tying run in the ninth, he struck out on three pitches. Brooklyn went down, 2-1, and "the American Leaguers were beginning to think [Pete] had won the National League batting championship under false pretenses," wrote Whitney Martin.

Game Four would be a different story. In the first inning, Yankee lefty Atley Donald got the best of Pete, striking him out on a three-two count with a high, inside fastball. However, when he tried that again in the third, Pete bounced a single to right field past Gordon. Finally, in the fifth, Pete provided the moment for which the Brooklyn fans were waiting. Dixie Walker had just doubled when Pete stepped to the plate with the Dodgers losing 3-2. Doing the radio play-by-play, Bob Elson barely had time to say "Here's Reiser" before listeners heard a loud *crack* and an escalating roar from the crowd. Pete had blasted the first pitch toward the thirty-five-foot-high scoreboard in right-center. "Right fielder Henrich goes back, against the scoreboard, it's gonna hit . . . it's a home run!" Elson shouted as thirty-four thousand Dodger rooters opened their throats and made a din equal to a squadron of B-52 bombers. "Well, fans, that was a mighty wallop," Elson informed his audience once he could be heard again. The Dodgers now led, 4-3.

Hugh Casey replaced Johnny Allen after the fifth and set down the Yankees in the sixth, seventh and eighth innings with no trouble. In the top of the ninth, he retired Johnny Sturm and Red Rolfe on ground-outs and got two quick strikes on Tommy Henrich. Ebbets Field buzzed with anticipation; one more strike and the Dodgers would even the series at two games apiece, something no team had done against the Yankees since 1926. Casey peered in at catcher Mickey Owen for the signal. Owen called for a curve.

"Casey gets by Henrich; it's all over," Elson reminded listeners. Then: "Pitcher starting his windup out there again. He's all ready now, watch it, here it comes—heeeeeee *swung*," Elson exclaimed, preparing to announce strike three. But Elson had to slam the brakes because Casey's sharp-breaking pitch—rumored to be an illegal spitter rather than a curve—caromed off Owen's glove and bounced toward the Dodger dugout. Henrich immediately saw what happened and dashed down the baseline. The crowd, which had let out the beginnings of a roar, fell into a state of agitated confusion as the reality dawned on them; Owen had dropped the game-winning third strike, enabling Henrich to reach first safely. "Fortune still smiling here in this ninth inning on the Yankees," commented Elson, dryly, as DiMaggio came to bat.

He didn't know the half of it. The Dodgers still led 4-3 with two outs. The game wasn't over. But Casey proceeded to give up a single to DiMaggio, a double to Charlie Keller, a walk to Joe Gordon, and another double to Bill Dickey. By the time he settled down and retired the side, the Yankees led 7-4. Amazingly, Durocher didn't change pitchers or visit the mound to calm Casey down. "It was like a punch on the chin," Owen explained years later. "You're stunned. You don't react. I should have gone out to the mound and stalled around a little. It was more my fault than Leo's."

Durocher, to his credit, tried to direct the blame to himself. "My mistake was, for the first time in my life, I was shell-shocked. I should have gotten off the bench and gone out to the mound to talk to my pitcher . . . Instead, I sat on my ass and didn't do anything," he said.

The Dodgers went down meekly in the bottom of the ninth, with Pete making the final out on a grounder to first base. Owen's error would live on as one of the worst blunders in World Series history. The loss was a backbreaker for the Dodgers, Pete included. "I remember talking to him about the '41 Series, and he said he was still mad at Mickey Owen for dropping that third strike," remembers Rick Tuber. Pete's daughter Shirley interjects: "He'd laugh and say it jokingly."

The next day, the Dodgers showed little life, managing just four hits and one run as the Yankees wrapped up the title. Pete did what he could. In the bottom of the first, he cracked a triple off the center-field wall, bringing the Ebbets Field faithful to their feet. But Camilli popped up to end the inning. Two innings later, Pete came to bat with Wyatt on third and hit a high fly toward the scoreboard. Would it get out again? No, the ball settled into Henrich's glove. It was enough to score Wyatt and give the Dodgers their only run.

Overall, Pete managed four hits in twenty at-bats during the series, a .200 batting average. The whole team struggled against Yankee pitching, hitting a collective .182 and scoring only eleven runs in five games. It was a disappointing coda to a majestic if unruly symphony of a season. Pete had to be satisfied with one thing: his World Series share. Each player on the losing team got a check for four thousand eight hundred and twenty-nine dollars. The money more than doubled Pete's salary for the year.

The day after the series, Pete drove back to St. Louis and settled in for what figured to be a fun off-season. He saw Durocher and Reese in mid-October at the wedding of Leo's daughter in St. Louis. He went to Louisville to play golf and hang out with Pee Wee. He and a friend made a cross-country drive to California, stopping off in Denver, Salt Lake City, Reno, and at Dolph Camilli's cattle ranch in Northern California before arriving in San Francisco, where he visited the DiMaggio family's restaurant on Fisherman's Wharf. Silent home movies taken there show Pete in a fine mood, wearing a sharp gray suit, tieless white shirt, and a smile as he and some pals dig into fresh lobsters.

And he began to collect awards. The writers had decided that despite his fifty-eight games in 1940, Reiser was indeed a freshman, and *The Sporting News* named him the National League Rookie of the Year, as did the Chicago chapter of the baseball writers association. The *Sporting News* and the national writers' association picked him for the 1941 major league all-star team. Incongruously, the women's magazine *Redbook* named him one of the "10 Luckiest People" of 1941, as if his stellar performance had been the work of four-leaf clover.

When he returned to St. Louis, life got eventful there too. Pete and his parents had done some house hunting and using his postseason earnings, Pete purchased the family a two-story, ten-room house in Pasadena Hills, just outside the St. Louis city limits. They moved in shortly after Thanksgiving.

As if enough wasn't happening, Pete found love. He met nineteen-year-old Patricia Hurst right after he came back to St. Louis from the World Series. A friend had invited him to a party; he explained the following year. "I declined his invite because I didn't have a girlfriend to bring with me," he said. "'Don't let that bother you,' he said. 'My girl has a friend she'd like you to meet.' So, I joined them. It was the first time I had ever seen Patricia in my life. I didn't look at another girl after that.'" Pete and Pat were married in Florida the following April as the Dodgers wrapped up spring training. Pee Wee got married to his gal Dorothy the same day, with the two Dodgers serving as best men at each other's weddings.

Only one cloud darkened Pete's horizon, and it was a big one. On the afternoon on Sunday, December 7th, the radio networks interrupted their programming with a news flash: Japanese planes had bombed the U.S. Navy base in Pearl Harbor, Hawaii. The United States was in the war. The next day, recruitment offices for the Army, Navy, and Marines nationwide were jammed with volunteers. Bob Feller, baseball's brightest pitching star, winner of a hundred big league games before his twenty-third birthday, was among the first to sign up. "In light of events of the past few days, I believe and sincerely hope that I can be of more value to the Navy than to the Cleveland Indians," Feller said. Hank Greenberg, discharged from the Army just two days earlier when Congress released men twenty-eight and over from service, quickly announced he was re-enlisting. "We are in trouble, and there's only one thing to do—return to the service," he said.

Within weeks, a stream of major leaguers had enlisted or were being drafted into the armed forces. Commissioner Landis wrote a public letter to President Franklin D. Roosevelt, asking whether baseball should shut down for the duration of the war. Roosevelt quickly responded with an emphatic no. "I honestly feel that it would be best for the country to keep baseball going," he wrote. Everyone would be working harder, and for longer hours, he said; the public deserved the opportunity for recreation and to take their minds off work. In fact, the president added, he'd like to see the leagues add more night games to their schedules, so people working the dayshift could enjoy baseball too.

This was music to the team owners' ears and a heavenly choir to many of the players. Professional athletes have a limited number of years to play their sport and make big money before time or injuries end their careers. Yes, the president said in his letter that professional ballplayers should not be exempt from the draft. Still, if the big leagues continued to operate, the majority of players would get another year, maybe two, before they'd have to exchange their cleats for army boots and their bats for guns.

So, no one raised a stink—not publicly at least—when Pete and the Dodgers agreed to a contract for the 1942 season. MacPhail more than doubled Pete's salary to ten thousand dollars. It was about half of what more established teammates like Medwick and Camilli earned but still an excellent income for a youngster with only a year and two months in the major leagues. And for a guy with Pete's talents, it was just the start. There were so many good things waiting in his future: more batting titles, more pennants, more money, more fame. All he had to do was stay healthy, or in the words of Casey Stengel, stand up. Casey was right about that. A star can't deliver unless he stands up.

5

Hitting the Wall

If Pete Reiser could be likened to a space rocket—an apt comparison, given the speed and power he unleashed on the field every day—he reached the zenith of his career, maybe his life, in the early evening of Saturday, July 18, 1942.

Pete was back in his hometown St. Louis, where the Dodgers played a four-game set with the second-place Cardinals. It was a tight schedule—doubleheaders on consecutive days, four games packed into the span of thirty hours, all in that godawful St. Louis heat and humidity. But for the Dodger center fielder, good things far outweighed the bad. The Dodgers finished Saturday with a solid grip on first place in the National League, eight games ahead of the Cardinals. Pete was playing in front of siblings, his parents, and the family of his new bride. If he had time that weekend, he probably stopped by his folks' new house on Roland Boulevard, the one he had bought with his World Series money. And any observer of the baseball world who looked at his '42 stats and his growing renown would have to say: This man is a lock for MVP.

On several occasions later in life, Reiser said that going into the next day's doubleheader, his batting average stood at .381, or .383, or another figure in that vicinity. Many well-known sportswriters repeated those claims as fact over the years, with some adding Pete's assertion that he was destined to finish the season above the hallowed .400 mark, a feat Ted Williams had accomplished one year earlier at .406, but no major leaguer has done in the eight-plus decades since. In reality, Reiser's average never soared to such stratospheric heights. But he was doing just fine, thank you. At the end of Saturday's action, he led the National League in batting average (.356), hits (104), doubles (26), runs (62), stolen bases (12), and slugging percentage (.531). No one calculated the numbers back then, but Reiser was also tops in on-base percentage at .416 and OPS at .947.

To put his hitting in perspective, Pete's batting average at that moment was twenty points higher than that of Ted Williams, nearly thirty points ahead of Stan Musial's, and well above the average of every other future Hall of Famer playing ball in 1942, including Joe DiMaggio, Joe Gordon, Johnny Mize, Mel Ott, Enos Slaughter, Bobby Doerr, Joe Medwick , and Bill Dickey. He outranked them all in OPS, too, except for Williams at 1.082.

The esteemed Grantland Rice took note of Reiser's hot hitting in his column that week. Many players had complained about the ball being less lively than normal that season, Rice wrote. There were suspicions that a shortage of natural rubber, caused by the wartime cutoff of supplies from the Pacific, was forcing ball manufacturer Spalding to use less springy "reclaimed" or recycled rubber in the core of the ball. "But this doesn't account for Pete Reiser keeping his same fast pace," Rice said. "Reiser is the only hitter who has been able to park himself consistently over the .350 grading. That .350 mark is a good bet to lead both major leagues this season."

A few days later, New York betting expert Jimmy Doyle proclaimed the Yankees and Dodgers to be virtual locks for the two pennant races and predicted the Yankees would be only a slight favorite in the World Series, still more than two months away. "And Brooklyn will be tougher than it was last season," he told a United Press reporter. "That Reiser-Medwick combination is deadly, as the Yanks will learn, and the Dodgers have better pitching than any club in the American League, with the possible exception of Detroit. This will be a great series."

In the July 18th doubleheader, a perspiration fest played in muggy ninety-two-degree weather, Reiser had given the Cardinals all they could handle. In game one, won by the Cardinals 7-4, he knocked in one run on a fielder's choice and a second with a solo home run that hit the roof of the Sportsman's Park right-field pavilion. In game two, he doubled in the fourth inning and came around to score on a single, helping the Dodgers to a 4-3 victory. He was now working on a thirteen-game hitting streak and hitting .385 for July.

More than thirty-four thousand fans, the Cardinals' biggest crowd of the season, jammed Sportsman's Park on July 19th for the second twin bill. Reiser's balloon deflated a little in the first game as Cardinals pitched their ace, Mort Cooper, a tall, fireballing right-hander amid a magnificent twenty-two-win, 1.78 ERA season. Cooper and reliever Max Lanier held Pete hitless in five at-bats as the Cardinals jumped out to an early lead and held on for an 8-5 victory.

Game two was more of a see-saw thriller. The Dodgers grabbed a 2-0 in the first inning, with Reiser walking and scoring from second base on a single by Camilli. The Cardinals roared back to knock out starter Kirby Higbe and take a 6-2 lead, only for the Dodgers to tie it with a fifth-inning rally in which Reiser again walked and scored. The deadlock held for the next six innings, with the Cardinals' Lanier and the Dodgers' Curt Davis snuffing out multiple uprisings. Reiser hit a one-out single in the tenth and advanced to second on an error by center fielder Harry Walker but was stranded when Camilli hit into a double play.

The clock atop the ballpark's left-field scoreboard read 7:37 pm when Enos Slaughter strode to the plate for the Cardinals in the bottom of the eleventh. Sunlight was fading, and as noted previously, under National League rules, the Cards could not turn on the stadium lights to extend the game. There was no formal announcement, but reporters in the press box agreed: if the Dodgers could set down the Cards, the umpires would have to call the game and declare a tie, allowing Brooklyn to escape town with a seven-game lead.

Johnny Rizzo had pinch-hit for Davis in the top of the inning, so Durocher sent in a fresh pitcher, Johnny Allen. Allen worked Slaughter to a count of two balls, one strike. On the fourth pitch, Slaughter connected and smashed a long fly to deep center field. Pete turned on the jets and zoomed back for a rendezvous with the ball. In his path stood a flagpole, located in the field of play near the centerfield wall, and the wall itself, a dark green concrete barrier nearly twelve feet high. There was no warning track and no padding on the wall to cushion an outfielder trying to make a catch.

A large contingent of newspapermen were on hand that day for the Bums-Redbirds showdown. In their stories, they gave readers a detailed account of what happened next:

> Martin J. Haley, *St. Louis Globe-Democrat*: "Racing back at top speed, all but unmindful of the wall, Reiser stretched high and grabbed the ball with his glove at the 405-foot mark."
>
> Tommy Holmes, *Brooklyn Daily Eagle*: "'It might have been the greatest catch I've ever seen,' said Joseph [Medwick]. 'I'll swear that Slaughter hit the ball beyond Reiser and that Pete overtook it. He was traveling like a bullet when he hit the fence.'"
>
> Haley, *Globe-Democrat*: "Just as it appeared as if he had made a clean catch, the back of his head struck the concrete a fearful blow."
>
> W. Vernon Tietjen, *St. Louis Star and Times*: ". . . he crashed against the concrete between the 422-foot and 405-foot markings, and when

the back of his head struck the wall with what must have been a sickening thud, the ball popped out of his glove and bounded toward the flagpole."

Unbylined article, *Brooklyn Citizen*: "Pete dropped to the ground as though he had been shot."

Dick McCann, *New York Daily News*: "Dazed by the collision, Petey lurched like a punch-drunk fighter after the ball and flung it desperately toward the infield where Slaughter was digging up great divots in a mad dash around the bases."

Tietjen: *Star and Times*: "He managed to get it in partway to shortstop Pee Wee Reese, and Billy Herman's subsequent relay sped toward the plate. But the speedy Slaughter now was pedaling faster than a horse headed for oats, with manager Southworth waving him on in windmill fashion at third base, and he slid under the throw in a cloud of dust with the winning run."

Holmes, *Daily Eagle*: "Slaughter wouldn't have completed his home run if he weren't unusually fast."

Roscoe McGowen, *New York Times*: "As Slaughter crossed the plate, an extraordinary crowd of 34,443 went wild, and [seat] cushions came sailing from every section onto the field . . . The cushion-throwing continued for ten minutes despite frantic appeals over the public address system."

McCann, *Daily News*: "Reiser meanwhile slumped against the bleacher wall. Through a deluge of scorecards and cushions, his mates raced out to him and helped him from the field through mobs of taunting Card rooters."

Holmes, *Daily Eagle*: "The delegation of Dodgers in center field found Reiser weaving and groggy. They escorted him to the clubhouse, and he was still badly shaken."

McCann, *Daily News*: "His head badly bruised, Pete was then hustled into an ambulance and rushed to St. John's Hospital for X-rays. As he left the clubhouse, the doughty outfielder said he felt all right, but the Dodger management wanted to make sure nothing serious had happened to him."

Reiser gave his account of the play several times, the most complete in his 1974 interview with Donald Honig. "Enos Slaughter leads off the inning, and he ties into one," Reiser recalled. "It's a line drive directly over my head, and my first thought was that it can be caught. Which is pretty much the way I felt about any ball that was hit. I'm a firm believer in positive thinking. I used to stand out there in center field and say to myself, 'Hit it to me, hit it to me.' Every pitch. I wanted that ball."

"Well, if this ball isn't caught, it's a cinch triple, and [Allen] can be beat, and above all the Dodgers. I caught it, going at top speed. I just missed the flagpole in center field, but I hit the wall hard. I dropped the ball, picked it up, relayed it to Pee Wee—how I did that, I'll never know—but we just missed getting Slaughter at the plate. Inside the park home run . . . And I'm out cold in center field. It was like a hand grenade had gone off in my head."

On a separate occasion, Reiser said, "I'd hit fences before, but not like this . . . I don't remember a thing until I woke up the next morning in the hospital, still wearing my uniform."

Fearful blow, sickening thud, punch-drunk fighter, hand grenade going off . . . from the descriptions, it sounds like Reiser suffered a catastrophic injury on the play. Pete always said he did. At St. John's Hospital, he was examined by Dr. Robert Hyland, the chief physician for the Cardinals, and the same doctor who had taken out Pete's appendix three years earlier. "Dr. Hyland, who was a very good friend of mine and all ballplayers, said I had suffered a severe concussion and a fractured skull. He recommended that I not play anymore that year," Reiser told Honig. The skull fracture became part of the Pete Reiser legend, mentioned by Pete in numerous interviews after his career ended, and invariably brought up by his many friends in the press, such as Jim Murray, Jimmy Cannon, Red Smith, and Dick Young, whenever those men reminisced and marveled about the young Reiser's capabilities.

The problem with these accounts is that outside Pete's recollection, there's no evidence his skull was actually cracked on the fateful play. In their July 20th editions, multiple St. Louis and New York newspapers, citing Dr. Hyland, reported that X-rays of Pete's head had come back negative—no skull fracture. They quoted Hyland as saying Reiser had sustained a mild (in some reports, moderate) concussion and would need to stay in the hospital a few days. He might be able to play in a week, the doctor said.

Which reports were correct—those of the sportswriters or Pete's? Pete's hospital records are long lost, but the available evidence points strongly toward concussion. One might think a patient would remember his diagnosis, especially if that diagnosis was something as serious as a fractured skull. But as we've seen, Reiser was not above exaggerating his feats and downfalls or simply misremembering events. For instance, in talking to W.C. Heinz, Pete placed the wall collision in August, not July 1942, and said it came at the end of a 1-0 game pitched by Whitlow Wyatt.

There is also this telling newspaper report, published the day after the crash:

> *"Pete's dad entered the clubhouse, found the stocky Dodger sitting up, smoking a cigarette, an ice pack on his head, a cold towel wrapped around an elbow.*
> *"I'm all right, Dad," said Pete.*
> *Reiser Sr. playfully punched his boy in the chin.*
> *"You should have caught the ball," he said, whirling on his heel and walking out to make his report to the family.*

Perhaps most telling of all is a photo of Reiser taken that night at St. John's Hospital. A *St. Louis Star and Times* photographer snapped Reiser's picture as he sat up in bed—and Pete's face showed no signs of the swelling or bruising or the "raccoon eyes" that often accompany a skull fracture. In fact, the patient was well enough to wave and smile for the camera.

That doesn't mean that Reiser's injury was minor. Concussions are a form of brain trauma, explains Dr. Daniel Zimet, a sports psychologist and Ph.D. who has helped treat dozens of athletes at the amateur, Olympic, and professional levels. "Concussions occur when the brain hits the inside of your skull, which is not a smooth surface, and your brain is not meant to move. It isn't like a muscle that is meant to stretch and contract," he explains.

Short-term symptoms of concussions include headaches, dizziness, confusion, fatigue, and nausea, among other ill effects. Zimet says these symptoms can disappear within days or a couple of weeks—*if* the patient allows him or herself adequate time to rest, then makes a gradual return to normal activities. "The science is still out on this, but it does seem that you prolong the impact of a concussion by going back to life as normal too soon," he says. If the recovery protocols are ignored, he says, the patient can develop complex post-concussion syndrome, a condition where symptoms persist for months, even years, and are accompanied by poor focus, irritability, sleep disturbances, and impulsivity.

In light of studies that showed concussions could lead to impaired functioning, Major League Baseball and the other major U.S. sports leagues adopted concussion protocols in the early 2000s. The programs require players to go through a series of medical checks and evaluations before returning to action. Under current MLB rules, if doctors clear a player, he can sidestep the injured list and return to action within seven days. However, many players take longer to recover; a 2018 medical study published by the National Center for Biotechnology Information, a branch of the National Institutes of Health, found that MLB players with concussions sat out an average of thirty-one days.

In 1942, that health-and-safety-first approach was still light-years in the future. Dr. Hyland's wish for his patient to rest and recover in the hospital was not to be. On the evening of Monday, July 20th, less than twenty-four hours after the collision, Pete checked out of St. John's Hospital. Contemporary news reports said he spent the night at his parents' house and caught a noontime train heading east the next day.

"I don't like hospitals," Pete later told Heinz, "So after two days [actually, one], I took the bandage off and got up. The room started to spin, but I got dressed, and I took off."

Another time, he described his decision this way: "I wasn't supposed to, but I told Dr. Hyland that I had to get back to Brooklyn. I insisted on leaving, whether they liked it or not. I was kind of bullheaded. Probably still am."

That bullheadedness cost Reiser dearly. He didn't know it at the time, but when he left that hospital bed early, he left behind a chunk of his God-given talents. He would get many more hits, steal many more bases, bring the Dodgers more victories with his bat, feet, and glove. But after July 19, 1942, Pete Reiser was damaged goods, always playing at something less than his full natural abilities. Never would he give his concussed brain a full chance to rest and heal.

More than one observer said the events in St. Louis essentially cost Reiser his career. "He was never the same again," lamented the *New York Times*' Arthur Daley years later. "He was only twenty-two years old at the time, and that was the tragedy of it."

* * *

In later years, when he talked to sportswriters, Pete often spun a tale about getting off his Brooklyn-bound train early and catching up with the Dodgers as they played a three-game series in Pittsburgh. He told Heinz that he went to Forbes Field and took a seat in the stands, close to the Dodgers' dugout.

"Leo saw me, and he said, 'Go get your uniform on, Pistol,'" Reiser recalled. "I said, 'Not tonight, Skipper.' Leo said, 'Aw, I'm not gonna let you hit. I want these guys to see you. It'll give 'em that little spark they need. Besides, it'll change the pitching plans on that other bench when they see you sittin' here in uniform.'"

Pete said he complied with Durocher's request and suited up. Then, according to Heinz:

> "In the 14th inning, the Dodgers had a runner on second, and Ken Heintzelman, the left-hander, came in for the Pirates. He walked Johnny Rizzo, and Durocher had run out of pinch hitters. "Damn," Leo was saying, walking up and down. "I want to win this one. Who can I use? Anybody here who can hit?"
>
> Pete walked up to the bat rack. He pulled out his stick. "You got yourself a hitter," he said to Leo.
>
> He walked up there and hit a line drive over the second baseman's head that was good for three bases. The two runs scored, and Pete rounded first base and collapsed.
>
> "When I woke up, I was in a hospital again [Pete said]. I could just make out that somebody was standin' there, and then I saw it was Leo." He said, 'You awake?' I said, 'Yep.' He said, 'By God, we beat 'em! How do you feel?' I said, 'How do you think I feel?' He said, 'Aw, you're better with one leg and one eye than anybody else I've got.' I said, 'Yeah, and that's the way I'll end up—on one leg and with one eye!'"

That story, too, has been regurgitated in other books and articles, including Heinz's own *They Heard the Cheers*, which contains an entire chapter on Reiser. But like the alleged skull fracture, the tale is a myth. The Dodgers did beat the Pirates on July 20th in Pittsburgh, but Reiser wasn't even there. Augie Galan played center field in his place and helped spark the Dodger attack with two hits and two RBI.

However, once the Dodgers returned to Brooklyn, Pete defied the doctor's orders and tried to storm his way back into the lineup. Arriving at Ebbets Field on the afternoon of July 22nd, he pulled on his uniform and stepped up to the plate for batting practice before anyone could object. Within minutes, wrote Lee Scott of the *Citizen*, Reiser demonstrated "there was nothing wrong with his vision or his clubbing, for he walloped five pitches out of the ballpark. Then to top it off, he shagged his quota of flies in the outfield. Later he told Durocher he wanted to play."

Leo vetoed the idea but was nonetheless pleased with the demonstration. "Nothing wrong with him," he said to Scott.

Reiser later said that MacPhail got incensed when Dr. Hyland recommended that he sit out the rest of the '42 season. He said the Dodgers general manager, known for his volatility, accused the doctor of trying to sabotage

Brooklyn's season. It wouldn't be a far-fetched notion, given that Hyland was the Cardinals' team doctor.

However, Scott's contemporaneous report shows a different MacPhail:

> *Pete sat on the bench with the boys that evening waiting for the game to start when President Larry MacPhail spotted him. "What are you doing here?" he asked.*
>
> *"Why, I'm ready to play," replied Pete with a big boyish grin.*
>
> *"No, you don't," came back Larry. "Dr. Hyland said you were to be rested up for ten days."*
>
> *"Hey Leo," Larry called to the Brooklyn skipper. "What about this guy? He should be in bed."*
>
> *Leo laughed out loud. "Whattaya mean in bed? He's alright. There's nothing wrong with him...."*
>
> *"But I thought Hyland said he was to be rested for a few days."*
>
> *"What does that guy Hyland want to do, lose the pennant for us?" chimed in Larry French. "That's why he advised Pete to be out for ten days so the Cardinals could catch up. He's no dope." MacPhail laughed, and so did the other players on the bench.*

In the end, Reiser came back earlier than Hyland, MacPhail, or any responsible party would have preferred—July 25th, just six days after he smacked into the wall. Durocher put him in center field, batting third, for that afternoon's game against the Pirates. The Dodgers lost, but Reiser played well. In his first at-bat, he singled to left, driving in a run. In the sixth inning, he threw out the Pirates' Johnny Barrett, trying to take third base on a fly to center.

Pete admitted to teammates and reporters that he was feeling less than 100 percent. But his drive to play was strong as ever, and Durocher didn't seem to think a longer rest was in order. In fact, for the next week, it looked like Pistol Pete had shrugged off the collision the same way he shook off the beaning from Ike Pearson. In three games against the Pirates, he got five hits in eleven times up, knocking in two runs, scoring three. He didn't hit as well when the Cardinals came to town, but the Dodgers took two out of three games to tighten their hold on first place. On the last day of July, Reiser slashed three hits against the Cubs. On the first day of August, he slugged a three-run homer that proved to be the margin in a 9-6 Dodger win.

It wasn't until August 3rd that the effects of the collision really hit home. Reiser took batting practice late afternoon but sat out that evening's contest against the Giants at the Polo Grounds, undoubtedly disappointing a crowd of fifty-seven thousand in the stands. An upset stomach, the papers reported the next day. Nothing to worry about. But Reiser missed the entire four-game series against the Giants and two games against the Braves. Tommy Holmes of the *Brooklyn Daily Eagle* finally broke the story: Reiser suffered headaches and dizzy spells, no doubt related to his crash into the wall.

> *"Not so good," was Reiser's answer when asked last night at the Polo Grounds how he felt.*
> *"Well, how badly do you feel? Could you play if the club needed you badly?"*
> *"Not the way I feel," answered Pete. "I just don't think I could make it. I have headaches off and on, and I just feel plain lousy."*

So lousy in fact, that the Dodgers considered sending him to the renowned Johns Hopkins Hospital in Baltimore for treatment, although in the end, Reiser simply rested for a few days under the watch of a Brooklyn physician, Dr. Charles Weeth. With their sparkplug out of the lineup, the Dodgers won two games, lost three, and tied another that was called on account of darkness. Ominously, they scored only thirteen runs in the six-game span. "The team does not seem to be the same without Reiser in there," wrote Scott.

Cardinals' outfielder Harry Walker noticed the same thing. "Reiser was one of their star players, and his hustle kept them fired up. With him out of the lineup, we had a chance to catch up," he said. The Cardinals took the opportunity. On August 5th, the Dodgers held a ten-game lead over St. Louis. But from that point onward, the Cards kicked into overdrive, winning forty-three of their final fifty-one games, and started whittling away at the Dodger lead.

Pete returned on August 10th for a series against the Phillies. In the first inning of the first game, he reached base on a force out and then raced home on a double by Medwick. "Another player would have stopped at third," wrote Scott, noting that Reiser's speed gave the Dodgers their first run in thirteen innings. The Dodgers won that game 6-0, and, after a rainout, beat the Phils again two days later, this time squeaking out a 1-0 win on a ninth-inning rally fueled in part by Reiser's bunt single. Again, all seemed well.

MacPhail made headlines on August 12th when he ripped what he considered his team's lackadaisical effort. "This club isn't as good as the one we had in 1941," he said to reporters and a group of players. Only six Dodgers were playing heads-up ball, he asserted—among them Reiser and his roomie, Reese. It was an odd thing to say, given that the team's record stood at 76-33, six full games ahead of their pennant-winning 1941 pace and eight games ahead of the second-place Cardinals. Dixie Walker stood up and challenged the boss, saying, "I'll bet a hundred that we finish twenty games ahead."

"Don't gamble on it," MacPhail snapped.

The Dodger players shook their heads in wonderment and pressed on, sweeping a doubleheader two days later, with Reiser belting a home run in the finale. He slammed another round-tripper the next day, helping the Dodgers cap a come-from-behind 5-4 win over the Braves.

That home run—his tenth of the season—would be the last he hit all year.

He was still leading the league in hitting and was still performing at a high level, but Reiser later said that as the treadmill of hot August days rolled on, he became weaker and weaker. At some point, he strained muscles on his left side on one of his patented hard swings. Even worse, he was having trouble with his vision. "I was in pretty bad shape, and I was ordered to stay inactive for some time," he told *The Sporting News* in 1949. "However, the club needed me, and I wanted to play. So back I went, despite the fact that I was having dizzy spells and was missing fly balls regularly. At the plate, I'd see two balls coming toward me. In the outfield, I'd see two grandstands in front of me."

Defensive stats bear out Reiser's assessment. In 1941, he led all National League center fielders in assists (14) and putouts (355). In '42, playing in only eight fewer games in center, his putouts fell by almost eighty, and his assists dropped to nine. He also led all NL center fielders in errors.

"Leo kept me in there, but I probably shouldn't have played," he later said. "Fly balls I could [normally] stick in my back pocket, I didn't see them until they were almost past me."

Maybe that's what happened on August 22nd, during a home game against the Giants. In the second inning, the Giants' Bill Werber walloped a long fly toward left-center. Reiser initially misjudged the ball, forcing him to race back at top speed. A few feet in front of the wall, he dove and made a somersaulting catch. The grab preserved a 2-1 Dodger lead. But as Pete got up, he felt sharp pains in his left thigh. He limped through another few innings before Augie Galan replaced him in the sixth.

The Dodger lead had slipped to six games, so Reiser was back in the lineup for a doubleheader the next day. He managed two hits in the first game, including a triple. Then, his bat fell silent, his swing impeded by the gnawing pains in his left leg and side. He went the next five games without a hit. The slump crippled Brooklyn's offense at the worst possible time, a series in St. Louis against the hard-charging Cardinals. The Dodgers dropped three of four games, including a fourteen-inning nail biter in which Reiser failed to reach base in six times at-bat. In another St. Louis game, Durocher pulled him in the sixth inning after he struck out twice against Max Lainer. ("And St. Louis is Petey's hometown!" noted *The Sporting News*. The young Mrs. Reiser was also in attendance.)

While in St. Louis, Reiser was treated by Dr. Hyland for what the papers now described as a strained leg muscle. But the leg didn't respond, and on August 28th in Chicago, he was forced to leave in the second inning, unable to run or swing properly. Durocher finally stopped denying the undeniable and sat him down the next day. That afternoon, Pete submitted to an hour of hot towel therapy for his aching muscles. When that didn't help, the Dodgers sent him east to Johns Hopkins to see specialists. Doctors there diagnosed him with torn ligaments in his back and left thigh and gave him diathermy treatments. They couldn't do much else except recommend that he rest—something Pete found hard to do. When a reporter visited him in his Baltimore hotel room, he complained, "It's too fidgety sitting around doing nothing." After a few days there, the Dodgers sent him to MacPhail's farm in Maryland, where he could rest and resist the temptation to return to Brooklyn and jump the line in batting practice.

In his absence, Brooklyn managed to win five of seven, but all were squeakers. In a 2-0 victory over the Reds, the team managed just five hits and scored the two runs on an error and sacrifice fly.

On Saturday, September 5th, Pete rejoined the Dodgers at the Polo Grounds, still in pain from his leg and side injuries. "It hurts only a little when I run or throw. It's okay when I swing and hit the ball, but when I miss, it hurts the worst," he told a reporter. The pain must have flared something fierce the next few games; after doubling his first time up, he went seventeen plate appearances without a hit. The Dodgers dropped two of three to the Giants, reducing their lead to two and a half games. In game two of a September 7th doubleheader in Boston, Pete finally enjoyed a three-hit day and even stole two bases, but none of his contributions resulted in runs, and the Dodgers lost.

Friday, September 11th, brought the inevitable. The Cardinals whipped the underpowered Dodgers 3-0 in Brooklyn and drew even in the standings. Pete's bat was church-mouse quiet, 0-for-4, and the team managed only three hits overall. Pete was benched the next day as Durocher juggled the lineup, trying to light a spark. But Brooklyn went down, 2-1, and the Cardinals pushed them aside to claim first place.

On the same weekend, Pete lost his hold on the batting race, falling behind the Braves' Ernie Lombardi. His batting average had shriveled more than 40 points in less than two months, to below .320.

Dodger fans were in shock, as were the sportswriters, none more so than Tom Meany. Over the summer, Meany had written a long, laudatory piece on Reiser for the *Saturday Evening Post*, then one of the nation's most-read magazines, with a circulation north of three million. The piece, published in late September, was titled "Pistol Pete—National Leaguer No. 1" and adorned with a subhead that boasted, "Many experts rate Harold Patrick Reiser over them all—Ted Williams, DiMag, and Flash Gordon included." When Meany finished the piece in mid-August, those headlines were defensible. Now, not so much. In his gig as sports editor for New York's newest daily, the left-wing *PM*, Meany aired his dismay at the fall of both the Dodgers and their leading hitter: "Reputations are pretty much punctured down the line," he wrote after a Brooklyn loss to woeful, last-place Philadelphia. "In mid-August, Pete Reiser seemed a lead pipe cinch to be named the National League's most valuable player. And when the Dodgers dropped the opener Sunday, Pete couldn't get the ball out of the infield. Against the Phillies, mind you."

To invert Yogi Berra's famous truism, it wasn't over, but it was over. The Dodgers righted themselves down the stretch and reeled off eight straight wins to keep the pressure on the Cardinals. The race went down to the season's final day. But the Cards never stopped winning. The Dodgers finished second, two games behind. Their final record: one hundred four wins, fifty losses. At the time, it was the most games ever won by a second-place team. Today, they'd earn a wild card spot or the division title. In 1942, there was no such thing. If you didn't finish first, you went home.

As for Pete, he had a few more two- and three-hit games down the stretch but contributed few decisive blows. In July, he had batted .364 and racked up an OPS of .968. In September, he batted .233, and his OPS shrunk to .589.

What's amazing in retrospect is that no one—not MacPhail, not Durocher, not a single player, coach, or team official—spoke up during the last two months of the season and said, "This man has to rest." Reiser was never put on the disabled list, was never given more than a few days off to recuperate. For the Dodgers, getting back to the World Series was all that mattered, and everyone connected with the team seemed to see Reiser as the only ticket to get them there.

In a post-mortem of the season with Grantland Rice, MacPhail acted like an innocent bystander. Checking through a list of reasons why the Dodgers didn't repeat as champions, he bluntly said, "Then there came the injury to Pete Reiser, who suddenly changed from a .355 hitter to a .240 hitter." Rice didn't challenge him, didn't note that MacPhail could have ordered Reiser to the bench and told Durocher to play Galan, a career .287 hitter who was the regular center fielder for two pennant winners in Chicago and would hit over .300 for the Dodgers in 1944, '45 and '46.

Years later, *Daily Eagle* sportswriter Harold Parrott, who also served as the Dodgers' traveling secretary for a time, ripped MacPhail for what he called the "destruction" of Reiser's talents. "It was as heartbreaking and messy a thing as I had ever seen pulled in any sport," Parrott wrote. "MacPhail, the hungry magnate, bending and breaking a crippled superstar like a kid in a tantrum might twist out of shape an expensive toy because it wouldn't work just that minute." But to be fair, it was Durocher making the day-to-day decisions about who to put in the lineup. And Reiser completely shared in the Dodgers' team-first, health-be-damned philosophy, even though he eventually learned it was counterproductive.

"I was always the kind of fellow who couldn't say no when the manager or the front office asked me if I thought I could make it," he said in 1949 after his Brooklyn days came to an end. "Leo Durocher appreciated by my do-or-die try for him. But beyond that, the idea never worked out. I not only hurt myself; I hurt the ballclub by playing when I should have been in a dispensary."

"There's no question in my mind that being stubborn, I cost the Dodgers the pennant in 1942," he told Honig. "Do I blame Leo for keeping me in there? Listen, if you'd ever played for him, you wouldn't ask that. You have to have played for him. He wanted to win so bad it hurt, and I wanted to win so bad it hurt. I don't blame Leo. I blame myself."

"Listen, when you're twenty-three years old, you don't want to sit on the bench and watch a game," he said at another point. "You want to be in there. I couldn't have sat out in a pennant race any more than I could have swum the Atlantic Ocean."

Dr. Zimet thinks it's remarkable that Pete, battling headaches, dizziness, and double vision, could play at all. "I don't know how a person is able to hit a baseball with those deficits," he says. "It's not like hitting a golf ball, which is a stationary object. You're hitting something that's moving about ninety miles an hour."

For the last game of the season, several hundred Dodger faithful, Hilda Chester among them, trekked to Shibe Park in Philadelphia to see their heroes go down fighting. When word came through that the Cardinals had clinched the pennant, the Brooklynites took the news with a stiff upper lip. "We don't need no crying towels," Hilda said. The Dodgers themselves accepted their defeat with a minimum of teeth-gnashing and fuss. The war naturally made it easier to put things in perspective, and of course, the team had no reason to feel ashamed. They had actually improved on their '41 record by four games. Still, the outcome of the season hurt. "I've lost some tough pennant races before," said Billy Herman. "I was with the Cubs when we were nosed out of three or four championships. But this is the hardest thing I've ever gone through. When you win one hundred four ballgames and finish second, there isn't anything to say."

After the Sunday afternoon game, most Dodgers caught a train back to New York, but Pete wasn't among them. He and Pat left straight for St. Louis to see his parents and the extended Reiser and Hurst clans. Why go back to Brooklyn? There would be no celebration in the streets this year, no World Series—and no World Series check, although each Dodger picked up a few hundred extra dollars in second-place money. Once he got home, he laid low, aside from a quick trip to Seymour, Indiana, for an exhibition game with Pee Wee, who had played there in the minors. If he went to Sportsman's Park to watch any of the Series—the Cardinals pulled off a huge upset, downing the mighty Yankees four games to one—his presence wasn't reported.

Really, the only big news in his life was on the family front: Pat was pregnant and due to deliver sometime in the spring. Pete let the New York papers know about it. The *Daily News* got the date wrong, announcing the baby was set to arrive in late December. That would have been nice, the ultimate Christmas gift.

But Pete was girding himself for another kind of delivery—his draft notice. He quietly returned to Brooklyn the first week of December to take his preliminary physical and passed it despite his lingering concussion symptoms and other injuries. Soon after, he got a letter from his draft board informing him he had been reclassified as 1-A, ripe for induction. The first time he was deemed 1-A, his mom and dad appealed, arguing that Pete financially supported the family. Now, neither he nor his parents argued the decision, making it only a matter of time, a short time, until Uncle Sam called him up. "I'm ready to go," he told a St. Louis paper on the day his reclassification became known. "I've been expecting this for some time."

Induction day arrived on January 13th, 1943. Pete reported to the Jefferson Barracks military post south of St. Louis for another brief physical and swearing-in. He came smartly dressed for the photographers, sporting a light-colored button-down sweater over a white shirt and tie. Flashbulbs popped as he raised his right hand and took the oath of enlistment, becoming U.S. Army Private #37510553. Afterward, he was given the standard one-week furlough for new draftees to get their affairs in order.

Pete had dutifully smiled for the photo-takers but had little time for the reporters on hand to document the occasion. "Gotta go now, fellas, because I only have seven days," he said as he was leaving. "This looks like the real thing."

The real thing it was. Pete would spend the next thirty-four months in the service, wearing army green instead of Dodger blue, living and working on remote bases, out of sight to all but a tiny percentage of baseball fans. He was far from alone in this—by war's end, more than five hundred players from the major leagues, and another four thousand from the minors, would put their baseball careers on hold to serve their country. Two major leaguers—Elmer Gedeon and Harry O'Neill, "cup of coffee" guys with the Senators and A's, respectively—would be killed in action, along with at least one hundred twenty-five minor leaguers. More suffered injuries, both physical and psychological that ended or drastically affected their careers.

Pete would be spared such fates. War wouldn't be outright hell for him. Nor would it be a day at the ballpark.

6
"A Wild and Frightening Beauty"

The walls that crumbled the career of Pete Reiser could have also brought down Junior—Ken Griffey Jr., to be precise.

May 25, 1991, at the Kingdome in Seattle. Ruben Sierra of the Rangers reaches down on a low pitch from the Mariners' Rich DeLucia and slams a high fly toward the wall in right-center field. Griffey, just twenty-one years old, at the peak of his breathtaking, home run-stealing defensive powers, races back from center field for a rendezvous with the ball. Two steps onto the warning track, he leaps, not upward so much as forward, and snares the ball with his glove about one body length in front of the 380-foot marker. Goal accomplished, Griffey quickly flips into protection mode, throwing up his hands and feet to brace himself for impact with the outfield wall. He slams into the wall at bone-jarring speed, and for a split second, he's positioned on it like Spider-Man, clinging to the side of a New York skyscraper. Then he falls back to the ground, landing on his behind and doing a backward somersault across the warning track.

Now freeze that image for a second and consider: What if Griffey didn't get up? What if medics had to carry him off the field and rush him to a hospital for treatment of a serious neck or head injury? Worst-case scenario, career over. Medium-case scenario, Griffey suffers long-term effects from his injury, knocking his Hall of Fame-bound career into a much lower orbit. No more spectacular catches, no SportsCenter highlights. No Gold Gloves, or MVP awards, or endorsement contracts. No fifty-homer seasons, no playoff-winning dash home against the Yankees. Maybe, in the long run, no baseball in Seattle.

But that's not what happened. After his catch, Griffey stayed down for a moment, looking like a man who had just taken a bullet, or at least an uppercut from a young Mike Tyson. But within ten seconds, he bounced to his feet and coolly trotted back to the dugout, past his teammates, past the Mariners staffer who ran on to the field to see if he was ok. His body language said: hey, no big deal. The inning's over. Leave me alone; I'm fine.

So, what was the difference between Griffey and Reiser? Why did Griffey, who was equally if not more gifted than Reiser, spend twenty-two years in the majors, hit more than six hundred homers, and become an icon for high-flying outfielders everywhere, whereas Pete became a cautionary tale, one of baseball's all-time coulda-woulda-shoulda beens?

The answer comes down to two things: better playing conditions and superior outfield skills.

In terms of eras, Griffey was fortunate to play a half-century after Reiser, in an era when outfield walls were much, much less hazardous to a player's health. In 1941, when Reiser took over center field for the Dodgers, the walls were virtual danger zones—brick or concrete barriers that had no warning tracks and no padding of any kind. Several Hall of Famers had at least one bad encounter with them, including Babe Ruth, who knocked himself unconscious chasing a ball at Washington's Griffith Stadium in 1924; Ted Williams, who broke his elbow against the left-field wall at Chicago's Comiskey Park in the 1950 All-Star Game; and Mickey Mantle, who broke his foot when his cleats caught in the quirky chain link fence at Baltimore's Memorial Stadium in 1963.

"There was always talk about doing something with those walls because guys would run into them, and that was it, you know," recalled Pete's friend Lonny Frey, who played fourteen seasons in the big leagues. "There was no warning track—we didn't have any of that stuff in those days. You were on your own."

The walls also had a surprising number of obstacles placed in front of them. Centerfield flagpoles were the most common; Reiser had to sidestep one en route to his fateful 1942 rendezvous with Sportsman's Park's wall. At Forbes Field in Pittsburgh, players had to avoid a flagpole and a giant batting cage stored in deep center field because there was nowhere else to put it. At Crosley Field in Cincinnati, the field sloped *up* in front of the walls, a feature that caused many an outfielder to stumble, fall and spit out a stream of then-unprintable words. Centerfield at Yankee Stadium, where Reiser played in two World Series, had a flagpole and stone monuments to the departed Lou Gehrig and manager Miller Huggins. (Babe Ruth was added later.) Ebbets Field was thankfully free of in-field obstructions, but the wall in the deepest part of center field had an iron exit gate on which Reiser cut his back in 1941.

By the time Griffey Jr. came along, all such hazards had been removed, and today the walls of every major-league stadium are covered with some kind of vinyl or polyurethane padding except at Wrigley Field in Chicago, where tradition keeps the brick barriers thickly coated in ivy. In addition, every park has a roughly fifteen-foot-wide warning track to alert outfielders that they are running out of room. The tracks are always made of a different substance than the playing field and colored brown or reddish-brown so that fly-chasers—in theory at least—can both see and feel the change beneath their feet while pursuing their prey. Many parks also have walls made of detachable (and padded) four-foot-wide panels designed to bend or fall away when a player crashes into them. In 1991, Griffey made a full-body slam into a paneled wall at Baltimore's Memorial Stadium to catch a blast from the Orioles' Chris Hoiles. The collision briefly knocked him to the ground, but the battle was a draw: a panel came toppling down too. Griffey glanced back at the fallen piece with a "too bad" look as he jogged back toward the dugout and nonchalantly flipped the ball to the umpire.

"They've got those walls up there now, [players] bounce into them, and the wall gives. You can run head-on into those things and survive without any problem," said Frey.

However, Griffey's greatness was hardly the product of outfielder-friendly stadiums. Even in his early twenties, Junior was already a master at playing the walls safely and with the greatest expertise. His father, Ken Sr., a major league outfielder for nineteen years, no doubt taught him some tricks of the trade. However, Junior has always credited Hall of Fame slugger Willie Stargell—not a defensive stalwart but a left fielder for the bulk of his career—for giving him important pointers soon after the Seattle Mariners made Griffey the overall number-one pick in the 1987 draft. Stargell was then a coach for the Atlanta Braves, for whom the elder Griffey was playing left field. "[He] stuck me in the outfield, and we worked on footwork for three hours," Griffey Jr. remembered. "We didn't even touch a baseball. I didn't get to hit, and that's all we really wanted to do, is hit. He told me, 'You're going to learn how to play the outfield right now.'"

Reiser never talked about receiving such detailed outfield instruction at either the major or minor league level.

Junior put his lessons to good use as soon as he reached the majors, making a seemingly endless string of running, diving, and leaping catches, many of them made at or *above* outfield walls, all without suffering severe injury. After he made the "Spider Man" catch, the Mariners' announcers noted that there were dents in the Kingdome padding, one in each place where Griffey had dug in his spikes. Those dents were no accident, Griffey explained in a subsequent TV interview. "I was running full speed, and I ran so far, and I said, "Well, if I hit the wall . . . I might as well do it the best way I can, and that's to use my feet and hands, rather than my chest," he said. In other words, he knew how to protect himself. He explained in the same interview that when he made a diving catch, he lifted his elbows off the ground to avoid turf burns. Griffey also stressed the importance of studying outfield layouts before game time. "Number one, you count how many steps [to the wall] from when you hit the warning track because some warning tracks are smaller than others," he told Harold Reynolds on MLB Network. "You've got to know where you are on the field, all the time . . . [You] hit the warning track, you feel it or hear it, the difference from grass to dirt or cinder or rocks."

These lessons might seem obvious, but some players don't pay heed. In May 2013, Bryce Harper, then of the Nationals, chased after a long fly to deep right at Dodger Stadium. Tracking the ball, Harper made no visible attempt to locate the warning track and charged face-first into the right-field scoreboard, making a loud *thud* that echoed throughout the ballpark. Harper stayed conscious, but the collision left an ugly, bloody gash on his neck that required eleven stitches. As he was being led off the field, Dodger announcer Vin Scully said, "All I can think of . . . is a name that is a legend in Dodger history, an outfielder named Pete Reiser." ESPN's Buster Olney made the same comparison the next day in a piece that warned Harper to lower his intensity a notch. "And if he's too sore to play on Tuesday, he might want to take a few minutes to read about Pete Reiser," Olney wrote.

Even with his body-sparing techniques, Griffey also suffered injuries—he broke his wrist against the Kingdome wall in May 1995, and during the second half of his career, his hamstrings and other leg muscles seemed to fail him on an annual basis. But he never experienced a Reiser-like crash that knocked him out cold or required a fast trip to the hospital.

In contrast to Griffey and subsequent wall crawlers like Torii Hunter, Mike Trout, and Mookie Betts, Pete played the outfield kamikaze style, with no real safeguards, either external or within. He said he took one protective measure in the field, wearing the cap with the plastic lining that Larry MacPhail mandated for Dodger hitters in 1941. If that's true, the cap might have saved his life in his two worst collisions at Sportsman's Park in 1942 and Ebbets Field in 1947. But ultimately, a thin layer of plastic provided little protection to a man who tore after fly balls like a racehorse with tunnel vision.

"Some people can feel the wall close to them, you follow me?" said 1940s Dodger outfielder Gene Hermanski. "I know I would. I wouldn't look back, but

I could feel like it's there. And I would slow down . . . However, Pete, I guess, was never aware of the wall. He'd just go right through the goddamn thing."

"He played so hard, even in batting practice," recalled Brooklyn pitcher Ralph Branca. "Pitchers would be shagging flies, and Pete would come out there, and a fly ball would go up, and Pete would take off. You'd have to yell 'no, no, no,' because he would run into the wall in practice just to catch a ball. The guy had no fear."

"Reiser had blinding running speed, and he started instantly," said Dodgers' announcer Red Barber. "Reiser was in full speed on his first stride. When he started after a fly ball, he just kept going, and no matter how many times he bounced back from concrete walls, he never gave up. He tried them again and again."

Tommy Holmes of the *Brooklyn Daily Eagle* once wrote: "He continually tries to build new doors in the outfield barriers, a task too rugged for even the flesh, blood and bone that Pete possesses. Someday, the other Dodgers fear, they'll have to go out there and scrape Pete off the wall with a putty knife."

Said Barber: "It was frightening to see Reiser charge into a wall. He would crash into the concrete, bounce back, and lie crumpled and still on the grass. If Reiser could have played in the old days of baseball before they had fences, he might still be playing. If he had played at Yankee Stadium, in the big ballpark, he might have added years to his records." Barber could have added the Giants' Polo Grounds and its next-county center field walls as another safe haven for Pete. The fast-running and free-roaming Willie Mays never hit a barrier there, even when zooming back at full throttle to make "The Catch" in the 1954 World Series. When Mays made his famous back-to-the-infield, over the shoulder grab of Vic Wertz's blast, he had run about thirty yards and was approximately four hundred twenty-five feet from home plate. Yet, he was still several steps short of the wall.

In contrast, Ebbets Field may have been the worst possible place for Pete's runaway train fielding style. Its deepest point, the notch in center field with the exit gate, was just three hundred ninety-nine feet from home plate, one of the shortest such distances in the major leagues. The left-center and right-center field walls were short too because Ebbets Field was crammed into the space of a city block; behind the right field walls, there were no stands, just the busy foot and car traffic of Brooklyn's Bedford Avenue. For someone running as fast as Reiser, the walls arrived all too soon, with disastrous consequences.

"This is supposition, but if I had played with the Yankees, I probably never would have run into a wall, 'cause they wouldn't have used me out there [in center field]. I'm not going to beat DiMaggio out," Pete told his son-in-law late in life. Nor did he think he would have displaced the Yankee Clipper's outfield mates, Tommy Henrich and Charlie Keller, both stars in their own right. The position he really wanted to play—and play for the Cardinals, incidentally—was third base, far away from any body-breaking outfield barriers. "I could have played third base in St. Louis until I was fifty years old," he said. "I was a hell of a third baseman. [Reds' manager] Bill McKechnie told me I was. [Yankees manager] Joe McCarthy told me I was the best third baseman he ever saw. I thought it was the easiest position in baseball. I could play third base, believe me. I could have played there for thirty years."

* * *

The question—often asked but never quite answered—is *why* Reiser played the outfield so recklessly and why he couldn't or wouldn't change. Both during and after his career, reporters pressed him on the matter, and he always said, essentially, that he couldn't help it.

"It was my way of playing. If I hadn't played that way, I wouldn't have been whatever I was," he told W.C. Heinz in 1957. "God gave me those legs and the speed, and when they took me into the walls, that's the way it had to be. I couldn't play any other way."

"Why did all those fences happen to me? Well, I guess I was extra fast, and I guess I played extra hard. I wasn't cautious. I played all out to win," he told the *Los Angeles Times* in 1960.

To Donald Honig in 1974, he said, "It was my style of playing, the only way I knew how. You can't turn a thing like that off. Why should you? It's born in you; it's part of you. It *is* you."

But at least once, in a 1980 interview with a Salinas, California newspaper, Pete went a little deeper in his response. "It's hard to explain. I had great speed. I knew the ball could be caught, *so you actually forget where you're at*," he said. (Italics added.) Put another way, when chasing a fly ball, Pete screened out his surroundings—fans, fellow outfielders, and the location of the walls. It was as though everything except the ball became a blank.

Journalists didn't challenge Reiser when he made such remarks but could have legitimately asked: why not try to be more aware? Since the first fly balls were lofted into early nineteenth-century outfields, players have been taught to yell out warnings ("Got it!" "Wall!") and to listen for those commands to avoid harmful collisions. But for all his talents, Pete had trouble internalizing that rule. In the early part of his career, his main problem was colliding with teammates. Dixie Walker explained during spring training 1942: "Reiser and I have collided in the outfield when we both went after the same fly ball a number of times, you know. I don't remember ever hearing him yell, and he swears he doesn't hear me." Dixie wasn't exaggerating. In the latter half of the 1941 season alone, Reiser collided with Walker in July, rookie outfielder Tommy Tatum in August, and Walker again in September. In a key late-season game against the Cardinals, he nearly plowed into Pee Wee Reese, but the Dodger shortstop got out of the way at the last second.

Walker said he worked out a system with Reiser where he put up his hand like a traffic signal to indicate he was going to catch the ball. That worked to an extent: Reiser had no reported collisions with teammates in 1942. Unfortunately, the system did nothing to save Pete from inanimate objects. Just three days after Walker made his comments, Pete hit the center field fence during a Dodger exhibition game in Norfolk—one of his less serious collisions but a scary harbinger of what was to come.

Sportswriter Jimmy Cannon, always one of the more thoughtful and literate of his profession, pondered Reiser's fielding style at length in a 1949 essay for *Esquire* magazine and theorized on what might be stopping Pete from exercising the restraint needed to save his body and career:

> *"He is motivated by a wonderful devotion to the petty art of catching a baseball hit by a bat. There is little grace in his flights to the fences. There is dreadful panic in his reckless speed. He always seems alone, unconnected with other players, unmolested by the crowd as he goes back after a fly ball . . . There is terror in this act every time he does it. It is like watching a blind bird fly crazily around a room, brushing the walls with his wings.*
>
> *They give you many explanations for Pete's recklessness. But to me, it is as though he becomes trapped in a mobile dream. The dimensions of his field cease to exist in his mind, so great is his concentration. The shouts of the other outfielders warning him are unheard. The running fielder seeks to alter the frontiers of the field. The glades where big-league baseball is played are too pinched for Reiser, and in a remote way, this is similar to [Irish author] James Joyce trying to break out of the English language.*
>
> *Nothing else on the field is related to this feat. There is only the ball and Reiser. The ecstasy of the chase seems to cause a suicidal amnesia once he goes after a fly ball which is falling behind him. It must confuse the gamblers who make book on games in this country to watch one guy risk his life for one out in a ballgame in a schedule of one hundred fifty-four. It*

is beyond me, and Reiser can't explain why he does it. It is a man betrayed by a creative frenzy and is the artist achieving a supreme devotion to his craft. It is more manual labor than anything else, but Reiser gives baseball a wild and frightening beauty when he is after a fly ball, and there is a fence behind him."

Sports psychologist Dr. Daniel Zimet says intense focus is the norm among elite athletes like Pete. "That's not unique to him. That's almost universally true to athletes when they get to that level," he says. But, he adds, Pete's single-mindedness was probably stronger than most, and Pete might have had deeper motivations pushing him on. The early experience of trying to impress an older brother who then tragically died was likely one factor. Another might have been buried anger over his delayed arrival in the majors. "He might have needed to prove something, to show the decision-makers, 'I'm ready to move up.' You do that by giving one hundred fifty percent effort," Zimet says.

And at some point, says the doctor, the concussions themselves might have brought about more concussions. Brain injuries can disrupt the higher orders of thinking that make people exercise restraint, Zimet says. "It takes mental effort to be cautious and inhibit our behavior. A huge amount of brain activity has to take place to stop us from impulsivity and recklessly pursuing our desires." When that activity is impaired, he says, people can become more prone to anger and more careless in their general behavior. For the average person, that can lead to things like excessive drinking and road rage. For Pete, it led him right into the outfield walls.

For the record, Reiser himself spoke neither of artistry nor anger when talking about his feats and foibles in the outfield. He just wanted to make a catch.

"I know that he was so focused on catching the ball that sometimes that's all he thought about and didn't think about the consequences," says his son-in-law, Rick Tuber.

Incidentally, in the *Esquire* article, Cannon quoted Leo Durocher raving about Pete's abilities, and one gets the impression that Durocher *admired* Pete for repeatedly charging into hard, immovable things. "He's great, great, great," Leo said. "Three or four times, he's run into a wall. One time, and a lot of guys get wall shy. But he's still running right up after them." With that kind of encouragement, it's a wonder Pete didn't smash into walls once a week.

The year Cannon wrote his essay, the major leagues were finally taking steps to save outfielders like Reiser from themselves. In the spring of 1948, the

Dodgers became the first team to install foam rubber padding on their outfield walls at a reported cost of five thousand dollars. "[I] don't believe that it is fool-proof protection, but it offers Pete some safety," explained general manager Branch Rickey. The following season, team owners mandated warning tracks—"cinder paths" in the jargon of the day—for all major league ballparks. Pete, ironically, never got to benefit much from either innovation. By the turn of the decade, he was so banged up and plagued by dizziness that he only occasionally played the outfield. The bulk of his appearances now came as a pinch hitter or pinch-runner.

Years later, when the Dodgers built their dream stadium in Los Angeles, team executives recalled Reiser's experience and accepted a suggestion by consulting engineer Emil Praeger to make the outfield fences out of plywood instead of the traditional brick or concrete. "The Reiser case was familiar to all of us with the Dodgers," explained general manager Buzzie Bavasi. "He may have prompted Captain Praeger to come up with his suggestion, and I know it was a factor in our decision to use the light wooden wall." Pete, by then a coach with the Dodgers, looked over Dodger Stadium's plywood wall when it was finished and gave it his full endorsement. "There's no question that if we had a wall like this back in my day, I wouldn't have been so badly hurt," he said.

By then, running into walls had become Pete's defining feature, and he could make jokes about it. In February 1960, when construction workers began to tear down the now-abandoned Ebbets Field, Pete told Dick Young: "I'm sure they won't have any trouble knocking down that center field wall. I softened it up for them." A few years later, Jim Murray of the *Los Angeles Times* went a step further and constructed a whole column out of Reiser hitting-the-fence jokes. He said the German army studied film of Reiser's technique before attacking the Maginot Line. "He's only got half as many bones as the average man," Murray wrote. "The rest are embedded in outfield walls someplace."

But when Pete died in 1981, Murray wrote perhaps the most fitting tribute to the silenced Pistol. "Wherever he is today, I hope they have a roomy outfield and a crushed-brick warning track because Pete would still go hard," Murray said. "Pete was one of the best of the Boys of Summer, and he never saw a ball he didn't think he could hit—or catch. That was the trouble."

Pistol vs. Wall

Pete Reiser's seven major collisions with outfield walls:

MAY 8, 1941: Hit the center field exit gate at Ebbets Field while hauling in a long fly from Enos Slaughter. Reiser suffered a two-inch long cut on his back and was taken to Caledonian Hospital for stitches. Returned to play on May 18.

APRIL 7, 1942: Ran into the wall during an exhibition game at Bain Field in Norfolk, Virginia, while chasing a long hit from the Yankees' Charlie Keller. He was pulled from the game by manager Durocher and reported "shaken up" but played the next day.

JULY 19, 1942: Banged his head against the center-field wall at Sportsman's Park, St. Louis, while running after a drive from Slaughter. He was taken to St. John's Hospital and diagnosed with a concussion. He left the hospital against doctor's orders the next day, caught a train to Brooklyn, and returned to action on July 25.

EARLY AUGUST 1945: Ran through a makeshift fence or hedge at Camp Lee, Virginia, and tumbled into a ditch, injuring his right shoulder. He sat out the remainder of his army team's schedule.

MAY 19, 1946: Collided with the left-field wall at Ebbets Field while chasing a ball hit by Reds' Gary Hutton. He re-injured his right shoulder but returned to action on May 22.

AUGUST 1, 1946: Hit his head against the left-field wall at Ebbets Field while leaping for double by Cardinals' Whitey Kurowski. He was taken to Peck Memorial Hospital, where doctors diagnosed him with a mild concussion. Returned to play on August 8.

JUNE 4, 1947: Cracked his head against Ebbets Field's center-field wall while trying to catch a drive from Pirates' Cully Rikard. Given last rites by two priests in the clubhouse. He was taken to Swedish Hospital and was diagnosed with concussion and scalp lacerations. Spent five days in the hospital, returned to play on July 12.

Pete at the peak, standing with four future Hall of Famers before the 1942 All-Star Game. Left to right: Joe Gordon, Joe DiMaggio, Reiser, Ted Williams, and Joe Medwick. Pete entered the game leading both major leagues in hitting at .361.

Reiser family portrait taken in the mid-1920s when Pete was around five years old. Pete is at bottom left. His older brother Mike, whom he idolized, is at top center. (Courtesy Shirley Reiser Tuber.)

Pete, about 12 years old, shows off his baseball uniform in the backyard of his family's St. Louis home. (Courtesy Shirley Reiser Tuber.)

Pete (top row, right) in 1937 with his first minor league team in Newport, Arkansas. "I wanted to be a Cardinal," he later said. Fate and Commissioner Landis had other plans. (Courtesy Shirley Reiser Tuber.)

The intense Reiser glare. Pete was all business in a baseball uniform, to the point of ignoring friendly greetings from the other team when he got on base.

Preparing to hit at spring training in Florida, 1939. Given a chance to play that March, Pete got on base his first eleven times up, with eight hits and three walks.

Pete was never known for keeping his uniform sparkling clean. His mother said of him as a boy: "I think he did a lot of sliding just to get dirty." (Courtesy Shirley Reiser Tuber.)

The three men who determined the arc of Pete's career in baseball. Left to right: Larry MacPhail, Branch Rickey, and Leo Durocher.

Is it fair or foul? Pete watches the ball after striking a long drive at Ebbets Field, 1941.

Pals Reese and Reiser head out on the town, 1941. (Courtesy Shirley Reiser Tuber).

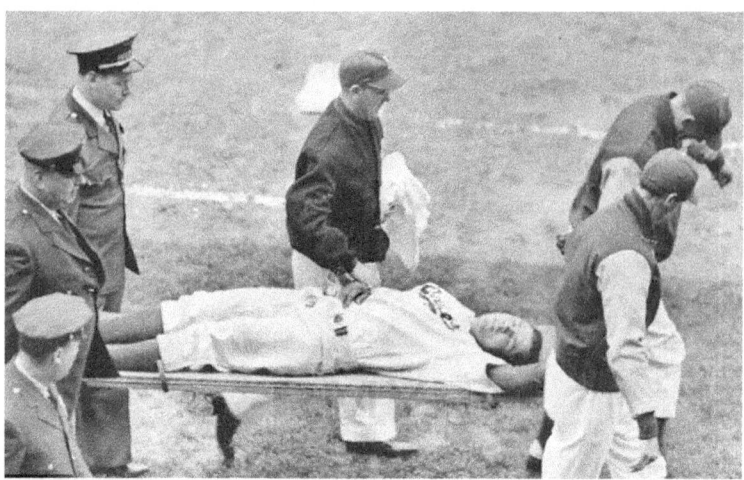

Pete is carried off the field after a pitch from Ike Pearson strikes him on his right cheekbone, April 23, 1941. He'd be stretchered or helped off the field several times more before his Dodger career was over.

Pete uncorks a practice swing during the 1941 season, when he led the National League in hitting at .343. (Ernie Harwell collection, Detroit Public Library)

Newlyweds: Pete and Patricia Reiser are all smiles along with Dorothy and Pee Wee Reese on opening day, 1942 at Ebbets Field.

By 1942, Pete's burgeoning stardom prompted Street & Smith publishing to put out a comic book version of his life story.

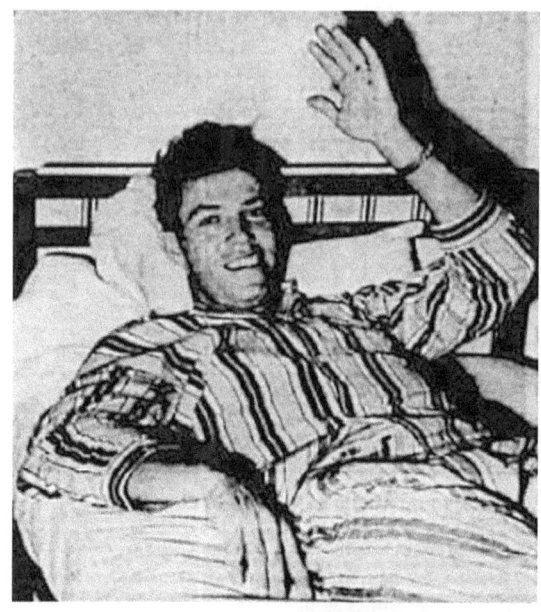

Pete in his hospital bed, July 20, 1942, the day after crashing into the center-field wall at Sportsman's Park. Contrary to his later claim, Pete did not suffer a fractured skull on the play. He did get a concussion, and ignored doctor's orders to rest for several days. He was plagued by headaches and dizziness afterward. (*St. Louis Star* and *Times*)

Drafted and lugging a duffel bag at the Jefferson Barracks in St. Louis, January 1943. Pete would miss three years of big-league ball to the service.

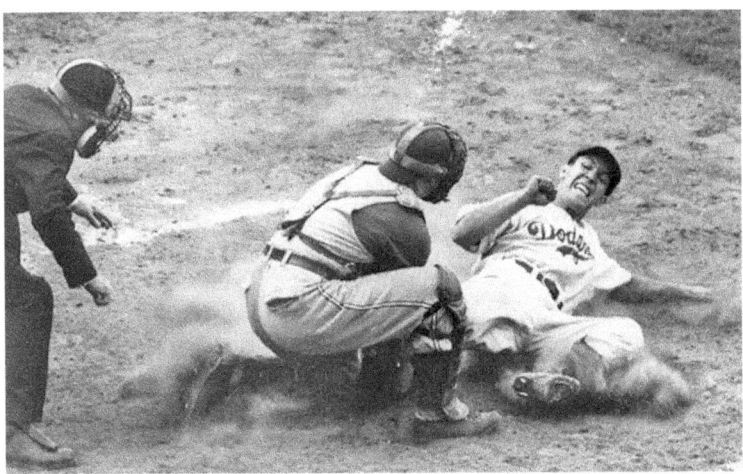

Back in Brooklyn in 1946, Pete perfected the art of stealing home and did it successfully seven times that season—still a major league record seventy-five years later, though it was tied by Rod Carew in 1969.

Pete slides home safely in September 1946, using his trademark "fallaway" slide to avoid a tag by lunging Cardinal catcher Del Rice. Pee Wee Reese watches.

Pete rushes past the attempted tag by Yankee first baseman George McQuinn in game one of the 1947 World Series. (1947 World Series film.)

Reiser forced the Dodgers to trade him to the Boston Braves before the 1949 season. He liked his new manager, Billy Southworth, but was so injury-prone he could rarely play more than a few games in a row. (Press photo).

The Reiser family, 1951: Sally, Pete, Shirley, and Pat. Pete was playing for the Pirates at the time. (Courtesy Shirley Reiser Tuber.)

After retiring Pete spent more than twenty years in baseball as a minor league manager and major league coach. Here, he teaches baserunning techniques to members of the Tokyo Giants during a brief stay in Japan, mid-1960s. (Courtesy Shirley Reiser Tuber.)

Pete takes part in his final old-timers day at Dodger Stadium in 1980. Next to him is Shirley's husband Rick Tuber. (Courtesy Shirley Reiser Tuber.)

Sixty-two-year-old Pete holds his grandson Peter Brian Tuber in 1981, a few months before his death that October. Peter would play in the 1994 Little League World Series. (Courtesy Shirley Reiser Tuber.)

7

Soldiering On

Jim Lehrer hosted the nightly *NewsHour* program on PBS for more than thirty-five years, first with Robert MacNeil, then solo. A journalist of the highest order, Lehrer covered the Kennedy assassination and Watergate, moderated a dozen presidential debates, won two Emmys and a Peabody Award, and, on the side, wrote twenty novels and a pair of screenplays.

But long before he ever stared into a camera, Lehrer was a childhood baseball fanatic whose world, to a large extent, revolved around Pete Reiser. "I had a comic-book biography of Reiser's life and career, and he had become my idol," the late Lehrer said in his memoir, *We Were Dreamers*. "I saw myself as him much of the time, in fact, rifling throws into the plate to catch Enos Slaughter and Whitey [Kurowski], lining game-winning doubles against the Ebbets Field fence, grabbing sinking liners off the grass in short center." Lehrer said his father even gave him a baseball outfit that mimicked the Dodgers' traveling uniform, gray with blue trim. His nickname around his Wichita, Kansas neighborhood—one suspects it was self-chosen—was Pistol Pete. It was an ironic name because, by his own admission, Lehrer wasn't very good at baseball. However, nine-year-old boys don't care about such things.

In the pre-television, pre-internet world of the early 1940s, Lehrer had no way of seeing his hero play ball outside brief flashes that popped up occasionally in movie theater newsreels. That suddenly changed in early 1943 when the newly drafted Reiser was sent to Fort Riley, an army base about one hundred twenty miles north of Wichita, and became the regular center fielder for Riley's baseball team, the Centaurs. The development added up to an extended birthday for the young Lehrer because the Centaurs drove down to Wichita at least twice a week to play games for soldiers and factory workers. A wide-eyed Lehrer was often in the stands. "I made Pop take me to as many of the Fort Riley games as possible," he remembered. When he couldn't see his hero in person, he recalled, he devoured the sports pages of Wichita's two daily newspapers, the *Eagle* and the *Beacon*, seeking news of Reiser's latest exploits.

Lehrer recalled that the ultimate thrill came one summer afternoon when a friend of his ran up to his house screaming out the news: the Centaurs were taking batting practice at the high school! Pete Reiser himself was there! Lehrer threw on his gray uniform, grabbed his glove, and dashed two blocks down the street to East High. He found Pete leaning on a bat next to the batting cage, waiting for his turn to hit. "He was stocky, well built. His arm muscles were huge," Lehrer remembered. "He slammed the first three pitches thrown him way over the heads of three or four players who were shagging flies at center. Then he hit several more to left and right just as hard and just as far. It was spectacular."

When Reiser was just about done, the young Lehrer edged toward the batting cage and initiated a conversation, which he recounted in his memoir:

"Hi, Pistol Pete," said I.
"Hello there," said Pistol Pete.
"You're great."
"Thanks."

That was it, Lehrer recalled. But, he added, "it was enough." He had spoken to his idol. More than sixty years later, he'd adorn the lead character in one of his novels with a strong Pete Reiser obsession, a personality trait that he no doubt borrowed from his younger self.

* * *

The elation felt by Lehrer and his cohorts in Kansas that spring was matched by the dejection felt by the Dodger faithful in Brooklyn. Sportswriters didn't mince words once Reiser was drafted: the Bums were doomed. "The definite loss of Reiser, of course, comes as a very serious blow to the Dodger pennant hopes in 1943," wrote John Drebinger in the *New York Times*. Tommy Holmes of the *Daily Eagle* summed up the general feeling: "[N]one of the considerable losses of the Brooklyn Dodgers to the armed service are as important as this one. It was entirely possible to replace Harry Lavagetto, and the club may stumble along without fellows like Larry French and Hugh Casey. But they'll not be able to replace the boy bomber from St. Louis with a reasonable facsimile of the same."

The prognosticators were correct. With Reiser in the army and Pee Wee Reese joining the Navy, the '43 Dodgers were, in one sportswriter's phrase, "slower than snails with fallen arches." Augie Galan did a capable job in center field, even led the league in walks, but the team's spark was gone, and Brooklyn finished third. Home attendance fell by three hundred seventy-five thousand, a drop of more than one-third from 1942. The following year the Dodgers would plunge to seventh place, and attendance slipped even more.

The only thing that gave Dodger fans hope was the new management. Near the end of the '42 season, after five tumultuous years at the helm, Larry MacPhail had resigned as GM to accept an officer's position in the army. To replace him, the Brooklyn board of directors hired none other than Branch Rickey, the genius who had built the Cardinals. Rickey was ready for a change of scene; his relationship with Cards owner Sam Breadon had gradually soured over issues of power and Rickey's very high pay. Meanwhile, the Dodger owners wanted a less temperamental chief executive, one without a drinking problem and one who would build the team through the farm system rather than dropping high-five and low-six figure sums on veteran ballplayers. Rickey did not come cheap: his contract called for a twenty-five-thousand-dollar salary, to be increased to fifty thousand upon the end of the war. He was also entitled to fifteen percent of the club's net profits before federal and state taxes, a figure that would drop to a still-substantial ten percent when hostilities ceased. The directors figured he was worth it; it was the Cardinals, after all, who stole the '42 pennant from the Bums with their one hundred six wins, the most by any National League club in over thirty years.

Rickey, naturally, was already familiar with Brooklyn's star centerfielder from his brief time in the Cardinal chain, and at his introductory press conference, the Mahatma briefly and eloquently name-checked Pete, saying he had "the gift to run and the urge to go."

The boy bomber may have smiled when he heard that compliment but was going through some difficulties. He had told the press he was ready for the army, but in private, "he didn't think he'd be drafted," recalled Pete's wife, Pat. His error was understandable. Yes, in 1942, the U.S. military's demands for manpower were enormous; approximately three hundred thousand young American men were joining the Army, Navy, or other branches of the service each month, as the U.S. geared up to fight a two-front war. Pete, however, was already walking wounded. Five months after crashing into the wall in St. Louis, he was still suffering chronic headaches plus periodic double vision and dizziness. Why would the army take a guy who couldn't always see straight? Add to that the other injuries—the bone chips in his arm from '39, the Ike Pearson concussion in '41, the torn ligaments from late in the '42 season. That fall, Doc Hyland discovered the Pistol also had a double hernia. And on top of everything, Pete had a nineteen-year-old wife who was due to give birth in two months. From a remove of eighty years, it seems like Pete could make a solid case to be declared 4-F—unfit for military service—or at least to retain his 3-A classification.

But certain army officers didn't see it that way. Pete told W.C. Heinz that on the day he reported to Jefferson Barracks, he took his pre-induction physical and got a thumbs-down from the doctors. Then . . . "I'm sittin' on a bench with the other guys who've been rejected," he recalled, "and a captain comes in and says, 'Which one of you is Reiser?' I stood up, and I said, 'I am.' In front of everybody, he said, 'So you're trying to pull a fast one, are you? At a time like this, with a war going on, you came in here under a false name. What do you mean, giving your name as Harold Patrick Reiser? Your name's Pete Reiser, and you're the ballplayer, aren't you?' I said, 'I'm the ballplayer, and they call me Pete, but my right name is Harold Patrick Reiser.' The captain says, 'I apologize. Sergeant, fingerprint him. This man is in.'"

The story sounds like something out of a movie, but Tommy Holmes later wrote that he heard the same tale from a sailor stationed in Brooklyn during the war. The unidentified sailor ("a little Italian fellow") said he got his medical exam at the same time and place as Pete. "I heard a doctor tell Reiser to go home and forget about it," he remembered. He said Pete was putting on his socks when a major walked in the room, recognized Pete, and accused him of the phony name scheme. "The officer told him to wait some more and went inside again," the sailor recalled. "After two more minutes, he came to the doorway and beckoned. And Reiser walked through the door and right into the army."

The story raises a question that Pete never addressed: was he actually hoping to slip through the physical unrecognized and walk free? It's unclear, but it wouldn't be the last time in the army his notoriety and talents worked against his overall interests.

He became a full-time soldier on January 20th, and within a week, the realities of army life hit hard. First, he was transferred three hundred eighty miles west to Fort Riley for basic training. All his life, Pete had been a city boy, growing up in the center of St. Louis, playing baseball in the heart of Flatbush. Now he was planted on a sprawling, rural army base that must have seemed a day's walk from nowhere. "Fort Riley was in rough country," remembered Cardinals' outfielder Harry Walker, also stationed at the base during the war. "Flat, no trees. Burning hot in the summer and cold in the winter. Snow would pile up." And initially, during boot camp, sergeants didn't give their star draftee any special treatment. Private Louis Miller was in the same troop unit as Pete. He told his hometown *Louisville Courier-Journal* in early 1943 that "Pete gets K.P. [kitchen patrol] and detail as well as the tough grind of guard duty." Same as everybody else, in other words.

A few weeks later, Pete got his first heavy dose of winter weather when his unit went on a two-day, fifty-mile march, lugging heavy packs in frigid temperatures. Pete made it through the march but caught pneumonia afterward and was soon laid up in Fort Riley's hospital. One day, he woke up to find a doctor sitting beside his bed. The doctor had been studying his medical records, Pete said, and initiated a conversation.

> *"Feeling better?" he asks.*
> *"Yeah."*
> *"How long you been in the army, son?"*
> *"Three weeks."*
> *"How'd you ever get in?"*
> *"They told them to fingerprint me and induct me."*
> *"You'll be out in two weeks," he says. Pats me on the shoulder and walks away.*

Given all that Reiser had endured in the previous eight months—the concussion, the dizziness, the leg and side injuries, and now, a bout with pneumonia, the doctor's words must have sounded reassuring and completely believable.

About ten days later, he recalled, a voice squawked over the PA, instructing "Private Reiser" to report to camp headquarters. Pete hoped this was it, his call to pick up his discharge papers and head home. Once he arrived, he was sent to see a colonel sitting behind a desk. The officer explained that he was a sports fan; he followed all sports, in fact, but he especially loved baseball. A little voice inside Pete said, "Uh-oh."

The colonel first wanted to establish the identity of his visitor. The discharge papers apparently named the private as "Harold Patrick Reiser," same as Pete's induction papers. Again, it's not clear whether Pete was deliberately trying to conceal his baseball fame. But the colonel, like the captain at Jefferson Barracks, was suspicious:

> *"You wouldn't happen to be related to Pete, would you?"*
> *"Yes, sir."*
> *"You're not Pete, are you?"*
> *"Yes, sir, I'm Pete."*

"You know, I always wanted to meet you."
"Thank you, Colonel."

After that exchange, which had to raise tension between the two men, the colonel picked up the papers. "They want me to discharge you. It's up to me to sign them or not. Tell me, what happens if I sign?" he said.

Pete replied that he'd play center field for the Dodgers—an honest but probably counterproductive answer.

"I was looking forward to having a hell of a ballclub here in Fort Riley," the colonel said, according to Pete. "Now, do you really want to go back to Brooklyn? The war's going bad, you know. I think it would be a shame if you left the Army."

And with that, he ripped up Pete's discharge papers.

"I can still hear that 'zip' when he tore them," Pete told W.C. Heinz.

I have to pause here again because this part of Pete's story—told in slightly different versions to Heinz in 1958 and Donald Honig in 1974—initially struck my ear as too starkly dramatic, too much a caricature of power-loving army types, to be entirely true. After all, why would a colonel keep a baseball player in the military against his will, especially if that player had already suffered so many well-documented injuries, injuries that might limit his usefulness as a ballplayer, not to mention as a soldier?

However, it turns out Pete's experience wasn't that uncommon. In January 1942, as noted, President Roosevelt had expressed a wish to keep baseball going during the war, on the grounds it would be good for the nation's morale. But as Pete was fast learning, a segment of American society, especially in the armed forces, felt any man healthy enough to play ball for a living was surely healthy enough to serve his country. Late in '42, Yankee pitcher Red Ruffing got an induction notice in his hometown of Long Beach, California. Ruffing was thirty-seven years old, was the sole means of support for his wife and son, and was missing four toes on his left foot due to a childhood accident when he worked in a coal mine. But none of that mattered, Ruffing recalled: "The regular doctors examined me. They turned me down. The last doctor I came to was an Army doctor. He put on his report that what I could do on the outside I could do on the inside. He would have drafted any ballplayer. So that's how I got in." Ruffing missed two and a half big league seasons, likely costing him a chance at winning three hundred games.

Reiser wasn't even the only player effectively trapped at Fort Riley. Harry Walker, the younger brother of Dixie Walker, arrived there in October 1943, days after playing for the Cardinals in the World Series. Soon after his induction, Walker came down with spinal meningitis, an infection of the membranes around the brain and spinal cord. If not treated quickly, meningitis can be fatal. Even with effective treatment, which Walker fortunately received, patients can take months to regain their strength. "They said, 'You'll never go overseas with that, you'll be going home,'" Walker recalled. "And everybody [else] that had it went home. But because I was in baseball, they said, 'You can't go because it'll be bad publicity and things like that.' So, I had to stay." Not only did Walker stay in the army—he and several other ballplayers trained at Fort Riley were sent to France in 1944 and fought in the Battle of the Bulge. Walker shot several German soldiers, suffered shrapnel wounds, and earned a Bronze Star and Purple Heart.

Reiser's ailments did have one upside—because of them, he would never face combat. "No one in authority in the service will take the responsibility of okaying him physically for overseas duty," the *Daily Eagle* once explained. However, military officials had another assignment for Reiser: entertaining the troops. Millions of soldiers passed through U.S. military bases during the war, and the army had to provide diversions to keep morale high. USO shows and Hollywood movies played important roles, but baseball was the perfect fit. A good ballgame kept the men occupied and away from mischief; a winning team on base spread cheer and gave the brass something to brag about. And even before Reiser's arrival, Fort Riley officers made sure they had a hell of a ballclub. The 1942 team had won the Kansas state semipro championship and reached the semifinals of the national semipro tournament, held each year in Wichita.

With his hopes for a discharge now literally in shreds, Pete adjusted to the situation. Fort Riley authorities made things easier by turning him into a full-time army ballplayer, at least during the spring and summer months. He said he was given a private room and assigned no duties, although he was technically classified as a physical training instructor. He had to perform occasional publicity tasks, like talking to boys' clubs or giving jeep rides to kids at a school. But his real job was to play center field for the Fort Riley base team, known as the Centaurs. And this was no ordinary team. Reiser's '43 teammates included five other major leaguers: infielders Frank Crespi, George Archie, and Joe Gantenbein, and pitchers Ken Heintzelman and Joe Lanning. No other service team in the region had such a concentration of talent. The result? "We whomped everybody we played," Reiser remembered. He wasn't exaggerating. In the spring, the team sailed to the pennant in the Kansas-Oklahoma Victory League, an association of regional service and factory teams. In July, they again won the Kansas state semipro tournament. And in August, they again reached the semifinals of the national tournament.

That was in '43. Ahead of the '44 season, Fort Riley's commanders grabbed hold of more major leaguers, including Walker, pitcher Al Brazle, and all-star second baseman Lonny Frey, as well as a couple of prospects who would hit the big leagues after the war, pitcher Rex Barney and catcher Joe Garagiola. Again, the Centaurs swept to the Victory League championship and won the Kansas state semipro tournament. Fort Riley authorities disbanded the team before the national tournament, stating that several players on the team had finished their basic training and were being transferred to other posts. But some observers suspected a different reason: the team was too good. Pete told a reporter that the team's record was eighteen wins and one loss. "We made up for that one by walloping the team that beat us 18 to 4 the next time out," he said.

As for Pete himself, the games were akin to batting practice. During the '43 state semipro tournament, he batted a reported .481. In a list of the Victory League's best hitters published in June 1944, Reiser sat on top with a .565 average, thirteen hits in twenty-three times at-bat. He did better still during the '44 state semipro tournament, hitting .583 and clinching the finale for Riley with a two-out single in the ninth that drove in Archie and Gantenbein with the championship runs.

And after getting hits, he wasn't jogging it on the basepaths. Rex Barney, who would be Pete's teammate again after the war with the Dodgers, recalled a Fort Riley game where Pete "slid headfirst into third so hard that he tore the bag off the hook and carried it ten feet into foul ground. He didn't know how to play the game any other way."

Not that they needed extra help, but the Fort Riley team could have been an even greater aggregation in these years. In 1942, a private from the Los Angeles area was transferred to the base. He had been a star running back at UCLA but had suffered a broken ankle that made him reluctant to play more football. He was still able and ready for baseball, though. Sometime in 1943, the athlete, recently promoted to lieutenant, asked to try out for the Riley team. "An officer told him he couldn't play," Pete recalled. "'You have to play with the colored team,' the officer said. That was a joke. There was no colored team. The lieutenant didn't say anything. He stood there for a while, watching us work out. Then he turned and walked away. I didn't know who he was then, but that was the first time I saw Jackie Robinson. I can still remember him walking away by himself."

Pete and Jackie would cross paths again after the war, at the start of a new era in American history.

* * *

Pete's romp through the Victory League raises another question: How might he have fared in the wartime majors, when nearly all of the top players and pitchers were in the service, leaving teams to struggle along with those deemed too old, too young, or too physically flawed for military duty? It's easier to project than one might think by looking at the stats of one Stanley Frank Musial.

Musial's life, talents, and early career were a close match for Reiser's in many ways. Born in November 1920, eighteen months later than Pete, Musial was raised in Western Pennsylvania, more of a football region than baseball-crazy St. Louis. But like Pete, Stan the Man came from a large Catholic family (six kids instead of twelve) and got his start playing semipro ball. Like Pete, he was pursued and signed by the Cardinals while still in his mid-teens. *Un*like Reiser, he was never freed from the vast Cardinal farm system by Judge Landis. But just like Pete, Stan spent four years in the minor leagues, overcame a bad arm injury, was moved from his original position, pitcher, and made a fast rise to the majors once he spent a few months playing the outfield full time at full strength. He made his debut with St. Louis in the home stretch of the 1941 season, batting a red-hot .426 in a dozen games.

If a comparison between Reiser and one of baseball's all-time greats seems far-fetched, consider that some very informed contemporaries considered them equals. In 1991, umpire Al Barlick, who worked twenty-eight years in the majors and umpired seven World Series, was asked about the best hitters he ever saw. "I'd have to say, Ted Williams, Musial, and if he hadn't gotten hurt early, it probably would have been Pete Reiser. What a talent, what a talent," Barlick replied. Asked who was better in 1943, Dodger coach and future manager Charley Dressen said, "It's close, but for my money, Musial cannot run or throw like our Pete." Post-war Dodger manager Burt Shotton had a tense, sour relationship with Pete but told *The Sporting News*, "He's the only one in the league who can touch Stanley Musial if he is well." Pee Wee Reese was Pete's close buddy, but it's still surprising to read an interview in which he said, "I thought Reiser would be better than Musial. He had everything. He was a natural."

In 1942, the first wartime season, Reiser and Musial were unquestionably the two best young players in the National League. Their final statistics for the year were remarkably similar, with the caveat that Musial didn't play the last two months of the season burdened by dizzy spells and torn ligaments in his back and leg:

Reiser .310 AVG, 10 HR, 64 RBI, 89 R, 149 H, 222 TB, .838 OPS
Musial .315 AVG, 10 HR, 72 RBI, 88 R, 147 H, 229 TB, .888 OPS

Musial had a better strikeout-to-walk ratio than Pete, while Reiser accomplished more on the basepaths, swiping twenty bases to Musial's six.

But their paths diverged after that season. Reiser got drafted; Musial did not. Musial had married in May 1940, and his wife gave birth to the couple's first child a year later, before Pearl Harbor. Along with an offseason job in a steel plant, that may have kept his Western Pennsylvania draft board from immediately claiming the Cardinal outfielder for the armed services. So, Stan got to play in 1943 and blossomed into a superstar, leading the National League in batting (.357), hits (220), doubles (48), triples (20), and several other categories. At season's end, he was named National League MVP. He'd play in 1944 too and put together an almost identical season as the Cardinals swept to their third straight pennant, followed by their second World Series title in three years.

No doubt Pete would have hammered the thinned-out pitching staffs of wartime just as hard had he been allowed to play. Arthur Daley wrote of Pete after the war: "If you concede that in the normal course of events Doc Hyland would have had him patched up for the '43 campaign, he'd have performed with such superlative brilliance for the past three years that possibly, he'd now be in a class by himself."

Instead, Pete had to settle for occasional batting practice with the Dodgers when he was on furlough in St. Louis, and the team happened to be in town. These brief glimpses of Pete were a little tough on Durocher. After one such visit in September 1943, a reporter wrote: "Reiser, on furlough from Fort Riley, worked out with the Dodgers again today and broke the Brooklyn manager's heart because he couldn't put Pete in the lineup."

* * *

Despite his success on army ballfields, despite his light duties, Pete found military life a trying experience. For one thing, he was still feeling the effects of crashing into the center-field wall at Sportsman's Park. "Once when we were driving to a game, he suddenly got dizzy and passed out," recalled Centaurs' manager Beryl Taylor after the war. Pete also said he was feeling incessant headaches. In July 1944, these got so bad that the army reportedly considered giving him a discharge on medical grounds. The *New York Post* hailed the development as "electric news." Leo Durocher announced that if Reiser returned, he'd put him at shortstop to replace Reese. But the same week the rumors were printed, Reiser smacked three hits in a 6-0 Fort Riley victory over a semipro outfit in Dodge City. Once again, a discharge failed to materialize.

"Considering what a lot of guys did in the war," Pete later said, "I had no complaints, but five times I was up for discharge, and each time something happened." Some of his supporters in the press were more condemnatory of his treatment. Tommy Holmes wrote that while Pete suffered less than many others in the war, "That doesn't make what happened to him right." Arthur Daley was more blunt, calling the Army's treatment of Reiser a disgrace. "It added up to three wasted years." he wrote.

Not surprisingly, Pete got down at times. Like a lot of soldiers, he missed life as a civilian. How could he not? Summer of '42, he was starting the All-Star Game in New York, getting profiled in magazines, pulling down his first five-figure salary, being hailed as one of the best, maybe the very best young player in baseball. Then, poof—he was somewhere on the prairie, stuck with a nonstop pounding in his head, chasing fly balls to please a colonel, making all of fifty bucks per month, the same money he made playing class-D ball at the start of his career. Sure, he was doing what he loved to do, play ball, but it was nothing, *nothing* like Brooklyn, where the Sym-Phony clattered away, and Hilda hollered from center field, and the roar of twenty or thirty thousand fans filled the ballpark as Camilli homered or Pete slid into third with a triple. Here, a big crowd might be four or five thousand for a game at Wichita's Lawrence Stadium. And even when Pete had a good day and the Centaurs won, no one outside Kansas noticed—or cared.

Worst of all, he was alone, hundreds of miles away from anyone who mattered in his life—Leo, Pee Wee, his old St. Louis pals, Mom and Dad, his siblings, and Pat. He could write and receive letters; he could make scratchy long-distance phone calls. Occasionally, he'd get a furlough to visit St. Louis and see everybody; the first one came in March of '43 when he was given leave to see Pat in the hospital after she gave birth to the couple's daughter, who they named Sally. But on a day-to-day basis, he was basically by himself. And it was tough.

"Probably the most unhappy period in Pete's life was the three years in the Army," wrote Tom Bernard in a July 1947 profile of Pete for *American* magazine. "Never was Reiser fit for Army life or Army duty."

When facing the public, as he sometimes had to, Pete wore a friendly face and put a patriotic foot forward. But signs of his unhappiness still leaked out.

Talking to a Marysville, Kansas newspaper in April 1943, he said, "I like the Army fine, except I wish my wife and baby could be with me." Asked how much of a pay cut he had taken, he replied, "I don't know. I'm afraid to figure it." In a letter to a soldier that June, he nostalgically wrote, "I miss hearing Hilda's cowbell out in center field and Durocher giving umpires a piece of his mind, and all the other things that make Brooklyn the best ballclub in the world." And to a newspaper columnist the following January, he said, "I'll never complain about playing an extra-inning doubleheader in August anymore. Army life is tough, but it's good for ballplayers because it teaches them how lucky they are."

Another future journalist, sportswriter Jim Montgomery, caught a glimpse of Reiser's state of mind one spring day when he approached the Fort Riley star for an autograph. Montgomery, then a boy of about ten, called out "Mr. Reiser?" while Pete sat on top of a dugout, presumably before a game or practice. But Pete stared straight ahead and said nothing for several seconds. "Finally, Reiser turned his head," Montgomery remembered. "He had brown eyes, a heavy jaw, an expression of boredom." The starstruck youngster asked Reiser to sign his mitt. Reiser looked at the glove while several more seconds passed. "Then, still with the same expression, he took the glove and the pen and carefully wrote his name, dotting the 'i' in Reiser with a small circle," Montgomery recalled. Nearly forty years later, as a writer for the *Cincinnati Enquirer*, Montgomery still had the glove and had gotten other stars like Musial and DiMaggio to sign it but stated that Reiser's name remained the prize, even though Pete never said a word to him.

In early 1944, life got tougher still for the prairie-locked star. On February 2nd, a few days Pete made another visit home; Pat filed a petition for divorce in St. Louis Circuit Court. In the petition, reported on by all three St. Louis newspapers, Pat described Pete as "morose and sullen" and said he had become indifferent to her and her general welfare about eighteen months before—notably, around the time he crashed into the Sportsman's Park wall. She accused Pete of failing to provide a home and forcing her and the baby to live with her parents. She also claimed that she and Pete had separated on January 6, 1943, a week before Pete was inducted into the army. Pat asked for custody of Sally, then eleven months old, as well as monthly alimony and child support payments.

Twelve days later, according to newspaper reports, the court granted Pat the divorce. The reports said Pete filed a general denial of Pat's charges but did not contest the suit. Judge Francis E. Williams approved a stipulation in which Pete agreed to pay fifty dollars per month in alimony and thirty dollars per month in child support.

Eighty years on, it's hard to know what to make of this because, without question, Pete and Pat remained married. In postwar stories, Pat was always referred to as Mrs. Reiser. She and Pete lived together, raised their kids, and stayed together until Pete died in 1981. There are no official records of a divorce or remarriage. It's as though the court approved the split, but Pete and Pat changed their minds at the last minute and asked the judge to set it aside. In all likelihood, Pat's petition was at least partly the result of loneliness and stress brought on by her physical separation from Pete while he served in the army, and she raised their baby daughter. Hundreds of thousands of couples went through similar dramas during the war.

Whatever happened legally, it's clear that Pete was in less-than-ideal shape as the war dragged on. Further evidence comes from correspondence between Pete and Branch Rickey. In early 1944, Pete wrote to the Dodger GM and requested an advance on his future salary. The club gave him twelve hundred fifty dollars—one thousand in January, the rest in June. In January 1945, Pete sent a letter to Rickey requesting another advance. "As you are well aware, I'm starting my third year in the Armed forces, and during that time, it has cost me a considerable amount of money not only to pay off different expenses, such as doctor bills, hospital bills, and last but not least, my Divorce case [cost] me more money than I was able to pay," he said in the typewritten letter, composed on U.S. Army stationery. He explained that he had to borrow money from friends and now wanted to pay off those debts. "I know that I have already made one advancement, but honestly, Mr. Rickey, I'd feel a lot better if it were possible to pay off these debts and get them off my mind now," he said. If the club helped him out, Pete added, he would be free of worry upon returning to the Dodgers and be "the hustlingest player that you ever did see."

Rickey was not moved by his plea. His response, preserved among his papers housed at the Library of Congress in Washington, was by turns preachy, condescending and accusatory:

> *Dear Pete:*
> *I was glad to have your letter, but I was sorry to learn of your further need for cash. At the present time, you owe our club $1250.00, which you borrowed last year.*
> *In the first place, I know the disappointment that comes to boys when they have to repay loans. Then, too, I am concerned quite naturally with the reasons, or possible reasons for your need of $2,000.00.*
> *For some time past, and from more than one source, there has come to me stories, really ugly stories, about yourself . . . These stories have to do with your drinking . . . If a man is going to drink and drink to excess, and from time to time and not infrequently goes hog wild about it, there*

usually isn't any cure for it. It doesn't get any better and he doesn't quit. He goes from bad to worse and in time it gets him."

Now I understand that this sounds like I am in the midst of a big lecture to you on the subject of drink based on the assumption that you have been drinking entirely too much. In the first place, if it does any good, I would be glad to have you call this a lecture in a dozen different ways, and in the second place your request for a loan of $2,000 convinces me beyond a doubt that the reports about your drinking are, most regrettably, true.

It is just too bad, and there isn't any reason for my pointing out to you all the reasons for changing your habits . . . You know just as well as I do that were supposed to have a great future ahead of you in baseball, and why you'll kick that future around like a boy with a football is mystifying, of course, to those who have never seen it done. I have seen it done a good many times. I have seen some great athletes go to hell pretty fast because they would rather get their snoots full whenever they wanted to, than they would to save their money, make a name for themselves, raise a family and become creditable citizens and amount to something."

So, I know, as I said above, that using words to a fellow who is determined to go to hell with his drinking doesn't ordinarily do much good. But there is one thing sure. I am not going to be a party to the push that sends you headlong in that direction at a faster gait than you would otherwise employ—by loaning you $2,000 or any other amount of money. That just isn't in the books and that decision is made not at all for my sake or for the Brooklyn team, but it is made for your sake—whether you know it or not.

I would give a good deal to see you and I would give a good deal to talk to your commanding officer, and I will make it a point to do both at the earliest opportunity.

With all good wishes,
I am very sincerely yours,
Branch Rickey

Did Pete have an alcohol problem? It sure doesn't seem so. Never during his career did teammates or managers accuse him of excessive drinking. Reporters didn't either, though to be fair, this was an era when many ballplayers were heavy drinkers, and sportswriters generally kept athletes' personal flaws out of the paper unless they became too obvious for the public to ignore. The only possible hint that Pete liked to imbibe came in a September 1942 *New York Post* profile of the then-newest Dodger wives, Dorothy Reese and Patricia Reiser. At the end of the piece, writer Harry Feeney noted, "the Reisers always have dozens of bottles of beer in the refrigerator." But Pat had an explanation. "It's not for us," she said. "Pete doesn't drink anything stronger than soda pop. The beer is for the company."

After Pete retired, two baseball writers—Roger Kahn, who authored the classic *The Boys of Summer*, and reporter-turned-Dodger employee Harold Parrott—suggested that he did tend to drink more as his career went on and the injuries piled up. But they were the lone voices.

Regarding the exchange of letters, it's not known whether Pete paid back the loan to the Dodgers or if Rickey eventually talked to Pete's commanding officer. In a couple of postwar interviews, Rickey dropped hints that he had played a role in sorting out his star outfielder's personal affairs. "I know all about Pete Reiser," he said in one. "I know his parents, his wife. I've been through all his difficulties with him. I've sat in the boat with him when he needed money and counsel."

For his part, Pete never said anything about Rickey getting involved in his life off the ballfield. What is clear is that after the war, Pete and the Dodgers GM seemed not to trust each other, as evidenced by public disagreements over salary, Pete's physical condition, and the level of medical care he required. In all likelihood, that mistrust took root with these letters, especially when Pete read Rickey's response, which had to feel like a hard slap in the face.

Pete's life wasn't all gloom and doom during the war years. Son-in-law Rick Tuber says to some extent, Pete enjoyed playing army ball. "He liked the guys," Rick says. "He liked playing the different major leaguers from other teams. It was kind of like an all-star team." He also made friends on the Fort Riley ballclub, among them his fellow St. Louisian, Joe Garagiola. When Rick approached the catcher-turned-broadcaster at a 1989 old-timers game and asked about his relationship with Pete, Garagiola virtually erupted with excitement: "Pete Reiser? You know how close I was to Pete Reiser? I was in the army with Pete Reiser. I was at Fort Riley with Pete Reiser. I love Pete Reiser. I *miss* Pete Reiser," he said. Garagiola explained that Pete "took care of me when I was a kid, an eighteen-year-old boy at Fort Riley . . . He taught me how to drive, coming back from Wichita to Fort Riley. He was always a happy guy and worried about other people. I don't have any funny stories [about him]; I just have good, pleasant memories. Pete Reiser was the kind of a guy that you always felt better after having been around him. I loved him."

Reiser became even closer pals with another Fort Riley teammate, Lonny Frey. Frey hailed from Pete's northern St. Louis neighborhood and even attended the same church as the Reiser family, but somehow never met Pete there, probably because Frey was nine years older. In the army, though, they became best buddies and stayed that way until the end of Pete's life. "The only player he really stayed in touch with and saw outside of the baseball season was Lonnie Frey," says Pete's daughter Shirley. "They were great friends."

Pete found other ways to make life as a soldier bearable. The occasional workouts with the Dodgers in St. Louis were one source of relief. On other furloughs, he'd stop by Sportsman's Park just to watch the Cardinals or Browns play. When the teams won their leagues' respective pennants and played in the first and only all-St. Louis World Series in 1944, Pete made sure he was there for multiple games. Dressed in his Army khakis, he visited players in the dugouts and talked to reporters about returning to the Dodgers after the war. To Dick Young of the *New York Daily News*, he said he wanted to change positions. "I was born at third base," he said, "and I'm tired of playing the outfield where hardly anything ever happens . . . I want to go back to the infield where you can get some action."

That fall, Pete got a different kind of a change when the Army transferred him to Camp Livingston in northern Louisiana, an infantry training base and internment center for thousands of German, Italian and Japanese prisoners-of-war. Like their Fort Riley counterparts, Livingston commanders took baseball seriously; Pete's Dodger teammate Kirby Higbe led the pitching staff, future Yankee player and manager Ralph Houk was the catcher, and the team had finished fourth in the national semipro tournament, the one the Fort Riley squad had skipped that August. When spring training rolled around in March 1945, Pete found himself promoted to sergeant and installed as team captain. Higbe had moved on, but the Livingston Blues still overwhelmed their competition. By mid-June, the team had won twenty-two of twenty-six games, and Pete was batting a reported .429.

No question he still missed the Brooklyn crowds, though. A newspaper photo of a June '45 game at Livingston shows the third-base bleachers standing stark and empty. The lack of audience didn't seem to stop Pete, however. The picture shows him charging toward home plate, about to launch into one of his patented fadeaway slides—playing to win as always, even if no one is there to see.

* * *

In July 1945, Pete was reassigned again, this time to Camp Lee in Petersburg, Virginia—and there, his health and career took another fateful turn. Throughout the war years, he had managed to sidestep serious injury. There were some close calls: the pneumonia at Camp Riley, a car accident while traveling to Wichita in May of '43, and stomach trouble that caused a reported fifteen-pound weight loss at the Kansas state semipro tournament in '44. However, Pete had so far avoided another calamitous crash into an outfield wall. The small-town ballparks of Pete's wartime world didn't lend themselves to such crashes; most had outfield fences made of wood, solid enough to shake up an outfielder who flung his body against them but less able to cause concussions, fractures, and the like.

This was demonstrated during one of his first games with Camp Lee, when his new team, known as the Travelers, traveled south to Newport News on August 1st to face the Camp Patrick Henry Pirates. Camp Henry had a strong team studded with major leaguers like former Yankee pitcher Steve Sundra and Philadelphia A's outfielder Elmer Valo. In the ninth inning, with the Travelers trying to rally from a 9-2 deficit, one of Reiser's teammates smashed a fly ball to deep right that looked like a certain home run. But Valo had other ideas. "Running back at full speed, Valo leaped into the air and speared the ball just as it was going over the right-field fence, at the same time crashing into the fence and knocking a piece out of it," reported the *Newport News Daily Press*. Put another way, it was the wooden fence, not the outfielder, which suffered a break. Valo not only emerged from the collision unharmed but also hung onto the ball, earning huge cheers from the crowd of about a thousand soldiers, most of them wounded war vets.

Maybe Valo's sensational catch was still on Pete's mind a few days later when the Travelers played a game at Camp Lee's Nowak Field. Maybe it wouldn't have mattered what Valo did because Pete Reiser was programmed to chase fly balls like a bird is born to fly. In any case, someone on the opposing team hit a long fly ball, and Pete charged after it. There was no concrete wall in his path, just a barrier of some kind, either a hedge or a temporary wooden fence, according to different accounts Pete gave over the years. Whatever it was, Pete ran right through it in pursuit of the ball—and tumbled into a drainage ditch located off the edge of the field. He landed hard on his throwing arm, injuring his shoulder.

The accident was severe enough that Pete came out of the game and was taken to the camp hospital. "The X-ray examination showed no injury," he later explained. "The next day, I played short and felt fine until I had to make a long throw. Then my arm felt like it had been slashed by a knife."

Wisely and somewhat uncharacteristically, Pete did not attempt to play through the pain. He shut himself down for the rest of the season—and effectively for the rest of the war because Japan surrendered on August 14th. The

Travelers didn't need him anyhow. With big leaguers like Hank Steinbacher, Johnny Lindell, Buster Maynard, and Dave Philley on the roster, the team swept to the championship of the Third Service Command, covering bases in Virginia, Pennsylvania, and Maryland.

Reiser kept the injury to himself for a while, hoping it would heal. The first time he mentioned it to a reporter came, of all places, in Millvale, New Jersey. His brother was a union organizer there, and Pete accepted an invitation to speak at a union dance and rally late that October. The *Millville Daily* noted that he was accompanied by "his very attractive wife," signaling that by this time, Pete and Pat's separation was over. The paper also reported: "Pete played some baseball while in the service, but he stopped playing last August because of an injury to his shoulder. The Army offered to operate on the throwing arm, Pete says, but he declined the offer, feeling it is just a matter of rest." For the moment, he said nothing about his arm to the Dodgers. But the shoulder kept aching as fall turned to winter.

Pete still had a bigger problem—the army didn't want to let him go. Other ballplayers were being released from military duty. A handful had been discharged during the '45 season and rejoined their teams, stars like Bob Feller, Charlie Keller, and Red Ruffing among them. Hank Greenberg came back after four and a half years away and batted .311 with sixty RBI, helping the Tigers grab the American League pennant and beat the Cubs in the World Series. Hundreds of others, including Pete's Brooklyn teammates Pee Wee Reese, Kirby Higbe, Hugh Casey, Billy Herman, and Cookie Lavagetto, were discharged soon after the season and started getting in shape to return to big-league ball the following spring.

But incredibly, some unknown officer ticketed Pete for post-war overseas duty. In mid-September, an ominous filler item appeared in many newspapers: "The Dodgers fear Pete Reiser will not be back until 1947. The outfielder, in the army for three years, is in California and believes he will be sent to Japan with occupation troops for nine months or longer." The report was unattributed but essentially true; chatting with reporters that fall about Brooklyn's 1946 roster, Branch Rickey said he had a question mark next to Pete's name. No development could have been more unfair to Pete, who had already missed out on his age twenty-four, twenty-five, and twenty-six seasons, and the major league salaries he would have earned.

Fortunately, after three years in the grip of army control and high-handedness, Pete finally encountered a fair-minded officer. "Now it's November, and the war is over, but they're still shippin' guys out, and I'm on the list to go," he told W.C. Heinz. "I report to the overseas major, and he looks at my papers and says, 'I can't send you overseas. With everything that's wrong with you, you shouldn't even be in this Army. I'll have you out in three hours." Pete must have laughed; he had heard that line before. But this time—maybe because the war was over, maybe because Pete was injured and couldn't play—no one overruled the major.

"In three hours, sure enough," said Pete, "I've got those papers in my hand, stamped, and I'm startin' out the door." A Red Cross representative tried to get Pete to wait. "He says, 'I can get you some pretty good pension benefits for the physical and mental injuries you've sustained.' I said, 'You can?' He said, 'Yes, you're entitled to them.' I said, 'Good. You get 'em. You keep 'em. I'm goin' home.'"

Pete later told Donald Honig he was released from the army in January 1946, but his official U.S. Department of Veterans Affairs file confirms the discharge date was November 30, 1945. He must have called ahead to his family because the *St. Louis Star and Times* published a brief story that evening headlined, "Pete Reiser is Bound for Home." The lead: "Harold (Pete) Reiser is motoring along southern highways today, en route to St. Louis. He has been discharged by the army, checking out at Camp Lee, Va."

Eight days later, the same paper published a profile of civilian Pete, complete with a photo of the smiling ex-sergeant taking his two-year-old daughter for a walk. He refrained from criticizing his treatment in the army, terming it "fair enough." He raved about a catcher he had seen at Fort Riley—"Joe Garagiola, this kid catcher the Cardinals have. He is major leagues, right now."(Garagiola would indeed make the majors in 1946 and earn a share of the Cards' starting catcher job.) Pete also told Tietjen about the troubles with his throwing arm. He neglected to mention his crash and tumble at Camp Lee, passing off the arm's condition as the result of his 1942 collision with the wall at Sportsman's Park or a "growth in the right elbow." Maybe Doc Hyland could operate on it, he suggested, though he added there might not be time for an operation before spring training. "But I'm not worried," he added. "I can throw left-handed if necessary."

He could; that much was true. He seemed to overlook the fact that the Dodgers might look askance at their star center fielder firing off-target throws. With all the regulars coming back, the team's fans and brain trust were fervently hoping for a return to pre-war glory, which would require the full resurrection of the pre-war Pete. Pete would certainly do his best to deliver—but could he?

8
"He's the Difference, Brother"

The opportunity arrived in the fifth. Pete stood at third, two men out, bases otherwise empty. The pitcher was unfamiliar—Jack Brewer, a thin, tall righty for the Giants who had come up during the war. Pete studied him for a moment. A few pitches told the story: hard thrower, good stuff, leisurely windup. Too leisurely. The catcher, thirty-eight-year-old Ernie Lombardi, wasn't known for moving fast either.

Jimmy Cannon detailed the duel that followed.

> *Pete had lunged up the line from third toward home, flapping his arms, kicking the dust, and dancing a taunting jog. Although Pete had just stolen second and advanced to third on Nosey Lombardi's bad throw, Brewer ignored him. He glanced at Pete, halfway home, and turned away with an insulting indifference.*

"The first time when I faked, he practically dared me," Pete explained.

On the next pitcher, Brewer raised his hands like a man in a stickup, which he was.

"He gave me that a la carte look," Pete said. "He thought I was bluffing. I saw the way he was coming up with the ball, and I figured, if he does this again, I'll go. He did it again, and I took off."

Pete charged down the baseline with his trademark burst of speed. Brewer threw home, and Lombardi applied the tag. But it was too late. With a clenched-teeth, feet-first slide, Pete skittered across the plate for a steal of home.

The crowd inside Ebbets Field erupted. This was the day they had waited for—the return of the real players, *real* major league baseball, after three years of watching 4Fs and banana-green teenagers and graying old men. Thirty-two thousand fans had packed the ballpark for the 1946 home opener—another fifteen thousand were turned away—and the Dodgers gave them exactly what they wanted, an 8-1 blowout of the Giants. These weren't quite the same Dodgers as before the war; older players like Wyatt, Camilli, Medwick, and Fitzsimmons had retired or moved on, and in their place were kids barely old enough to vote, with unfamiliar names like Furillo, Hermanski, and Branca, the first fruits of the youth movement that Branch Rickey had planted upon taking over after the '42 season. But no one seemed to care. "Peace and contentment settled over Flatbush yesterday," wrote *Times* columnist Arthur Daley. "The sun came out to chase away brooding and ominous clouds. And the Dodgers vanquished the hated Giants with ridiculous ease. What more could a Brooklynite want?"

The returning Pistol was feeling good as well. After three years of playing for small-to-vanishing crowds in the heartland, all polite farm kids and blasé servicemen, this was what *he* had waited for: Brooklyn in its half-crazed glory, with fans roaring for hits, booing and taunting the umpires, wailing away on drums, whistles, and trumpets as the inspiration struck. The Dodger Sym-Phony was strangely absent that afternoon, but Hilda Chester was in the bleachers, yelling at top volume, clanging away on her cowbell. Running out on the field, Pete had a pleasant sense of déjà vu. "I looked around me. I said to myself, 'Where did the three years go?'" he told Cannon.

However, that might have been the only nostalgia Pete allowed himself as the new season began. In fact, his attitude toward the baseball world had begun to turn downright unsentimental.

It started in the winter with the brouhaha over his shoulder. From the minute Branch Rickey learned his star's throwing arm wasn't right, that he might need an operation, the Mahatma had been in a dander. "This is very disturbing," he told reporters upon hearing the news, adding: "I'm upset. I'll get Reiser on long-distance immediately. Why, Leo liked Pete to plug the gap at third base." Durocher, who indeed pictured Reiser manning the hot corner in '46, was simply puzzled by Pete's condition. "He worked out with us last summer, and he could throw as well as ever," the manager said. "If he hurt his arm, it must have been in the last seven months, but I can't figure out how." At this point, Pete had not informed Rickey and Durocher about his tumble into the ditch at Camp Lee, possibly an unwise decision.

What Rickey did understand was that Reiser might be damaged goods. And Rickey, long known for his parsimonious nature—Jimmy Powers of the *Daily News* famously dubbed him "El Cheapo"—wasn't about to give a hefty contract to an injured player, even if that player was the presumed centerpiece of the team. In early February, he sent Pete a salary offer of nine thousand dollars for the 1946 season, with the proviso that Pete would get ten thousand if he were healthy enough to play.

Pete was not happy. Ten thousand would be the same as he made in 1942. Nine thousand would be an ignominious ten percent cut. He returned the contract to Rickey unsigned and let word of his unhappiness leak to hometown reporter Sid Keener. "The St. Louis boy is dissatisfied with the salary figure in his 1946 contract," Keener reported.

In later decades, the matter of Pete's salary would have been handled by an agent and taken to arbitration. After six years in the majors, he could have entered free agency and escaped to a more generous team. None of these options existed in 1946. All baseball contracts in that era contained the reserve clause, the language that allowed teams to own players in perpetuity unless the team chose to rid itself of the player through a trade, sale, release, or minor league assignment. If a player didn't like his club's contract offer, he had little option but to hold out, hoping that management would negotiate. And that particular strategy, always something of a risk, was even chancier that spring because of the sheer glut of candidates for major league rosters. The majority of the pre-war players, plus most of the wartime players, *plus* the youngsters whose careers had been delayed by the war . . . all were now competing for the precious roster slots. The Dodgers entered the new year with no fewer than eight outfielders capable of being big league regulars, including three past or future National League batting champions (Reiser, Dixie Walker, and Carl Furillo), a three-time NL all-star (Augie Galan), two guys who topped .300 during the last year of the war (Goody Rosen and Luis Olmo), and two rookies who would each last several years in the majors without ever getting a real crack at a full-time job (Dick Whitman and Gene Hermanski).

Under those circumstances, especially after going three years without a real salary, many players would take the club's first offer and get into uniform pronto. Not Pete, who stubbornly stood his ground and remained at home, working out at a St. Louis athletic club. He may have been emboldened by articles that hailed him as one of baseball's biggest returning stars. "Pete Reiser is to the Brooklyns what Joe DiMaggio is to the Yankees, Hank Greenberg to the Tigers, Ted Williams to the Red Sox," wrote sports columnist Harry Grayson that winter. But Rickey was unmoved by such praise and held firm on his offer as February turned into March. When the Dodger GM visited St. Louis on March 6th, he passed on meeting with Pete in person. "No sir, absolutely not," he said when a reporter asked if he would see Reiser while in town. "I'm on my way to Fort Worth to look over our farm club there." It was another sign of the deep chill that had taken hold in Rickey-Reiser relations.

The second week in March, with the season closing in, Pete finally capitulated, accepting the Mahatma's terms. He reported to the Dodgers' training camp in Daytona Beach, Florida but remained dissatisfied and notably said nothing to the press about being happy to return to big-league ball. Pete had lost the salary battle—but the war was not over, as Rickey would soon learn.

In the meantime, Pete let his bat do the talking. In his very first post-war exhibition game against the Braves, he banged out two doubles, a single, walked three times, and made a nice running catch to take away a hit in center. "In the flick of an eyelash, one could see why he was rated one of the greats of the game before he was siphoned into the maw of GI life," wrote Arch Murray in the *New York Post*. The only warning sign was his arm; reporters noted that he lobbed in all his throws from the outfield. Durocher didn't seem concerned and went ahead with his plan to put Pete at third base, where the Dodgers were notably weak. In '45, Leo had rotated four players at third, including outfielders Olmo and Galan, all of whom proved inadequate. "Reiser isn't a total stranger to third base," Durocher said when he announced the shift on March 30th. "He played a few games there at Ebbets Field for us, if you remember," referring to Pete's rookie season.

The experiment almost immediately backfired. In the March 31st exhibition game, Pete fielded a ninth-inning bouncer from the Senators' Al Evans, fired a throw across the infield, and grimaced in pain. X-rays after the game confirmed the bad news: he had a separated shoulder—a tearing of the ligaments that connect one's clavicle, or collarbone, to the shoulder blade. Pete linked the injury to his tumble into the ditch at Camp Lee. "The shoulder I fell on in an army camp last summer has been growing tender for a week," he said. "I guess the throw I made did it."

Initial reports said he might be sidelined for a month—but that talk quickly ended as Durocher concocted other schemes to keep Pete's bat in the lineup. Before the injury, Pete had been swatting two or three hits nearly every time he played, and his batting average for the spring was an otherworldly .652. Leo talked about putting Pete in left field—"you don't have to throw much out there," he said—and also worked him out at second base. Pete even revisited his old talent of throwing left-handed, something he hadn't done for several years. "If my right whip is washed out, my left might keep me in the big leagues," he said.

In the end, the idea of a southpaw Pistol was shelved, and Pete was sent to Johns Hopkins for examination by a surgeon, Dr. George Bennett. As the Dodgers no doubt wanted, Bennett encouraged Pete to get out on the field, throwing sidearm if necessary. "He told me it wouldn't do any harm to play if I could stand it," Pete said the next day. "There's nothing broken, and throwing ought to strengthen my arm."

When the season began in Boston, Pete was indeed the Dodgers' third baseman—a testament to his desire to play, his disdain for the consequences, and the Dodgers' disregard for their star's long-term well-being.

After Pete's pilfering in the April 18th home opener against the Giants—he stole three bases on the day—Durocher poured on the praise that helped keep his star happy and in the lineup. "How about that Reiser?" he told Cannon. "Take him out of there, and it's a different ballclub. He's the difference, brother. The difference. Don't think I don't know it."

Durocher's point was proven four days later as the Dodgers hosted the Braves, with Pete batting third and playing third. In the first inning, he doubled and came around to score on an infield error. In the second inning, he foiled a squeeze play by throwing out the Braves' Skippy Roberge at home. In the fourth and seventh innings, he singled. In the ninth, he hit a two-RBI double, tying the score at 4-4. Minutes later, he and Dixie Walker pulled off a double steal, putting the winning run ninety feet away. The Dodgers couldn't push him across but won the game on a Billy Herman single in the tenth.

Pete freely admitted after the game that his throwing arm hurt like hell. "The pain is killing me, but I'm getting used to it," he told Lee Scott of the *Citizen*. I want to play, and it doesn't matter if it hurts when I throw, and it certainly does." Durocher made a concession the first week in May, moving Pete from third back to center field. But he gave no rest days to his slugger, who opened the season hitting like it was 1941 all over again. On April 23rd, Pete drove in the Dodgers' first run and scored the second and third as an old Elmira teammate, Ed Head, pitched a no-hitter. The next day, he initiated an 11-3 slaughter of the Phillies with a first-inning homer. Two days later, a first-inning RBI double served the same role in an 11-3 walkover of the Giants. By the start of May, he was batting .354 and leading the league in doubles, runs, and hits.

Meanwhile, the Cardinals were off and running too, bolstered by the military's discharge of their two big sluggers, Stan Musial and Enos Slaughter. By early May, the Bums and Redbirds were locked in the same kind of tight race they fought in '41 and '42, trading the number one and two spots atop the National League multiple times per week. In the heat of a pennant race, grueling shoulder pain was merely a nuisance, a little problem that could be swept under the rug. That's how Leo saw things anyhow. And if that's how his manager saw things, Pete was willing to see it that way too—at least for the time being.

* * *

At that moment, a more existential threat to the Dodgers' resurgence came to the fore. The problem had first emerged that February. Ever concerned about keeping profits high and players' salaries low, Branch Rickey had mailed outfielder Luis Olmo a contract offer of seventy-five hundred dollars for the 1946 season. The twenty-six-year-old Olmo, insulted, returned the contract unsigned. He had batted .313 in '45, drove in one hundred ten runs, and placed among the National League's batting leaders in several categories—an excellent year, even taking weakened wartime pitching into account. Speaking to reporters in his hometown of San Juan, Puerto Rico, Olmo said he wanted at least ten thousand from the Dodgers, preferably twelve. "I had a good season last year, and I think I am worth that much," he said. Rickey, undoubtedly comfited by his team's abundance of good outfielders, disagreed and refused to raise his offer.

There the matter might have stood unresolved, an open wound, until a wild card entered the picture. Jorge Pasquel was a wealthy, well-connected Mexican businessman and *de facto* owner and operator of the Mexican League, baseball's top league south of the American mainland. Pasquel and his four brothers had made millions building a business empire that started with a cigar factory and expanded into banks, ranches, real estate, and Mexico's largest import-export business. But Pasquel's real passion was building up his six-team league. Starting in the late 1930s, he began to recruit Negro League stars from the U.S. to boost attendance and the level of play. Dozens of players accepted his offers and played in Mexico for a season or more, including but by no means limited to Satchel Paige, Josh Gibson, Monte Irvin, Cool Papa Bell, Ray Dandridge, and Roy Campanella. Black players looked kindly on the Mexican League, partially because of the generous salaries they received—three to five hundred dollars per month above what they earned in the U.S.—and because in Mexico, they could live free of the open discrimination they faced in housing, shopping, public facilities, law enforcement, and so many other things at home. "For the first time in my life, I felt really free," recalled Irvin. "You could go anywhere, go to any theater, do anything, eat in any restaurant, just like anybody else, and it was wonderful."

Now, with the war over, and a surplus of players sloshing around the baseball world, Pasquel turned his sights to White major leaguers. Olmo was a natural place to start; he was a budding star, spoke Spanish, and was highly unhappy with his treatment by the Dodgers. When his talks with Rickey made no progress, Olmo spurned Brooklyn and signed a contract to play for the

Mexican League's Vera Cruz franchise. He got the ten thousand dollars per year that he wanted—a thirty percent increase from his previous Dodger pay—and received a three-year contract to boot. The signing grabbed the attention of the American press and players alike, who previously weren't sure what to make of the ambitious, mustachioed Pasquel. Now they knew he was serious.

Pasquel made it clear he was thinking big, telling reporters he was prepared to invest twenty million dollars into his league. "We are building seven ballparks in Mexico, including the big stadium in Mexico City," he said that February. "All will be lighted for night games, and we are out to get the top-quality players that are available now."

The Pasquels sent agents into U.S. spring training camps, dangling fat contracts and signing bonuses in front of returning war vets, urging them to jump their teams. The Mexicans' targets included most of the game's top stars. Ted Williams and Bob Feller turned down offers of over one hundred thousand dollars per year, an unheard-of sum for any ballplayer at that time. Stan Musial considered, then rejected a five-year deal almost as rich. St. Louis Browns shortstop Vern Stephens, the American League's home run leader in '45, accepted an offer, played two games in Mexico, then changed his mind and snuck back across the border. In the end, none of the biggest names made the leap, but several lesser-known players on tight-fisted teams found it hard to resist Pasquel's wide-open checkbook. The Senators lost a steady relief pitcher, Alex Carrasquel; the Philadelphia A's were deprived of speedy outfielder Bobby Estalella; the New York Giants lost several regulars, most notably a young, future twenty-game winner named Sal Maglie. The Cardinals would suffer a major blow that May when pitcher Max Lanier, who had begun the season with six straight complete-game wins, signed a contract with Pasquel and jumped the Cards during a road trip, pulling pitcher Fred Martin and backup second baseman Lou Klein along with him.

In a bid to stop the outflow, new baseball commissioner Happy Chandler, who had replaced Judge Landis after his death in December 1944, announced that any player who jumped to Mexico would be banned from "organized ball" for five years. The warning made many would-be jumpers think twice, but some chose to take the risk anyway. On April 1st, the Dodgers' starting catcher Mickey Owen, returning from a one-year stint in the Navy, signed a deal to become player-manager of the Mexico City franchise at a reported twenty thousand dollars per year. Rickey was furious. "He can go to Mexico and good riddance," the Mahatma said with uncharacteristic bluntness. "No man is bigger than the Brooklyn ball club. He must be taught to understand that."

But Rickey's bluster couldn't stop Pasquel's agents from making their pitches or disgruntled players from listening with open ears. Pete's turn to be wooed came on Friday, May 3rd, soon after the Dodgers arrived in St. Louis for a two-game set with the Cardinals. One of the Pasquels' agents, Mario Loussac, contacted Pete at his hotel and asked for a meeting. Pete, still unhappy with his salary, readily agreed. According to Pete, Loussac first offered a five-year contract at fifteen thousand dollars per year. Pete said no. Then Loussac proposed three years at twenty-five thousand per season. Again, Pete turned it down. Finally, the agent upped the ante: a three-year deal for one hundred thousand dollars, with half of the money paid upon signing. With one signature, Pete could recoup all the money he had lost during his long stint with Uncle Sam and then some. He acknowledged the proposal was "mighty tempting."

"Sure, I'm considering their offer. I'd be crazy not to," Pete told the *New York Times*, though he added, "there are several things they'll have to show me before I sign."

The Dodger-Cardinal game was rained out that day, giving Pete more time to ponder his decision. "I don't know what to do," he said that night. "I would have to be in the big leagues a long time to make an equal amount." Dazzled and confused at the same time, Pete went from teammate to teammate, asking for advice. Several told him to consider the downsides of the deal—he'd have to live in a foreign, less-developed country, with harder living and travel conditions, and deal with the language barrier. There'd be the loneliness factor; only a handful of other major leaguers had made the jump. And of course, if Mexico didn't work out, he'd be banned from returning to the Dodgers for five years until he was thirty-two years old. Pat was reported to be against the deal. Pete listened to everyone but couldn't shrug off the financial implications. "How long would it take me to save a hundred grand up here?" he asked.

Durocher must have reported the conversations to Rickey, for the next morning, the Mahatma chartered a private plane to make an emergency visit to St. Louis. Loussac, hearing that Rickey was on his way, called Pete and pushed for an immediate decision. There's a magnificent car downstairs waiting to take you to Mexico City, he purred. Pete put him off and waited for Rickey. Bad weather, which had rained out another Dodger-Cardinal game, delayed the Mahatma's arrival, but he finally landed around 5 P.M. and drove straight to the Dodgers' hotel for conferences with Reiser and rookie shortstop Stan Rojek, who was also entertaining a Mexican offer.

Rojek capitulated quickly, agreeing within a few minutes to stay with Brooklyn. Then it was Pete's turn. Pete later claimed that when he entered the hotel room, Rickey threw his hands in the air and said: "Are you going to cut my throat? Or is the knife already in my back?" Pete said he assured the GM there was no need for such drama, that he had already decided to stay with the Dodgers. Still, the two talked for nearly an hour, keeping the reporters waiting elsewhere in the hotel on edge. Maybe Rickey had to explain his rejection of Pete's last wartime loan request. Maybe Pete had to assure his boss he wasn't a heavy drinker.

Whatever they discussed, the outcome was to Rickey's liking. Pete called Loussac and told him no deal.

Reporters cornered both men when they finished their talk. "Pete Reiser remained with the Brooklyn club because I don't believe he wanted to be a man without a country," Rickey said. Pete acknowledged that was an issue—along with the fact that he'd lose most of his six-figure windfall to U.S. income taxes. One year after the war, the rate for top earners was still almost ninety percent. The Pasquels had promised his salary would be tax-free, but that would only work if Pete became a Mexican citizen and banked his money there.

"I think I did the wise thing in passing up that offer," Pete said that night as the Dodgers' train chugged toward Pittsburgh. He said he and Rickey had not discussed a new contract but expressed confidence the GM would take care of that. And Rickey did—sort of. Two weeks later, the New York newspapers reported that Pete had received a modest salary bump. "A two thousand five hundred dollar raise for turning down a hundred thousand," Pete later said, perhaps a little ruefully. His 1946 salary now stood at twelve thousand five hundred dollars—not a bad paycheck in that era for the average major league player, but nowhere near the highest figure on the team. It was also well, *well* below the amounts earned by the stars he was often grouped with, such as Williams and DiMaggio. Playing his prime years for Rickey, Pete would never land a truly big contract, a fact that gave him low-level bother for years.

If it was any consolation to Pete, all of the major leaguers who signed with the Pasquels returned home by the end of the 1947 season. For all of the brothers' grandiose promises, the Mexican League operated something like a class-A circuit in the United States, with small ballparks, poor fields, and low attendance. Players got tired of the conditions or the local food, and low revenues made it hard for even the wealthy Pasquels to pay the agreed-upon salaries. For major-league ballplayers, the era of free agency, big money, and long-term deals—and the strong union that made those things a reality—still lay decades in the future.

* * *

One way Pete could still earn a big chunk of cash was to get back to the World Series, and that May, he seemed hellbent on making that happen. Prime example: the Dodgers' contest with the Phillies on May 11th, a cool Sunday at Ebbets Field. The visitors started Ike Pearson, whose high, tight fastball had sent Pete to the hospital with a concussion five years earlier. The Phillies batted around in the top of the first inning and handed Pearson a 4-0 lead. However, Pearson was shaky from pitch one, giving up back-to-back walks, an infield single to Pete, and a two-run single to Dixie Walker. Quickly, the Phils yanked him and replaced him with a wartime holdover, Tommy Hughes. Pete, now standing on third with nobody out, noticed immediately that Hughes was paying him little attention. On the second pitch, he stormed down the line and slid under the tag from catcher Andy Seminck for a theft of home, his second of the young season.

Pete's feet weren't done for the day. The game turned into a see-saw affair, with Phillies blowing additional leads of 7-3 and 11-5, as the Dodgers teed off on seven Philly pitchers. The Dodgers tied it up 11-all in the eighth when second baseman Eddie Stanky doubled home Reese. Pete led off the bottom of the ninth, with fourteen thousand Dodger fans screaming for a rally. He gave them something even better: a drive to the deepest part of center field that hit the wall on the fly and caromed to the left, dodging both center fielder Johnny Wyrostek and left fielder Del Ennis. By the time Ennis finally got the ball and heaved it to the infield, Reiser had zoomed around the bases and crossed home plate in for that most electrifying of plays, a walk-off inside-the-park home run.

Pete's torture of the Phillies continued two days later. In the fifth inning, with Brooklyn trailing 3-2, he reached base by outrunning a double-play ball, then moved up to third on a single and a walk. With Reese at-bat, he began dancing down the baseline, trying to unnerve veteran pitcher Oscar Judd. On the fourth pitch, he finally charged for the plate. Judd hurried his throw, but Pete slid under catcher Seminick's tag for the tying run and his third steal of home on the year. An inning later, he knocked in the go-ahead run as the Dodgers went on to a 6-3 win.

"Shades of Ty Cobb and Max Carey!" Hy Turkin declared in his lead the next day. Columnist Jimmy Powers wrote: "Baseball men say Pete Reiser will be the NL's player of the year. Pistol Pete can do everything."

The Pirates got the next dose of the Reiser treatment. On May 17th, Pete came to bat in the fourth inning with Reese and Herman on base and the Dodgers down 6-5. Once again, he smacked a line drive to the deepest part of Ebbets Field. This time, the ball fell just short of the fence, bounced in and out of the notch, and came to a complete stop. Outfielders Ralph Kiner and Johnny Barrett both froze, waiting for each other to pick up the ball. Pete took advantage and motored around the bases for his second inside-the-park homer within a week. The three-run shot put the Bums on top for good as they romped to a 16-6 win.

By month's end, Pete had become the Dodgers' magic bullet, their on-call stroke of lighting, cutting down opponents seemingly at will when the game was on the line. On the 23rd against the Cubs, he tripled to lead off the eleventh inning and scored the winning run minutes later on a sacrifice fly by Reese. On the 26th in Philadelphia, he homered in the third inning, threw out a runner at home in the ninth to preserve a 4-4 tie, and doubled with two outs in the eleventh, setting up a game-winning single from rookie Carl Furillo. In between, on the 25th, he fleeced the Phillies with yet another theft of home. This one came with an asterisk. Reiser, who had doubled and moved to third on a groundout, rushed toward the plate as Hugh Mulcahy delivered his pitch. Catcher Seminick, no doubt sick of watching Reiser's foot slide under his glove, stepped forward to get the ball and apply the tag. But in doing so, he made contact with the bat of hitter Augie Galan, who had swung defensively at the pitch. Umpire Al Barlick charged Seminick with catcher's interference, awarding Galan a free pass to first and allowing Reiser to score, his fourth steal of home on the year.

All this derring-do on the bases was necessary because, in 1946, Dodger bats alone couldn't carry the team to victory. The lineup had absolutely no long-ball threats; only one player finished the season with more than ten home runs, and that was Pete, who hit eleven. The team also had no solid regulars at first base, third, or catcher, forcing Durocher to shift and substitute players daily, hoping to find the hot hand or the right matchup to generate some offense. To compensate for the lack of firepower, the Dodgers made frequent use of tactics that originated in baseball's Deadball Era, like sacrifice bunts and hit-and-run plays, and embraced plain old aggressive baserunning. "Most other managers are too conservative," opined one sportswriter. "As their shortstop, Durocher learned the Cardinals' old rule well: make them throw you out. Under Durocher, the Dodgers run, take the extra base, steal." The team stats tell the story. The Dodgers finished near the bottom of the National League in homers (with 55) but topped the circuit in sacrifice hits (141), triples (66), stolen bases (100, a high number for the era). They also led in a modern-day statistic called XBT, or extra bases taken. Dodger runners were grabbing two bases on a single or three on a double whenever they could.

Along with running, these Dodgers believed in walking. The player that personified the team, even more so than Pete, was the regular second baseman, Eddie Stanky. A runty, five-foot-eight player nicknamed The Brat, Stanky had a fraction of Pete's natural athletic talent. He didn't reach the majors until age twenty-seven, during the war, and the Dodgers gave up a barely used relief pitcher to obtain him from the Cubs. (The trade itself was barely noticed; it went through on D-Day, June 6, 1944). However, Stanky had a scrappy, edge-seeking style of play that Durocher adored. "He can't hit, he can't run, he can't throw—all he does is beat you," was the line attached to his career, first uttered by Rickey, often used by Durocher. One way he beat you was by bending the rules: Stanky was known for sign stealing, faking catches to confuse baserunners, kicking balls out of infielders' hands on steal attempts, even waving his arms to distract opposing batters—the last ploy a trick that was eventually outlawed. Another tactic, perfectly legal but frustrating to the other team, was to foul off pitch after pitch, waiting for one he could slap for a single, or in the absence of that, ones that would add up to a base on balls.

Stanky came to bat six hundred forty-two times in 1946 and hit not a single home run—but earned his keep by topping the league in sacrifice hits (20), walks (137), and on-base percentage (.436). Durocher wisely deployed him as the leadoff batter, followed by either Reese, Herman, or Galan, three capable singles hitters who also knew how to get a free pass. Reiser, cleanup hitter Dixie Walker or any of the ten different players who batted fifth during the season would then be responsible for producing the RBIs. The combination of patience and hard running paid off: the Dodgers scored seven hundred one runs, second-best in the league.

They probably would have scored even more had Pete finally learned *when* to stop running. On May 19th, as the Dodgers hosted Cincinnati, the Reds' Grady Hatton hit a smash to deep left-center. Pete raced back for the ball, made a leaping attempt to catch it, and slammed into the unpadded wall with his right shoulder. This was one of Pete's less calamitous collisions; he landed on his feet, picked up the ball, and made an off-balance throw to the infield, holding Hatton to a triple. But the collision, or perhaps the throw after it, aggravated his already damaged shoulder. It could have been worse. "It's lucky that I stumbled just before I reached the wall," Pete said after the game. "Otherwise, I'd have crashed into the concrete really hard."

The Dodgers, true to form, downplayed the extent of the injury; the team doctor proclaimed it "not serious." Pete didn't think it was either and sat out only one game. A few days later, though, he admitted the pain was increasing.

"I tried to return to the lineup too soon," he said. "The pain in my shoulder has gone down into the elbow, and I even feel a tingling in my fingertips." After a game against the Giants on May 28th, Durocher was forced to put Reiser on backup duty, limiting him to pinch-hitting appearances for the next two weeks. In his absence, the Dodgers flattened out, winning seven, losing six, though they maintained a slim lead over the Cardinals.

Doc Hyland examined the shoulder when the Dodgers rolled into St. Louis on June 10th. The doctor recommended a few more days of rest. Pete, as usual, was a bad patient and suited up that night for the start of the crucial three-game series against the Cardinals. Brooklyn dropped the first two, letting the Cardinals climb within a game of first, but Pete saved them in the finale, hitting an RBI single in the third inning, an RBI triple in the seventh, and a leadoff double in the ninth that ignited a four-run rally. The Dodgers won 10-7. Along with the hits, he pulled off yet another steal of home—number five on the year—this time off the Cardinals' top pitcher, Howie Pollet, who was on his way to a twenty-win, 2.10 ERA season.

"Durocher can thank Pete Reiser for the win," said one writer the next day. "Pistol Pete made the difference between victory and defeat."

By now, National League pitchers were getting nervous the minute Pete stepped on third base. The ninety feet to home plate looked more like sixty when Pete started dancing off the bag. "Other base runners have to be watched to keep 'em from stealing second, but Reiser has perfected the art of stealing home," wrote Harold Burr in the *Daily Eagle*. "The enemy has one foot on the pitching slab and the other on a banana peel every time Peter [sic] reaches third. He doesn't dare take his eye off Pete for a second. He's afraid to go into his windup."

"He worries the pitchers to death," said Dixie Walker that summer. "Do you know that with Pete on third, the pitchers act just as if he were on first?"

Said Jimmy Cannon after Pete reached base seven times in a doubleheader in the Polo Grounds: "When Pete was on, spasms of panic ran through the Giants. He taunted them with his presence."

Pete was not shy about explaining his home-stealing technique. "I rely on the pitcher's fear of the balk," he told the *Sporting News* later that year. "And I've got to lull him into something like a feeling of security. That means playing poker with your face and your feet. First, you have to get a good lead. You play fast and loose with the hurler. And you've got to know a lot of things about him. You study little quirks. This pitcher drops his head when he is about to deliver the ball to the batter. That one grits his teeth; another sticks out his tongue. You watch for these telltale actions."

Besides reading the pitcher, he explained, stealing home was a matter of choosing the proper moment. Having a right-handed hitter at the plate was a big help. "The righthanded batter helps to block the catcher's view," he said. The proper slide was also key. "I slide by the catcher and stick out a hand. I run all bases that way," he said. "In one of my steals, I threw my hand over the catcher's glove. I never bowl over the catcher. You see, the hand is quicker than the eye or the foot."

Photos indicate this wasn't always the way Pete stole his bases. Sometimes, he aimed his feet directly toward the base first, his cleats kicking up clouds of dust, his teeth clenched tight in a way that could be taken for a grimace or a grin. However he did it, the result in 1946 was usually positive—a steal for Reiser, embarrassment for the other team, and often, another run for the Dodgers.

* * *

If only Pete could concentrate full time on hitting and running. Alas, baseball did not have a designated hitter rule in 1946, which meant he had to play the field, which meant he had to throw, the act of which continued to cause him significant pain. During his examination of Pete, Doc Hyland recommended immediate surgery to fix the shoulder separation. "The doctor said if it became worse, he could wire it together, and it wouldn't bother me again," Pete said during the St. Louis series. The downside to the operation? He'd be out three to five weeks, a big chunk of time in the middle of a burning pennant race.

Pete was open to Hyland's suggestion—but at the same time was picking up signals that many folks expected him to tough it out and keep playing, no matter how much his shoulder throbbed. Leo, of course, wanted Pete in there at all costs. "Nobody makes more a difference than Reiser—even a one-armed Reiser," Durocher told reporters repeatedly that season. The writers increased the pressure by passing along Leo's line of thought to their readers. "The Durochermen have a strong chance to win the pennant with a disabled Reiser in the lineup. They would have a heap of trouble trying to win without Pete," wrote Edward T. Murphy of the *Sun*. Arch Murray of the *Post* chimed in: "There is no doubt that the Dodgers must have [Pete] in there if they are to win the pennant. Without him, they are just another ballclub."

Dixie Walker agreed. "Speaking of Reiser, there is the big question," he said that July. "We ask it every day in the clubhouse; we ask it every night of ourselves. Will Pete be able to play through the season? If he makes it, we make it. If he fails—well, it will be tough." (If only Branch Rickey valued me this much, Pete must have thought.)

Pete accommodated the press and his teammates much as possible; despite his bad arm and the May 19th wall collision, he started thirty-two of the Dodgers' first thirty-four games and pinch-hit seven times during the period when shoulder pain kept him from starting. In mid-June, Durocher moved him from center field to left, where, in theory, he'd have fewer throws to make. In fact, Pete had no trouble adjusting and showed runners they could not take an easy extra base off him. On June 19th in Brooklyn, Ralph Kiner of the Pirates tried to score from second on a single. Pete scooped up the hit and fired a throw to nab Kiner at the plate. "The peg was perfect and had plenty on it," reported Burr. As if to prove a point, the next day, Pete threw out Al Lopez in the eighth, trying to stretch a single into a double. He also piled up three hits and four RBI on the day, powering Brooklyn to a 7-3 victory. The Cardinals came to town next, and Pete whacked out five hits as the Dodgers took two out of three and expanded their slender hold on first place.

But the throws and the hits didn't mean his arm was okay, and as June turned into July, Pete began to get unusually frank about what he was going through. One day Arthur Daley of the *Times* asked how his shoulder was feeling. "Terrible, just terrible. It hurts here and here, and here and here," Pete said, pointing to various spots in his shoulder area. "Do you know what?" he added. "It bothers me when I'm hitting 'cause I can't get a full swing. And I can just make one throw a day. Then it's gone."

To Jimmy Cannon, he said: "It feels like it's coming off every time I throw. It has no strength in it when I throw. It takes twenty minutes or a half an hour for the life to come back to it."

Talking to Dick Young of the *Daily News*, he went further, suggesting obliquely that the Dodgers didn't care about his condition. Doc Hyland wanted him to have the shoulder operation right away; he said, "but didn't want to be the one to advise the Dodgers of it." Well, Pete, Young asked, why can't *you* advise the Dodgers? "No, I don't want to be the one to suggest it either," he replied.

Young, then at the start of a long, controversial sports writing career—built on reporting unusually frank comments along with his own blunt, provocative opinions—went on give readers an inside look at the Dodgers' behind-the-dugout drama:

> *It should be mentioned here, by way of explanation of the rather peculiar situation, that Reiser has developed a substantial resentment toward Dodger management's attitude concerning his injured arm. He pictures them as contending his pain is 'imaginary' to a great extent and that*

> he can throw if he convinces himself he is capable of doing so. It is this strained relationship between Pete and club on this one matter that makes Reiser reluctant to demand a showdown.
>
> "If I were sure that Doc Hyland could perform the operation and have me back in the minimum time of his estimate (three weeks), then I'd go right the office and demand that it be done. But . . ."
>
> Reiser's thoughts trailed off into nothingness, but it was easy to see what he was trying to say. If the operation were to take five weeks, or maybe more, he figured that the club wouldn't look favorably upon losing his services for that length of time.
>
> Even so, there was no doubt about where Pete stands in the matter. He would prefer to have it over and done as soon as possible. Each throw, even the forceless sidearm heaves he resorts to when the play is not imperative, stabs the muscles at the rear of his shoulder due to the lack of support from the separated clavicle.

Young, writing with his typically sharp-edged pen, went on to compare Dodger management to a "feelingless ogre which is placing [Pete] in jeopardy of permanent injury to his shoulder," while likening Reiser to "the kid who's lost confidence in his old man to such an extent that he won't have a heart-to-heart talk with him." He finished the story with his own suggestion: "Let you fellows get together, for the good of everyone concerned."

If Reiser, Durocher, and Rickey ever did have a heart-to-heart, it ended in a two-to-one vote, with Reiser on the losing side. He continued to play without surgical intervention, his shoulder wrapped in elastic bandages and tape, and he continued to play outstanding ball. After a slump in late June, he caught fire again, racking up six straight multi-hit games right before the All-Star Game. The best of these was a July 4th matchup against the Giants in the Polo Grounds in which Pete singled, walked three times, and most importantly delivered a two-out RBI double in the ninth inning to help the Dodgers seal an 8-5 win. He also kept manufacturing runs with his feet. In a July 7th game against Boston, he reached base with a first-inning single. With Dixie Walker batting, Pete took off for a steal attempt. He made it and kept going when catcher Phil Masi's throw sailed into center field. Most runners would have been satisfied with one extra base, but when outfielder Mike McCormick bobbled the ball slightly, Pete raced around third to score.

Pete ended the first half of the season hitting .326 with seven homers, thirty-nine RBI, and a league-leading nineteen stolen bases. They weren't quite

1941 numbers but were damn good considering he had started just fifty-four of the Dodgers' seventy-four games. For the third time, National League managers voted him onto the all-star team. In a concession to his shoulder, the Dodgers and the league allowed him to skip the game itself. The move rankled some fans and sportswriters. "Without him, the all-star game is a hoax," protested Jimmy Cannon. However, Pete had full backing from Durocher, who said, "I don't think it's fair, with him meaning so much to our pennant fight, that he be asked to strain his shoulder in that game when I have to rest him during our regular-season games." Thus, Pete got a few days off while the NL squad got whomped by their American League counterparts 12-0 at Fenway Park, in a game highlighted by Ted Williams' two home runs, the second coming off a loopy "eephus" pitch from the Pirates' Rip Sewell.

"The Nationals displayed no fight," wrote one reporter covering the game. "We missed the Dodgers' Pete Reiser. The Pistol might have started something."

During the break, Dick Young talked to Pete again and gave New Yorkers an expanded look at his history of injuries, from the bone chips in his elbow in Elmira to the Pearson beaning and the concussions and the shoulder separation. He also gave further insight into Pete's state of mind. "Pete is pretty depressed about the entire strange sequence of mishaps, and no wonder," Young wrote. "Not only has it hit his development, but it has stunted his salary, which is where it really hurts."

* * *

The second half of the season began at Wrigley Field with a bad omen. Pete was at his favorite spot on the field, third base, having just knocked starter Claude Passeau out of the game with a two-run triple that put the Dodgers up 3-0 in the fifth. The Cubs sent in lefty Bob Chipman to relieve. On Chipman's second pitch, Pete broke for the plate. Chipman threw, Pete slid, and according to several press box observers, his right foot touched home safely under the tag. But umpire George Magerkurth called him out. For the rest of his life, Pete insisted that after making the call, Magerkurth reversed it under his breath. "In Chicago, I stole home, and Magerkurth hollered, 'You're out!' Then he dropped his voice, and he said, 'Sonofabitch! I missed it.' He'd already had his thumb in the air," Pete said. Magerkurth, for the record, never confirmed Pete's tale.

The Dodgers won that game, but they and their star outfielder were heading into a rough stretch. Before the all-star break, the club had begun a five-city, sixteen-game road trip, with most of the games played under the sun in sweltering summer temperatures, even though every National League team except the

Cubs now had lights for night games. Except for Dixie Walker, who was on a tear that pushed his batting average above .370, the whole offense began to struggle. The first day after the break, the club was shut out on three hits by the Cubs' Johnny Schmitz and scratched out only four hits the next day in another loss. Burr wrote that the team looked weary, including Reiser, of whom he said, "Pete isn't hitting those long drives that break up games anymore."

Pete's triple against Passeau undercut that observation, but overall, Burr was on target. After Chicago, the Dodgers traveled to St. Louis for a showdown with the second-place Cardinals. If not quite a massacre, it was a disaster. The Cards swept four close contests, slicing Brooklyn's lead in the standings to a half-game. Stan Musial was lethal, slamming out nine hits in eighteen at-bats, including a game-winning homer in the second game, a twelve-inning 2-1 nail-biter. Pete, meanwhile, was almost helpless, getting just one hit in the series. He further hurt the team by getting ejected from the third game after a vehement dispute with umpire Al Barlick over whether or not he caught a sinking line drive off the bat of Enos Slaughter. "It appeared to most spectators that Reiser had made a shoestring catch of the ball," said one writer. Barlick disagreed, threw out Reiser, and tossed Durocher too for arguing alongside his outfielder.

Pete's bat was still quiet as the Dodgers dropped two of three in Cincinnati and remained so even as the Bums rebounded by sweeping three games in Pittsburgh. By the end of the road trip, his batting average had sunk below .300 for the first time all season, and the Cardinals had climbed into a tie for the league lead. Durocher pulled no punches on a road trip post-mortem. "Reiser hurt us badly," he said. "He hit only about .100 on the trip. That's bad. We need Pete in our business."

Burr asked Pete about his struggles. Pete said he wasn't feeling well and had lost weight during the trip, dipping as low as one hundred sixty-five pounds, at least fifteen below his norm. He said he didn't know why, except for the hot weather.

The one highlight during this time was a July 29th game against the Reds in Brooklyn. Bucky Walters of the Reds was cruising along with a 3-1 lead until he allowed two rookies, Bruce Edwards and Gene Hermanski, to reach base in the bottom of the fifth. Up came Pete, whose batting average had now declined forty points since the all-star break. But he had always hit the Reds' ace well, and on a one-ball, two-strike count, he smashed a Walters offering into deep center. Pete's St. Louis pal Lonny Frey, a career-long second baseman making his debut in center field that day, made an ill-timed leap for the ball and allowed it to sail over his head. "Practically jet-propelled," in the words of one observer,

Pete raced around the bases for his third inside-the-park homer of the season, crossing the plate well before the incoming throw. The Dodgers won 7-3.

Unfortunately, the hot-foot homer did not trigger one of Pete's exhilarating hot streaks. On August 1st, the Dodgers played host to the Cardinals for the rubber match of a crucial three-game series. In the fifth, Brooklyn was down 3-0 when Whitey Kurowski smashed one toward the lower leftfield stands. Pete, desperate to prevent another run, raced back and attempted a jumping catch. He missed—and once again paid the price for trying, cracking the back of his head against the concrete wall. Carl Furillo raced over to retrieve the ball, holding Kurowski to a double, then checked on his teammate and beckoned frantically for help. Pete lay motionless on the outfield grass.

Within minutes, he was placed on a stretcher, with four Ebbets Field attendants carrying him off the field. Pat, who was in the stands, rushed down to the clubhouse to check on her husband. She found him lying on a massage table, blood seeping through his hair. He had regained consciousness by that point and opened his eyes. I've got a *baaad* headache, he said. Can somebody get me a smoke?

A cigarette was produced, and Pete breathed in the (lung-killing) fumes to calm his nerves while Dr. Dominic Rossi examined his head. The doctor called for an ambulance to take Pete to Peck Memorial Hospital, though he doubted there were any brain or skull injuries. "I don't think it's anything serious, but we'll take the X-rays, of course, and he may have to remain in the hospital for two days for rest and observation," he said. Explaining the situation to a reporter, he turned to the Reisers and reiterated, "I assure you this is not serious."

Rossi's reassurance aside, it was serious enough that doctors at Peck diagnosed Pete with a concussion, his third (at least) in the past five years. He slept overnight at the hospital, but per his custom, ignored the doctor's request for a longer stay and checked out within twenty-four hours. "In view of his eagerness to go home, it wouldn't help any to tie him down," said Rossi, resignedly.

After a few days of recuperation, Pete was set to return on August 7th when the injury bug bit him again, this time at home. Pat was about to make dinner, and Pete offered to light the gas stove. Somehow, he set off an explosion. It wasn't a huge blast, but it was enough to burn his fingers, singe the hair on his right arm and forehead, and force him to miss that night's game against the Giants, which the Dodgers proceeded to lose 5-2. One report said that to a man, the Dodgers were "incensed" about the incident.

Maybe that's why Pete came back the next afternoon; burned fingers be damned, and proceeded to slay the hated Giants all by himself. In his first at-bat in a week, he slammed a pitch from starter Ken Trinkle some three hundred forty feet into the Polo Grounds' right-field stands. The 1-0 lead held until the sixth when the Giants' Willard Marshall hit a tying solo shot. Trinkle kept pitching as the game went into extra innings. In the top of the tenth, with the score still knotted 1-1, the Dodgers got two men on. Up came Reiser, who hit a savage, sinking liner to left. Outfielder Sid Gordon charged it, trying for a diving catch, but he came up short, and the ball scooted by. If Pete's legs weren't tight from sitting down for a week, he might have raced around the bases for yet another inside-the-park homer. Instead, he settled for a triple and two RBIs, accounting for all the runs in the Dodgers' 3-1 victory.

The writers promptly expended a new gush of ink on Pistol Pete. "Without him," said Jimmy Cannon, "the Dodgers are just a lot of guys riding around the National League with a trunk full of bats and balls." Lee Scott of the *Citizen* put it more simply: "When Reiser plays, the Dodgers win, but when he's forced to take a rest, the Dodgers don't fare too well."

Since he *had* taken a rest, Pete seemed to have renewed life in his game, and he carried the team through the hot, humid days of August. On the 9th, his eighth-inning RBI single, a broken-bat blooper, gave the Dodgers a 1-0 win in Philadelphia. The next day, another RBI single started the scoring in a 6-0 victory. Four days later, in the opener of a day-night doubleheader in Brooklyn, the Dodgers trailed the Giants 4-3 in the fifth when Pete singled in Stanky with the tying run. He advanced to second on the throw-in to home, and a pair of walks moved him up another ninety feet. The crowd began to murmur: "Reiser's on third!"

The pitcher, six-foot-four Big Bill Voiselle, sensed the electricity in the air and called out to Reiser, trying to defuse it.

"Bill Voiselle of the Giants challenged me," Pete recalled. "He said, 'Go ahead and steal if you dare.' I could not ignore this. I went about five feet off third, and I laughed. I made out that I was going to leap back. He dropped his head, and I ran on. Halfway through his windup, I was halfway home and made it." He made it with a big smile plastered on his face, judging from the photos published the next day. It was Pete's sixth steal of home on the year—a new major league record—and it gave the Dodgers a 5-4 lead. They hung on to win that game and won the back half of the doubleheader as well, with Pete scoring what turned out to be the winning run.

Pete continued to deliver timely hits and stolen bases for the rest of the month, although his average remained under the then-magic .300 mark, and on several occasions, Durocher removed him early from games because of lingering aches and pains. Leo was now juggling players at a frantic pace anyway. The team's one consistent heavy hitter besides Pete, Dixie Walker, pounded the ball at a .380 clip through July but was now on a downward slide that would trim sixty points off his average by season's end. The Dodgers had unwisely sold Billy Herman to Boston in June, and old reliable third baseman Cookie Lavagetto, a late returnee from the war, was out again with injuries. Durocher had no choice but to rely on the team's ample supply of untested youth. That season, the team had eight rookies—outfielders Furillo, Hermanski, and Whitman, catchers Bruce Edwards and Ferrell Anderson, third baseman Bob Ramazzotti, and pitchers Hank Behrman and Joe Hatten. On some days, Durocher played four of them in the starting lineup and used two or three others by the game's end. That rawness showed in the field, where the Dodgers committed one hundred seventy-four errors, a whopping fifty more than the Cardinals. But with Leo teaching and cajoling the youngsters, giving quick hooks to pitchers in trouble, and making liberal use of pinch hitters, runners and fielders as he saw fit, the Dodgers squeezed out win after win and hung in the pennant race with the more experienced, more powerful Cardinals.

"It's not a secret the odd collection of youngsters and oldsters wearing the Dodger flannels this season is not a great team," said a United Press writer. But, he said, "a biting criticism from Durocher, a 'college try' lecture or a slap on the back from their flamboyant boss, and they become champions."

"A born gambler through and through, Leo has gambled on countless occasions. Lady Luck has smiled on him," said Leonard Cohen, a columnist for the *Post*. "But any way you look at them, Durocher is the chief reason [the Dodgers] are slugging toe to toe with the Cardinals today."

Sun writer Herbert Goren noted something else about the team after their twin bill triumph over the Giants: "More than most teams, the Dodgers wear a hungry look. There are a lot of kids on the club who do not make more than five thousand dollars, and several seasoned players, such as Pee Wee Reese and Pete Reiser, who missed out on big money by time in the service. They are battling for a big world series [sic] check."

* * *

Late in August, that check seemed to be drifting out of reach. On August 22nd, the Dodgers were shut out by Johnny Vander Meer in Cincinnati, getting only three hits, and dropped into a first-place tie with the Cardinals. It was the first time the Cards had caught them in a month. St. Louis inched ahead a few days later by beating Durocher's men 2-1 in front of a gleeful thirty-four thousand at Sportsman's Park. Pete helped pull the Dodgers back even the following day, racking up three hits, a walk, and a stolen base in a 7-3 victory. But a trio of losses to end the month pushed the Dodgers into second place.

To make matters worse, on the last day of August, Pete took one of his characteristic hard swings and felt pain cascade through his body. "It felt as though every muscle in the back of my shoulder ripped way down deep," he said. He had to leave the game in the sixth inning, after knocking in the Dodgers' only run in a 2-1 loss, and to the dismay of Brooklyn fans everywhere, he was sidelined for a week.

The injury solidified his determination to get the shoulder surgically fixed after the season. "What good am I like this?" he said. "In for two weeks, out for two weeks. In for another week, and back out for four of five days. Even when I'm playing, the pull in my shoulder is so bad at times I'd swear the catcher is holding my bat." While he was out, the Dodgers scored an average of fewer than three runs per game but managed to win six of eight due to excellent pitching, including a 1-0 win over Boston in which their only run came on a Johnny Sain wild pitch.

Pete returned September 7th with his arm feeling no better, but his legs were still in top condition. He proved that the next day against the Giants at Ebbets Field. Batting in the third inning, he walked, then scampered to third base while Reese got caught in an extended rundown near home. The crowd began to buzz, suspecting what was next. The pitcher, Monty Kennedy, was known for having a slow windup. Pete didn't disappoint. After a couple of false starts, he stormed down the line and made a dust-raising, feet-first slide. Kennedy threw hurriedly to the plate but had no chance. Safe again. Pete's seventh steal of home on the year gave the Dodgers a 2-0 lead.

For the entire game, Giant pitchers were in abject terror whenever Reiser reached base. Reiser gave them a reason to be, stealing second base in the first inning and third base in the fourth in addition to his theft of home. He reached third again in the seventh with the bases loaded and six-foot-nine Johnny Gee on the mound. One, two, three times, he faked dashes for the plate. "The towering Mr. Gee took off his cap to mop a feverish brow," Burr reported. Gee finally dealt with his problem by plunking Bruce Edwards, forcing Pete in with another run. It didn't count as a steal of home, but it was larceny just the same.

Arthur Daley marveled at Pete in the *Times* the next day. When Reiser is on base, he wrote, the fans get excited, and the other team gets the jitters. "He's the only man in the game who can upset the opposition entirely by doing no more than stand a few feet off base, a quizzical, mischievous grin on his face," Daley said.

Twenty games to go, the Dodgers were now two games out of first. On the 10th, they walloped the Reds 8-0 in Brooklyn, with Pete playing just six innings. The next day, the same teams got mired in a scoreless, five-hour marathon. Pete's arm was having one of its better days, and he threw out two runners, one at third, the other at home, to help keep the Reds off the scoreboard. Unfortunately, the Dodgers were helpless against Vander Meer, who hurled fifteen innings of goose eggs, and equally so against Harry Gumbert, who threw another four. The game was finally called on account of darkness, as National League rules still blocked teams from turning on the lights during a day game.

Next up: a three-game visit from the Cardinals. St. Louis won the first in a 10-2 rout, Musial getting three hits and Pete's wartime buddy Joe Garagiola bashing a three-run homer. The Dodgers played with desperation the following day. Galan slashed a first-inning single and advanced on a wild pitch. Pete singled to bring him home and then moved up to second on a walk. When Ed Stevens punched out another single, Pete rumbled around third, determined to score. It was going to be a close play at the plate. Enos Slaughter fired a throw from right field. Catcher Del Rice received it, whirled to his left to make the tag . . . but there was nothing for him to tag. Pete had executed a perfect, picturesque fallaway slide, patting home with his left hand as the rest of him sailed past the plate, beyond the reach of Rice's full-body lunge.

The crowd of twenty-two thousand erupted, and Brooklyn led 2-0. Only one problem: Pete got up limping. When he tried to run out to left field in the top of the second, the limp was so obvious that Durocher called him back and sent Dick Whitman to replace him. He had pulled a hamstring muscle, his fourth significant injury of the season.

Hamstrung or not, there was a pennant in sight, so Pete returned against the Cubs on the 16th, his thigh now tightly wrapped up as his shoulder. Durocher sent him to bat as a pinch-hitter in the fifth with the Dodgers down 5-4 and a man on third. Pete hit a line drive off pitcher Hank Borowy's glove and somehow raced down to first as the tying run scored.

"It was a grand exhibition of pure guts, and Petey, giving way to a pinch-runner for about the only time in his speedy career, received a standing ovation," reported Dick Young.

The Dodgers won that game, then split a doubleheader with Pittsburgh, with Pete unable to play. In the starting lineup on the 19th against the Pirates, he walked his first time up, scored on Furillo's double, but aggravated the hamstring running home and was replaced by Whitman. Durocher played him only once over the next six days, a fruitless pinch-hitting appearance in a loss to Boston.

The season entered its final week, with the Dodgers a half-game behind the Cardinals. They beat the Phillies on Monday, September 23rd, to keep pace. Tuesday's game was rained out. On Wednesday, Pete tried again and finally made it through an entire game, though he went hitless. The Dodgers were on top 9-6 going into the ninth, usually a secure lead against the perennial doormat Phillies. But the roof caved in: Philly batters exploded for five runs, with four pitchers needed to stop the bleeding. Down 11-9, the Dodgers tried to rally. With two outs in the bottom of the ninth, Stevens singled, and Pete walked, giving the Brooklyn faithful some hope. But Dixie Walker, with a chance to be the hero, flied out to end the game. Only a Cardinal loss to Cincinnati kept Brooklyn from falling into total despair. The Dodgers were one game back with three to go.

The next day more than thirty thousand crammed Ebbets Field to see if their beloved Bums could stay alive. With two out in the first inning, no score, Pete stood on first base as Walker came to bat. He was still nursing his pulled hamstring and had not swiped a base in two weeks. But when he looked into the dugout, there it was—the steal sign. "Jesus Christ," Reiser muttered to himself.

Never one to embrace caution, Pete took a long lead off first base. The Phillies' pitcher, a righty named Charlie Schanz, saw what he was doing and fired a pickoff throw. Pete dashed back to the bag, sliding feet first. As he did, his spikes got caught in the infield dirt. And everyone nearby heard a loud, sickening *snap*.

Peter later said that Durocher rushed out on the field and told him he was okay, to get up and walk it off. But contemporary reporting shows otherwise. The *Eagle* quoted Leo the next day: "I knew right away that this finished Reiser for the season. I could hear something like a stick breaking. There wasn't a chance he'd get up."

Pete, rolling in the dirt, writhing in agony, his face twisted with pain, was quickly surrounded by teammates and put on a stretcher for transport to the clubhouse. An ambulance took him, once again, to Peck Memorial Hospital. There, X-rays confirmed the bad news: he had fractured his left fibula just above the ankle. Pete's season was done. This wasn't like the concussions, the shoulder separation, or the hamstring injury. No one, not even one so driven as Pete Reiser, could play baseball on a broken ankle—though Pete would one day try, with surprising results.

Durocher blamed what he called the rock-hard dirt of the infield for the injury. Pete blamed his pulled hamstring. "I tried to slide back in a way that favored that leg, and then the spikes caught under the bag," he said. He couldn't help but add, with a touch of self-pity, "Can you think of anything else that might happen to me?"

Three days later, the Dodgers and Cardinals finished the regular season in a tie, with identical records of ninety-six wins and fifty-six losses. The National League held an unprecedented three-game playoff to decide the pennant. Pete, leaning on crutches, his foot in a cast, accompanied the team by train to St. Louis for game one. He watched the first inning from the dugout but was so jittery that he painfully banged his leg against the steps. He had to retreat under the stands, where his teammates relayed the action to him. "I just can't watch a game I'm not in," he told Dick Young. Eventually, he went to the dressing room to follow the action on the radio—restlessly hopping and hobbling around the room, puffing cigarettes, cheering the good news, cursing the bad. The bad news prevailed as Howie Pollet beat the Dodgers 4-2.

Two days later, the teams met in Brooklyn, with Pete now parked in a box seat behind the dugout. Durocher used eighteen players, including seven rookies, trying to light a spark under his team. But Musial, Slaughter, and company romped out to an 8-1 lead before the Dodgers rallied for three runs in the ninth to make it interesting. With the bases loaded and Ebbets Field in a tizzy, Eddie Stanky came to the plate. How Durocher would have loved to insert Pete as a pinch hitter here. But he couldn't, and The Brat struck out. So did the next batter, Howie Schultz. The Dodgers' season was over. For the second time in Pete's still-young career, the Cardinals had nipped them at the wire for the pennant.

The Cardinals would defeat Ted Williams and the favored Boston Red Sox in the World Series, four games to three. For the Cards, it was their third championship in five years. And for Stan Musial, it was the perfect ending to an almost-perfect season. People still likened Pete to Stan in terms of raw talent, but there was no longer any comparison when it came to on-field production. Despite playing out of position at first base for most of the year, Musial had thrashed away at NL pitching staffs from start to finish, topping the league in hits, runs, doubles, triples, slugging percentage, and total bases while claiming his second batting crown at .365. If there had been an OPS title back then, he would have won that too, at 1.021. He also started and completed every game on the St. Louis schedule, including the two-game playoff. When the season was over, baseball writers rightfully voted him the league's MVP by a two-to-one margin over runner-up Dixie Walker. At the age of twenty-five, Stan's trophy case was filling up fast.

Pete didn't lug any prizes home at season's end. His final numbers were modest: a .277 batting average, eleven home runs, seventy-three runs batted in. He led the league in stolen bases (34) but didn't crack the top five in any other categories. A modern-day stathead would not be overly impressed by his .789 OPS, the fact that he was thrown out on one-fourth of his steal attempts, or the fact that he played only eighty-nine complete games out of just one hundred twenty-two appearances overall.

But this was a case where the stats didn't reflect the true value of the player. Nineteen forty-one was definitely Reiser's best season, but 1946 was his most heroic. In the span of six months, he had suffered a shoulder separation, two collisions with outfield walls, a burnt hand, a pulled hamstring, and a broken ankle. He played not a single game without pain pulsing somewhere in his battered body. And yet, in the view of many observers, it was Pete who drove the Dodgers to the brink of a pennant, and his injuries were the hurdle the team couldn't overcome.

"In the last month of play, the Dodgers lost Pete Reiser—not only a great ballplayer, but an inspirational force," wrote Grantland Rice. "With Reiser in shape, the Dodgers would have been a kick-in down the stretch, where all races are won or lost."

"I will say this emphatically: If Pete Reiser had been available every day, Brooklyn would have won the pennant by eight games," wrote Dan Daniel in *The Sporting News*. Arthur Daley opined: "If Pistol Pete had played one hundred and fifty-four games, the Brooks would have won in a breeze."

Pete's colleagues felt the same way. "We didn't have the service of Pete Reiser during those late games, and without him, we just couldn't make the grade this year," said Stanky in a post-season interview. Durocher unsurprisingly agreed. He was talking to columnist Leonard Cohen during the playoff when Reiser hobbled by with a cane. Durocher took a long pull on his cigarette and sighed. "If we'd only had him the last ten days," he said. "If we had Reiser in the lineup daily during the final drive, we'd have won the pennant without any playoff."

To another writer, Durocher offered this observation: "Pete Reiser came near wrecking himself in trying to win. A head, a back, an arm, or leg meant nothing to Pete with a run at stake," he said, all too accurately.

Pete himself took no issue with such remarks. "Had I been able to play every game during the summer, there would have been no race after Max Lanier, Fred Martin, and Lou Klein jumped the Cardinals," he said.

Instead, Pete and his teammates had to settle for a few hundred dollars in second-place money and the knowledge they had battled a generally superior team down to the last day of the season and then some. Astute observers predicted that if the same teams got locked in a pennant race in 1947, the Dodgers would prevail. Cardinals' owner Sam Breadon had been emphasizing short-term profits over long-term success. The Cards' minor league system had shrunk by forty percent since Rickey's heyday running the club, and the team was starting to come up empty with good replacements for veterans who aged, fell victim to injury or, in the case of all-star brothers Mort and Walker Cooper, were sold for big sums of cash. Meanwhile, Rickey had doubled the Dodgers' scouting staff and built the farm system up to twenty-one teams. With the war over, those teams seemed to be swarming with talented young ballplayers, kids with names like Campanella, Hodges, Snider, Newcombe, Erskine, Labine—and Robinson. Jackie Robinson, second baseman down at Montreal. Very good ballplayer, said the scouts and sportswriters. Fast runner. Plays with fire. Might stick with the Dodgers '47. Might make quite an impact.

9

The Other Great What Ifs

"It's defeatist to harp on what might have been, and yet it's hard to resist considering what might have been."
—*Christopher Reeve, actor and horseman, 2002.*

There must be dozens, maybe hundreds of players scattered across baseball history who had the requisites to be big league superstars but saw their careers derailed by forces beyond their control. Injuries, accidents, drinking, drugs, segregation, war . . . They've all unraveled the hopes of young men who could hit a ball unusually far or throw it unusually fast. Years from now, we might hear about guys who were ticketed for stardom only to be cut down by COVID-19.

However—not every Mike Trout-in-the-making who was hit by misfortune qualifies as one of the game's great what-ifs. Not in my book, anyway.

So, what exactly defines a great "what if" player? In this author's view, it's a player who showed the ability to build an extraordinary, impact-making career at the major league level, only to see that potential stripped away *before* the player could reach his peak.

The timing is important. One could ask, "What if doctors in 1966 had been able to cure Sandy Koufax's arthritic pitching arm?" If they had, the "Left Arm of God" might have blown away National League hitters for another decade. But Koufax dominated the league for five glorious years before he retired. He won an MVP award, three Cy Youngs, pitched four no-hitters, captured five straight ERA titles, set the single-season strikeout record, had seasons of twenty-five, twenty-six, and twenty-seven wins, and carried the Dodgers to a pair of World Series titles. The man reached his full potential. So did Thurman

Munson before the plane crash, Kirby Puckett before glaucoma, Don Mattingly before the back problems, Denny McLain before his general implosion, and Shoeless Joe Jackson before being barred for life. The baseball-going public got to see everything they could do. There's no real what-if question hanging over their heads.

Also excluded . . . players who had sky-high ceilings in terms of talent but ultimately just weren't much help to their teams. Steve Dalkowski purportedly threw the ball one hundred ten miles per hour but walked ten to twenty batters per game and never made the major leagues. Alex Johnson had a champion batting stroke but refused to run hard on the basepaths or the outfield. Bo Jackson was the greatest athlete of his generation but wore down his body and ruined his hip playing in the NFL. They never put it all together on the field, never really showed they were meant for Cooperstown.

What about players with great potential who met tragic ends? Those guys can certainly qualify—if they enjoyed success in the big leagues before their death. But beware a tendency to romanticize such players. Prime example: Cubs second baseman Ken Hubbs. Hubbs won the NL Rookie of the Year award in 1962, mainly for his fielding: he went seventy-eight games and over four hundred chances without an error and became the first rookie to nab a Gold Glove award. Unfortunately, he died at age twenty-two when a small plane he was piloting crashed near Provo, Utah, in February 1964. Three decades later, *Sports Illustrated* asked some baseball writers to compose "What If" articles, and SI staffer Steve Rushin conjured up a scenario in which Hubbs lives on, the '64 Cubs play improved ball, and the team decides not to trade Lou Brock to the Cardinals that June for sore-armed Ernie Broglio. In this alternate universe, the Cubs then build a powerhouse around Brock, Hubbs, Billy Williams, Fergie Jenkins, and Ron Santo and become the "Big Blue Machine," sweeping to five World Series titles in seven years starting in 1969.

Now, Rushin was writing somewhat tongue-in-cheek, but . . . whoa. Ken Hubbs' survival wouldn't have changed the Cubs' fortunes one whit. He was an excellent fielder and a popular guy, but his bat was full of holes. In his rookie year, he batted .260 with five home runs while leading the league in both strikeouts (129) and hitting into double plays (20). In his second year, he cut down on the strikeouts somewhat, but his average slipped to .235, with very little power, very few walks. The guy who eventually replaced him at second, Glenn Beckert, was unspectacular but perfectly adequate in the field and a reliable .290 hitter who rarely struck out and made four all-star teams. And incidentally, the Cubs weren't doing too bad when they traded Brock in '64; they had a .500

record and sat just five and a half games out of first place. Hubbs might have enjoyed a long, productive career, but seeing him as one of baseball's great what-ifs requires a haze of nostalgia tinted Cubbie blue.

Along the same lines . . . Oscar Taveras. Taveras was one of the most highly touted prospects of the 2010s but played only a single season in the majors before a car crash in his native Dominican Republic took his life in October 2014. It was unquestionably a big loss for the Cardinals. St. Louis had signed Taveras when he was just sixteen years old. His self-chosen nickname was *El Fenomeno*—The Phenomenon. It was a lot to live up to, but Taveras had the talent. Playing single-A ball in 2011, he batted .386 and won the Midwest League batting title. The following year, he captured the same title in the double-A Texas League, batting .321 and adding twenty-three homers. On May 30, 2014, the Cardinals brought him up to the big leagues, and in his second major league at-bat, Taveras launched a homer to right field that proved to be the winning run. He hit another dramatic homer in that year's NLCS against the Giants; a pinch-hit shot in Game Two that tied the game and brought forty-six thousand towel-twirling Redbird fans at Busch Stadium to their feet.

However, in between those two homers, Taveras . . . floundered. He was sent back down to the minors in mid-June after batting .189 in eleven games. He was called back up in July, played regularly, and did better but ended the season at .239 with three home runs in eighty games and an OPS of .590. The Cards remained very high on him, as they should have, and projected him as their starting right fielder or center fielder for years to come. Still, based on his actual performance in the majors, it would be a stretch to list him as one of the greatest what-ifs.

How about Lyman Bostock? At age twenty-five in 1976, Bostock batted .323, fourth-best in the American League, and the following year he blossomed into one of the league's top players, hitting .336 with good power, scoring more than a hundred runs, helping the Twins make a surprising run for the AL West title. That offseason, he signed a five-year, two-million-dollar contract with the Angels, a giant contract at the time. He got off to a horrendous start in '78, batting .209 through the end of May, and famously donated his first month's salary from the Angels to charity because he thought he didn't deserve it. His bat caught fire in June, and by September 23rd, he was hitting a team-high .296. That night, after a day game in Chicago, he went to Gary, Indiana, to visit his uncle. The two men met up with two old family friends, both female. They were driving through Gary when the estranged husband of one of the women, in a fit of jealous rage, pulled up beside the vehicle and opened fire.

Buckshot pellets hit Bostock in the head, and he died three hours later in a Gary hospital. The murder was especially tragic because Bostock's killer pleaded insanity, and under a now-defunct loophole in Indiana law, he was able to walk free from a state mental hospital less than two years after the shooting. All that said, Bostock falls a bit short of being one of the great what-ifs. He was a very good player, but not a dominant one. If his '78 season had been as good as '77, I might see it differently.

Then there are the imitation Reisers, talented guys who played the game a wee bit too hard. Reiser actually had a contemporary, Slovakian-born Elmer Valo of the Philadelphia A's, who shared his tendency to crash into outfield walls. On May 15, 1948, in front of sixty-nine thousand fans at Yankee Stadium, Valo slammed into the right-field wall while taking a home run away from Yogi Berra, preserving a 3-1 victory and knocking himself unconscious. The A's surprisingly held first place in the American League at the time, so Valo returned to the lineup just six days later but promptly broke a rib making another fence-crashing catch in St. Louis. Sportswriters subsequently gave him sobriquets such as "neck-risking outfielder" and the "American League's Pete Reiser." Valo once explained, in words that could have come straight from Pistol Pete: "When that ball comes out there in my direction, I forget all about everything else. I just think the one thing to do is catch that ball, get that thing before it lands for a double or a triple." It got to the point where the A's eighty-six-year-old owner and manager, Connie Mack, couldn't remember Valo's name (or the names of most of his teammates) but identified his right fielder as "the fellow who runs into walls." These crashes usually forced Valo to miss twenty to forty games per season, which was a shame because when he played, he walked a lot and hit well, topping .300 in five of his nine seasons as an A's regular, including an eye-catching .364 in 1955. His bat lacked Pete's extra-base pop, but still, a healthy Valo could have been a perennial all-star.

More talented than Valo but almost as injury prone as Reiser was the brilliant Eric Davis. A string bean who stood six feet two but weighed just one hundred sixty-five pounds, Davis burst into the majors in the mid-1980s with a combination of speed, power, and fielding ability that inspired comparisons to Willie Mays. In his first full season as the Reds' center fielder, in 1986, he swiped eighty bases and bashed twenty-seven homers. In 1987, he enjoyed a half-season for the ages, batting over .320 and matching his '86 home run total by the all-star break. Davis was still going strong in early September when he chased a long fly into the brick outfield wall of Wrigley Field. His left shoulder, not his head, took the force of the blow, but he laid on the warning track for over a minute, writhing in pain. The shoulder injury forced him to miss ten days, and forevermore Davis seemed snake-bitten, prone to collisions, hamstring pulls, knee problems, and other, more freakish injuries that usually cost him at least thirty games per year. Diving for a ball in the 1990 World Series, he lacerated a kidney. In 1997, playing for Baltimore, he was diagnosed with colon cancer. He fought his way through the treatment and even hit a game-winning homer for the Orioles in that year's ALCS; the next season, he rebounded to hit a career-high .327.

In the end, Davis enjoyed a productive seventeen-year career and got the big contracts that always evaded Pistol Pete. But similar to Reiser, his career was shadowed by what could have been. No less an authority than Paul O'Neill, an outfielder on the late 1990s Yankees dynasty and a member of the Reds 1990 world championship squad, said that Davis was "the best hitter, best runner, best outfielder, best everything I ever saw"—some very Reiser-esque compliments when you think about it.

My picks for the greatest "what if" players in baseball history not named Harold Patrick Reiser:

Charlie Ferguson

The Philadelphia Phillies had to wait nearly one hundred years to win their first championship, delivered by the firm of Carlton, Schmidt & McGraw in 1980. The franchise might have reached the summit a lot sooner had fate been kinder to one Charles J. Ferguson.

At age twenty-four in 1887, "Fergy" put together a two-way season that rivals the best of Babe Ruth or Shohei Ohtani. Batting, he hit a team-high .337 and racked up eighty-five RBI in less than three hundred at-bats. Pitching, he won twenty-two games, finished with a 3.00 ERA, and posted the second-best strikeout/walk ratio in the National League. He did his best work down the home stretch, winning seven of the Phils' final eighteen games, playing second base when he wasn't pitching, and batting .361 during that span. The Phils finished a strong second, just three and a half games behind the Detroit Wolverines, and many baseball scribes tabbed them as a likely pennant winner in 1888.

Granted, major league baseball was a very different game during the Grover Cleveland (not Alexander) era. Rosters were limited to fourteen men, ensuring that many pitchers took turns at other positions. The pitcher's box—there were no mounds yet—was only fifty feet from home plate, easing the strain on hurlers' arms. But nobody else on the Phillies or around the league stood out as both pitcher and hitter the way Ferguson did. And none of the others made such a lasting impression. In the late nineteenth and early twentieth century, it wasn't uncommon for insiders to name Ferguson as one of the greatest players of all time:

Wilbert Robinson, Hall of Fame catcher and manager: "It's unfair to name just a few . . . But if I have to name the best five, you can put down Cobb, Keeler, Ruth, Wagner, and Ferguson for me."

Jack Clements, a catcher with the Phillies and four other teams: "I recognize the greatness of Mike Kelly, Buck Ewing, Charlie Bennett, and others in their prime, but I cannot get away from my high regard for Charlie Ferguson. He was the greatest all-around ballplayer that ever lived."

Alfred H. Spink, founder of *The Sporting News*: "He had a magnificent arm, a clear eye, pluck, and control. He could throw a ball with terrific speed, and he had absolute control of the sphere at all times. He was of great use to his team outside of his aid in the pitcher's points, for he was one of the best left-handed batsmen known to the game."

Born and raised in Charlottesville, Virginia, Ferguson joined the Phillies in the spring of 1884 after impressing scouts with his play on a Richmond semipro team. In his very first outing with the Phils, he collected three hits and threw a complete-game victory over the Wolverines, with "Ferguson's pitching completely puzzling them," according to the *Philadelphia Inquirer*. He wasn't always quite so good; in fact, he gave up more earned runs than any pitcher in the National League that season. But he quickly improved. On August 9, 1885, he threw the first no-hitter in Phillies' history against the defending NL champion Providence Grays. In 1886, he won thirty games, struck out two hundred twelve batters, and lowered his ERA to 1.98, second-best in the league. His hitting was getting more consistent too, and Phillies manager Harry Wright began to play him on days he wasn't pitching, initially in the outfield.

At times Ferguson seemed to overwork himself, and he acquired a reputation as a "crank," or hypochondriac. In August 1886, he left the team against Wright's orders during a western road trip, insisting that he was ill and needed treatment back in Charlottesville. "I left because I feared a long spell of sickness," he later explained in a letter to *The Sporting News*, "Mr. Wright may have—I will say he did have—doubts about the seriousness of my case, or he would surely have let me go home. When I arrived home, I was confined to my bed for ten days, and here is a physician's certificate to that effect." Whatever tensions existed between Wright and his star player; they were apparently set aside as Ferguson rejoined the team in September. On the final day of the season, he defeated Detroit in both halves of a doubleheader, 5-1 and 6-1, denying the Wolverines a shot at the pennant. "The great feature of both contests was the pitching of Ferguson," reported the *Philadelphia Times*. "He pitched in fifteen consecutive innings, and at the finish, he was just as effective and seemed as fresh as when he started. Ferguson proved his claim to the title of the champion pitcher of the League, and the crowd gave him a royal ovation as he left at the end of the second game."

He left the team briefly again in June 1887, this time for an undeniably legitimate reason: his infant daughter had died. During the week he was in Charlottesville, the club lost five out of six games. When he returned on June 15th, he pitched the Phils to an 18-4 victory over Washington, adding three hits and a pair of stolen bases.

Ferguson performed such feats for a very average salary: twenty-five hundred dollars for the season, well below the four to five thousand paid to top stars like Mike Kelly of Boston and Cap Anson of Chicago. As the Philly *Times* pointed out, "Ferguson thinks his salary is much too small for a man of his ability," and he had held out during the 1887 preseason, seeking a boost to three thousand. The Phils, one of the league's lower-paying teams, wouldn't go that high. When the season ended, he had a chance to fatten his wallet by playing a national exhibition tour with some of his teammates. The tour was a success, with the traveling Phillies playing to sizeable crowds in Denver, Santa Fe, San Francisco, Los Angeles, and other young cities in the expanding West. Ferguson, however, backed out at the last minute; it was reported that he was "detained in the east" due to his mother being ill. It seems just as likely he was simply tired.

Ahead of the 1888 season, "Fergy" got in shape coaching the Princeton College baseball team, waiting until the last day in March to join the Phillies for preseason games. All seemed fine until a week before opening day when the Philly papers reported he was sick. "Ferguson is not seriously ill. He may play to-day," the *Times* assured readers. But what was initially thought to be a bad cold was soon diagnosed as typhoid fever. Typhoid, a bacterial infection transmitted mainly through food or water, was tantamount to a death sentence in the nineteenth century, as doctors of the time could do little except to prescribe rest and prayer.

As his condition deteriorated, Philly sportswriters saw the team's pennant chances slipping away too. "His loss is irreparable," said the *Inquirer*. The *Times* chimed in: "Ferguson will be badly missed just now. He has been pitching well and playing a great game on second, and there is no one to take his place." That wasn't literally true; when the season opened, manager Wright put utility infielder Charlie Bastian at second and tapped rookie Kid Gleason to pitch. But it soon became apparent that neither man could fill the spikes of their ailing teammate. Bastian would hit a feeble .193 that season and Gleason (future manager of the infamous 1919 "Black Sox") would win seven games while losing sixteen.

The players made daily visits to Charlie and his wife, who were staying at the house of Phillies' shortstop Arthur Irwin on North Broad Street. Ferguson seemed to improve at times, and his teammates occasionally gave semi-hopeful updates to the press. "He is very thin and weak, and I don't believe he will be able to pitch any this season. But he may get in shape to play second base," said pitcher Dan Casey. But even that prognosis was too optimistic, and Ferguson expired on the evening of April 29th, less than two weeks after turning twenty-five.

The end had been expected, and nearly every member of the Phillies was present when Ferguson died. In a remarkable tribute to their fallen teammate, the Phillies played their regularly scheduled game the next afternoon, wearing black armbands on their sleeves, and beat the visiting Washington Nationals 3-1. Immediately after the game, members of both teams attended Ferguson's funeral at Irwin's house. When it was over, several Philly players lifted his casket onto the hearse and accompanied it to the Broad Street train station, where it was placed on the 4:30 P.M. "Southern Express" for Ferguson's final trip home to Charlottesville.

Cecil Travis

In the 2000 version of his *Historical Baseball Abstract*, Bill James devoted a section to players whose service in World War II kept them out of the Hall of Fame. Number one on the list, and rightfully so, was Cecil Howell Travis. It is an incontestable fact: no other major league star lost more of his talent to the war than the Georgia native and Washington Senators shortstop.

In the last year of pre-war baseball, Travis had ascended from the ranks of the good to the spectacular. When baseball fans think of 1941, they tend to remember Ted Williams' .406 average and Joe DiMaggio's fifty-six-game hitting streak, but Travis actually hit for a higher batting average (.359) than Joltin' Joe and hammered out more hits (218) than the Splendid Splinter. The latter figure led both major leagues. He had been a first-rank ballplayer for several years before then, consistently hitting well above .300 and making two all-star teams while playing in Washington's Griffith Stadium, a pitcher-friendly park with distant outfield walls and ample foul territory. However, during the '41 season, Travis switched to a heavier bat and altered his grip and stance, transforming himself into a pull hitter. The result was career highs in doubles, triples, and homers, allowing him to top one hundred RBI and a hundred runs scored for the first time. He started and played the entire All-Star Game and made a key take-out slide of NL second baseman Billy Herman in the ninth inning, stopping the National League from turning a game-ending double play. The next batter, Williams, smashed a three-run homer that gave the American League a 7-5 win.

Day in and day out, not many folks got to *see* Travis, mind you. During his prime years, the Senators were usually out of the pennant race by Flag Day. Most afternoons, the team was lucky to draw five thousand fans. (In one September 1939 game against the Indians, they drew three hundred.) Sportswriters would have adorned their profiles of Travis with words like dependable, modest, and unpretentious, except that nobody wrote such articles during his career, so unnoticed were his efforts on such a lowly team. "I never did care much for publicity, anyway. That was always the last of my concerns," Travis said years later. Virtually the only time he made national headlines was after his first major league game on May 16, 1933. Arriving at Griffith Stadium just a half-hour before game time, he was written into the lineup and tied a record by banging out five hits in his major league debut. That year was the one time in his career the Senators made the World Series. Travis hit .302 in eighteen games during the season but was left off the postseason roster.

At the end of the '41 season, Travis was twenty-eight years old and in perfect health; under normal circumstances, he could have bashed away at AL pitchers with his newfound power for another five to ten years and cemented a place as a historically great shortstop, maybe even raised the Senators out of their perennial sixth-place gloom. Alas, the war. Travis had narrowly sidestepped the draft in the summer of '41, receiving a sixty-day deferment that allowed him to finish the season. Pearl Harbor ended such respites, and he received his draft notice the day before Christmas. When he reported at Fort McPherson in Atlanta, a colonel greeted him with a sly putdown of his former team: "Well, son, you've finally caught on with a world championship outfit." Travis spent much of the next two summers playing ball with the Camp Wheeler squad in Georgia. It was a good team, as good or better than the one surrounding Reiser at Fort Riley in Kansas, and both squads reached the final stages of the 1943 national semipro tournament in Wichita, though Reiser and Travis never went head-to-head. Fort Riley, as noted, finished fourth in the tourney, while Camp Wheeler went all the way to win the championship.

Travis told a newspaper in early 1944 that he was keeping himself in "very good playing shape" and predicted he would make a successful return to big-league ball. That was before he got shipped to Europe as part of a combat unit in the Army's 76th Infantry Division. The unit was deployed in Belgium in January 1945, during the final stages of the Battle of the Bulge, just behind the frontline troops. The Senator-turned-soldier avoided combat injuries but suffered from the extreme cold. "Heck, you was in that snow," he recalled, "and you was out in that weather, and you was lucky you got to stay in an old barn at night. The thing about it, you'd sit there in those boots, and you might not get 'em off for days at a time. And cold! You'd just shake at night. Your feet would start swelling, and that's how you'd find out there was something really wrong—you'd pull your boots off, and your feet is swelling." The swelling, it turned out, was the result of frostbite. Travis was pulled off the line and sent to an Army hospital in France. Doctors there saved his feet, but they remained tender after being shipped back to the U.S. that summer, still in the army, awaiting further orders.

That fall, Travis finally had a shot at a World Series. The Senators were in a neck-and-neck pennant race with the Tigers, and when Travis was unexpectedly discharged from the army in Georgia on September 5th, he hopped in his car and drove all night to get to Washington. After just two days of batting and infield practice, he tried to jump back into the lineup. It didn't work out. After a year without playing serious ball, he looked slow afoot and hit mostly inconsequential singles down the stretch as the Senators came up a game short to Detroit. After the season, Senators owner Clark Griffith acknowledged that Travis "found it difficult to run properly after his return to us."

"I was just dead last year," Travis said the following February. "I couldn't move around. Nothing hurt me, but I just didn't feel right."

The problems persisted the next spring as Travis tried in vain to find his old form. After a fast start in 1946, he leveled off at .252, the worst performance of returning pre-war stars. He was benched in '47 as he struggled to keep his batting average above .200 and retired at the end of the season, just thirty-four years old. He refused to blame his wartime frozen feet for his downfall. "My problem when I got back to baseball was my timing," he explained decades later. "I could never seem to get it back the way it was after laying out for so long. I saw I wasn't helping the club, so I gave it up." He remained a popular player, and in August 1947, the Senators honored him with a Cecil Travis night. Fifteen thousand fans—a big crowd by Washington standards—turned out to pay tribute, among them Travis' commander in Belgium, Major General

William Morris Hoge. General Dwight Eisenhower sent a message expressing his deep "respect and admiration." Appreciative fans showered Travis with ten thousand dollars worth of gifts, including an electric oven, a six-piece bedroom set, leather chairs, a De Soto automobile, and a fifteen-hundred-pound Hereford bull for his farm.

Travis was largely forgotten for several decades until several contemporaries—notably Ted Williams, Bob Feller, and former baseball commissioner Bowie Kuhn, who had been a Senators batboy—began mentioning him as a candidate for the Hall of Fame. "If it had not been for the war, he would have had a lifetime batting average of .325, .335," Feller said. "He'd be a major Hall of Famer. No questions asked." Interviewed by researchers and newspaper columnists, Travis expressed appreciation for the compliments but refused to say he was worthy of induction. "There are a lot of players with records as good or better than mine who are not in it," he said. "I just don't think it would look right. Now, if I had had several seasons like 1941, then it might be different."

Jose Fernandez

He should be at his peak now, mowing down hitters with that ninety-five mile per hour fastball, making them swing and miss at the changeup or the slurve. He should be limbering up for pitching duels with Buehler, Fried, and DeGrom and showdowns against Tatis, Alonso, and Judge. There should be highlight videos from his playoff starts, especially from 2017, when his teammate and close pal Giancarlo Stanton launched fifty-eight homers and won MVP. He should have a shelf adorned with at least one Cy Young award, next to the Rookie of the Year prize he picked up in 2013 and the Comeback Player of the Year trophy he won three years later after recovering from Tommy John surgery.

But none of that is happening or will happen because of an ill-advised motorboat ride that Jose Fernandez took in the pre-dawn darkness of September 25th, 2016. Investigators said Fernandez, drunk on tequila and high on cocaine, piloted his boat into a rock jetty in Miami's Government Cut shipping channel, killing himself and two fellow passengers. A family attorney challenged the official report, insisting one of the other passengers was at the wheel and suggesting that someone had drugged Fernandez to steal fifteen thousand dollars in cash he was carrying in his backpack, apparently meant for end-of-season tips to Marlins Park employees. It didn't matter. Either way, the ace of the Marlins' staff lost his life that morning, prematurely ending what should have been a glorious career.

In four short years, Fernandez had become the face and the spark of the Miami franchise. Fans never tired of hearing his story: born in communist Cuba, he made three escape attempts before succeeding at age fifteen. During the fourth attempt, he dove into the water and saved his mother from drowning. After one spectacular season in the minors, he reached the Marlins at twenty-one and made the National League all-star team his rookie year. In the game itself, he pitched a one-two-three inning, striking out two. Later that season, he blasted his first major league home run, a shot to left field against the Braves. He took a second to admire the hit, prompting some testy remarks from catcher Brian McCann and a clearing of the benches. The incident reflected a side of Jose's personality: cocky, bordering on arrogance, a quality that bothered his teammates occasionally and especially bothered Marlins management when he criticized them for failing to build a winner.

The fans in Miami's sea-green ballpark never cared about things like that. They loved Jose's ever-present smile, his infectious youthful energy, and of course, his lights-out pitching. His lifetime record at Marlins Park was an astonishing 29-2, with a 1.49 ERA. The Marlins stayed stubbornly under .500, but Fernandez raised hopes that the team's lengthening history of futility and bad faith management was nearing an end. The Fish were certainly on the upswing, with talented young hitters like Stanton, Christian Yelich, and Marcell Ozuna in the lineup. Maybe 2017 was meant to be their breakthrough year. Maybe attendance would have shot through the retractable roof. Maybe the Marlins would've stopped losing money and not conducted the fire sale that happened after the season when they traded Stanton and every other live bat on the roster for Triple-A players and cash.

Fernandez's statistics strongly suggest he was headed for Cooperstown. In four seasons with Marlins, two of them partial because of the Tommy John injury, Fernandez posted a 2.58 ERA, a better than four-to-one strikeout/walk ratio, and a .691 winning percentage. The last is most impressive because the Marlins were a losing team in all four years. In Jose's rookie year, the Fish went 18-10 in games that he started, 44-90 the rest of the time. And at the time of his death, he was getting stronger and better. In his final season, he won sixteen games and piled up two hundred fifty-three strikeouts, second-best in the National League. In his last start before his untimely end, against the playoff-bound Nationals, he pitched eight scoreless innings, giving up just three hits, striking out twelve.

"I think we're going to remember him as one of the great pitchers to come along in quite some time," said ESPN analyst Tim Kurkjian on the day

Fernandez died. "We're going to look at him as one of the great success stories, overcoming adversity, and we're going to look at him as someone that just lit up a ballpark whether he was pitching or not, but especially when he was pitching. That was worth viewing in Miami because of how great he was and what he brought to the competition every single time he started."

Mark Fidrych

Great as Jose Fernandez was, he was a Miami star. Nearly half a century ago—can it be that long?—Mark Fidrych was an American phenomenon. Virtually every time he pitched, regardless of the city, the day of the week, the quality or popularity of the opposing team, an extra fifteen to thirty-thousand people poured through the turnstiles to see "The Bird" take flight. In a sport that often emphasizes conformity, he oozed individuality. He talked to himself on the mound. He talked to the ball. He aimed it like a dart. He bent down and smoothed out the dirt in front of the rubber. He bobbed up and down before starting his delivery. He charged, not jogged off the field at the end of an inning. And with his lanky 6'3" frame and mop of blond curls, he really did resemble Big Bird from Sesame Street—thus the nickname. The two once shared a *Sports Illustrated* cover.

Behind the personality, however, was one top-notch pitcher. In 1976, at age twenty-one, Fidrych won nineteen games for the Tigers, completed twenty-four of twenty-nine starts, and led the American League with a 2.34 ERA. He started the All-Star Game, finished second in the Cy Young voting, and was named AL Rookie of the Year. The following season, after missing several weeks with torn cartilage in his right knee, he ripped off six straight wins, all complete games, in which his ERA was just 1.33. The best of those was a dominating 2-1 victory over the Yankees in which he held Reggie Jackson, Thurman Munson, and company to three singles. Fidrych needed only eighty-six pitches to set down the eventual world champions in a game that lasted just one hour, fifty-seven minutes. "Tonight, we didn't win because a great pitcher shoved our bats down our throats," said Reggie after the game. "Mark Fidrych beat us."

Remarkably, Fidrych didn't have an overpowering fastball and rarely struck out more than four or five batters per game. What he did have was excellent control and a top-of-the-line sinker, making batter after batter hit ground balls. In one July 1976 win against Minnesota, he gave up ten hits, including four to Tony Oliva, but all were singles, and three of the runners were erased on double plays. For the month as a whole, he started six games, pitched fifty-one innings, and didn't allow a single home run.

Over thirty thousand fans attended that game in Minneapolis—a big crowd for the Twins back then, but a relatively small turnout for The Bird. Five of his starts that summer attracted crowds of at least fifty thousand, and several others drew forty thousand plus. Fans could not get enough of his pitching, his eccentricities, and his youthful enthusiasm. The game people tend to remember was his national debut, so to speak, a June 1976 game against the Yankees that was televised by ABC and gets rerun periodically by MLB Network. From the first batter, a packed Tiger Stadium was roaring, and Fidrych gave the TV audience a great show, limiting the Bronx Bombers to a run and seven hits while keeping up a stream of animated gestures and talking that visibly irritated the Yankees but riveted the fans. By the ninth inning, announcer Bob Uecker was exclaiming, "I love this guy!" as an excited Fidrych pumped his fist after striking out Chris Chambliss and yelled, "Nice play!" to his second baseman for fielding a routine grounder. After the game, Tigers' fans stood and chanted "We want Mark!" until a beaming Fidrych came out, tipped his cap, and shook hands with fans as well as policemen guarding the dugout. "I've been in baseball for 35 years, and I have never in my life ever seen anything equal to this," said Uecker's broadcast partner Bob Prince.

It was just over one year later, July 1977, that it all came to a screeching halt. He was pitching in Baltimore, in front of an Independence Day crowd of forty-five thousand, when he threw an awkward pitch. "I thought, 'That really looked weird. His motion was different. The next pitches were all hit hard," remembered teammate Dave Rozema. Fidrych's personal catcher, Bruce Kimm, also noticed an immediate difference: "All of the sudden, he couldn't get anyone out . . . When [manager] Ralph Houk came to the mound to relieve him, Mark said, 'I feel fine, but the ball went dead.'" In actuality, it was the Bird's wing, er, arm that went dead. He struggled through his next start against the White Sox, in front of forty-six thousand at Tiger Stadium, then threw just fifteen pitches against the expansion Blue Jays before he asked to be taken out. "I was throwing great. Then it hurt. On one pitch, it semi-hurt. Then another hurt and another hurt," Fidrych said after the game.

He didn't pitch again that season. Puzzled team doctors diagnosed him with tendinitis in his right shoulder. But that wasn't the real problem. It wasn't until 1985, after advances in MRI technology, Fidrych discovered he had two severe tears in his rotator cuff. Even if he had known, there wasn't much that doctors in 1977 could do. Just a year earlier, Dr. Frank Jobe had performed the first rotator cuff surgery on an active pitcher, Steve Busby of the Royals. Busby, a former twenty-game winner, never came close to regaining his form, and time would show that the surgery had a low success rate; for every pitcher who bounced back from it, like the young Roger Clemens, there were several others whose careers foundered. More useful innovations like platelet-rich plasma shots and stem cell treatments were still decades away.

After a year and a month of exhilarating success, Fidrych's career was essentially over. He pitched a few more games over the next three seasons, even winning an opening day start in 1978 in front of his biggest crowd ever, fifty-two thousand plus at Tiger Stadium. But the pain and weakness in his arm never disappeared.

More so than most what-if players, Fidrych's career implosion was avoidable. Some observers thought he tried to come back too early from his knee injury and subtly changed his mechanics, straining his shoulder. More than a few wondered, especially in retrospect, why the Tigers let their prized youngster throw so many complete games. Yes, the Tigers had only one effective relief pitcher in John Hiller at the time. Yes, it was standard procedure to let top pitchers finish their starts back then; in 1976, ten other American League pitchers completed at least eighteen games. But most of those were older, well-established stars like Jim Palmer, Gaylord Perry, Catfish Hunter, and Vida Blue, who were used to carrying the heavy load. Fidrych was just twenty-one years old. Two years earlier, pitching in rookie league ball, he had thrown a total of thirty-four innings. In '76, he threw two hundred fifty.

Worse yet, no one was monitoring his pitch count. Four times that season, manager Houk let his star rookie go eleven innings or more. In each of those starts, Fidrych faced more than forty batters and, in all likelihood, threw at least one hundred fifty pitches. In today's game, Houk would be fired, it not hauled into court for abuse of an irreplaceable, unforgettable young pitcher.

Smoky Joe Wood

Of course, if you really want to hear about a pitcher wearing out his arm, look no further than the case of Smoky Joe Wood. In 1912, at the tender age of twenty-two, the fireballing young Kansan hurled the Red Sox to a world championship, winning thirty-four games and losing only five. He then pitched four games in the World Series, winning three, including the finale, where Giants center fielder Fred Snodgrass infamously muffed an easy fly ball in the tenth inning to set off the Sox' winning rally. By season's end, including the Series, Wood had thrown three hundred sixty-six innings, a heavy load even for the pitcher-friendly Deadball Era.

There was no Cy Young award then—Cy Young had just retired a year earlier—but Wood would have been the winner in all likelihood. Yeah, this other guy named Walter Johnson had the best season yet in his brilliant, batter-humbling career. But Wood topped him in several key categories, including wins (34-33), complete games (35-33) and shutouts, (10-7), even though Johnston took the strikeout and ERA titles. Better still, when the two aces faced off in a September 8th pitching duel, Wood came out on top, beating "Barney" and the Senators 1-0, striking out nine. Fenway Park was so packed for the game that the Red Sox set up ropes and let customers sit on the edge of the field, one of the last times that ever happened in a big-league ballgame.

Wood and the Red Sox thought that magnificent season was only the beginning. But in the spring of 1913, Smoky Joe came down with a sore arm and, in the words of one reporter, lost the smoke on his pitches. "That was it. That was it right then and there," Wood recalled to Lawrence Ritter more than half a century later. "My arm went bad . . . and all my dreams came tumbling down around my ears like a damn house of cards." Wood traced his misfortune to an incident where he slipped on wet grass while chasing a ground ball and fractured the thumb on his pitching hand. "It was in a cast for two or three weeks," he said. "I don't know whether I tried to pitch too soon after that or whether maybe something happened to my shoulder at the same time. But whatever it was, I never pitched again without a terrific amount of pain in my right shoulder. Never again."

Unlike many other sore-armed hurlers who try to push through their pain, Wood remained a very effective pitcher when he could take the mound. From 1913 to 1915, not-so-Smoky Joe won thirty-six games, lost thirteen, and compiled a 2.08 ERA. In 1915, his 1.49 ERA topped the American League, and his fifteen wins helped the Red Sox secure a tight pennant race over the Tigers. But he couldn't pitch in that year's World Series, and he decided to call it quits the following spring. "I stayed on the farm because my arm was too bad," he explained almost seventy years later, talking to an enterprising high school reporter. "And then they got this theatrical bird in there, Frazee, and he just sold the ballclub out. He cut my contract twenty-five hundred dollars, and I wouldn't report." The bird in question, Harry Frazee, would sell Babe Ruth and several other stars to New York a few years later, triggering the start of the long Yankee dynasty.

At age twenty-six, Smoky Joe's baseball career seemed over . . . until he picked up a bat. When player shortages hit teams in 1918 due to World War I, Wood made it back to the majors as an outfielder for the Cleveland Indians.

In that role, he won another World Series with the Indians in 1920 and batted .366 for them in part-time play the following season. After another good year in 1922, he retired to become baseball coach at Yale, where he led the team for twenty years and even trained his son, Joe Wood Jr., who pitched three games for the wartime 1944 Red Sox.

But in his heart, Joe Wood was never a batsman or an outfielder. "Hitting is very nice," he said near the end of his life, "but it's much nicer to be like I was— practically among the best of them, pitching."

Josh Hamilton

How feared was Josh Hamilton's bat at his peak? In an August 2008 game, Hamilton came to bat in the ninth inning with the bases loaded and his Rangers trailing the Tampa Bay Rays 7-3. Fans at Rangers Ballpark stood up, anticipating a showdown between Hamilton and pitcher Grant Balfour. But Rays manager Joe Maddon was having none of it. He ordered an intentional walk, letting Texas score one run to prevent Hamilton from crushing a homer and knocking in four. Only one other player in the previous sixty years—Barry Bonds—had received such a tribute. "I just didn't want to see Hamilton there," said Maddon after the game. "I mean, listen—it's his year. And why have him hit a grand slam there and really screw up ours?" The strategy worked: the Rays won the game 7-4 and rolled on to win the division title and reach the World Series. Hamilton had to settle for a pair of runs batted in that night, two of the one hundred thirty he'd rack up by year's end, topping the American League.

During that season and a couple of others, no opposing manager or pitcher wanted to see Hamilton at the plate in any situation. Quoting the *Charlotte Observer* in his native North Carolina: "Hamilton had been blessed genetically and had put in the work. He was six-foot-four, weighed about two hundred forty pounds, and he could move his size nineteen shoes with the speed of a much smaller man. He could throw a baseball faster than ninety-five miles per hour, and he routinely hit baseballs more than four hundred feet." But Hamilton also had a curse—drug and alcohol addiction. It had begun in 2001, during his minor league days, when he was idled by a lower back injury, fell in with a dead-end crowd at a tattoo parlor, and slipped into heavy use of cocaine and alcohol. By 2004, after five failed drug tests, he was suspended from baseball and spent much of his time in treatment clinics. He got married, became a dad, and would manage to stay clean for weeks, even months at a time. Then he'd fall back. During one relapse, he was arrested for smashing in the windshield of a friend's truck. During another, he gave his wife's wedding ring to a coke dealer as payment. During still another, he claimed to have spent one hundred thousand dollars on crack. In his own words, he was disintegrating.

Somehow, with the help of his grandmother and strong Christian faith, Hamilton got sober and made it to the major leagues with the Reds. He played one season with them, hit .292 with nineteen homers, then got traded to the Rangers. The 2008 season was his breakthrough year. That July, he not only made the All-Star Game, but he also stole the show at the Home Run Derby, crushing a new record of twenty-eight homers in the first round, several of which reached Yankee Stadium's upper deck. At one point, he crashed homers on thirteen pitches in a row. The crowd was electrified. He lost the final round to Minnesota's Justin Morneau, but Hamilton didn't care by then. "Standing at home plate and having Yankee Stadium chant your name, is there a better feeling?" he said.

In 2010, his finest year, he hit thirty-two homers and led the American League in batting average, slugging average, and OPS, giving an otherwise so-so Rangers' offense enough oomph to win the AL West. In that year's ALCS, he whacked four homers in the first four games, prompting the Yankees to walk him intentionally three times in the finale as they tried in vain to stave off defeat. His 2011 season wasn't as good, but he nearly achieved baseball immortality in that year's World Series. With Game Six knotted 7-7 in the top of the tenth inning, Hamilton blasted a two-run homer to right-center. In the dugout, Rangers manager Ron Washington jumped for joy; in the stands, team president Nolan Ryan started high-fiving the fans. Hamilton himself seemed oddly unemotional, crossing the plate but explained to reporters after the game that he was simply feeling the presence of God. "He told me, 'You haven't hit one in a while, and this is the time you're going to,'" said Hamilton. He added: "You know what? I probably had the most relaxed, peaceful at-bat I've had of the whole series at that moment."

Unfortunately, the Rangers lost the lead, the game, and the series, and Josh Hamilton couldn't hold onto that feeling of peace. He had relapsed briefly in early 2009, getting drunk at a bar in Tempe, Arizona. It happened again in early 2012, this time at a bar in Dallas. Hamilton remained an awesome force at bat—in a May 2012 game, he launched four homers against the Orioles, tying the major-league record—but his performance that season grew more erratic. He slumped badly toward the end of the year, striking out sixteen times in his last thirty-five at-bats, and dropped an easy pop-up in the season finale, costing Texas the game and the division title. Rangers fans lustily booed him, and the front office made less than an all-out effort to re-sign him when he hit free agency that winter.

Instead, Angels owner Arte Moreno opened his wallet and inked Hamilton to a five-year deal worth one hundred twenty-five million dollars. It may have been the worst free-agent signing of the decade. In his first season with Los Angeles, Hamilton stayed clean and healthy but hit just twenty-one homers, led AL outfielders in errors, and struck out three times for every time he walked. He missed nearly half the games in season two due to thumb, shoulder, and rib injuries and failed to get a single hit during the American League division series, triggering boos from the Angels fans. After he relapsed again in early 2015, this time with cocaine, the Angels decided they'd seen enough and traded him back to Texas. He lasted there one fairly unproductive year before multiple knee surgeries forced him to retire at age thirty-four.

It would be nice to say that away from the pressures of big-league baseball, Hamilton found the inner peace he sought. In May 2019, he told reporters he had stayed away from his addictions and was focused on being a good dad to his four daughters. "Surround yourself with good people, people who love you and people who want you to do good, and now I've become a good contributing part of the community," he said. Five months later, he was arrested and charged with injury to a child after allegedly punching and assaulting his oldest daughter. In April 2020, he was indicted on the charge and faced a possible ten years in prison, though he had not gone on trial more than sixteen months later. His life story isn't over, but his baseball career is, and for a guy who was compared at various times to Mickey Mantle and Ken Griffey Jr., it's hard not to wonder what might have been.

Herb Score

For two years, the Indians thought they had the second coming of Bob Feller. Herb Score didn't reach the majors at seventeen like Rapid Robert but threw nearly as hard and effectively. In 1955, he won sixteen games, led the American League in strikeouts, and was named AL Rookie of the Year. In 1956, he won twenty, led the league in strikeouts again, and pitched five shutouts to boot. Like Feller, he had trouble hitting the strike zone, but even the walks were coming down. He was the new bedrock of the Indians' pitching staff, a guy to keep the team in pennant hunts for years to come.

Nineteen fifty-seven, it all came to a screeching halt. May 7th that year, a line drive off the bat of the Yankees' Gil McDougald smashed into Score's right eye. He was rushed to a Cleveland hospital, where doctors diagnosed him with damage to the right cheekbone, a broken nose, a lacerated eyelid, and damage to the eye itself. He would spend three weeks in the hospital and be sidelined for the rest of the season. Without their ace, the Indians slumped to their first losing season since 1946, leading to the dismissal of rookie manager Kirby Ferrell. Casey Stengel told Ferrell after the year that he had really lost his job on May 7th.

There's not much else to say except that Score never came all the way back. His eye healed, he returned in '58, pitched a brilliant thirteen-K shutout against the White Sox, then tore a tendon in his left elbow. That healed, but afterward, Score could never recapture his previous speed and mastery. After several seasons of declining fortunes, he retired at age thirty in 1963. He found a second career as the Indians' radio voice, doing play-by-play and color commentary for thirty seasons before retiring in 1997. Unlike some other "what if" players, he expressed no resentment for the turn his career had taken. "You know, maybe I was fortunate to get hit in the eye, and I lost that year," he said late in his broadcasting career. "It gave me a chance to reflect and think about the future. And I also found out there are a lot of nice people in the world."

J.R. Richard

In 1980, I was ten years old, already a baseball fanatic, and plunked down eagerly in front of the family Zenith to watch the All-Star Game. The starting pitcher for the National League was J.R. Richard, and . . . wow. For years afterward, I carried a mental image of his six-foot-eight frame atop the pitcher's mound at Dodger Stadium. Richard looked huge under any conditions, but with sun splashed across the field that day, with his orange-striped Astros jersey and white pants standing out against the blue outfield walls, he looked bigger than life. He pitched that way too, rearing back with an already old-fashioned high leg hick, and the ball came zooming out of his hand, a tiny white pellet passing through the late-afternoon L.A. shadows. He walked a couple of guys, as always, but for the most part, the American League hitters either waved helplessly at the ball or tapped it weakly to the infielders. Richard was dominant.

It had taken nearly a decade for James Rodney Richard to reach this peak. Some fastball pitchers, the guys who can touch one hundred miles per hour, take a few years to harness their control. Randy Johnson and Nolan Ryan each needed six seasons in the big leagues. Sandy Koufax required seven. J.R. Richard was like that. He reached the majors in September 1971, struck out fifteen

Giants in his first start, then bounced in and out of the minors for the next three years, trying to consistently hit the strike zone with his fastball and equally lethal slider. When he finally cracked the Astros' starting rotation in 1975, he led the National League in wild pitches and walks. But each year, he got a little better. The strikeouts shot up, the walks dropped to a manageable level, and his ERA got lower and lower.

By '79, he was possibly the best hurler in the game, winning eighteen games and topping the NL in strikeouts (313) and ERA (2.71). And it wasn't the pitcher-friendly Astrodome causing his success. In '79, opposing teams hit .200 against him in Houston and just .221 everywhere else. He should have won the Cy Young Award that season; he was third in the voting, behind a reliever, Bruce Sutter, and teammate Joe Niekro, a knuckleballer who won twenty-one games but had nearly two hundred fewer strikeouts than J.R.

That offseason, the Astros signed Richard to a new four-year contract worth about eight hundred thousand dollars per year, then turned around and made Ryan the first guy to get a million. If that bothered him, Richard kept it to himself and focused on getting the Astros to their first postseason berth. In 1980, he came out on fire, striking out thirteen Dodgers in a 3-2 win on opening day. Nine days later, he shut them out on one hit and struck out twelve. He tossed three shutouts in a row in May and June, racking up thirty-one consecutive scoreless innings before the Cubs nicked him for a single run. "He was the best pitcher in baseball, no question about it," former Astro manager Bill Virdon said a few years later. "He probably created more headaches and stomachaches for right-handed hitters than anybody who ever played."

Richard reveled in his success. "I felt like I was the baddest lion in the valley," he later said. In his 2015 book *Still Throwing Heat*, he added: "I thought I was invulnerable. [I was] the only guy in the world who could throw a ball through a car wash and not get it wet."

How could he know it was all about to end? For some weeks before the All-Star Game, Richard had complained about numbness and fatigue in his right arm. Doctors examined him and could not find anything physically wrong. But in his last start against Atlanta, Richard lasted just three innings, saying his arm had gone "dead." Some Astros officials and reporters covering the team publicly questioned his training habits and fortitude; the team physician insultingly suggested he cut back on socializing and get more sleep. Finally, at the end of July, a more thorough exam found blocked arteries reducing circulation to his pitching arm. Doctors recommended rest, not surgery, and cleared Richard to continue light workouts. During one of these workouts, on July 30th, Richard heard a loud ringing in his left ear, got dizzy and nauseous, and collapsed in the outfield at the Astrodome, the victim of a stroke. An ambulance rushed him to Houston's Memorial Hospital for surgery to remove a blood clot. He survived, but the stroke temporarily paralyzed his left side. He spent weeks in the hospital and missed the rest of the '80 season, watching from home as the Astros finally made the playoffs, losing a tough five-game series to Philadelphia.

Spring of '81, after a second operation to restore circulation to his arm, he tried to come back. The fluid pitching motion was still there, and so was most of the fastball. His depth perception and reaction times were not, and the Astros limited him to workouts and throwing batting practice for his teammates. That June, he rejected his own agent's suggestion that he pitch in triple-A. "I'm not working out twice a day to go to the minor leagues," he said. After he donned glasses and showed some improvement, the Astros reactivated him in early September as they drove for a playoff spot. Virdon organized a simulated game at the Astrodome as a final test. It didn't pan out; Richard touched ninety-one miles per hour on the radar gun but was wild high on most of his pitches and stumbled when he had to move laterally. He sat on the bench the rest of the way as the Astros reached the playoffs again and lost another five-game series, this time to the Dodgers.

In the spring of '82, Richard tried again. After battling back tendinitis and a significant weight gain, he agreed to go to the minors. He did well at single-A Daytona Beach, pitching two complete-game victories, the crowd cheering him on with chants of "J.R! J.R!" The Astros promoted him to triple-A Tucson. "He doesn't look like he's been sick in his life . . . He looks like he could whip anyone or anything if he had the urge," wrote a reporter upon his arrival. But in his second start, it all fell apart: eight hits, seven walks, three wild pitches, and fifteen runs in just three and a third innings. The manager left him in, hoping he would find a groove, but by the end, Richard was taking frequent breaks behind the mound, his face a vacant stare, like that of a shell-shocked World War I veteran.

He pitched a few more games that season, but the comeback attempt may as well have ended there. After one more season spent in rookie league ball, Richard was released with little fanfare in the spring of '84. When he became eligible for the Hall of Fame, he dropped off the ballot after one year, getting less than two percent of the vote. He won a one-point-five-million-dollar settlement against the Astros and their medical staff, but his life spiraled downward—he lost jobs, two wives, his money, his home, and for a while in the mid-1990s, he was living part-time under an overpass in Houston. Eventually, Richard straightened out with help from local churches and a new wife, and he stabilized financially when his baseball pension kicked in. He told reporters he didn't feel bitter toward those he felt had wronged him, though he added qualifications. "God said love everybody, which is not easy, because some people are tough," he said in 2018. "I forgive, but I haven't forgotten."

For some years before his death in August 2021, fans and sportswriters conducted an intermittent campaign for the Astros to retire the big righty's number 50. Had he stayed healthy, there wouldn't be any such need: he would have retired with Cy Young Awards, a World Series ring or two, and a spot in the Hall of Fame.

Ray Dandridge

A whole separate "What If" book could be written about the hundreds of players in baseball's segregated era who were barred from the White majors and denied national fame and big salaries because of the color of their skin. Black ballplayers would have altered the majors' pre-1947 history. Who knows what might have happened had, say, the Senators bolstered their lineup by adding Josh Gibson, or had some team thrown a young Satchel Paige against the Ruth-Gehrig Yankees, or had great players like Oscar Charleston, Judy Johnson, Buck Leonard, John Henry Lloyd, Cool Papa Bell, Leon Day, and many, many others not been shunted into a separate and unequal baseball existence. When Jackie Robinson finally busted the color line, more than fifty players from the Negro Leagues followed in his path, among them still-familiar names like Roy Campanella, Monte Irvin, and Minnie Minoso, as well as all-time greats in Ernie Banks, Hank Aaron, and Willie Mays.

In this author's view, the greatest "what if" question among these players hangs over a third baseman from Richmond, Virginia named Ray Dandridge. When Robinson signed with the Dodgers in October 1945, Dandridge had been an all-star shortstop and third baseman for over a decade in the Negro National League, the Caribbean, and Mexico. He didn't look much like a ballplayer, standing a mere five-foot-seven with bowed legs that seemed out of place on an athlete. People routinely described him as "squat." But the looks were deceiving. To the infield, he brought a wide range, a rifle arm, and sure hands; it was said a freight train could pass through his legs, but never a ground ball. Hitting-wise, stats are incomplete, but he is credited with batting averages of .403, .372, and .370 in different seasons. He started with the NNL's Newark Eagles, playing in three East-West all-star games, then decamped for Mexico, where a friendship with league president Jorge Pasquel helped ensure a better salary and good all-around treatment. By the early 1940s, he was in demand year-round, playing games in Cuba, Venezuela, and Puerto Rico when not manning an infield slot for Mexico City or making one of his periodic returns to play for Effa Manley in Newark.

Monte Irvin picked Dandridge as the best third baseman in Negro League history. "He could play third base like Pie Traynor, Brooks Robinson, Mike Schmidt, Graig Nettles, and anybody else you want to name," he said in his book, *Few and Chosen*. Kansas City Monarchs' first baseman Buck O'Neil gave Dandridge the same honor in his book, *I Was Right on Time*. "With Willie Wells at short and [Dandridge] at third, a grounder his against the Eagles had no chance of surviving until the outfield. Ray could hit a little too—line drives every which way." Testimony like that was instrumental in getting Dandridge into the Hall of Fame in 1987.

What makes Dandridge so intriguing is that with different breaks, he could have capped his already-great career with a few years in the major leagues . . . and possibly, a role alongside Jackie Robinson in breaking the color line.

When Robinson signed with the Dodgers in October 1945, Dandridge was thirty-two years old, far past the age of being a "prospect," but not so aged that integration-minded owners and executives could pass him by. He was on the Mexico City Reds at the time, and the Mexican League's raids on American baseball in 1946 raised his profile; suddenly, he was playing with or against well-known major leaguers like Luis Olmo, Max Lanier, and Mickey Owen and began to get mentions in the U.S. mainstream press. "There is a Negro shortstop down here named Dandridge who is sensational," wrote New York columnist Jimmy Powers, attending that year's Mexican League all-star game. *Cleveland Plain Dealer* sports editor Gordon Cobbledick devoted a column to Dandridge during his own visit to the Mexican capital. He said former Cardinals Lanier and Fred Martin had practically hounded him into interviewing Dandridge and raved at length about his infield range and clutch hitting. "Wait a minute," Cobbledick said to them. "You fellows are from the South. How do you feel about playing with a colored boy?"

"Well, I'll tell you," said Martin, "he hasn't asked me to his house for dinner, but I wish there were three more like him in the infield when I'm pitching."

Comments like that apparently got the attention of the man who purchased the Cleveland Indians that summer, Bill Veeck. Veeck, a groundbreaker by nature, ever one to upset the apple cart, wanted to integrate the Indians, both for his passionate belief in equal opportunity and his certainty that it would strengthen the team. He launched a search for candidates. Friends provided scouting reports. Cobbledick was a friend. In all likelihood, Cobbledick praised Dandridge to Veeck. So, according to Dandridge, Veeck contacted him and asked if he'd like to try out for the Indians. He told the story in different ways at different times, but his tellings all came to the same conclusion: he turned Veeck down, mainly because life was good in Mexico. "I thought about it a lot," he said in one 1980 interview. "I was making ten thousand dollars a year. I had two children. I didn't want to rock my boat. So, I said, 'No.'" He added: "It was the spring of 1947, the year the Dodgers called Jackie from Montreal. I can't imagine what my life would have been if I had said yes to Veeck."

Veeck, it should be noted, never confirmed that he tried to sign Dandridge. But later that season, he signed another former Newark Eagle, Larry Doby. A year later, he also signed Satchel Paige. Both players made huge contributions to the Indians 1948 AL pennant and World Series victory.

Developments like eased the way for other Black players into "organized ball," and Dandridge, now ready to take a shot at the majors, signed a minor-league contract with the New York Giants in 1949. He tried to conceal his age, telling the Giants he was twenty-nine instead of thirty-six. Few, if any, insiders were fooled, but he *played* like a youngster. Sent to the Giants' triple-A club, the Minneapolis Millers, he tore apart the American Association, batting .362, the second-highest average in the league. This was against high-quality opposition, mind you; more than fifty pitchers in the league that year had spent or would spend time in the majors, including future notables like Lew Burdette, Harvey Haddix, and Clem Labine. To everyone's surprise, he also became one of the most popular players on the Millers' roster. Meanwhile, in New York, owner Horace Stoneham had integrated the Giants, bringing in Irvin, who was already thirty, and youngster Hank Thompson. All the signs pointed toward "Dandy" getting a shot at the big time in the near future.

It should have happened in 1950. Dandridge continued to lash triple-A pitching, hitting .311, scoring over a hundred runs, playing stonewall defense, and leading the Millers to a first-place finish. At the season's end, he was named American Association MVP. In New York, both Irvin and pitcher Sal Maglie urged club management to bring Dandridge to the majors. The Giants finished a strong third that season, and Maglie, who had played against Dandridge in Mexico, was convinced the veteran could push the team over the top. "I told our scout, 'Why don't you get Dandridge?' He says, 'Too old.' I say, 'What the heck, play him for a month; we could win the pennant.' No, too old. Just bring him up for one month, for crying out loud. Sure, he was old, bowlegged. He'd have helped us; we would've won it."

It could have happened in '51. Early in the year, Dandridge watched as twenty-year-old Willie Mays spent a month in Minneapolis, hit a torrid .477, and got called up to the big club. In July, the Giants also called up the Millers' second baseman, Davey Williams, hitting about forty points lower than Dandridge's .324. A week later, the Giants sent a struggling Thompson, their regular third baseman, down to the minors. That could have been the moment, the golden door opening for Dandridge. Unfortunately, just three days earlier, he had undergone an emergency appendectomy. By the time he was back at full strength, Thompson had regained his batting stroke and was recalled to New York. Dandridge watched from afar as the Giants made up a thirteen-game gap with Brooklyn and won the pennant on Bobby Thomson's "Shot Heard 'Round the World."

It still could have happened in '52. The Giants lost Irvin to a broken ankle and Mays to army service that spring. Calling up Dandridge to play third and letting the younger Thompson and Thomson patrol the outfield would have made sense. But again, the Giants kept him in triple-A. Dandridge later said the Phillies, at the urging of Judy Johnson, asked to purchase his contract that season but that the Giants wouldn't let him go. It remains an unproven claim. At the end of that season, the Giants sold Dandridge, now thirty-nine, to the Sacramento Solons, an independent Pacific Coast League team. He never got anywhere near the majors again.

Why wouldn't the Giants give Dandridge a shot at the big time or just allow him a proverbial "cup of coffee?" Other Negro League stars on the wrong side of thirty—Paige, Irvin, Quincy Trouppe, Willard Brown, Luke Easter, Sam Jethroe—got to experience the thrill and vindication of playing for the leagues that barred them for so long. And the Giants were one of the first and fastest teams to integrate, having five Black players on the roster during the '51 season, including three in the regular lineup.

Part of the problem was that the team wasn't in much need of infield help. Before the '50 season, the Giants had acquired Boston's all-star double-play combination, Eddie Stanky and Alvin Dark, to man second base and shortstop. Hank Thompson was no Dandy with the glove, leading all NL third basemen in errors, but hit .289 with twenty homers, enough to keep his spot at third. When Thompson slumped in '51, Durocher simply moved in Bobby Thomson from the outfield. Given that Bobby hit .440 with nine homers in September and crashed the most famous home run in baseball history, it's hard to find fault with Durocher's move.

In the 1980s, former Giants executive Chub Feeney said the team thought about bringing Dandridge to the majors. "Ray was considered several times, and the strange thing about it was that Horace [Stoneham] loved him," he told author Jules Tygiel. But, he added, "Ray was probably in his early forties, and by that time, we had Henry Thompson and then Bobby Thomson at third base. There just never came a time where there was a real need." Looking back, Feeney said, the Giants could have brought Dandridge up at the end of the season "if we'd recognized the fact that he had felt that need."

Dandridge very much felt that need, and in later years was not shy in expressing his bitterness at never playing in the major leagues. One time, he recalled, Stoneham tried to approach him at an old-timer's game. "I said to Horace Stoneham, right in front of his face, I told Horace, I don't wanna even talk to you. I said, 'You had a chance to sell my contract, you had a chance to bring me up, and everything else, and you wouldn't do it.' I said, 'Onliest thing I wanted to do was hit the *major* leagues. I did everything in the minor leagues that I could do for you, and still, you wouldn't bring me up.' I said, 'You could've called me up even if I stayed up for one week.' You know what Horace told me? He said the reason I didn't let you go, is because you was the drawing power up in Minnesota. That's the break I got."

In one sense, Dandridge got the last laugh. In 1987, the Hall of Fame Veteran's Committee voted him into Cooperstown, an honor that Stoneham to date has been denied. At his induction speech, Dandridge expressed his gratitude but couldn't help but take a last, only half-in-jest poke at baseball's powers-that-be. "I want to sincerely thank each and every veteran on the committee for allowing me to smell the roses," he said. "My only question is: why'd you take so long?"

10

Jackie and the Last Rites

On the most groundbreaking, momentous day in baseball history, Pete Reiser grabbed the headlines—only this time, he didn't really deserve them.

At about 2 P.M. on April 15, 1947, Jackie Robinson slipped on his first baseman's mitt and trotted onto the Ebbets Field grass to make his regular-season debut with the Brooklyn Dodgers. The Braves' leadoff hitter slapped a ground ball to third baseman Spider Jorgensen, Jorgensen fired it to Robinson for the putout—and with that, sixty-three years of racial segregation in the national pastime was officially over. A Black man was playing major league baseball. Never again would his kind be banned from the game. Never again would great young talents be relegated to separate, unequal leagues because of their skin color. Robinson had traveled a rough road during his year in the Dodger organization, getting run out of small Florida towns, hearing calls of "nigger" and "coon" from the stands, living in segregated, substandard housing while his teammates stayed in nice hotels. Just a few weeks earlier, several Dodgers had signed a petition to have him removed from the team.

But Jackie was holding up under pressure and turned in a solid performance that day. He made eleven put-outs and no errors at first base, despite never playing the position until a month earlier. He got no hits but reached base when his speed caused the Braves' Earl Torgeson to mishandle a bunt in the seventh inning, and he soon scored the go-ahead run in what turned out to be an opening day Dodger victory.

All of which makes it baffling, almost incomprehensible, that not one of the ten mainstream daily newspapers New York City boasted in this era chose to shine a spotlight on Robinson's premiere. Instead, the sportswriters built their game stories around the familiar figure of Pistol Pete.

"Dodgers Trip Braves, 5-3; Reiser Is One-Man Show," blared the headline in the city's most widely read paper, the *Daily News*. "Reiser Shows Old-Time Form," said the *Sun*, while the Reiser-centric headline in the *Journal-American* added, "Doubtful Shoulder Passes First Test." The *New York Times* sports page boasted a headline with the game's result and no fewer than four subheads, two of which featured Reiser, and none of which mentioned Robinson. Talk about burying the lead.

The text of the stories was no different. The *Daily News* article by Dick Young didn't mention Robinson until the fifth paragraph. That was better than the story in the *Journal-American*, which didn't refer to him at all, or accounts in other papers, some of which relegated Jackie to paragraph eight, ten, or thirteen. Dodger announcer Red Barber downplayed Jackie too, failing to mention him even once during a fifteen-minute national sports recap that night on CBS radio. But Barber did say, "If Pete Reiser can play a full season, the Dodgers still must be rated among the National League's most formidable teams." It was as if the New York sports media made a collective decision to divert attention away from the landmark sociological change unfolding before their eyes. Whether this reflected a myopic focus on events between the baselines, an act of benign neglect to ease the pressure on Robinson, or a sign of their discomfort with the idea of integration and racial equality in American society . . . that is a subject for another day.

Pete did have a good if not extraordinary afternoon against the Braves and their ace, twenty-game winner Johnny Sain. The first time up, he walked. The second time, he walked and scored the Dodgers' first run. The third time, he singled, dashed to third on a single by Walker, and came home on a groundout. His fourth at-bat was the turning point of the game. With the Dodgers down 3-2, Pete came up in the seventh inning with two outs, Robinson on second base and Stanky on third. He tore into a pitch from Sain, smacking a long drive down the right-field line. There was a moment of suspense: would it stay fair or curve foul? The ball struck the fence above a giant Burma Shave ad, inches left of the foul pole. Fair ball, double, and two runs batted in. Minutes later, Hermanski drove in Pete from third with a sacrifice fly, meaning Pete scored or knocked in all five of the Dodgers' runs that day.

For this, the writers gave him the press box equivalent of a royal salute. "Potentially the best player in the business, Pistol Pete could even mean a pennant if he could escape injury and play every day. He's that good," wrote Michael Gavan in the *Journal-American*. Said Bob Cooke of the *Herald Tribune*: "A number of observers had been attracted by the presence of Jackie Robinson, Brooklyn's

Negro first baseman, but as the innings passed, it was all anyone could do [but] to keep their eyes on Reiser." That's how Cooke's eyes saw it, anyhow. Black fans made up slightly more than half of the twenty-six thousand people who bought tickets to Ebbets Field that day; without question, they were there to see how Jackie fared, not Pete.

After the game, reporters chatted separately with Pete and Jackie, getting their opening day impressions. Pete tried to assure everyone that he was in playing shape after his injury-filled '46 season. "My ankle hurts a little, but up here, I felt good," he said, pointing to the area where his collarbone met his shoulder. He also expressed the belief that his new teammate would soon start getting hits. "He'll be all right," Pete said. "He'll steady down, and he'll be fine."

As for Robinson, he met with reporters on a stool in the corner of the locker room, waiting for the other players to finish their showers before using the facilities himself. He insisted he wasn't nervous or even excited about his major league debut. "I was as loose as could be," he said, though he expressed disappointment that he failed to get a hit. The Dodgers' clubhouse attendant broke in to remind him that Johnny Sain was one of the best pitchers in the league. "If he wasn't, I'm in for a rough season," Robinson said with a grin.

At that moment, Reiser walked past Robinson's stool.

"What a player that man is," Robinson said soon as Reiser was out of earshot. "He's a real one."

To be more precise, those were the words reported at the time. Three decades later, newsman Bill Roeder, who covered the game for the *New York World-Telegram*, expanded on that moment in a souvenir book for the New York Baseball Writers Association. He recalled that reporters naturally wanted to know how Robinson felt about his first game in the majors. He wrote: "The writers are all gathered around Jackie in the clubhouse afterward, waiting for the historic comment, and he looks over toward Pete and says in a tone of awe: 'Does he play like that every day?'"

Maybe in Robinson's mind, the opening day headlines weren't entirely off-target.

* * *

It was something of an achievement for Pete to be playing at all that spring. The off-season had been one long rehab. After the season, he spent six weeks letting his broken ankle heal, getting the cast off in mid-November. Then it was decision time on whether his shoulder required surgery. The Dodgers sent him to three different specialists to get opinions, one of them as always Doc

Hyland in St. Louis. Only Hyland was fully in favor of the operation. Branch Rickey was reported to still be against it, allegedly because he worried the wire used to fix the shoulder separation would permanently inhibit Pete's throwing. Pete told *The Sporting News* he discussed the issue with Rickey's son Branch Jr., who ran the Dodgers' farm system. "He said, 'You can play ball as you are. Why take a chance that you will never be able to play again?'" Pete explained that he didn't look at the surgery like that. "I figured that even if the operation wasn't a complete success, the arm could be no worse than it was," he said.

In the end, Pete got his way, and Hyland performed the surgery on December 17th at St. John's Hospital in St. Louis, reattaching the clavicle to the shoulder blade. After the two-hour operation, Hyland declared it a success. "I am sure that Pete will throw much more effectively next season and without pain," he said. The patient posed for pictures in his hospital bed the next day, with a smile on his face and his right arm in a sling.

This was Pete's third hospital visit in five months, and it helped him win an unusual honor: he was named "sport king" of a fundraising drive to fight polio. "Reiser knows what it is like to be bedridden with limb injuries," explained the chairman of the Brooklyn March of Dimes campaign, "and his courage exemplifies what some polio sufferers are going through."

Pete appreciated the honor and later attended the campaign's kick-off banquet, but he remained unhappy with the real king of sport in Brooklyn, Branch Rickey Sr. Again, he felt the Dodgers general manager was showing callous disregard for his well-being. Talking to reporters the first week in January, Pete said he had not spoken directly to Rickey for over two months, despite repeated long-distance calls to the Dodgers' front office, both before the surgery and after. The silence, he confessed, left him ill at ease. "I'm supposed to be one of the valuable players on the Brooklyn club," he said, "so you'd think they'd show a little interest and ask how I am getting along. That would make me feel better."

"I don't quite get the idea," he added. "Maybe it's because it is getting to be contract time, and they don't want me to think I am too important."

It took a week, but Rickey eventually responded to Pete's remarks. "I understand that Reiser believes we don't care about him. Well, that is far from the truth," he told a reporter, asserting that he had kept in contact with Dr. Hyland and received encouraging reports about Pete's shoulder. He added: "I guess Pete just felt lonely last week. I have helped him in matters outside of baseball in the past and think highly of him." Despite its condescending tone, the comment seemed to calm the waters, and Pete visited Brooklyn at the end of January to let team doctors examine his throwing arm and talk contract with Rickey.

Negotiating face to face with the Mahatma was never easy; no one knew what gears were turning behind those impossibly tall, thick eyebrows or what points he might make with a jab of his fat, ever-present cigar. But after a couple of negotiating sessions, Pete signed for an unspecified raise over his '46 contract, probably in the neighborhood of fifteen thousand dollars, and declared himself satisfied.

That was for the best because Rickey had two much larger issues on his plate as the season drew near. The first was of his own enthusiastic making. Soon after taking control of the Dodgers in 1942, Rickey had launched a secret plan to break baseball's long-unassailable color line. A small but growing army of activists had pressed the sixteen major league teams to integrate for more than a decade. Black sportswriters, led by Wendell Smith of the *Pittsburgh Courier* and Sam Lacy of the *Baltimore Afro-American*, made baseball part of their papers' larger crusade to take down Jim Crow laws. The cause was taken up by the Communist Party, in particular the party's newspaper paper, the *Daily Worker*, which ran dozens of stories on the issue from the late 1930s onward. In 1940, sympathetic unions held rallies outside several big-league ballparks, including all three stadiums in New York City, and by the mid-'40s, politicians in New York and Boston were making noise about penalizing their local clubs unless they reconsidered their hiring practices.

Under pressure, the Red Sox reluctantly gave a tryout at Fenway Park to three Negro League players in 1945. The Pirates and White Sox held perfunctory tryouts as well. Nothing came of it, and at the end of World War II, the world of so-called organized baseball—the National League, the American League, and the affiliated minor league circuits—still had a sign on its door that read Whites Only.

Behind that door, however, Rickey was plotting. During the war, he had his scouts check out exhibitions and military games in which major leaguers played against Negro League stars. He told them to look for Black players who had great baseball skills and possessed the mental toughness to withstand the verbal abuse, possibly physical abuse, that the first player, the trailblazer, would have to face. Gradually, the scouts and Rickey zeroed in on Jack Roosevelt Robinson, a fleet, highly intelligent, and intensely competitive former UCLA football star who in 1945 was playing shortstop for the Negro American League's Kansas City Monarchs. As mentioned, Pete had first laid eyes on Jackie at Fort Riley, where both were stationed in 1943. While Pete was starring in center field for Riley's baseball team, Jackie, a second lieutenant and the morale officer for his "colored" unit, was sparring with senior officers, trying to win basic seating rights for his men at the post exchange.

In 1944, Robinson was transferred to an even more segregated army base, Camp Hood (now Fort Hood) in Texas. There, he ran into what a later generation of civil rights leaders might call "good trouble." It started when he disobeyed a bus driver's order to move to the back of the vehicle. Robinson pointed out, correctly, that a recent War Department order had desegregated military buses. The driver and fellow passengers, accustomed to Negroes being confined to the back seats of public transportation, started yelling insults and threats, but Jackie refused to budge. The matter eventually resulted in Robinson facing a court-martial in August 1944, charged with two counts of insubordination. With the help of a sympathetic lawyer, he proved the charges were both racist and unjustified and was found not guilty on all counts. In a subsequent letter to Truman Gibson, a War Department official who had helped him get into officer school, he wrote, "I don't mind trouble, but I do believe in fair play and justice."

Branch Rickey had found his man. In August 1945, the two had their famous first meeting in Brooklyn, where Rickey tested Robinson by playing out scenarios: an angry opponent throwing a punch, a pitcher hurling fastballs at his head, a southern hotel clerk refusing to give him a room. Robinson asked: "Mr. Rickey, do you want a ballplayer who's afraid to fight back?" Rickey thundered: "I want a ballplayer with guts enough *not* to fight back!"

Convinced Robinson was the right one, the Dodgers signed Robinson in October 1945 to a contract with their top farm team in Montreal. The milestone generated notably different reactions from two of the Dodgers' key players. In St. Louis, newspaperman Vernon Tietjen asked Reiser what he thought about it and reported: "Pete could find no fault with the Dodgers' signing of Jackie Robinson, Negro star. 'If he's good enough, more power to him,' he commented."

In Birmingham, Alabama, a reporter posed the same question to Dixie Walker. Walker pointed out that Robinson had only been signed to a minor-league deal and added, "as long as he isn't with the Dodgers, I'm not worried." The comment, of course, suggested that if Robinson did join the Dodgers, Walker would be one worried man.

Robinson's 1946 season in Montreal was an unqualified success. He won the International League batting title at .349, led his team in runs, hits, and walks, and was the key man in every way as the triple-A Royals cruised to the league title, winning the pennant by nineteen games, and then swept the Little World Series. Even more importantly, from Rickey's perspective, Robinson won the acceptance of his teammates, the Montreal fans, and his Mississippi-born and raised manager Clay Hopper. Rickey had worried about Hopper. During spring training, Rickey and the manager watched a Montreal practice when Robinson made a diving attempt for a ball. Rickey declared that Robinson's effort was superhuman. Hopper replied, "Mr. Rickey, do you really think a nigger is a human being?"

But by season's end, Hopper had come around. "You're a great ballplayer and a fine gentleman," the manager told Robinson. "It's been wonderful having you on the team."

Rickey hoped a similar process would unfold during spring training in 1947 when he planned to ease Robinson onto the big club. He arranged for the Dodgers and Royals to train together, not in segregated Florida but racially mixed Cuba. Not wanting to push too far too fast, Rickey maintained segregation in housing. White players stayed at Havana's deluxe Hotel Nacional, which had a pool, a restaurant, and room service, while Robinson stayed at the dingy Hotel Los Angeles, which had cockroaches. But Robinson played through his anger. When the Dodgers asked him to learn first base, he quickly picked up a basic knack for the position. When the Royals joined the Dodgers for some exhibition games in Panama, he regularly bashed out two or three hits a day. Rickey refused to be nailed down about Robinson's prospects, but others were less cagey. The president of the Montreal club, Hector Racine, said he would not be surprised to see Robinson "go up and stay up." Dodger coach Jake Pitler said Robinson was ready for the majors. "It would be a crime not to bring this boy up because of his color. You ought to see him play first base. He's as much at home on the bag as if he played it all his life," he said.

However, some players didn't like the changes in the air, particularly Dixie Walker. As his nickname implied, Walker was born and raised in the South and made his adult off-season home in Birmingham, where he ran a hardware store. He was used to a segregated world, with Blacks kept separate and unequal. Rickey had hoped that Walker and his teammates would see Robinson as a great ballplayer who could finally bring the Dodgers that elusive world championship. And some players came around to that point of view. But Walker couldn't see past the newcomer's dark skin. Though he sometimes denied it in later years, multiple witnesses said that while the Dodgers were in Panama, Walker initiated a petition to keep Robinson off the team.

According to sportswriter and author Roger Kahn, the petition read, "We the undersigned will not play on the same team as Jackie Robinson." Several established Dodgers allegedly signed it, including Eddie Stanky, Hugh Casey, Kirby Higbe, and Carl Furillo. They were joined by two backups trying to make the team, Dixie Howell and Bobby Bragan. Then the petitioners approached Pete, hoping that his Missouri upbringing was southern enough to make him sympathetic to their cause. He gave them an absolute no.

At least twice later in life, Pete explained his reasoning. In a 1972 interview with the *Pittsburgh Courier*, shortly after Robinson died, he said: "Pee Wee Reese and I were the last ones they came to for signatures. We both refused to sign. My attitude was that if he was capable of playing big-league baseball, he should be allowed to play. I learned my lesson when I was in the service at Fort Riley, and my wife became ill. The only doctor available was a Black man, and he was wonderful. I never forgot it."

Speaking to Donald Honig two years later, Pete changed some details of the story but reached the same conclusion. "I'd had an experience when I was in the Army. This was in Richmond, Virginia," he said. "I'd just been transferred there. My daughter got very sick. So, I looked up a doctor in the phone book. He told me to bring my daughter to the office. The office was in a Negro neighborhood. The doctor was a Negro. I didn't think anything of it. What the hell was the difference? He gave her a shot, penicillin, I think it was, and cured her. I told that story to one of the players who wanted me to sign the petition against Robinson. I said, 'What would you have done?' He said, "I would have turned around and walked away from the neighborhood.' I told him I thought he was a goddamn fool, and then I told him what he could do with his petition."

Pete's daughter Shirley heard the doctor story and confirmed her dad was firmly against segregation and racism. "He grew up in North St. Louis, very integrated. He didn't grow up with those preconceived racial bigotry feelings. I don't think it would even enter his mind," she says.

As Pete mentioned, the petitioners also got a thumbs-down from his pal Pee Wee Reese, a native of Louisville, Kentucky. Reese later explained: "I wasn't trying to think of myself as being the great White father, really. I just wanted to play the game, especially after being in the Navy for three years and needing the money, and it didn't matter to me whether [Robinson] was black or green. He had a right to be there too."

The petition lost momentum after Higbe drank at a local bar and muttered some words about it to the team's traveling secretary, Harold Parrott. Parrott told Durocher, who proceeded to call a late-night meeting of all the players in the kitchen of the team's hotel. Wearing pajamas and a yellow bathrobe, Durocher tore into the petitioners and made it clear, in his salty way, that skin color would be no barrier on any team of his. "I don't care if a guy is yellow or black or if he has stripes like an f---ing zebra. I'm the manager of this team, and I say he plays,"

Durocher said. He told the players that Robinson was "going to put money in your pockets and money in mine." As for Walker and his pals, he said they could take their petition and—this is an exact quote—"wipe your ass with it!"

The manager's stand, recreated for the Jackie Robinson biopic *42*, brought the ban-Robinson movement on the team to a screeching halt. On the eve the season, *Pittsburgh Courier* sports editor Wendell Smith praised Leo for his open-mindedness. "He seems to be all for Robinson," Smith wrote. "He does not care what color he is or anything else . . . Robinson will not have a lot of trouble with him. Durocher is definitely in his corner."

In the same column, Smith, who had traveled with the Dodgers throughout the spring as Robinson's roommate and confidant, gave his take on what some key players thought of Jackie:

"Eddie Stanky: He appears to be prejudiced but will play with him."

"Pee Wee Reese: He will play. His attitude is not known, nor has it been revealed in any way."

"Arky Vaughn: He will go along with the mob. If they want Robinson, he will be for him. If they are against him, Vaughn will be too."

"Dixie Walker: He is against Robinson. Would rather have him elsewhere. But will tolerate him because he (Walker) is one of the highest-paid players in the majors."

"Pete Reiser: A great ball player. He will play with anyone."

Unfortunately for Rickey, he had a second major issue to deal with that spring, and it was Durocher himself. For years, Leo had flirted with undeniably bad kinds of trouble. In June 1945, he was arrested for allegedly assaulting and breaking the jaw of a fan who had heckled him from the stands. A friendly Brooklyn jury acquitted him, but Durocher had to pay nearly seven thousand dollars to settle a civil suit. The following year, baseball officials grew concerned about the Dodger manager's off-field association with gamblers like bookmaker Max "Memphis" Engleberg and mob figures like Bugsy Siegel and the actor George Raft. As far back as 1941, Judge Landis had advised Durocher to steer away from such types, lest anyone think they might persuade Leo to throw a game. The concerns re-emerged in 1946 when Raft, a particularly close pal of Durocher's, was accused of hosting a rigged craps game in Leo's New York apartment when Leo was away at spring training. One player allegedly lost ten thousand dollars, very heavy money in the 1940s.

Rickey, hoping to rein in his wayward manager, asked baseball's new commissioner, former U.S. Senator Happy Chandler, to scare Durocher straight. At a face-to-face meeting in November 1946, Chandler told Leo to avoid Raft and several other undesirables. Durocher agreed to do so, albeit reluctantly. "They'll call me a louse, but I'll do it," he said.

Leo's reputation took another hit that winter due to his relationship with Hollywood actress Laraine Day. The Durocher/Day affair is a complicated, seamy tale not worth recounting in full detail here. In short, Day's husband of five years accused Durocher of seducing his wife inside the couple's West Hollywood home. Day had wanted to leave her husband anyway, and in January 1947, a California judge granted her a divorce, with the stipulation that she not remarry until the provisional decree became final in one year. The actress flouted the ruling, getting a second divorce in Mexico the next day and marrying Durocher a few hours later. The California judge threatened to annul his ruling, raising the possibility that Day would be married to two men simultaneously, one of whom was the manager of the Brooklyn Dodgers.

In Brooklyn, the Catholic Youth Organization—a strong supporter of the Dodgers' Knothole Gang program for kids—threatened to boycott the team because of Durocher's "moral looseness." Rickey voiced support for his manager, and the storm might have blown over. But Durocher stirred the pot yet again in March when he accused his old boss Larry MacPhail, now general manager of the Yankees, of playing host to a pair of prominent gamblers at an exhibition game in Havana. "Where does MacPhail come off flaunting his company with known gamblers right in the players' faces? If I even said hello to one of those guys, I'd be called up before Commissioner Chandler and probably barred," he told the ever-present Dick Young.

Leo had pissed off one too many authority figures one too many times. After an investigation that found MacPhail innocent, Chandler announced on April 9th that Durocher was suspended for the entire 1947 season. Chandler did not specify the reasons for banning Leo, except to say it was "a result of the accumulated unpleasant incidents in which he has been involved."

The news sparked a public outcry in Brooklyn, where Leo was very much the face of the Dodgers. Many players didn't like it either. "I hate like hell to see him go," said Higbe. "I just wish Leo could be with us," said Reese. Pete commented, too, suggesting the players would stay loyal to Durocher even while another manager took his place. "I'm pretty sure," he said, "the club will hustle for Leo whether he's with us or not."

* * *

Pete had exchanged the '27' on the back of his uniform for a lucky '7' and seemed to have good fortune on his season as the season began. Opening day, as noted, he got on base all four times he came to bat. Day two, he banged out singles in the first, second, and fourth innings, coming around to score twice, as the Dodgers built an early eight-run lead over the Braves and cruised to a 12-6 victory. However, success came with a warning sign: he had to leave the game in the seventh when his left ankle swelled up. Carl Furillo filled the gap in center field, with rookie Duke Snider taking over in left.

A few days later, Dick Young gave *Daily News* readers their first medical update on Pete of the 1947 season, and it was not good. Pete's ankle, he reported, was swollen to twice its normal size. But, he added, the owner of the ailing joint refused to consider sitting down. "Sure, it hurts during the game," Pete said. "But the doctors tell me I can't do any permanent harm by playing, so I'll keep right on. Staying out for a week won't cure it." Indeed, Pete was in the lineup as the Dodgers swept a three-game set from the Phillies, racking up four hits and three walks while making so many running, sensational catches in the finale, a 2-0 squeaker, that Harold Burr called him a one-man outfield.

That said, '47 Pete wasn't the Pete of the year before. The ankle, which team trainer Harold Wendler heavily taped before every game, was slowing him down. Against the Phils, he was thrown out trying to go from first to third on a Dixie Walker hit. Two days later, he was called out on his first attempt of the season to steal home. The day after that, he drove in a runner from first with a two-bagger but was cut down again as he tried to extend it to a triple.

"Though he still covers considerable ground in center field and has come up with a couple of corking catches, he seems to have lost, temporarily at least, that vital extra step which is the difference between a steal and an out," Young wrote.

The loss of that extra step didn't hurt the Dodgers as much as it might have because of the new guy on the club. Jackie Robinson wasn't setting the National League afire with his bat in the early going. He batted just .225 in April and went hitless in twenty-five straight plate appearances at the end of the month. "Robinson's Job in Jeopardy," read a headline in the *New York Sun*. But Rickey remained supportive partly because when Robinson did get on base, he was putting pressure on the opposition, much like Reiser had in '46. In the fifth game of the season, the Dodgers and Phillies were locked in a scoreless tie entering the bottom of the eighth. Robinson led off the inning with a short but well-placed poke that landed in center for a single. With Reiser batting, he took a long lead off first and dashed for a second on a three-two pitch. Pete swung and missed for strike three, but catcher Andy Seminick fumbled the ball, then threw wildly into center field. Robinson bounced up from his slide and scampered to third. Minutes later, Gene Hermanski's single drove him in. It was the only run in the team's 1-0 victory.

The rookie's speed and skills drew quick praise from the Dodgers' new manager. Two games into the season, Rickey had hired Burt Shotton, a former coach and minor-league manager within the Cardinal system, to replace Durocher. Shotton remarked a few days later: "The first time I watched Robinson go down to first base, I didn't think he could run . . . Then I saw him go careening around the bases and changed my mind. That boy can travel." He added: "He makes 'em pitch to him and doesn't go after many bad balls. I've noticed too that he's a good hitter with two strikes on him."

Bespectacled, sixty-two-year-old Burt Shotton was probably the perfect manager for Robinson as he went through the crucible of being the majors' first Black player. Shotton was low-key, amiable, and dignified—dignified to the point where he chose to manage from the dugout in street clothes rather than don a Dodger uniform. Dick Young referred to him as KOBS, which stood for Kindly Old Burt Shotton. This was fine with Robinson; the last thing he needed right then was a manager who stirred up tension and anger a la Durocher, and he appreciated that Shotton was patient with him as he struggled at the plate. Other Dodgers weren't so enamored with their new leader. They felt Shotton lacked Durocher's ability to fire up players or outsmart the other team.

That group included Reiser, who declared himself more than once to be a "Durocher man." In fact, the day after Durocher's suspension, Pete was photographed shaking his hand in the Dodger clubhouse as Leo said his goodbyes for the season. Shotton couldn't possibly miss the signals, and from the start, his relationship with Pete veered between lukewarm and sour, though he publicly lauded Pete's abilities. It counted as one more pulled string in the fraying relationship between Pete and between the Dodger front office.

The Dodgers thrived under Shotton at first, opening the season with ten wins in thirteen games. Then they hit reverse and lost ten of fourteen, slipping from first place to fourth. The controversy around Robinson was proving to be a distraction. In Philadelphia, Phillies manager Ben Chapman had his players unleash a volley of racial insults so crude and nasty that even Stanky, no supporter of Robinson's, yelled at Chapman to knock it off. In St. Louis, several Cardinal players allegedly discussed going on strike rather than take the field with Robinson; NL President Ford Frick sent a warning, and the strike talk fizzled, but not before the story blew sky high in the papers. In New York, the police announced they were investigating death threats that had been mailed to Jackie. "At least two letters of a nature that I felt called for investigation were received by Robinson," Rickey confirmed. No attacks materialized, but Jackie remained understandably on edge, worried someone might take a shot from the stands or harm his wife and baby son.

It would be false to say that Robinson's teammates were befriending him or giving him support in his time of need. But Wendell Smith of the *Pittsburgh Courier* noted this small exchange: "Pete Reiser went out of his way to introduce Jackie to his father in the dressing room in St. Louis. Pete's father told Robbie he was glad to meet him and wished him luck."

Amid the turmoil, Pete continued to play good, if slightly erratic ball. Case in point: May 10th, Dodgers vs. Phillies at Shibe Park. Pete hit a solo homer in the first inning to give the Dodgers a 1-0 lead. Two innings later, he gave it right back, badly misplaying a drive to deep center by Andy Seminick and letting the Phillies' catcher rumble around the bases for an inside-the-park home run. In the eighth, Pete singled to fuel a rally that put the Dodgers ahead again. But after advancing to third, he tried to swipe home on a double steal with Dixie Walker and was thrown out by several feet.

There were other days when Pete was still, as Durocher liked to call him, the difference. May 21st in St. Louis, the Cardinals and Dodgers played another one of their tight, tense games, going into extra innings with the score tied 3-3. With one out in the top of the tenth, Pete slashed a single to center and moved to second on another hit by Furillo. Walker popped up for the second out, but Lavagetto came through and smacked a liner into left field. Running on contact, Reiser zipped around third and headed for home. Arriving at the plate just ahead of the incoming throw, he uncorked one of his trademark fadeaway slides to get past catcher Joe Garagiola. It worked beautifully—so beautifully that Pete's outstretched hand missed home plate as he slid by. Fortunately, Garagiola didn't notice, and while the young catcher shifted his focus to the other Dodger runners, Pete darted back to the plate and touched it for what would be the winning run.

As the calendar turned to June, both Pete and the Dodgers remained somewhat stuck in second gear. But then, so was the whole National League. The defending champion Cardinals had gotten off a shockingly bad start, dropping eleven of their first thirteen games and plunging into the NL cellar, where they stayed for weeks. They were handicapped by a lack of production from their slugger, Stan Musial, who insisted on playing despite an inflamed appendix. Doc Hyland oddly recommended that Stan try an old-fashioned treatment and "freeze" the appendix by applying ice bags to his abdomen. It worked in the sense that the organ didn't burst, and Musial continued to breathe. But a weakened Stan ended May with a puny .198 batting average. As the Cardinals stumbled, the Giants, a team of prodigious home run production, so-so pitching, and a pronounced lack of foot speed, took hold of first place. The Braves, Cubs, and Dodgers trailed close behind, with none of the teams much above .500.

The evening of June 4th rolled around with Pete and friends hoping to gain ground against the Pirates, another team with lots of power and not much else. The day before, the Dodgers swept the Bucs in an afternoon doubleheader at Ebbets Field. Pete had to be happy with the wins but frustrated by his own play. In game one, he went hitless. In game two, he contributed an RBI triple in the fifth inning but was thrown out again as he tried to steal home. Burr noted his failure in the next day's *Daily Eagle*. "Pete Reiser isn't getting the jump on the pitcher he did last year," he wrote.

The whole Dodger lineup jumped all over starter Elmer Singleton that night, running up an early 7-2 lead, the key blow being a grand slam by Reese. On the mound, Ralph Branca was more or less cruising along, giving up only two hits through five innings—one a homer by budding superstar Ralph Kiner, the other a homer by Hank Greenberg, who the Tigers had sold to the Pirates during the off-season.

Branca retired the first hitter he faced in the sixth, Billy Cox, on a routine popup. Next up: thirty-three-year-old journeyman outfielder Culley Rikard. The '47 season was Rikard's first taste of the majors in five years, after time in the military and the minors. He normally wasn't seen as a threat but had recently earned a spot in the Pirates' lineup with a hot bat. The day before, he banged out four hits off four different Dodger pitchers.

Branca worked him to a count of three balls, two strikes, then fired a pitch that Rikard walloped and sent sailing toward the center-field wall. The only man between the ball and the barrier: Pete Reiser.

The reporters on hand described what happened next in gripping, chilling detail:

> Dick Young, *New York Daily News*: "Back flew Reiser, his eyes glued to the ball as he raced closer and closer to the wall. 'Look out!' warned scattered cries from the stands. But Pete, with characteristic disregard for all walls, never reduced speed."
>
> Herbert Goren, *New York Sun:* "The ball was hit on a line directly over his head, and he raced back with the drive, sticking up his gloved hand and making the grab at the moment his head struck the concrete."
>
> Harold C. Burr, *Brooklyn Daily Eagle*: "Reiser dashed back and intrepidly made the catch. But suddenly, he was seen to crumple at the base of the wall and lie still."

Carl Lundquist, United Press: "Reiser was unconscious when teammates reached him. But still clutched firmly in his globe was the ball he risked his neck to catch."

Vince Johnson, *Pittsburgh Post-Gazette*: "After Rikard had trotted around the paths, umpire Butch Henline, who had investigated the catch, told plate umpire Bill Stewart the ball had been legally caught. Stewart called Rikard out. There was no protest from the Pirate bench."

Burr, *Daily Eagle*: "Gene Hermanski was the first to reach Pistol Pete, lying there so ominously still. He took the ball from Pete's unresisting hand. Dixie Walker came rushing up and knelt down, his own uniform quickly stained with Reiser's blood from a wicked V-shaped cut on his forehead."

Al Laney, *New York Herald Tribune*: "The crowd, which watched silently while Reiser was being carried away, did not know he had held on to the ball until two outs were posted on the scoreboard after play was resumed. Then they let out a tremendous roar."

Young, *Daily News*: "And while the comparatively meaningless ballgame continued, Pete was being worked on under the stands. At first, it appeared Pete had argued with the wall once too often. As club physician Dominick Rossi made a nimble precursory examination of the bleeding skull, two priests were summoned . . . Through the partially open door, one priest could be observed in the foreboding administration of the last rites—it was that frightening, at first."

It was probably the closest a major leaguer had come to dying because of an on-field injury since Cleveland's Ray Chapman was fatally beaned in 1920. However, Reiser soon woke up, very much alive, though not feeling well. Someone handed him a cigarette, which he smoked ("shakily," according to Burr) while waiting for an ambulance to take him to Swedish Hospital, five minutes away on Bedford Avenue. Dr. Rossi said there was no skull fracture, a diagnosis confirmed by X-rays at the hospital. Instead, he had another concussion, along with cuts and lacerations to his scalp.

The "meaningless" game continued to the end, with young Duke Snider replacing Reiser in center field and the Dodgers hanging on for a 9-4 victory. After the game, the Dodgers talked about their fallen teammate in hushed tones.

"He was bleeding pretty badly," Walker said. "Sure gave me a fright when I raced out there. I still have some of the blood on my uniform. When I got out there, Pete was conscious, and he was saying, 'Hell, fellas,' as if he was terribly sorry he had let us down."

Of course, Reiser hadn't let the team down; he had just made a tremendous catch. Or had he? Here, some chicanery enters the story, enough to make even Leo Durocher or a trashcan-banging Houston Astro blush.

Reiser himself always said he caught the ball, though he admitted his information was second-hand. Right after the collision, he talked to reporters and said, "I don't even remember making the catch." Years later, he told the *Los Angeles Times*, "I took off and caught the ball and, they told me later, held onto it." Still another time, he said, "The remarkable thing was that somehow I held on to the ball and kept Cully Rikard from getting an inside [the park] homer."

However, two key witnesses said that, in reality, Pete *dropped* the ball after slamming into the concrete.

So, who fooled the umpires into thinking he had caught it?

Who else? The witnesses.

Dodger left fielder Gene Hermanski claimed responsibility several times, most extensively in an interview with baseball researcher Rod Roberts.

> "Someone hits a hell of a shot towards center. I broke [toward the ball], I knew I couldn't get it. If anybody could get it, Pete could. Pete's running like hell, boom boom boom boom. He jumps up, and the ball hits his glove. As the ball hits his glove, his head hits the concrete, and he drops. Now the ball trickled along down the wall, almost like water, and it lands between the wall and Pete. And Pete's cradled, so no one can see the ball—really the God's honest truth. So, I'm in there within seconds, I see the ball, I get the ball, put it in his glove. Meantime, I know he's hurt, cause he's out cold, smashed his head against that damn wall. But within three four seconds, the umpire's out there, he looks and goes "OUT!" Calls the batter out."

Telling the same tale to Pete's son-in-law Rick Tuber, Hermanski added: "That's one of the best things I did in baseball."

However, . . . the Dodgers' right fielder that day, Dixie Walker, later insisted *he* was the one who pulled off the sleight of hand. "I got to Pete first and saw the ball laying near his glove," Walker said shortly before his death from cancer in 1982. "Nobody was nearby, so I just put it in his mitt. When Pittsburgh manager Billy Herman ran up, he asked, 'Did he catch it?' and I said, 'Look in his glove.'" In the end, Reiser got credit for the putout, credit that perhaps should be reassigned to Hermanski and Walker, a half-putout each.

Burt Shotton, flashing the usual Dodger indifference to injury, predicted his concussed outfielder would be back in the lineup in about a week. Rickey's assistant Arthur Mann said he would be released from the hospital within a day. But the next afternoon, Pete was still at Swedish Hospital and uncharacteristically stayed there for another four days. In later life, Pete claimed that he was paralyzed for ten days after the crash. That certainly wasn't true, but it may be that for once, Pete listened to good advice and let himself rest so he could start to recover. When he did leave the hospital on June 9th, he did not attempt to force his way back into the lineup, although he did attend the Dodgers-Reds game that night at Ebbets Field, watching the action in street clothes from behind the Brooklyn dugout.

Asked about his condition the next day, Reiser told the *Times*, "'I'm just sore all over. My left side, my neck, my left wrist—everywhere. Haven't had any headaches, but I've had a kind of groggy feeling." Despite that status report, Pete was still facing pressure for a fast return. On June 12th, ahead of a four-game series in St. Louis, the *Daily Eagle* reported that "Manager Burt Shotton is anxious to have his injured outfielder in the lineup against the Cardinals." Pete may have been willing but proved unable to ease Shotton's anxieties, sitting out the entire series with shoulder pain and dizzy spells.

In his place, Shotton played a twenty-year-old who was in just his third season of professional baseball. In the future, Duke Snider would turn into a consistent forty-homer-a-year man, annual all-star, and the cleanup hitter for one of baseball's most famous teams, the "Boys of Summer" Dodgers of the early and mid-1950s, winner of five National League pennants. In 1947 however, Snider was green as an avocado from his native California, and with him batting third and playing center, the Dodgers dropped four in a row to the Cardinals by a cumulative, unsettling score of 31-8.

Shotton said of Snider during the series: "He's done better than I expected, but you just can't replace Reiser and get the same value. I can do things with Pete as a hitter, runner, and fielder that I can't do with any other player. He knows how to win ball games."

The manager's hope for a quick comeback by Pete was further dashed when the Dodgers, licking their wounds, arrived at Wrigley Field on the 16th for a three-game series with the Cubs. It was kind of a freak thing; Pete was standing in the outfield before the first game, just chatting with Carl Furillo, when relief pitcher Clyde King inadvertently barreled into the pair as he ran after a fly ball during warmups. Reiser got the worst of the collision, getting knocked to the ground and taking another jolt his aching body and head didn't need.

In later years, Pete said the collision with King caused a blood clot inside his skull and that he was flown to Johns Hopkins Hospital in Baltimore the next day for an emergency operation. It appears that, again, Pete was telling tall tales. He did go to Hopkins, but not until June 24th, after his concussion symptoms persisted, and after the cut on his head became infected. When he finally went, there was no surgery for a blood clot, which would require, at minimum, several days of hospitalization followed by two or three months of recovery. Instead, he was examined by neurologist Dr. James Arnold, who ordered him to go home to St. Louis and take it easy for two weeks. Arnold told reporters that Pete's concussion was "not serious enough to warrant hospitalization" but added that his dizzy spells made a period of rest advisable.

The Dodgers didn't put up a squawk for a change, and Pete spent the next fortnight at home in St. Louis with Pat and Sally, doing little except taking his daughter on daily walks to a nearby park. He did give an interview on July 7th to a St. Louis newspaper, in which he swore that he was following doctors' orders to stay away from ballfields. "That's why they sent me home," he said. "They didn't want me watching games. I get too anxious, too irritable, and itchy. I want to get right back in there and play." He admitted that after a month out of action, he wasn't fully recovered—he still felt dizzy any time he changed positions quickly, even when he sat up in bed. But he added, "I'm feeling better all the time."

Not surprisingly, he also called for the installation of a warning track at Ebbets Field. "The best thing they could do," he said, "is to build a cinder path about three or four feet wide, about ten feet from the fence. As soon as your spikes touch the path, you'll subconsciously break stride, and while you may still hit the fence, it won't be head-on." The Cubs had installed such a path at Wrigley Field, he said, "and I've never had any trouble there."

The day after Reiser's crash, the newspapers had been full of calls for the Dodgers to make Ebbets Field safe for outfielders, and Arthur Mann announced the Dodgers were considering some protective measures. The team might install rubber padding on the concrete walls, he said, or lay down a cinder path of the kind Pete suggested. But after about a week, the talk and the stories faded away, and nothing changed, not in the short run anyway. As for Pete's safety, Rickey had an alternate plan. "We are going to ask Pete to wear a helmet in the field," the Mahatma said.

* * *

Pete returned to Brooklyn on July 9th, after two weeks at home, after five weeks of rest in all. It was the longest recovery period he'd ever enjoyed after a concussion, and in retrospect, it may not have been enough. But at least Rickey and Shotton let it happen. Maybe they didn't rush Pete back sooner because an unexpected thing was happening in his absence: the Dodgers were playing great ball.

For several seasons, going back to 1941, fans, coaches, sportswriters, and players alike had looked at Pistol Pete as the premium fuel in the Dodger engine. With him in the lineup, the thinking went, the club was a pennant winner. Without him, the Dodgers were something less; not the Daffiness Boys of yore necessarily, just . . . bums. That mindset held after Pete's June 4th crash, when the club dropped seven of ten games, including the debacle in St. Louis, falling from a first-place tie to fourth, albeit only three games off the league lead.

But as soon as Pete went down, other Dodgers stepped up. On the day Clyde King smashed into Pete, the team broke a five-game losing streak with a 2-1 victory. Snider drove in one run, and Jackie Robinson drove in the other. The victory launched a streak in which the team won twenty of twenty-six games, reclaiming first place. Snider struggled and was returned to the minors for more seasoning, but Furillo stepped in and played a capable center field while keeping his batting average over .300. Walker, Spider Jorgensen, and Robinson were also hitting, Reese and Stanky were turning double plays, and an underwhelming pitching staff stabilized when Branca caught fire and won several complete-game victories starting in mid-June. Amid the winning, the tension between Robinson and the team's southern contingent receded, although it never entirely went away.

And quietly but definitively, the Dodgers began to move on from Pete Reiser.

In terms of offense, it was Jackie Robinson who filled Pete's shoes. Facing the enormous pressure of being the first "Negro" player in the majors, forced to hold his tongue in the face of unrelenting taunts, and playing an unfamiliar position to boot, Robinson's bat had been relatively quiet in the early weeks of the season. By Memorial Day, he was hitting just .264, and it was an empty .264, with just six extra-base hits. But the minute Reiser went down, Robinson raised his game to a higher level. On June 5th, he homered and got two other hits in a 3-0 win over the Cubs. The next day, he broke open the game with a bases-loaded single that drove in two runs, then created two more when he gunned for second base and drew a wild throw, allowing Eddie Stanky and himself to storm home.

On June 11th, Robinson enjoyed his best game yet as a Dodger, stroking four hits against the Reds, including a double and a triple. The one time he didn't bat safely, he laid down a sacrifice bunt that advanced Stanky to second and set up the Dodgers' first run. The Dodgers lost, but the perfect day pushed Robinson's batting average above the prized .300 mark. "Jackie Robinson tried to beat the Reds in yesterday's getaway game at Ebbets Field all by himself," wrote Harold Burr in the next day's *Daily Eagle*.

The rookie's hitting was only half the story. From day one, he had used his speed and aggressive baserunning to help manufacture runs. Now he stepped up the pressure whenever he got on base, taking giant leads, feinting once, feinting twice like he was going to steal, darting back to the bag when the pickoff throw came in but repeating the dance as soon the ball was returned to the pitcher. It was partly a psychology game meant to worry and distract the other team in hopes of provoking a balk, a wild pitch, an error . . . anything to help the Dodgers score. And it was reminiscent of the pre-broken ankle Pete Reiser.

Robinson completed the impression against Pittsburgh on June 24th. Standing on third, he broke for home as pitcher Fritz Ostermueller went through a long, complicated windup. Alerted by the crowd's roar, Ostermueller quickly fired the ball to catcher Dixie Howell. "The ball actually beat Robinson to the plate by a split second, but Jackie zipped across the plate with a beautiful hook slide to the inside of the diamond just ahead of Howell's forward lunge," reported Dick Young. The theft of home broke a tie, and the Dodgers went on to win 4-2.

A little more than a week later, Jackie's number one tormentor, Phillies manager Ben Chapman, uttered words that must have pained him to say, even though they were true. "Robinson is the principal factor keeping the Brooklyn Dodgers in the pennant race," Chapman told reporters. "He can run, hit, is fast, and is quick with the ball."

So, when Pete rejoined the team, the Dodgers were happy—"It's what the doctor ordered," Shotton said—but didn't rush him back into the lineup. Pete took batting practice for a few days, then made three pinch-hitting appearances. Not until July 15th did Shotton reinstall him in center field. He played both ends of a doubleheader, getting a hit and RBI in each game, and made it through the day without re-injuring himself. "He came close to the wall once to make a catch of a long fly but didn't bump his cranium, although the concrete was seen to shrink back defensively," joked Burr.

After six weeks of rest, some players might be rusty, but the long layoff seemed to revitalize Pete. His ankle was stronger, his right shoulder less troublesome. To Rickey's relief and surprise, he was finally able to play the large majority of the Dodgers' games, batting third and ably covering either left or center field. Better still, he hit. In the first fifty games after his return, he batted .364, easily the best on the club over that stretch. His best day was probably a July 27th doubleheader in Pittsburgh. In front of an overcapacity crowd of forty-two thousand, he reached base seven times (via five hits and two walks), scored four runs, and crunched his first post-concussion homer, a shot over Forbes Field's new, shortened wall in left field, dubbed "Greenberg Gardens" for the slugger it was intended to benefit. The Dodgers swept the twin bill, in fact, swept everything in the latter part of July, reeling off a thirteen-game winning streak, all but two of the wins on the road. It's still the second-longest streak in Dodger franchise history. They capped it off with a three-game sweep of the Cardinals in St. Louis, no doubt with an assortment of Reisers young and old watching from the stands.

But . . . those crowds weren't seeing the same Pete Reiser as before the war, or even before the broken ankle. This Pete was less of a pistol. He got fewer extra-base hits, drove in fewer runs, stole fewer bases. The whip swing was still there, but the ball didn't travel as far. He still ran plenty fast, but the *dangerous* speed had not returned. There were no steals of home, not even any steals of third. He caught most of the balls hit his way but seldom threw out a runner, rarely made a spectacular grab. The oooh-and-ahh side of his game had disappeared, wiped away by the concussions and broken bones. Accordingly, the newspapermen stopped referring to him as the best player in the National League. From July onward, he noticeably receded from the headlines.

When he did get attention, it was usually for a fresh injury. On July 21st, he made a diving attempt to catch a long drive off the bat of the Reds' Babe Young. He missed and landed heavily on his left shoulder. Doc Wendler jogged out to center after Young circled the bases. "I think it's dislocated," Pete said, grimacing with pain. It was. Wendler, who had worked with football teams and was familiar with this type of injury, snapped the shoulder back into place right there in the outfield. Pete gritted it out for another three innings before the pain forced him to leave the game. A year earlier, he had separated his right shoulder; now, he had dislocated his left. Both troubled him for the rest of his career and beyond.

The effects of the June concussion also lingered. On August 6th in Boston, Pete experienced dizzy spells and misplayed two fly balls "like a deserter from

Alcoholics Anonymous" (Dick Young's words), giving the Braves a double, a triple, and two undeserved runs. "I know I played both of them badly, but the grandstand was spinning like a merry-go-round," Pete explained after the game. He sat out for one day, then returned for a weekend series against the Phillies, where he went six-for-thirteen.

Pete wasn't even safe running the basepaths. During a September 9th game in Chicago, charging down the first base line to beat out a slow roller, he crashed into the Cubs' Eddie Waitkus—and took a knee to the groin area. He was down for five minutes but somehow stayed in the game.

A year earlier, such injuries would have caused wails and handwringing among the Brooklyn populace. Now they were met with a shrug. The Dodgers simply weren't as dependent on Pete as before. If anything, they were sailing toward the pennant. The long winning streak in July had put them in front by ten games.

The race wasn't quite over. As Stan Musial regained his strength and returned to his hard-hitting ways, the Redbirds surged into second place in August and shortened the gap. They got their best opportunity to close it when the Dodgers pulled into St. Louis for a three-game series on September 11th. Some eleven hundred Brooklynites made the thousand-mile journey to cheer on their Bums, leading by five games with sixteen to go.

The Cardinals jumped out to a 2-0 lead in the opener, only to see Jackie Robinson tie it up with a two-run homer in the fifth. The game was still tied in the seventh when Jorgensen doubled, and Robinson walked with two out. Up came Pete. Hitting against Howie Pollet, always a tough customer, he lined a single to right to drive in the go-ahead run. The Dodgers went on to win 4-3.

The Cardinals rebounded to take the second game and needed the third to stay within striking distance. The Dodgers upset those plans, bashing out nineteen hits, the last one a single from Pete in the top of the ninth that drove in Stanky and gave the visitors an 8-4 lead. The insurance run proved to be huge. In the last of the ninth, Musial led off by lofting a fly to center field. Pete ran in a few steps, stopped, then began to wave his arms; he had lost the ball in the late afternoon sun. It dropped an embarrassing twenty feet behind him, and Musial motored to third with a triple. The next batter popped a short fly behind second base. Stanky faded back, but he too lost the ball in the glare; it fell for a single, allowing Musial to score. After Slaughter grounded out, Terry Moore hit a grounder toward third. Jorgensen reached out to glove the ball, only to see it take a bad-hop bounce over his arm and into left. Another single. The next batter lifted a high fly to right-center. Both Reiser and Walker converged on the area, but the sun still had the upper hand. The ball dropped for yet another single, and the Cardinals had the bases loaded.

Shotton changed pitchers while the Dodgers caught their breath and wondered if the heavens and earth were conspiring against them. New hurler Hank Behrman struck out Joe Garagiola for the second out. But pinch hitter Red Schoendienst smacked a line-drive single that made the score 8-7. That brought up Erv Dusak with the tying run on third. Dusak swung at Behrman's first pitch and drove a fly toward the wall in right. Thirty-three thousand fans held their breath as Walker, fighting the sun again, faded back, reached out for the ball—and caught it. The game was over, and in essence, so was the pennant race.

The Dodgers officially clinched the pennant on the night of September 22nd, an off-day on the schedule. Hugh Casey had recently opened up a restaurant and tavern on Flatbush Avenue in Brooklyn. Several players and wives or girlfriends were enjoying a late dinner when word came through that the Cardinals had lost to the Cubs, mathematically eliminating them from the race. Brooklyn exploded into a late-night party, with thousands milling and cheering and parading in the streets around the restaurant. The front page of the next day's *Daily Eagle* showed a half-dozen Dodgers and their companions dancing in a conga line led by an accordion player, among them a very happy-looking Pete and Pat Reiser.

Pete didn't care that the Dodgers won the pennant on an off-day. "It's good no matter when it comes," he said. "This time, people were saying to me, 'You don't want to back in, do you?' I said I'll take it any way they want to give it to me. It's been a long year."

In 1946, Pete's play during the season and his absence at the end were seen as deciding factors in the Dodgers' drive for the pennant. In 1947, no one suggested he was the main man. When he played, he was still very good. His final batting average of .309 topped the Brooklyn regulars, and his .415 on-base percentage would have ranked fifth-best in the NL had he batted more often and qualified for the league leaders. But there was a decline that couldn't be ignored. His crash into the wall and the now-usual array of other mishaps limited him to just one hundred ten games and four hundred sixty-two times at-bat. His fourteen stolen bases ranked second in the league, but his eleven failed steal attempts ranked first. He hit only five home runs, his lowest total since 1940, and drove in only forty-eight, a steep drop from his '46 total. The drop in RBI was partly attributable to clutch hitting, or lack thereof. In 1946, Pete had batted .347 with two outs and runners in scoring position. In the same situation a year later, he hit just .250.

At the same time, the team around him was stronger. Reese, Furillo, Branca, and Hermanski all significantly improved on their '46 performances. Jorgensen had filled the void at third. Bruce Edwards was a workhorse behind the plate. And at first base, Jackie Robinson withstood the pressures heaped on his back and produced an outstanding year. Playing in all but three games, Jackie batted .297, led the team in homers (12), total bases (252), and runs (125), and topped the National League in stolen bases with twenty-nine, including three steals of home. That November, the Baseball Writers' Association of America would name him the major leagues' first official Rookie of the Year. The award carries his name today.

Shotton chose to be diplomatic when a reporter asked which player was most responsible for the Dodgers' success. "I couldn't point to any one player and say, 'There is the man who won the pennant for us!' It was a team victory by being a hustling young ball club," he said the day after the pennant was secured. Rickey was equally democratic and unusually jolly. "I like this ballclub of Shotton's," he said. "Everybody has done a great job—Barney, the coaches, the players. I like everybody!"

* * *

Just as in 1941, the Dodgers would play the Yankees in the World Series. It was the seventh time New York City would enjoy a "Subway Series," the kind where the Bronx's Yankees faced either Brooklyn's Dodgers or Manhattan's Giants, and fans could hop on the trains and attend all the games. If they could get in, that is. This was the first time any New York team had reached the fall classic in four years, an eternity by Gotham standards, and ticket demand was through the roof. The Yankees added thousands of temporary seats along the foul lines, but ahead of the opener, scalpers reported getting offers of fifty dollars for tickets that sold at face value for six or eight. Attendance for all the games at Yankee Stadium would top seventy thousand, and for games at tiny Ebbets Field, the Dodgers would stuff in around thirty-four.

Folks who couldn't get gain entry had other options to follow the games. As in 1941, the New York Telephone Company set up a number to call for minute-by-minute updates. The *Daily Eagle* publicized the number with a plea: "Please do not call the *Eagle* for scores." The Mutual Broadcasting System fed the action to a record five hundred sixty-four stations across North America and overseas on Armed Forces Radio. And for the very first time, fans were able to watch the games on television—if they were lucky enough to live in New York, Philadelphia, Washington, or Schenectady, the only cities connected to NBC's network at the time. TV stores advertised heavily as the series approached. "Have a box seat at the World's Series... Right in the comfort of your living room... Simple as a radio to operate," read one newspaper ad for the Philco #1000 table model, sold by Namm's furniture store in Brooklyn. Buyers got a ten-inch-wide screen encased in a stylish mahogany cabinet, which delivered slightly fuzzy black and white pictures and mono sound pulled in through a metal rooftop antenna. The total cost, including the set-up of the antenna, was four hundred forty dollars. It was huge money in 1947 and such a little set—but there were tens of thousands of early adopters.

As technicians installed antennas, betting experts installed the Yankees as eight-to-five favorites for the series. The press leaned that way too; in a poll of more than sixty sportswriters by the Associated Press, scribes picked the Yankees to win by more than a two-to-one margin. That said, these were not the Bronx Bombers that regularly stomped their opponents in the late '30s and early '40s. Yes, the Yankees led the American League in home runs and scoring. Yes, they had ripped off a nineteen-game winning streak in mid-summer, setting a new American League record, and won the pennant by a dozen games over the Tigers. The team had some fine young players on the rise: starting pitchers Allie Reynolds and Vic Raschi, both future twenty-game winners; fireballing Joe Page, the team's relief ace as long as he kept his drinking under control; and a hard-hitting rookie catcher, Larry Berra, gradually becoming better known by his nickname, Yogi. But there were no Ruths and Gehrigs in this lineup to make pitchers quake with fear. Joe DiMaggio was still in there, batting cleanup and manning center field, but he hadn't been Joltin' Joe since returning from the war. He hit just twenty homers in '47, the lowest total of his career, and his .315 average was nearly twenty points below his career mark entering the season.

The sportswriters still rated Joe a notch or two higher than his counterpart in Brooklyn. "The Dodgers have no power to match [DiMaggio] even though they have a mighty solid baseball citizen out there in centerfield," said one pre-series prognosis. "Reiser is hitting .309 but because of a series of injuries, appears to have lost much of long-ball hitting power." Another article said: "A sound Reiser would come closest to matching DiMaggio, but he has been broken up so frequently that there is something missing. A shoulder separation deprived Reiser of his rifle arm and affected his batting swing." The same writer noted Pete's diminished base-stealing ability. "He has stolen fourteen bases this season, but that used to be nothing for him. Last year he stole home seven times."

Pete's old boss Larry MacPhail, now GM of the Yankees, expressed the same general view in a pre-series talk with sports scribes. "I consider the Dodgers that won the pennant for me in 1941 to be superior to this year's Brooklyn club. For one thing, Pete Reiser was a better ballplayer then," he said.

Burt Shotton said nothing about Pete but wasn't having any talk about a Yankee victory. "Favorites have been beaten before, and we're going to do it again," he said on the eve of the series. At a gigantic pre-series rally on the steps of Brooklyn's Borough Hall, attended by an estimated quarter-million fans, Dixie Walker backed up his boss. "We've won two pennants for you now but never a World Series. However, I think we're going to do that this time," he said. The streets of Brooklyn thundered with cheers.

Pete was batting third and playing center field as the series opened at Yankee Stadium on September 30th. Instead of his biggest winner in Reynolds, Yankee manager Bucky Harris chose to pitch Frank (Spec) Shea, a hard-throwing rookie right-hander who had overcome neck and arm injuries to win fourteen games. The Dodgers nicked Shea in the first inning. Robinson drew a walk with one out. With Pete batting, he stole second base. Pete then hit a one-bouncer right back to Shea. Rather than take the easy out at first, Shea turned toward Robinson, who had unwisely run on contact, and trapped him in a rundown near third base. However, Jackie avoided the tag long enough for Pete to dash all the way to second. Moments later, Dixie Walker blooped a single to left, and Reiser stormed home with the Dodgers' first run.

Pete helped manufacture another run in the sixth. He came to bat with one out, Robinson on first, and Joe Page now pitching. Again, he hit a weak infield chopper, this time to first baseman George McQuinn. McQuinn, a career-long American Leaguer, was unfamiliar with his opponent's speed. When he ran toward Pete to apply the tag, Pete kicked into higher gear, arching his back and accelerating to avoid the ball in McQuinn's left hand. Pete lost his footing as he ran and went tumbling, not sliding into first base. But the ump called him safe, overruling the Yankees' protest that he had stepped outside the baseline. The hit advanced Robinson to second, and one out later, Furillo lined a single to center to drive him home. Unfortunately, this kind of scratch-and-claw offense wasn't enough to overcome a five-run outburst by the Yankees in the fifth, and the Dodgers lost the opener 5-3.

Game Two demonstrated that after all the collisions and injuries and dizziness, Pete was simply not the player he used to be. Shotton played him in center field, always a tall task in Yankee Stadium with its vast territory and stone monuments to Lou Gehrig and Miller Huggins near the 461-foot sign. (The Babe Ruth monument was added later, after his death.) Pete had done fine in Game One, catching three routine fly balls. But a bright sun was out for Game Two, and the

Yankees were pounding longer drives. The fiasco began in the third inning when Stuffy Stirnweiss of the Yankees hit a liner that dropped into right-center field. Pete bobbled the ball while chasing it down, allowing Stirnweiss to advance to third and get credit for a triple. Two batters later, Johnny Lindell blasted a fly to deep right-center. Pete, running with sunglasses down, raced back and tried for a diving catch, but the ball caromed off his glove, giving Lindell his triple and allowing Stirnweiss to score for a 2-1 Yankee lead.

The next inning, Billy Johnson of the Yanks crushed another long drive to deep center. Pete, frantically pedaling backward, fell and somersaulted in reverse as the ball landed behind him for yet another Yankee triple. Johnson scored a few minutes later on a hit by Phil Rizzuto. Finally, in the seventh, Pete let a single by Johnson roll through his legs and go all the way to the fence, allowing another run to score. He was charged with only one official error on the day, but his miscues contributed mightily to the 10-3 Yankee victory.

After the game, several players, including Joe DiMaggio, defended Reiser, noting that the bright sun and a smoky haze, presumably from cigarettes smoked by the crowd, made fielding difficult for everybody that afternoon. "I've seen better outfielders than Reiser look like bums out there. You have to be used to it," said former Philadelphia A's outfielder Al Simmons. However, Dodger manager Burt Shotton could not hide his irritation. "I don't think the fellow in center field was good, either," he said to reporters amid a volley of post-game questions. The press was harsh too. "Big leaguers are paid for catching the kind of long hits Reiser misjudged so badly yesterday," wrote Leonard Cohen in the *Post*.

Nevertheless, Shotton put Reiser back in center as the Series moved to the small, familiar confines of Ebbets Field the next afternoon. Pete, no doubt trying to make up for the disaster of the previous day, walked in the bottom of the first and promptly tried to steal second. But he was called out on a strong throw from Yankee catcher Sherm Lollar. And that wasn't even the bad news. On the slide, Pete jammed his right ankle into the base. He tried to keep playing, but Shotton removed him after another half inning as the joint swelled. The Dodgers sent him to Swedish Hospital for X-rays while his teammates squeaked out a 9-8 victory.

Here begins another key chapter in the saga of Pete Reiser, wounded but willing warrior. The next day's newspapers reported that Pete had a badly sprained ankle. Dodger physician Dr. Harold Wendler said Pete would play in Game Four "only by some miracle." Pete told reporters the same thing. "I won't be able to play tomorrow, if at all this Series," he said. "They strapped up the ankle and told me to walk on it as much as possible to keep the swelling from stiffening up. But it just hurts too much to stand up. I don't see how I can even pinch-hit tomorrow."

But . . . in later years, Pete said reports of a sprain were for public consumption. In reality, he said, the ankle was broken. He told Honig: "The doctor X-rayed it that night. 'You've got a broken ankle,' he says, 'a very slight fracture.' Boy, was I ticked off! Did it have to happen right in the middle of a World Series? 'Listen,' I told the doctor, 'Don't say anything. Just put a tight bandage on it, say it's a bad sprain, and that I'm through for the rest of the Series. That's all.' I was afraid that if he said it was broken, Rickey would give me a dollar-a-year contract next year, meaning I would have to prove I was physically fit to play before I could sign a regular contract."

The next day, Pete tried to take batting practice but could not stride and put weight on his right foot. As the game started, he sat dejectedly on the bench in uniform, watching Furillo fill his spot in center field. He might have been the only downcast person in the ballpark. More than thirty-three thousand rabid fans had packed tiny Ebbets Field, hoping to see the Dodgers even up the series. From the start, they got their money's worth. The Yankees threatened to break it open in the top of the first, producing one run on back-to-back singles, an error by Reese, and a bases-loaded walk to DiMaggio. Shotton hurriedly removed starter Harry Taylor and inserted Hal Gregg, who pulled Brooklyn out of the fire by inducing a pop fly and a double play. Gregg pitched seven strong innings afterward, allowing only one other run, on an RBI double by Pete's wartime teammate Johnny Lindell.

Meanwhile, Yankee starter Bill Bevens walked both Stanky and Walker in the bottom of the first but escaped the jam by retiring Hermanski on a pop-up. The inning set pattern for one of the oddest pitching performances in World Series history. Frame after frame, Bevens struggled with his control, walking a Series record ten men, adding a wild pitch for good measure. The Dodgers scored in the fifth on a fielder's choice after Bevens gave free passes to Jorgensen and Gregg to start the inning, and Stanky bunted them over. But Yankee manager Bucky Harris left Bevens in the game because when the Dodgers swung at his offerings, they seemed to be helpless, hitting mostly weak grounders and pop-ups. Modern analysts would deem the Yankee righty "effectively wild." And as the afternoon shadows at Ebbets Field grew long, it gradually dawned on all present that Bevens, the owner of a mediocre 7-13 record during the regular season, was pitching a no-hitter.

Pete saw only some of the action. His ankle pained him, so after the third inning, he went back to the Brooklyn clubhouse, stripped off his uniform, and soaked his foot in the whirlpool. Four innings later, he suited up again and reappeared in the dugout. Shotton looked surprised.

"What are you doing here?" he asked. "You can't even stand."

"If you need me, I can give it one hell of a try," Pete replied.

Shotton turned his attention back to the game. In the bottom of the eighth, three of the Dodgers' best hitters—Robinson, Walker, and Hermanski—went down without a peep. It was Bevens' second one-two-three inning of the day. In the top of the ninth, the Yankees loaded the bases with one out. Shotton pulled Hank Behrman and brought in his relief ace, Hugh Casey, to face the Yankees' always-dangerous Tommy Henrich. The move paid off as Henrich hit a grounder that Casey grabbed and whipped to catcher Bruce Edwards for the force at home. Edwards then fired the ball to first in time to nab Henrich. Double play. The score remained Yankees 2, Dodgers 1.

Bevens went to work in the bottom of the ninth with the crowd in an edge-of-their-seats state of anxiety. Edwards batted first and hit a fly to deep left field. Lindell ran back and caught it chest-high in front of the wall. One out. Furillo was up next, and Bevens walked him on five pitches, the fifth bouncing past catcher Yogi Berra. One out, one on. Next batter, Jorgensen. On Bevens' fourth pitch, Jorgensen lofted a high pop-up above first base that McQuinn pulled down. Two out. Bevens needed to retire just one more batter to throw a World Series no-hitter, a feat which had never been accomplished in the Series' forty-four-year history. Due up: the pitcher, Casey, who owned a batting average of .056 that season, one hit in twenty-one at-bats.

Shotton looked down his bench for a pinch-hitter. He had used his top reserve, Arky Vaughn, in the seventh. Several capable hitters were available, but to face the righty Bevens, Shotton wanted a left-handed batter. He had only one good lefty available: the hobbled Pete Reiser.

The exact words Shotton used vary in the retellings, but the Dodger manager looked at Pete and said something like: "Ain't you going to volunteer to hit?"

The ever-game Reiser grabbed a bat. Striving to conceal his limp as much as possible, he walked to the plate. At the same time, Shotton sent speedy Al Gionfriddo in to run for Furillo.

Had the Yankees known Pete's ankle was broken, not merely sprained, Bevens might have relaxed a touch, concentrated on throwing good fastballs, and simply blown Pete away. "There's no way I could have ran," Pete told Curt Gowdy on a mid-1970s TV show, *The Way It Was*. "If I had hit the ball for a single, I don't think I'd have made first base." But with athletic immortality just one out away, with the Ebbets Field crowd standing and roaring at top volume, with tens of millions listening on radios and uncounted more watching on tiny, primitive TVs, Bevens couldn't settle down. His first pitch was a ball. His second pitch was a ball. On the third, Reiser swung and hit a foul tip for a strike. The fourth pitch, ball. More significantly, Gionfriddo stole second, sliding in head-first under a high, late throw from Berra.

At that point, Yankee manager Harris made a decision that would be discussed, dissected, and dissed for decades to come, ordering an intentional walk to the ailing Reiser. Nearly thirty years later, DiMaggio told Gowdy he was still surprised. "You don't just put that winning run on first base, and that's the first time I'd ever seen that happen in all the time I was in the major leagues. It shocked me to see that happen," DiMaggio said. Pete himself said it was a "pretty unorthodox move."

Harris, however, defended his decision as the correct one, given who was standing at the plate. "You've got the tying run on second after Gionfriddo steals," he said after the game. "A single drives it home, and the winning run's on first anyhow. The count is three-and-one, and Reiser is a longball hitter. I'm not going to give him a chance to whack one over the fence."

He got support from an unlikely source: Branch Rickey. "Barney [Shotton] sent up his best pinch-hitter in Reiser," he said. "You can't criticize Harris for his reluctance to pitch to Pete."

In his fine book *1947: The Year All Hell Broke Loose in Baseball*, Red Barber also supported Harris' move. "He knew Reiser was hitting off his left foot, which was healthy and strong," Barber wrote. "He was afraid Bevens, in his effort not to throw ball four, would groove the pitch and that Reiser would hit it against or even over the nearby right-field wall. He didn't want Reiser hitting a fat pitch. Instead, he wanted him on first base."

Bevens threw ball four, and Pete did a fast limp down to first. Shotton sent in Eddie Miksis to run for him. The next batter was another pinch hitter, Cookie Lavagetto, now a utility player who had played just forty-one games all season and gotten all of eighteen hits. That didn't matter against the depleted Bevens. Lavagetto cracked Bevens' second pitch against the right-field wall, scoring both Gionfriddo and Miksis, giving Brooklyn a 3-2 victory that sent the fans into a state of bedlam and topped off what remains one of the most famous and memorable games in World Series history.

"DiMaggio told me years later that Harris knew I had a broken ankle but that he still didn't want to pitch to me," Reiser told Honig. "'He'll still swing, ankle or no ankle,' Harris said. That was a nice tribute to me, but it cost him."

The sincerity of Harris's concern about Pete became even clearer in Game Five. The Dodger bats were feeble again, not getting a hit off Spec Shea until Gene Hermanski singled in the fifth. When Brooklyn scored an inning later, it came off two walks and a single by Robinson. Fortunately, the Yankee hitters weren't much better, and the Dodgers were trailing only 2-1 when a walk to Edwards and a double by pinch-hitter Vaughn put runners on second and third with two outs in the seventh. Up next was leadoff man Eddie Stanky, a base-on-balls machine but a subpar hitter, not the run producer Shotton wanted to see at the plate in that situation.

Again, Shotton turned to Reiser, broken ankle and all. Again, Pete limped out to the plate as a full house of Brooklyn fans yelled and stamped and pleaded for a hit. And again, Harris ordered an intentional walk. This time, the move paid off; the next batter, Reese, struck out on three pitches.

That brief plate appearance was the last stand for Pete and his throbbing ankle. In Game Six, an 8-6 Dodger victory, Shotton used three pinch hitters, but Reiser stayed on the bench. In Game Seven, the Yankees jumped out to an early lead and handed the game to Joe Page, who mowed down the Dodgers with five innings of scoreless ball. In the final frames, a desperate Shotton sent up Miksis, Lavagetto, and young Gil Hodges as pinch-hitters to try and generate some offense. All were retired, and Reiser watched helplessly from the dugout as Brooklyn went down 5-2 and the Yankees sealed their eleventh world championship.

Pete had to content himself with the loser's share of the series money—a sum of just over four thousand dollars—and the knowledge that on back-to-back days, with World Series games on the line, the Yankees gave him free passes because they feared his bat.

The outcome left Brooklyn in an utter state of gloom. This was the closest the Dodgers had ever come to winning the World Series, and the heartbreak was almost too much for some of their rooters to bear. "I would have rather have seen them lose in four games than have them drag it out that long," said Frank Sullivan, a policeman. "The letdown is indescribable. I probably won't be able to sleep for another week." Estelle Fopeck, a waitress, blamed the manager. "If Durocher were managing, we would have won in four straight games," she said. Pete himself blamed nobody for the loss, although a few newspaper scribes singled him out in the series post-mortem for his poor fielding in the second game.

One day after the series, there were newspaper reports that the Dodgers were planning to trade Pete, either to the Reds, who needed offense, or the

Braves, whose owner, Lou Perini, was investing heavily for what turned out to be a successful run at the pennant in 1948. The rumors would persist throughout the fall and winter and intensify in the spring until Branch Rickey finally shot them down. "Pete Reiser is not for sale or trade," the Mahatma said. "He may play on one leg or with one hand, but it will be with this club."

As a sign of his commitment to Reiser, Rickey finally undertook a project the writers demanded all summer—padding the outfield walls of Ebbets Field. In January, Rickey agreed to pay five thousand dollars to install a protective barrier on the walls. "It's a new substance called foam rubber, and it's claimed you can throw an egg against it without breaking the shell," reported the *Eagle*.

Rickey touted the product's safety features but notably expressed doubt that his star outfielder could avoid injuries entirely. "Pete Reiser will always be getting hurt. That's the way he plays ball—all out," the Mahatma said. On the surface, it sounded like a compliment. But it also showed Rickey had lost hope his star would stay healthy.

Asked about the Dodgers' plans to pad the walls, Pete's cynicism toward Rickey shone through. "I'll believe that when I see it," he said.

11

Baseball Afterlife

By the spring of 1948, Pete Reiser was a baseball zombie. He still wore a Dodger uniform, still went up to bat, and strived to give Brooklyn that desperately wanted world championship. But the life in his game had vanished. Two broken ankles had slackened his speed. Shoulder troubles shortened his throws. Hitting and fielding were complicated by headaches and dizziness that lingered from the concussions. On occasion, he still whacked the ball against the outfield fences like old times and made Ebbets Field roar. But all too often, the Pistol was firing blanks now, and worst of all, he knew his guns were broken.

"In '48, Rickey didn't want me to play at all. He said he would pay me if I sat down all year," Pete later told Donald Honig. "Being bullheaded, I said I wanted to play. But by that time, all of those injuries were beginning to take their toll . . . Something was gone. It had always been so easy for me, but now it was a struggle. I was only twenty-nine, but the fun and pure joy of it were gone." Would a year off have made a difference? Possibly, but it seems doubtful. One writer that season described him as "held together by adhesive tape and baling wire." In the words of *Eagle* writer Tommy Holmes, "poor Pete has been banged around so much that he can't go nine innings without bursting apart somewhere at the seams."

However, he still had a family to provide for and knew no way outside baseball to make a living, so he tried. The first task was to negotiate a new contract with Branch Rickey. For all his injuries, Pete batted .309 in 1947 and hit especially well in late July and August as the Dodgers put a stranglehold on the pennant. He felt deserving of a significant raise. But Rickey's first offer was for the same fifteen thousand he earned in 1947. Pete refused to sign. Talking to the *Eagle*, he cited Brooklyn's high living expenses as a reason, while hinting that he sensed the downhill side of his career coming on. "If I don't get more money now, I never will," he said. He finally signed the last week in February, when the Dodgers upped their offer to a reported nineteen thousand dollars, the highest salary of Pete's career. Another plus: Rickey re-hired Durocher as manager after his year's suspension, meaning Pete would no longer have to deal with prickly Burt Shotton.

Still, even with Leo restored, even with the bump in salary, spring training quickly became a rocky affair. The Dodgers ventured overseas again, spending three weeks in the Dominican Republic. Boarding the team plane, Pete was unsmiling and carrying a very noticeable double chin. Harold Burr, who also made the trip, reported that the center fielder was twenty pounds overweight. "At the first workout yesterday morning . . . Pistol Pete was the first hitter to waddle up to the batting nets, looking like a grounded blimp with his old No. 7 on his back." he wrote. Durocher called Pete "hog fat." Pete resisted the pointed suggestion that he lose the weight. "I don't want to take off the winter fat quickly," he said. "I want to keep some of it after the season starts. Last season I was way underweight, down to a hundred sixty-five, and it weakened me. My best weight is one seventy-five, and I'll work down to that gradually."

Pete also clashed with management about certain travel restrictions. The Dodgers had prohibited players' wives from going on the Dominican trip but made an exception for Durocher's wife, actress Laraine Day. Pat Reiser flew down to Santo Domingo three days into the trip, and Pete defiantly refused to send her home. "Leo Durocher's wife is here, so why not mine? If my wife leaves, I go with her," he reportedly said. Pat stayed, and Laraine Day later expressed admiration for her act. "I always admired the spunk of Mrs. Pete Reiser, who stood on her rights as an American citizen, got a passport and visa, and appeared in Trujillo City at her own expense," Day wrote. She noted, however, that Pat's presence caused an uproar, "for now, the players were being besieged by their wives to sacrifice a bit of their hard-earned money to transport them to this paradise." The result was that the Dodgers sent Pete back to Florida just ten days after his arrival, with Pat having no choice but to follow dutifully.

The official reason Pete went back was to work on his first base skills. Jackie Robinson, who had manned first during the '47 season, was moving to second to replace Eddie Stanky, traded to Boston. Rickey hoped that by moving Pete to first, he'd both fill a hole and keep his one-time wunderkind away from the fences. The team recruited Hall of Famer George Sisler, one of the greatest first basemen of all time, to teach Pete the basics of the position. But the experiment fizzled out before the season began. "He lacks height and the physical advantages a left-hand thrower enjoys at the position," Augie Galan pointed out. The *Daily News* put it more bluntly: "It's obvious that as a first-sacker, Reiser is a terrific outfielder."

On opening day, Pete was neither at first nor the outfield. "Pete's too fat to please the Lip," reported the *Eagle*. Not until the second week of the season did he start a game. When he finally did, he exploded, bashing out a two-run triple and a three-run homer against the Giants. A day later, he doubled, tripled, and walked three times against the Phillies. Unfortunately, the resurgence was short-lived. By the first week in May, Pete was hobbled by a sharp pain in his left ankle, the one he broke in September 1946. A quick trip to St. Louis for examination by Dr. Hyland revealed he had a bone chip. Hyland said Pete could play without aggravating the condition. But it soon became obvious that Pete was too injured to help the team. In ten games that month, he batted just .103, and the Dodgers quickly plunged to seventh place. The team sent him home to St. Louis for several weeks to recover.

When the healing took longer than expected, the front office began flashing signs of exasperation. "If I don't get word from Reiser by tomorrow, I'll make it my business to call him," Rickey said on June 18th. The next day, this missive appeared in the *Ridgewood News*, one of the northern New Jersey papers that covered the Bums: "The Brooklyn organization's (meaning Branch Rickey's) patience has just about had the last thin veneer scraped off by Pete Reiser's visits to the medicos. His mounting collection of X-ray photos . . . has caused the Dodger chief a headache. New York sportswriters have long known that Reiser's hypochondria has bordered on the neurotic, but Pete's a handy guy with the bat and glove, so no one wanted to blow the whistle on him . . . Some of Pete's accidents have been the McCoy, of course, but his recoveries have been a trifle slow, to put it mildly. Even more of his ailments have been strictly on the mental side."

The writers began to pile on too. Jimmy Powers of the *Daily News* wrote, "Pete Reiser is a great guy, and we hope he will not feel bad to learn he is known as 'peanut brittle' in rival dugouts." Writing of other Dodgers who recovered from injuries, Dick Young said Reiser was the sole player "not ready to produce. Poor Pete, of course, is running only to doctors these days."

Pete returned at the end of June and played sporadically the rest of the season. He enjoyed one last moment of glory as a Dodger on July 4th. Brooklyn, floundering in sixth place, hosted the Giants at Ebbets Field in front of an Independence Day crowd of twenty-nine thousand. In a see-saw slugfest, the Giants built an 8-3 lead only to see the Dodgers come fighting back with three runs in the seventh and three more in the eighth to go on top, 9-8. The Giants rallied again, scoring four times in the top of the ninth to retake the lead, 12-9. But the Dodgers weren't through. In the bottom of the ninth, Gil Hodges singled, and rookie Roy Campanella, playing only his second game in the majors, launched a homer to deep center field, pulling the Dodgers within one run. Brooklyn then loaded the bases against reliever Sheldon Jones.

Earlier that day, during batting practice, the hobbled and increasingly disgruntled Pistol, batting a paltry .196, made an off-hand comment to some reporters and teammates: "I think I'll quit." No one took him seriously. Now, in the bottom of the ninth, with the crowd going nuts, Durocher sent his dispirited outfielder up to pinch-hit. "Up to the plate, accompanied by a deafening roar born of expectancy, limped Pete Reiser whose twisted right ankle had kept him out of the lineup," wrote Dick Young. Jones got a ball and two strikes on his opponent. But on the fourth pitch, Pete shot a bullet single into right field. In came Dick Whitman with the tying run, followed by Reese, who stomped down hard on home plate for the winner. Young compared the hit to Cookie Lavagetto's in the previous World Series, the game-winning double that broke up Bill Bevens' no-hitter. "This one was only a single," he wrote, "but it produced the same sort of hysteria on the field—grown men like Jackie Robinson and Pee Wee Reese jumping wildly in the air and smothering Reiser with their joyous slaps and embraces."

Most of the time, though, Pete's ankle pains and a recurrence of his right shoulder troubles left him unable to contribute, and he spent the rest of the season riding the bench. The Dodgers were starting to coalesce around a new group of regulars. Gil Hodges established himself at first base, with Robinson at second, Reese at short, and newly acquired Billy Cox at third. Campanella had seized the catcher's spot, and Duke Snider took over in center, with Carl Furillo holding down right. When Don Newcombe arrived the following year to anchor the starting rotation, the Dodgers would emerge as the clear-cut best team in the National League, on their way to winning five pennants in eight seasons, missing two others only in the final inning of the final day of the season. Except for Reese, most of the pre-war and immediate post-war Dodgers were pushed aside—and that included Durocher, who Rickey allowed to jump to the crosstown Giants on July 16th, a move that stunned fans, writers, and players alike and made Pete even more miserable. Pete had always been, in his own words, a "Durocher man." Leo's departure meant a return to Burt Shotton. Shotton, never much of a Reiser fan, played Pete in center field on his first day back, then limited him to pinch-hitting appearances for nearly two months.

When Cox went down with an injury in mid-September, Shotton gave Pete a shot at third base. For four games, Pete played well, handling hot grounders and firing throws across the infield with surprising zip. Then, the headaches and dizzy spells flared up again, and before a doubleheader with the Reds, he told Shotton he couldn't play. "I get a new third baseman—and only keep him three days," Shotton told a reporter with unconcealed disappointment.

The Dodgers, after climbing into pennant contention in August, faded down the stretch and finished third. Pete's last at-bat with the team came on the season's final day, October 3rd. He struck out on three pitches. The former batting and stealing champion ended the season with a .236 average. His stolen base total for the year was three.

Fed up with Rickey, with Shotton, with what he considered their unsympathetic treatment of his injuries, Pete declared after the season that his time with the Dodgers was over. "I'll play anywhere—anywhere but Brooklyn," he said. "I think the change will do me good. I'm pretty sure I can play a full season if I go somewhere else."

At least one team was willing to find out if that was true. In mid-December, the Boston Braves traded outfielder Mike McCormick—a .303 hitter in 1948—and a player to be named later in exchange for the former all-star. "Pete Reiser got what he wanted for Christmas," wrote Dick Young. A happy Pete told reporters he was looking forward to playing for the Braves—who had a cinder warning track in their outfield—and especially looking forward to playing for their manager, Billy Southworth. Southworth was one of the game's most successful skippers, known for being a smart strategist, a good teacher, and communicative and understanding with players. Over six seasons with the Cardinals, his teams posted a .618 winning percentage, winning three National League pennants and two World Series. After the '45 season, Braves owner Lou Perini lured Southworth to Boston with a three-year, hundred-thousand-dollar contract. In three years under his guidance, the long-downtrodden Braves rose from fourth to third to the pennant, the team's first in thirty-four years.

Pete had met with Southworth in Chicago ahead of the trade, gave assurances that he was healthy, and said all the right things in interviews ahead of the '49 season. "I don't think I've ever felt better," he said just before opening day. "My legs are fine again, and so is my arm. I'm running into no more walls." Southworth was optimistic about Pete too. "I'm not worried about his legs or his health," he said. "He is not only a fine ballplayer but a great hitter and a natural competitor. He can help us more than you might think." However, one prominent baseball writer was skeptical. "Practically everybody you meet down here [in Florida] is making Reiser, traded by Brooklyn to Boston, the key to the National League race," wrote Joe Williams of the *World-Telegram*. "But hasn't it been a terribly long time since Reiser dominated a ball club? It's been seven whole years since he was a top man." He also said Pete had become a brooder who complained too much about his ailments.

There were days in '49 where Pete helped the Braves plenty. The team came into Ebbets Field on May 28th in a first-place tie with Brooklyn, sharing an identical record of twenty wins, fifteen losses. The Dodgers' Preacher Roe had shut them out the day before, and the Braves started badly on this day, too, falling behind 6-0 by the fourth inning. Reiser, batting third and playing left field, was hitless in his first four at-bats but came up in the eighth with the bases loaded and Boston now trailing 6-3. Dodger reliever Erv Palica worked Pete to a full count, then tried to sneak a fastball by him for strike three. Pete took a mighty swing and, in the words of the *Daily News*, "hit it to the parking lot attendant across the street." The grand slam vaulted the Braves to a 7-6 win and sole possession of first place in the National League. The *Boston Globe* put Reiser's homer on the front page the next day and touted Pete as "the clouting cripple."

But the majority of the time in '49, Pete was too inconsistent or too banged up to play more than a few games in a row. He left a game on May 1st, saying his arm was sore. He missed several games in June with what he termed "bronchial trouble." For much of the season, he complained of inexplicable pain in his chest. And on July 28th, he was struck in the back of the head by a line drive during batting practice. Boston sportswriters grew weary of hearing the medical reports. "Reiser has had more ailments this season than one can recall offhand," wrote Bob Holbrook of the *Boston Globe*. "He's a lot like Luke 'Aches and Pains' Appling of the White Sox. The only difference is that Appling plays better when he complains." Pete ended the season hitting a decent .271 with eight homers in eighty-four games but left the team in early September because of a broken rib. Southworth was put on leave even earlier, in mid-August, due to a player revolt against his strict training rules and a growing drinking problem that stemmed from the loss of his beloved son in a plane crash during the war. The Braves finished fifth.

Both Southworth and Reiser were back in the spring of '50. Pete hit .476 in spring training but batted only twenty-seven times, and the *Globe* noted his throws from outfield were no better than a high schooler's. Once the season was underway, he struggled, batting just .205 in fifty-three games. In late May, he said he felt great and predicted the Braves could win the pennant. But he pulled a groin muscle in St. Louis, and after he returned in July, Southworth used him almost exclusively as a pinch hitter, and he got only five hits for the remainder of the year. The Braves gave him his unconditional release at the end of October.

Pete wasn't quite done. After losing a power struggle in Brooklyn to Walter O'Malley, Branch Rickey sold off his Dodgers stock and moved to Pittsburgh to rebuild the last-place Pirates. One of his first signings was Pete Reiser, his onetime wunderkind. With the Korean War heating up, Rickey reportedly wanted to acquire players who were immune to the draft—and Reiser, with his now-famous litany of injuries, was definitely not a target of Uncle Sam. His contract called for ten thousand dollars, about half of what he earned three years earlier.

In March, eyebrows rose precipitously when Rickey tried the thirty-two-year-old Reiser at catcher during spring training in San Bernadino, California. Reiser even caught a pair of exhibition games. In one against the UCLA team, he caught the entire nine innings and threw out two runners at second. Umpire Dusty Boggess joked, "Maybe if he had been a catcher all along, he wouldn't have hit those fences. But he probably would have fallen into dugouts chasing fouls." The catching experiment quietly ended after two weeks, and once the season began, Pete was relegated mostly to pinch-hitting with occasional starts in left field. When he played, though, he played fairly well. He looked like the Pistol of old in a May 1st victory against Brooklyn, getting on base five games with a single, two doubles, a walk, and an error. "Reiser Returns to Haunt Bums, 6-2," read the headline in the *Pittsburgh Post-Gazette*. Overall, he got eleven pinch hits in thirty-three tries. He made notably fewer complaints about injuries, and there were no reported collisions with walls. In early August, a pleased Rickey boosted Pete's salary.

But Pete's luck couldn't hold. On August 11th, he played in both games of a doubleheader in Chicago, delivering a pinch-hit single in the opener. The next day, he was playing pepper with some teammates when somehow, he dislocated his left shoulder, the one that had popped out in July of '47. After a few days of rest, the shoulder showed no improvement, and Reiser went home to St. Louis to recuperate. He missed the rest of the season. His arm was in a sling when Bob Broeg of the *Post-Dispatch* interviewed him at home at the end of August. He wrote that Reiser "is broken in body, wired together uncertainly like a battered doll that has been dropped once too often." The Pirates gave him his unconditional release in mid-November.

Pete still wasn't ready to quit. In early February, he signed as a free agent with Cleveland. "I don't see how Reiser can help but prove valuable," said Indians GM Hank Greenberg. As always, Pete gave it his all. Playing first base in a spring training intrasquad game, he reached for a wide throw and took a blow to the head from the knee of oncoming runner Dale Mitchell. The team doctor said his cranium was just bruised, not concussed. Despite the mishap, he made the team, with manager Al Lopez saying, "I like his fire and desire. He hasn't lost any of it. He keeps himself in good shape, and he's still pretty fast."

Fire and speed, however, couldn't compensate for a weakened bat. In thirty-four games, most of them pinch-hitting appearances, Pete managed just six hits. In early June, he was reportedly suffering from an ulcer. In a June 20th game, with the Indians and Senators tied 3-3 in the eighth, Pete tried his old signature move, a steal of home. He was thrown out, and the Indians went on to lose the game.

The end came on July 11th, when the Indians reassigned him to their AAA farm club in Indianapolis. Pete debated for a few days whether or not he'd report. Three days later, he was in St. Louis when the Dodgers came to town. He told a *Daily Eagle* reporter that he was washed up during a brief visit to the press box. "I can't throw or swing anymore," he said, writing his own baseball obituary.

In the end, he decided to hang it up, retiring with a lifetime batting average of .295. Jimmy Powers suggested the Dodgers hold a "Pete Reiser Day" for their onetime star. "It's no secret that Reiser ruined himself crashing into outfield walls in his strong effort to bring the pennant to the Brooklyn fans," the columnist wrote. It would be wonderful, he said, if the team recognized "a player who would have become the greatest Dodger of all time if he wasn't cursed by bad luck and too much hustle for his own good." But no such day materialized in '52 or any other season.

* * *

For the first time in his adult life, Pete now had to make a living outside baseball. He not only had to support Pat and daughter Sally but a second daughter, Shirley, who had come along in 1949. And it was clear now that Sally, whose mental development had been slow, was a special-needs child—retarded was the term used at the time. Pat and Pete got involved with associations to help such children and talked to reporters to raise awareness. "It's not an easy thing to face up to, but we made our minds we weren't going to feel sorry for ourselves or for Sally," he said in 1959. "There were times when other kids made fun of her. One day she said to me, 'I can't help it, can I, Daddy?' But through special schooling and our love and care, she's come along."

The schooling cost a reported one hundred fifty dollars per month, making it imperative that Pete secure a steady income. For a couple of years, he attempted to make it in the used car business in St. Louis with an old friend, Glen Schaeffer, an ace soccer goalie who also spent eight years playing minor league ball. As sales manager and namesake of Pete Reiser Motors, Pete tried to drum up business by giving baseball clinics in the service room. As many as a hundred kids showed up for the clinics. However, not many of their parents bought cars, and the business went under, taking a reported thirty thousand dollars of Pete's money with it. After that fiasco, Pete was reduced to running a St. Louis lumber mill, earning three dollars per hour.

In early 1955, he wrote to the Dodgers, asking for a job. The team's GM, Buzzie Bavasi, called and offered a class-D managing position in Thomasville, Georgia, a town of about fifteen thousand near the Florida border. Pete would be back where he started eighteen years before, working in tiny ballparks on brutally hot summer days and enduring long bus rides at night. He took the job, putting the best possible spin on the position. "I played in class D, didn't I?" he told a reporter that spring. "I rode them buses with straight back seats for three years. This bus has got reclining seats. This is great compared to them days."

Thus started Pete's itinerant career as a minor league manager. After a year in Thomasville, the Dodgers moved him to Kokomo, Indiana, still in class D. In '56, his team finished dead last in the Midwest League. In '57, they leaped to first, and Pete got to coach his first real major league prospect, an eighteen-year-old Brooklyn native named Tommy Davis. Under Pete's tutelage, Davis won the league batting title. The next year, Pete stayed up north managing a class B squad in Green Bay, Wisconsin. This team had another major league prospect, six-foot-seven Frank Howard. With Pete's guidance, Howard led the league in homers and RBI. Developments like that got Pete promoted to the Dodgers' AA squad in Victoria, Texas for the '59 season, where he won his second pennant in three years, helped by Howard, who won the batting title at .371.

Pete professed to like the managing life. "You know, I'm really happier today helping young kids than when I was playing for myself," he said. "Besides, I can thank the Lord that I'm alive." He wasn't referring just to his long list of concussions and broken bones. In June 1956, a car crashed head-on into the Kokomo team bus during a road trip; both men in the car were killed, and Pete, sitting up front next to the driver, suffered neck and side injuries that required brief hospitalization. In May 1957, after a heavy workout, Pete experienced chest pains that lingered for nearly two weeks. W.C. Heinz, an old writer friend from New York, met him at the Kokomo stadium. "When Pete came through the gate, he was walking like an old man," Heinz reported. "The Dodgers [once] offered to bet one thousand dollars that Reiser was the fastest man in baseball, and now it was taking forever for him to walk to me." Heinz ended up driving Pete to St. Louis to see a heart specialist, engaging him in long talks about his life and career along the way. The conversations formed the basis of Heinz's award-winning magazine article, "The Rocky Road of Pistol Pete," published the following year.

It was a hard existence in many ways, but like Pete's previous tenure in the minors, it paid off. At the end of the '59 season, *The Sporting News* named him Minor League Manager of the Year, and in December, the Dodgers gave him the promotion he wanted most of all, making him their hitting coach for the 1960 season. He wouldn't be going back to Brooklyn, as the Dodgers had made their historic move to Los Angeles two years earlier. Pete didn't care; after eight years, he was back in the big leagues.

Almost immediately, the hire paid dividends. Manager Walter Alston had little faith in the hitting of Dodger shortstop Maury Wills, replacing him almost nightly in the late innings for a pinch hitter, a trend which left Wills in deepening despair. By the end of May 1960, he was nearly ready to quit. Pete offered to help, and a desperate Wills accepted. "Pete started me from scratch—almost like a manager would do with a nine-year-old Little Leaguer," Wills said in his autobiography. "He selected a new bat for me, one I could whip around faster. He opened my batting stance and worked on fundamentals such as meeting the ball out in front of the plate—taking an even swing and not overstriding. It was almost like learning a new sport." For up to two hours a day, Pete tossed batting practice as Wills learned to hit with his new stance and swing. When Willis said it was no use, Pete told him to keep trying. When Wills complained about the heat inside the L.A. Coliseum, Pete asked if he preferred the weather in triple-A Spokane. After two weeks, something clicked, and Wills began to hit. His batting average rose from .222 to over .300 in less than a month. He ended the year at .295.

Now that Wills was hitting, Pete began to work on his base-stealing skills. A naturally fast runner, Wills had swiped six bases in April and May. Pete advised him to get longer leads and take "greater liberties" against certain pitchers. Willis had stolen fifty bases by season's end, more than any National Leaguer in thirty-seven years. Two years later, Wills really took liberties, swiping one hundred four bases, shattering Ty Cobb's record of ninety-six from 1915. He also batted .299, scored one hundred thirty runs, and won the NL MVP award. Wills dedicated his 1963 book to Pete. "They say in every man's life there's a guiding light—someone who believes in you, helps you over the hump, inspires you to greater heights. My champion was Pete Reiser. Even though I had quit on myself, he never gave up on me for a moment," Wills said.

Pete's proteges carried the Dodger offense in this era. Tommy Davis won back-to-back batting titles in '62 and '63, while Frank Howard led the team in homers four years out of five. The pitching staff, led by Don Drysdale and the incomparable Sandy Koufax, kept opponents waving at air, and the Dodgers steamrolled to a pennant in 1963, brushing off a late-season challenge from the Cardinals with a three-game sweep in mid-September. Prognosticators expected a tough World Series against the Yankees. They got the opposite—a four-game sweep by the Dodgers, with Koufax setting a series record by striking out fifteen Yankees in the opener and Drysdale pitching a three-hit, 1-0 shutout in Game Three.

After twenty-five years in professional baseball, Pete Reiser finally was part of a world championship team. "I know that was a great highlight for him," says daughter Shirley. "Finally got his ring." For the first time, he also got the winner's share of the World Series money, twelve thousand eight hundred dollars, more than he earned in most of his playing years.

With Pete, however, the good times never seemed to last. Before a home game in April 1964, he was hitting fungoes to the outfielders when he felt sharp pains in his chest. He walked off the field under his own power and was taken by ambulance to L.A.'s Daniel Freeman Hospital, where doctors found he had suffered a mild heart attack. Pete's shrug-it-off nature hadn't changed; team doctor Robert Woods said that after his hospital exam, the patient "wanted to leave the hospital and go home." Somehow, Woods succeeded where other doctors had failed and convinced Reiser to stay in the hospital for ten days and take an extended rest afterward.

He rejoined the team in July, but only temporarily. The Dodgers skidded to a sub-.500 record in 1964, and on the last day of the season, the team announced it was replacing the entire coaching staff. The Dodgers offered Pete another job managing their triple-A squad in Spokane. He accepted but never managed a game. During spring training in 1965 in Florida, the chest pains returned, and Pete flew home to Los Angeles. Doctors proclaimed it a "near heart attack." After a few weeks' rest, Pete decided to take off the entire year. The Dodgers did not offer him another position.

Lacking any better option, Pete accepted a job with a Japanese team for the '66 season but was unhappy and came home within a few weeks. Leo Durocher came riding to the rescue. Leo had just accepted his first managerial post in eleven years, leading the Cubs, and in June brought Pete aboard as the hitting and third-base coach. "Leo was very good to Pete. When he was looking for work, Leo would hire him. And really respected him," says Rick Tuber. Cubs owner Philip Wrigley soon took a liking to Pete as well, and Pete would serve the Cubs as a coach, scout, and minor league trainer off and on for the next fifteen years.

Most of those years are mere footnotes to Pete's career, with one big exception: 1969, a year that remains seared into memory for Cub fans of a certain age. When I raised the topic with Shirley for this book, her first reaction was, "Oh, don't talk about it!"

Entering that year, it had been nearly a quarter-century since the Cubs even sniffed a pennant, and as recently as '66, Leo's inaugural season, the team had finished dead last. Since then, Leo had implemented a massive turnaround, mainly by pushing the players to hustle more and completely overhauling the pitching staff. He found an ace in Fergie Jenkins, who reeled off six straight twenty-win seasons beginning in '67, and by 1969 the Cubs had a strong four-man rotation in Jenkins, Ken Holtzman, Bill Hands, and Dick Selma. The team also had ample home run power in Billy Williams, Ron Santo, and the aging but still dangerous Ernie Banks. Don Kessinger and Glenn Beckert formed an able if unspectacular double-play team and Randy Hundley was so good and durable behind the plate that Durocher barely needed a backup catcher—or didn't think he did.

The team had finished a distant third in 1968, but from opening day, an extra-inning win over the Phillies, the '69 Cubs seemed destined for glory. They burned through the early part of the season, winning thirty-six of their first fifty-two games, building an eight-game lead in the new National League East division by early June. Attendance soared, Durocher was the toast of Chicago, and it was headline news when Leo got married for the fourth time on June 19th to his girlfriend of three years, Windy City socialite Lynne Goldblatt. "I was visiting dad in Chicago, so I went to the wedding with him," Shirley remembers. "It was at a small room at the Ambassador Hotel. There were seats on each side and just a few ferns at the end of the aisle. Solemn music was playing, and people were speaking in hushed tones. So, my dad looks around and says out loud: 'Where's the casket?' Everyone laughed."

But at the stag party, a boozy affair in a Chicago pub two weeks before the wedding, Pete chatted with a reporter and admitted to having doubts about the Cubs' success. "The whole season has been going too good so far. Everybody thinks we've already won the pennant. What happens if we stop getting the breaks? What happens if we go into a losing streak? Do we panic and lose the whole thing? We've just been too lucky so far. The whole thing makes me scared," he said.

Pete was right to worry. Despite their rocket start, the Cubs had some glaring weaknesses. No one ran particularly fast, and the bench and the bullpen were both on the thin side. Worst of all, the team lacked a decent centerfielder. Durocher tried four different guys—Adolfo Phillips, Don Young, Jim Qualls, and Oscar Gamble—and they hit a combined .239 with seven home runs while providing subpar defense. Young hung on to the job for the longest, but Durocher damaged his confidence after a game in early July where Young misplayed two ninth-inning fly balls, allowing the second-place New York Mets to pull out a 4-3 victory. "The man [pitcher Jenkins] pitches his heart out, and one man can't catch a fly ball. It's a disgrace," Leo fumed to the press after the game.

Pete played a minor role in the next incident to upset the Cubs' momentum. Leo left early in a July 26th game at Wrigley, saying he felt ill and turned the managerial reins over to his old pal. With Pete in charge, the Cubs pulled out a 3-2 victory over the Dodgers in eleven innings. All seemed fine until the *Chicago Tribune* reported three days later that Leo hadn't been ill—instead, he had flown via private plane to Wisconsin to attend a party at a boys' camp where his new wife's son was spending the summer. When Cubs owner Phil Wrigley learned of Durocher's deception, he was furious and threatened to fire the less-than-repentant Lip. Wrigley reportedly called first base coach Herman Franks to offer him Leo's job. Franks, a Durocher loyalist, turned it down, saying the switch would disrupt the team too much.

Pete may have been getting tired of all the drama, for he told a Green Bay reporter that August: "It would be nice to win this year because this is my last one. I've got my twenty years in for my major league pension. So, I'm going to get me a part-time job in L.A. and spend some time with my family."

The Cubs looked like a sure winner as late as mid-August when a hot streak put them more than thirty games over .500. Few gave the surprising, second-place Mets a serious chance to catch up; in the first seven years of their existence, since joining the National League as an expansion team in 1962, the Mets had averaged one hundred five losses per season, and their personnel had not changed all that much from '68. But the Mets had a strong pitching staff, anchored by young superstar Tom Seaver, and manager Gil Hodges seemed to have the whole team hitting and fielding well above their presumed talent level. Meanwhile, Durocher was playing the same regulars game after game in the daytime heat of unlighted Wrigley Field, giving no rest even to the catcher,

Hundley, who caught a back-breaking one hundred fifty-one games, or thirty-eight-year-old first baseman Banks, who played one hundred fifty-five.

In essence, Durocher was repeating the mistake he made with Pete in 1942, pushing people beyond their physical capabilities. The results were much the same: every key player slumped in September, and the Cubs lost seventeen of twenty-five games, including eleven of twelve to start the month. It was as though the entire team, like their third base coach in his younger days, had slammed into a concrete wall.

"I just remember the feeling, we're gonna win, we're gonna win, and then, it not happening. Dad never said that should have happened, or I should have done this. But yeah, it was a huge disappointment," says Shirley. The Miracle Mets roared past the Cubs to win the NL East, then swept past the Braves in the playoffs and Orioles in the World Series to win one of baseball's most unlikely championships. Pete was officially an ex-Cub by then, having resigned his position on the last day of September.

His comments in August to the contrary, he wasn't ready for part-time work yet. He coached full-time with the California Angels in 1970 and 1971. Then it was back to Chicago and Durocher for '72. Leo got fired mid-season, but Pete stayed on and remained a Cubbie coach through '73. He got knocked out of a game one last time that May, when he unwisely waded into a fight between the Cubs and Giants at Candlestick Park and took an accidental punch to the throat from Cubs' pitcher Jack Aker, followed by a kick to the head after he fell near home plate. When the field was cleared, Pete was put on a stretcher and transported to a San Francisco hospital. Doctors there said he had suffered a concussion—his fifth, going by official diagnoses, though it's entirely possible he'd picked up more along the way.

From 1974 on, Pete stayed away from full-season coaching jobs and worked either as a scout or roving minor-league instructor. As early as 1945, he had expressed interest in scouting, telling Branch Rickey in a letter that "I believe I have a nack [sic] of knowing a prospect when I see one, and I well remember what Charley Barrett used to look for." Rick Tuber recalls accompanying Pete to a game in Riverside, California, and watching him take notes. "I think one guy hit two home runs, and I said, 'That guy looks really good.' And he just shook his head and said, 'No, not good enough. He just had a great day at the plate.' He saw things that I couldn't as an average fan. It was a hole in the swing; the guy missed a curveball or something. He really was a good judge of talent, and that's why he ended up scouting."

But rarely from this point on did he work outside southern California. Shirley says he was done with traveling. "He just didn't want to see a suitcase ever in his life again," she says. "He was tired. He was very physically tired." His health was getting shaky, too, both from his baseball injuries and decades of smoking. "He'd had a couple of heart attacks, and he'd grab his chest," Shirley says. "He had emphysema and heart problems and still had his other physical things. He didn't complain all the time, but you could see it."

In April 1979, Pete was running an extended spring training for the Cubs and Mets in St. Petersburg, Florida, when he checked into a hospital with what turned out to be pneumonia. While there, he got an unexpected visit from W.C. Heinz, who wanted to update his profile of Pete from twenty years earlier for a book he was writing. Heinz found him in a small private room, dealing with a persistent cough and labored breathing. When the nurse failed to respond to the call button, Heinz plugged in the oxygen machine himself and handed Pete the mask. For a minute, Pete drew in deep pulls of the life-giving air.

Then the two went back to talking about baseball. "As Mr. Rickey used to say," Pete said, pausing for breath between sentences, "it takes no talent to hustle. The easiest thing a man can do, outside of walking, is to run. I believed him."

In July 1980, Pete was healthy enough to attend an old-timers day in Los Angeles, donning the Dodger blue one last time. But with his bald head, well-lined face, and expanding gut, he looked older than his sixty-one years. One month later, a reporter for *The Californian* newspaper chatted him up as he scouted a class-A game in Salinas for the Angels. Pete admitted to feeling the effects of his old injuries. "They've really slowed me down. My shoulder comes out of place. Arthritis is setting in my elbows and knees and hips." The last time he tried to swing a bat was the previous year. He said, "I almost killed myself. It was during batting practice, trying to show off, I guess. Thought I could do the things I could do twenty years ago."

The writer asked if he enjoyed scouting.

"No," Pete said, then added: "I'm starting to like it. But ya sit too much. You get too itchy." Looking down at the infield, he added, "I'd like to be down there. Just to sit on the bench and shoot the bull with the kids."

At age sixty-one, even as his battered body gave out, Pete's spirit was still young. He still wanted to be part of the game.

* * *

On a Sunday, October 25, 1981, the end came at home in Palm Springs, after what the papers termed a long respiratory illness. The Dodgers were in the World Series and had beaten the Yankees in Game Five a few hours earlier. Pat said that Pete was aware of the victory but was too sick to follow the series closely. "He was laboring so for breath that he missed an awful lot of it," she said. She tried to be philosophical about his passing. "It was probably the best thing because to have Pete walking around with oxygen all the time would have been devastating. All things happen for the best," she said.

He had lived just long enough to see the baptism of Shirley and Rick's son, Peter Brian Tuber, born three months earlier. Peter would play in the 1994 Little League World Series.

About a hundred people attended Pete's funeral service three days later at St. Theresa's church in Palm Springs, including Leo Durocher. "This is quite a loss," Leo said. "He was one of my best friends."

His old pals in the press—Red Barber, Jim Murray, Red Smith, Dick Young, plus less famous names in places like Elmira, Kokomo, and Green Bay—paid tribute to him in their columns, testifying to his greatness as a player, lamenting the tendencies that stripped the greatness away. A transplanted Brooklynite near Tucson, one Anthony Sciretta, was as eloquent as any of them when he wrote, in a letter to the *Arizona Star*, "I have a warm smile on my face at this moment, for I can picture Pete Reiser running into the gate even before St. Peter had a chance to open it."

Pat survived Pete by twenty years. Sally lived another nineteen beyond that. Shirley still lives with Rick today in California. They still make it out to ballgames, and she still thinks about her father. "I miss him every day," she says.

12

Legacy

Eight decades have gone by since Pete Reiser won his lone batting title. Seven have passed since he took his last major league at-bat. Nearly all of his contemporaries have hit the showers in the sky, so to speak, and only a few of their names—Robinson, Musial, Williams, DiMaggio—still generate a flicker of recognition among the general MLB-watching public of the twenty-first century.

Yet Pete is not forgotten. In fact, hardly a week goes by on Twitter without a baseball history fanatic posting an article, a factoid, an old baseball card, or a photo to marvel at Pistol Pete Reiser. Here's the pre-war Reiser in a zippered Brooklyn uniform, eyes burning with game-ready intensity. Here's Pete stealing home, kicking up dust as he slides past an outstretched catcher's glove. Here's Pete being carried off the field after hurling his body against another hard outfield wall. Here's Pete as coach, head and neck tilted skyward to talk to six-foot-seven Frank Howard. Here's another post lamenting what might have been, what *should* have been . . . If only, if he hadn't, if he could've. What if, what if, what if.

One such article was posted by Daniel Brown, a senior editor and writer for the sports website *The Athletic* who covers events in the San Francisco Bay area. As a self-described baseball-mad kid in the late 1970s and early '80s, Brown discovered Reiser's story—as did I—through Lawrence Ritter and Donald Honig's book *The 100 Greatest Baseball Players of All-Time*. "His 'what if' story really captivated me," Brown says. "The notion that he was *so* good that even a bite-sized taste of his talent got him into the top 100 was just enthralling to me. I would have been ten when that book came out, so it had a comic book-like effect on me. It was hard to believe that there was a superhero who didn't save the world."

That feeling came unexpectedly rushing back years later when Brown—by now a well-seasoned baseball writer who spent parts of two decades covering the Giants—got to talking with former MLB pitcher and current Giants color analyst Mike Krukow. "I heard Krukow say during a TV broadcast that the first person who ever told him he was going to the big leagues was Leo Durocher," Brown recalls. "That was amazing to me, and I told him so when I saw him in person a few days later. That's when he said, 'That's nothing. Pete Reiser was my first minor league coach.' I was blown away! I felt ten years old again, and I couldn't believe that I knew someone who knew the comic book figure of my youth." In March 2021, Brown wrote a well-received story on Krukow and Reiser, memorably describing the latter as having "a career that left him cast in plaster instead of bronze."

Brown was far from the first writer inspired to put pen to paper, or fingers to keyboard, by Reiser's life and career. In fact, for decades, starting in the late 1940s, the Pete Reiser recap was a staple of sportswriters' columns across the country. Sometimes, they wrote it because of a personal encounter with Pete, who was usually willing to talk to journalists. Sometimes, it was triggered by boyhood nostalgia. Occasionally, it appeared to be the result of deadline pressure, written in the absence of a better way to fill the allotted twelve hundred words of newsprint. Whatever the reason, many of the best-known sportswriters of the second half of the twentieth century devoted one or more columns to Pete, including but not limited to Grantland Rice, Dick Young, Jim Murray, Furman Bisher, Bob Broeg, Red Smith, Joe Williams, Jimmy Cannon, Jimmy Powers, J.G. Taylor Spink, Phil Pepe, Dave Anderson, Arthur Daley, John Kieran, Harry Grayson, and Les Biederman. Most of the pieces shared a tone of awe and regret, as typified in a 1997 piece by Bisher, a pillar of the *Atlanta Journal-Constitution* for nearly sixty years: "[He] could have been the greatest baseball player of this century if he'd had more respect for outfield walls. That's right, *the* greatest. Instead, he was the most tragic. He left his career lying in a heap at the base of the outfield fence in Ebbets Field."

Writers outside the sports field incorporated Reiser into their works as well. One of the Dodger faithful was a Brooklyn-born and raised writer named Bernard Malamud. In the literary world, Malamud was and remains best known for novels that plumbed the American Jewish immigrant experience like *The Assistant* and *The Fixer*, the latter of which won the 1967 Pulitzer Prize for fiction. But for the general public, his best-known book is his first published novel, *The Natural*, a baseball-themed work that Robert Redford made into a 1984 movie which aired on MLB Network many, many, many, many, many, many, many,

many times as the network tried to weather the 2020 coronavirus shutdown. The novel is centered around Roy Hobbs, an outfielder for the fictional New York Knights. Hobbs is a semi-tragic figure attempting to make a comeback in his mid-thirties, some fifteen years after he was shot by a mysterious woman in a hotel, cutting short his career as a teenage pitching phenom. In one dramatic scene, Hobbs' athletic and romantic rival, Bump Bailey, is trying to outshine him and becomes a ballhawk in center field, catching one long hit with a spectacular dive, grabbing another on a running over-the-shoulder catch, Willie Mays style. Then, with his girlfriend watching from the stands, Bailey charges after a line drive headed toward the center-field wall and met a fate that could only be described as Reiseresque:

> *As Bump ran for it, he could feel fear leaking through his stomach, and his legs unwillingly slowed down, but then he had this vision of himself as the league's best outfielder, acknowledged so by fans and players alike, even Pop, whom he'd be nothing less than forever respectful to, and in love with and married to Memo. Thinking this way, he ran harder . . . and with a magnificent twisting jump, he trapped the ball in his iron fingers. Yet the wall continued to advance, and though the redheaded lady of his choice was on her feet shrieking, Bump bumped it with a skull-breaking bang, and the wall embraced his broken body.*

Unlike Reiser, Bailey died. Malamud never explicitly said that he fashioned Bailey's end on Reiser's real-life collisions but confirmed more than once that the Dodgers were the model for much of what occurred in his book. "The old Brooklyn Dodgers were our heroes, our stars, like something out of myths," he said in the 1980s as Redford's movie was being filmed.

Reiser also served as a touchstone for a generation of authors, somebody they could freely put into their stories, confident that strands of their audience—the Brooklynites, New Yorkers in general, and baseball fans—would remember him. Pulitzer Prize-winning author Philip Roth worked Reiser into a 1957 short story, "You Can't Tell a Man by the Song He Sings." The unnamed narrator in the story, presumably a stand-in for Roth, gets into a conversation with a high school classmate about the relative merits of Pistol Pete and a rival outfielder. "As a Dodger fan, I preferred Reiser to the Yankees' Henrich," says the narrator, "and besides, my tastes have always been a bit baroque, and Reiser, who repeatedly bounced off outfield walls to save the day for Brooklyn, had won a special trophy in the Cooperstown of my heart."

As noted, PBS news anchor Jim Lehrer was a huge Pistol Pete fan in his youth. In later life, Lehrer found both critical and commercial success as a writer, and in 2009, he published *Oh Johnny*, a novel about a young man in the 1940s who dreams of playing major league baseball. The character's idol, not surprisingly, is Pete Reiser. "You can call me anything. But mainly, call me a ballplayer. A center fielder," the young man writes in a letter to a girlfriend. "I'm good, and I'm going to be even better. As good as Pete. Pistol Pete Reiser. I'm sure you don't know about him, but trust me, he's the best."

Brooklyn-born and raised Pete Hamill built his long writing career on observations and memories of New York. So, it's hardly surprising that Reiser turned up repeatedly in his writing. In Hamill's novel *Snow in August*, the main character sits in the Ebbets Field stands when he spies Reiser trotting out to left field soon after one of his crashes into the wall. He says to himself, Holy God, there's Pete Reiser, back from the dead! He points Reiser out to his rabbi, sitting one seat over. "He looks okay, boychik," says the rabbi. "Maybe some prayers helped."

In Hamill's story *The Christmas Kid*, boys in a 1940s Brooklyn neighborhood befriend a young Jewish refugee from Poland and teach him about baseball.

> "He play baseball good?" Lev said, pointing at a picture of Reiser in the *Daily News*. "He play stickball good?"
> "Good?" Ralphie Boy said. "He's like Christmas every day!"

On one occasion, Reiser even met a legendary writer in person, though the writer was less than impressed. In the spring of 1942, the Dodgers trained in Havana, and one of their local admirers was none other than Ernest Hemingway. After hours, Hemingway took to hanging out with the Brooklyn club and even instigated an impromptu, late-night drunken boxing match at his house with Hugh Casey. (Casey won.) Hemingway later offered his impressions of several Dodgers in a letter to a journalist buddy of his. "Curt Davis, Billy Herman, Augie Galan, and Johnny Rizzo are really wonderful guys," he wrote. "Reese and Reiser are sweet ball players but ignorant punks."

One writer who did like Pistol Pete was the esteemed W.C. Heinz. Many contemporaries considered Wilford Charles Heinz the finest sportswriter of his time, though his fields of interest were not limited to sports. In the 1950s, he was a regular contributor to big-circulation magazines such as *Life*, *Esquire*, *Collier's*, and the *Saturday Evening Post*. Later he wrote two highly successful books: *Run to Daylight* with legendary Green Bay Packers coach Vince Lombardi and, working with a Maine doctor under the pseudonym Richard Hooker, *M*A*S*H*, the genesis for the hugely popular 1970 movie and the long-running TV series. But Heinz started out working for the *New York Sun*, first as a correspondent covering the war in Europe, later as a sports columnist pumping out spare, powerful writing and keen insights about the worlds of boxing, horse racing, football, and baseball. Take this 1946 column about the struggles of retired baseball players to survive financially in that era before a players' pension: "There are some things, though, that no athlete can put away. A base hit is spent the moment you touch the base. A fielding gem is a jewel that is stolen away the next time they hit one your way. There is no way that you can hoard the roar of the crowd calling your name. There is no bank that you can go to years later and say: 'Today I will withdraw a few decibels that I earned another day.'"

Maybe those thoughts were on Heinz's mind when in 1957, he got the inspiration to write about Pete, then managing a Dodger farm team in Kokomo, Indiana—at the class-D level, the lowest rung in professional baseball. Heinz went to the little ballpark and learned that Pete had been dealing with chest pain and planned to travel home to St. Louis to see a heart specialist. "I'll drive you," Heinz said and used the subsequent eight-hour trip as the backbone for a wistful look back at Pete's career of injuries, wall crashes, and bad breaks. Heinz liberally quoted baseball figures and sportswriters vouching for Pete's greatness, such as *New York Herald Tribune* sports editor Bob Cooke, who said, "I didn't see the old-timers, but Pete Reiser was the best ballplayer I ever saw," and of course, Leo Durocher, who said, "He was the best I ever had, with the possible exception of Mays. At that, he was even faster than Willie."

Heinz also did Pete the favor of letting him narrate his own tales, which by now Pete had told many times and knew how to deliver for a dramatic impact. He was best describing the callous, get-back-on-the-field attitude of the Dodgers and their doctors in those years. "Whitey Kurowski hit one in the seventh inning at Ebbets Field. I dove for it and woke up in the clubhouse. I was in Peck Memorial for four days. It really didn't take much to knock me out in those days. I was comin' apart all over. When I dislocated my [left] shoulder, they popped it back in, and Leo said, 'Hell, you'll be all right. You don't throw with it anyway.'"

The resulting piece, entitled "The Rocky Road of Pistol Pete," was published in the March 1958 issue of *True*, a popular men's magazine, to immediate acclaim. In 1959, it won the prestigious E.F. Dutton Prize for the best magazine article of the year. Heinz liked the story so much that he updated it for his 1979 book *Once They Heard the Cheers* and repurposed it for his 1982 book *American Mirror*. Since then, it's made the cut in multiple "best of" anthologies, notably a 1999 book entitled *The Best American Sportswriting of the Century*, and to this day pops up anew on the internet, posted by fans of Heinz, Reiser, and compelling baseball writing.

Overall, this is a good thing: it keeps Reiser's name alive to the public and introduces baseball history newbies to his story. There's a problem, though. Despite being published in *True* magazine, several anecdotes and details in "Rocky Road" are demonstrably false. Pete did not return just one day after the Ike Pearson beaning in April 1941 to crush a pinch-hit, game-winning grand slam against the Phillies. He did not deliver a game-winning hit in Pittsburgh two days after his July '42 crash into the Sportsman's Park wall. His peak batting average in 1942 never reached .391. His Fort Riley teams did not win the national semipro tournament. He was not in the hospital for four days after trying to catch the Kurowski hit. He was not paralyzed for eight days after crashing into the Ebbets Field wall in '47, and the Dodgers had not shortened center field by thirty feet the previous winter, the change that Pete blamed for the accident.

But like many a writer before and after him, Heinz chose to sidestep the truth and print the legend—which is a shame because Pete's true story was compelling on its own, without the embellishments, even if some of them came from Pete himself.

* * *

Pete's most tangible legacy, of course, can be found along the rim of the outfield. Each time a runner notices a warning track and slows down, each time he bounces off a wall unscathed instead of crumpling unconscious on the grass, he should say a quiet thank-you to Pete Reiser, who for all we know may be watching the game from a dugout in heaven and shouting at the player, "You shoulda caught that!"

Jim Murray of the *Los Angeles Times* once joked: "Every ballpark in America has a Pete Reiser memorial: the warning track in the outfield was put in to keep Pete Reiser from killing himself." Of course, the joke was not a joke at all; teams *did* install tracks and wall padding to prevent Reiser and fellow wall-crashers like Elmer Valo from destroying themselves for the sake of a fly ball. When Pete died in October 1981, Murray recycled the joke but put it in an appropriately solemn context. "When you watch the World Series on TV this week, you will notice a shaved portion of the outfield about four feet out from the fences. This is the warning track, the Pete Reiser Memorial. Pete's the reason there is one of these in every ballpark," he wrote.

Despite reminders from Murray, it's fair to say that even in 1981, only a minority of baseball fans and players knew of Pete's role in making outfield walls safe for fly-chasers everywhere. Even fewer are aware of it today, something that slightly bugs Pete's daughter, Shirley. "I think that only real baseball fans—baseball history fans—remember my dad," she wrote in an email to this author. "I have met a few people over the years who say they saw him play in Brooklyn. Alas, as we get older, there are fewer of them. Even young ballplayers today do not seem to relish too much of the history. Every time I watch a game today and an outfielder runs hard into the wall, only someone like Vin Scully would even know to mention my dad and the history that gave them those padded walls and warning tracks." Scully, who retired in 2016 after a mind-boggling sixty-seven years as a Dodger broadcaster, was the last active broadcaster who could be considered a contemporary of Pete's. And until the end of his career, he did, from time to time, mention Pete on the air, usually after a player lost his place on the field and crashed into an outfield wall.

Pete might be better known today if he was a member of the National Baseball Hall of Fame. Technically, he's eligible: he played the minimum ten years in the major leagues, even with missing three seasons due to the war, even with all the injuries that put him on the bench for big chunks of those ten years. But he'll never get elected. When he first appeared on the ballot in 1958, he got just two percent of the vote. When he appeared a second time in 1960, he got three. After that, he dropped off the ballot, and the various veterans' committees that re-examine overlooked candidates from time to time have never given Pete any real consideration. In all fairness, this outcome is the correct one. Whether measured in terms of statistics, awards, pennants, or overall impact, Pete's actual accomplishments do not rise to the level of typical Hall of Fame outfielder, even when compared to low-tier what-were-they-thinking picks like Chick Hafey and Harold Baines.

But before the walls got in the way, Pete was starting to build a bona fide Cooperstown resumé. Look at the pure numbers. Pete was in the major leagues for almost exactly two years before he slammed into the wall at Sportsman's Park. During that time, he played in two hundred seventy-two games and came to bat nearly twelve hundred times—not a small sample size. The results? He batted .335, had an on-base percentage of .393 and a slugging percentage of .517. That is a very, very good start to a major league career. In fact, it's hard to find other guys who batted .335 or higher during their first two full seasons in the bigs. Al Simmons, Chuck Klein, and the Waner brothers did it in the hitting-happy 1920s. Among Pete's contemporaries, only Williams, DiMaggio, and Musial pulled it off. Only Wade Boggs and Ichiro Suzuki have reached that plateau in the last half-century, both with significantly less power than Pete.

What makes Pete's accomplishment even more remarkable is that he did it at a time of declining offense in the National League. Between 1939 and 1942, the National League batting average dropped sharply four years in a row, falling from .272 to .264 to .258 to .249. On-base percentages and slugging percentages tumbled too, and total league scoring fell by nearly seven hundred runs. Why this happened is hard to say; none of the league's teams switched cities or ballparks, and there were no major changes in scheduling, rules, or equipment. The point is that while other top National League hitters like Mel Ott, Johnny Mize, Arky Vaughn, Joe Medwick, Ernie Lombardi, and Frank McCormick saw their numbers tapering off, Pete's were on the rise. He wasn't just hitting well; he was bucking a league-wide trend.

That must be partly why the renowned baseball analyst Bill James, in the 2000 version of his *Baseball Historical Abstract*, selected Pete as one of the ten best *young* center fielders—that is, center fielders under age twenty-five—in the history of the game. Other names on the list included DiMaggio, Mickey Mantle, Willie Mays, and Ken Griffey Jr. That's the kind of company Reiser walked in at his peak.

It didn't last, of course. After July 19, 1942, after he left that hospital bed in St. Louis against doctors' orders, Pete's career batting average was a decent but ordinary .269. He still did special things, like stealing home, getting game-winning hits, inspiring his teammates with his determination to play through pain. But the concussions, dizziness, shoulder injuries, broken ankles, and other accumulated cuts and pulls and bumps and burns gradually, inexorably, leached the magnificent talents out of his body.

Only his admirers remembered what could have been. Jim Murray wrote, "Pete Reiser would be in the Hall of Fame today if they had warning tracks when he was playing." Furman Bisher said: "The least they could have done was bury him in Cooperstown."

Shirley adds: "At least every year at Hall of Fame induction time, a light gets to shine on the great ones. But there are many great ones who do not get in the Hall."

Don't feel bad for Pete, though. He didn't want it that way.

Many a time, a reporter asked him: if you could get a do-over on your career, would you change the way you play? Sometimes, he said he'd like to reverse certain decisions, like signing with the Dodgers for only a hundred dollars or disregarding Branch Rickey's request to sit out a year. But those were off-field events. Regarding his on-field performance, he never changed his tune.

"I wouldn't play any differently if I had the chance to start all over," Reiser said as early as 1951, while he was still with the Pirates. "I wouldn't know how. I got to the top because I played to win. How else could I play?"

"Sure, if I could have avoided bouncing off fences, maybe I'd still be up there," he said in 1956 while managing in the minors. "I'm sure I would have lasted a lot longer than I did. But you can't say to yourself, 'I'm not going to get hurt.' At least I couldn't. I don't know, but if I were starting all over again, I couldn't promise anybody that I wouldn't play it just the same way."

And still, in 1976: "If I had to do over, I'd do it the same way, because that's the way I played ball."

During his long, bourbon-soaked talk with Pete in 1974, Donald Honig asked a slightly different question: do you have any regrets?

Pete's answer was unequivocal. "No, I don't have any regrets. Not about one damned thing," he said. "I've had a lot of good experiences in my life, and they far outnumber the bad. Good memories are the greatest thing in the world, and I've got a lot of those."

But—and this is a significant "but"—Shirley Tuber suggests that privately, her father's view on his career was not entirely regret-free.

"The one thing I do remember that he said a lot was, 'You get old too soon and smart too late,'" she says. "Maybe he was trying to give me a life lesson. Maybe that was him reflecting on what might have been."

Bibliography

Barber, Red, *1947: When All Hell Broke Loose in Baseball*. New York, Doubleday, 1982.
Durocher, Leo and Ed Linn, *Nice Guys Finish Last*. New York, Pocket Books, 1976.
Eig, Jonathan, *Opening Day: The Story of Jackie Robinson's First Season*. New York, Simon & Schuster, 2005.
Hamill, Pete, *The Christmas Kid and Other Brooklyn Stories*. New York, Little, Brown and Company, 2012.
———, *Snow in August*. New York, Little, Brown and Company, 1997.
Heinz, W.C., *Once They Heard the Cheers*. Garden City, NY, Doubleday, 1979.
———, *What a Time It Was: The Best of W.C. Heinz on Sports*. Da Capo Press, 2001.
Honig, Donald, *Baseball When the Grass Was Real: Baseball from the Twenties to the Forties Told by the Men Who Played It*. New York, Coward, McCann & Geoghegan, Inc. 1975.
———, *The Fifth Season: Tales of My Life in Baseball*. Chicago, Ivan R. Dee, 2009.
Jacobson, Sidney, *Pete Reiser: the Rough and Tumble Career of the Perfect Ballplayer*. New York, MacFarland, and Company, 2004.
James, Bill, *The New Bill James Baseball Historical Abstract*. New York, Free Press, a division of Simon and Schuster, 2001.
Kahn, Roger, *Rickey & Robinson: The True, Untold Story of the Integration of Baseball*. New York, Rodale, Inc., 2004.
Lehrer, James, *Oh Johnny: A Novel*. New York, Random House, 2009.
———, *We Were Dreamers*. New York, H. Wolff, 1975.
Malamud, Bernard, *The Natural*. New York, Harcourt, Brace and World, 1952.
Mileur, Jerome, *High-Flying Birds: the 1942 St. Louis Cardinals*. Columbia, Missouri, University of Missouri Press, 2009.
Nelson, Cary and Jefferson Hendricks, *Edwin Rolfe: a Biological Essay and Guide to the Rolfe Archive at the University of Illinois at Urbana-Champaign*. The University of Illinois Library, 1990.
Parrott, Harold, *The Lords of Baseball*. New York, Praeger Publishers, 1976.

Reichler, Joseph L. (Editor), *The World Series: A 75th Anniversary*, New York, Simon and Schuster, 1978.
Ritter, Lawrence, *The Glory of Their Times: The Story of the Early Days of Baseball Told by the Men Who Played It*. New York, MacMillan and Company, 1966.
Rosengren, *Hank Greenberg: The Hero of Heroes*. New York, New American Library, a division of Penguin Group, 2013.
Roth, Phillip, *Goodbye, Columbus*. New York, Houghton Mifflin, 1959.
Tygiel, Jules, *Baseball's Great Experiment: Jackie Robinson and His Legacy*. London, Oxford University Press, 1983.
Various, *The Score Book: Fifty-Third Annual Dinner New York Baseball Writers Association*. New York, New York Chapter of the Baseball Writers' Association of America, 1976.
Williams, Peter (Editor), *The Joe Williams Baseball Reader*. Chapel Hill, N.C., Algonquin Books of Chapel Hill, 1989.
Wills, Maury and Gardner, Steve, *It Pays to Steal*. Englewood Cliffs, N.J., Prentice-Hall, 1963.

Notes

All statistics and game information come from baseballreference.com unless otherwise indicated. Radio and TV broadcasts were found on YouTube unless otherwise noted.

Introduction

ix *"Grandpa, what was the best . . ."* The ad was for YouTube TV.
x   *"Boy, that was a wallop!"* Mutual radio broadcast, World Series Game Four, October 4, 1941.
x   *"At that moment . . ."* Joe Posnanski, "Catch 22," nbcsports.com, September 22, 2015.
x   *"There are knowing students . . ."* Red Smith column, *New York Herald Tribune*, August 5, 1958.
xii *"Of all the careers aborted . . ."* Lawrence Ritter and Donald Honig, *The 100 Greatest Baseball Players of All Time*, Crown Publishers, Inc., 1981, p. 153.
xii *"Soooo, the Dodgers are tied 4-4 . . ."* I recounted this game in a 2020 article for SABR, the Society for American Baseball Research. What I didn't realize at the time was that Captain America's screenwriters, Christopher Markus and Stephen McFeely, based the faux Red Barber call on a real call that Barber made in Game Six of the 1947 World Series. In the real call, when Barber said "this fella's capable of making it a brand-new game," he was talking about Joe DiMaggio. DiMaggio hit the next pitch to the right field fence of Yankee Stadium, but it was grabbed by a frantically backpedaling Al Gionfriddo, in one of the most famous catches in World Series history.

Chapter 1: Peak Reiser

1 *"So if the white shirt you wore . . ."* I grew up in Pittsburgh, and I heard stories like this all the time. Well into the late 20th century, many buildings in Pittsburgh were still blackened from decades of soot dumped on them during the years before pollution control.
1 *"I've always wanted to play . . ."* Joe Cummiskey column, *PM Daily*, June 28, 1942.
2 *"the NL pennant race might be over. . ."* Grantland Rice column, syndicated, *New York Sun*, June 2, 1942.
2 *"I know the Pirates aren't as bad . . ."* Associated Press, "Only Need Hits, Declares Frisch," *Cincinnati Enquirer*, June 2, 1942.
2 *"One of the principals . . ."* Turkin, "Dodgers Sweep Pair from Braves," *New York Daily News*, June 1, 1942.
2 *"Buy U.S. War Stamps."* The sign can be seen in photos taken at Ebbets Field during the 1942 season, viewable on the Getty Images website.
2 *"Reiser could be another Ty Cobb . . ."* Durocher said this on more than one occasion during the 1941 season, including a *Daily News* article published on June 1 and the Grantland Rice column of July 2.
3 *"Here is a lad who looks like . . ."* Tom Meany, "Reiser National Leaguer No. 1," *Saturday Evening Post*, September 26, 1942.

3 *"If you think he isn't..."* Tommy Holmes, "Heroics Cut No Ice with Pete Reiser," *Brooklyn Eagle*, May 26, 1941.
3 *"We've seen some who were smarter..."* Gerry Schumacher, International News Service, "Reiser One of the Loop's Best," *Pasadena Post*, May 31, 1942.
3 *"Do you think Reiser is as good..."* Donald Honig, *The Fifth Season: Tales of My Life in Baseball*, Ivan R. Dee, Chicago, 2009, p. 57.
3 *"Right now, there's little to choose..."* Edward T. Murphy, "Dodgers Deferred Games Mount Up," *New York Sun*, June 13, 1942.
3 *"I just wish he'd make more noise."* Elsa Maxwell, "Thunder Over Brooklyn Is Big, Booming Roar," syndicated, *Pittsburgh Post-Gazette*, June 17, 1942.
3 *"I sure wish he would holler more."* Robert Lewis Taylor, "Borough Defender: MacPhail and the Dodgers," *The New Yorker*, July 12, 1941.
3 *"Naw, I just get up there..."* Associated Press, "Pete Reiser Expects to be 'Farmed,'" *Elmira Star-Gazette*, April 5, 1939.
4 *"That Williams can hit."* Dick Farrington, "Petey, 'Grandest Boy That Ever Lived' to Mother, Buys House for His Parents With Dodger Earnings," *The Sporting News*, December 25, 1941.
4 *"I wouldn't mind batting five times..."* Associated Press, "Looks Like a Cinch for Reiser," *Dayton Daily News*, September 19, 1941.
4 *"Dad never talked about..."* author email interview with Shirley Tuber, September 2020.
5 *"When you lay in for that kid..."* Dick Young, "Reiser Looms as 2nd Flock 2-Time Champ," *New York Daily News*, July 26, 1942. Incidentally, New York and Brooklyn sportswriters of the 1940s often referred to the Dodgers and their fans as "the flock." The term originated during the years when the Dodgers were managed by Wilbert Robinson and were unofficially known as the Robins. Robins = birds = flock. Get it? Robinson retired after the 1931 season but the term remained in use for years thereafter, especially by headline writers seeking a short, colorful way to describe the team and its faithful rooters.
5 *"A lot of times a fellow..."* Honig, *Baseball When the Grass Was Real*, Coward, McCann and Geoghegan, New York, 1975, p. 68-69.
5 *Pete ran after the ball at full speed...* Associated Press, "Yankees Drub Dodgers 16-4 to Square Spring Series Count," *Richmond Times Dispatch*, April 8, 1942.
5 *"I always felt that he played too hard."* Honig, *Baseball Between the Lines: Baseball in the '40s and '50s as Told by the Men Who Played It*, Coward, McCann and Geoghegan, 1976, p. 60.
5 *"Pete has such tremendous will..."* Arthur Daley, "The $100 Bargain," *New York Times*, May 27, 1946.
6 *"Why rattle him like this..."* Turkin, "Leave Reiser Alone, Lip Pleads," *New York Daily News*, April 15, 1942.
6 *The draft board reclassified him.* "Reiser's Status Changed to 3A," *New York Daily News*, May 16, 1942.
6 *"There he was, inching..."* Honig, *Fifth Season*, p.58.
6 *"There wasn't a thing he couldn't do..."* Honig, *Baseball Between the Lines*, p. 209.
7 *"The feeling about him in 1942..."* Ibid.
7 *"Thousand bomber raids."* News about the raids on Cologne and the battles in Libya can be found on numerous front pages of newspapers from June 2, 1942. For instance, the *Brooklyn Eagle* ran a bolded, all-caps headline that read: "ESSEN DEVASTATED BY 1,036 RAF BOMBERS." Below that, in smaller type: "U.S. Tanks Smash Libya Rommel Drive."
7 *German sub U-404 claimed its second vessel.* Information on the submarine and the sinking can be found on uboat.net, which has details about all German subs in both world wars. (https://uboat.net/allies/merchants/ship/1728.html)

8   *"Hey, can YOU hit?"* Les Biederman, "The Scoreboard," *Pittsburgh Press*, June 2, 1942.
8   *"Every blow was a solid line drive..."* Roscoe McGowen, "Dodgers Set Scoring Record as Pirates Drop Tenth Straight," *New York Times*, June 3, 1942.
9   *"Pete is hitting the ball..."* Murphy, "Reiser Featured in Dodgers' Victory," *New York Sun*, June 3, 1942. The Joe Medwick quote about Pete comes from the same article.
10 *"He's so far ahead..."* Murphy, "Dodgers Grow Lyrical Over Reiser," *New York Sun*, June 5, 1942.
10 *"Reiser isn't just a hard hitter..."* Turkin, "Pete's Hitting a Hit With Mates," *New York Daily News*, June 4, 1942.
10 *"The boy has a great disposition..."* Ibid.
10 *"[I was] just starting to get warm."* Honig, *Baseball When the Grass Was Real*, p. 283-84.

Chapter 2: Like Father, Like Son

12 *"3018 North Taylor looks as though..."* All information about the Reiser family's old house comes from the website of the St. Louis Land Reutilization Authority. The house incidentally, was built in 1897. The photos of the house displayed on the LRA website date from 2014 and 2016. It's possible that the house has been fixed up since then, or decayed further. But it's doubtful anyone has made any significant changes, as the property remains on sale for $1,000 as of September 2021.
13 *"... ten to twenty murders per year."* Homicide statistics for all St. Louis neighborhoods can be found on the website of the St. Louis Metropolitan Police Department.
13 *"... murder rate there was three times higher than in Honduras."* Elizabeth Van Brocklin, "Is America Experiencing a Murder Outbreak? It Depends On Your Block." *The Trace*, December 27, 2016.
13 *"George had grown up poor."* Information on George Reiser's early life and his parents comes U.S. census records between 1860 and 1900, John Reiser's Civil War military records, and detailed research done by genealogist Ilya Zeldes. George's mother Antonia was John Reiser's second wife, whom he married just five months after the death of his first, Catherina, in January 1872.
14 *"The Repples finished seventh."* Trolley League standings published in the *St. Louis Post-Dispatch*, Oct. 13, 1907.
14 *"A sub-.900 fielding percentage."* Final Trolley League statistics were published in the December 1, 1907 edition of the *St. Louis Globe-Democrat*. These stats were also the source for George Reiser's pitching record.
14 *"...two of the best twirlers in the league."* "Two Games for Kulage's Park," *St. Louis Globe-Democrat*, July 14, 1907.
14 *"Reiser pitched great ball..."* "Repples 4, Alta Sitas 0," *St. Louis Globe-Democrat*, Sept. 30, 1907.
14 *"Reiser contributed a dumb play..."* "Maroons Give a Scare," *Winnipeg Tribune*, April 30, 1908.
14 *"Reiser was on the mound for the Maroons..."* "The Tide Is Turning," *Winnipeg Tribune*, May 9, 1908.
14 *"Reiser was let go in Minneapolis..." Winnipeg Tribune*, May 12, 1908.
14 *"... batting Reiser the Trolley League pitcher from the box."* *Arkansas Democrat*, August 9, 1908.
14 *"Reiser lasted nearly four innings..."* "Shamrocks Win in Eleventh, 7 to 6," *Arkansas Gazette*, August 12, 1908.
14 *"Reiser of the Argenta club was released..."* "Arkansaw League Notes," *Daily Arkansas Gazette*, August 13, 1908. That's not a misspelling; Arkansaw was the word used in the headline.

15 *"... applied for a St. Louis marriage license."* The issuance of the marriage license was reported in the July 1, 1908 *St. Louis Globe-Democrat*, although I was unable to find the actual marriage record for George and Stella.
15 *"The families were friends-slash-neighbors in DeSoto."* Gerry Meier email to author, August 2020.
15 *"... a virile son of the saddle."* Meany, *Saturday Evening Post*, September 1942.
15 *"He was Two-Gun Pete to the boys."* Farrington, "Young Pete Reiser, Who Bats Both Ways and Throws With Either Hand, Makes Two-Berth Bid on Dodgers," *The Sporting News*, February 6, 1941.
15 *"... insists that the name is pronounced 'Reeser.'"* W.J. McGoogan, "$100,000 Wouldn't Buy Reiser, Who Cost Brooklyn Only $100," *St. Louis Post-Dispatch*, August 1, 1941.
15 *"Ornery, mean, nice."* Honig, *Baseball When the Grass Was Real*, p. 285.
16 *"I was born in a rough neighborhood."* Interview of Pete by Rick Tuber. The exact date of the interview is uncertain but judging from references on the tape, it appears to be from the early part of 1981, a few months before Pete's death.
16 *"Harold Patrick was an altar boy..."* Vincent de Paul Fitzpatrick, "Top of the Morning to Pete," *The Tablet*, August 30, 1941.
16 *"Yes, yes—double yes."* Author interview of Rick and Shirley Tuber, September 2020.
16 *"As soon as you were old enough..."* Honig, *Baseball When the Grass Was Real*, 1975, p. 286.
16 *"We were a baseball-playing family."* Sidney Jacobson, *Pete Reiser: the Rough and Tumble Career of the Perfect Ballplayer*, McFarland and Company, 2004.
16 *"He was the dirtiest kid..."* Farrington, *The Sporting News*, December 25, 1941.
16 *"Over 300 major leaguers have been born or raised..."* The number is derived from baseball-reference.com and its page on players born in Missouri. In additions to the ones mentioned in the text, some of the more famous St. Louis natives to play big league ball include Harry Steinfeldt, the third baseman in the Cubs' famed Tinker-to-Evans-to Chance infield of the early 1900s; Dickie Kerr, one of the "clean" White Sox in the 1919 World Series; Elston Howard, who broke the color line on the Yankees and won the 1963 American League MVP; 1970s San Diego Padres slugger Nate Colbert; and Hall of Fame manager Dick Williams.
17 *"As agile as a cat..."* Schumacher, "Dodgers Owe Landis Thanks for Giving Them Reiser," International News Service, *Pittsburgh Sun-Telegraph*, June 30, 1941.
17 *"Sure, I wanted to be a ballplayer..."* Honig, *Baseball When the Grass was Real*, p. 285.
17 *"I was always a pretty good ballplayer..."* Ibid, p. 286.
18 *"My dad idolized Mike."* Author interview.
18 *"My brother was really good at it."* Harry Cross, "Pete Reiser to Bat Left-Handed and Throw Only with His Right," *New York Herald Tribune*, March 16, 1941.
18 *"The other guys would say..."* Honig, *Baseball When the Grass Was Real*, p. 283.
19 *"Operated on both of us..."* Ibid, p. 286
20 Mike Reiser's official Missouri death certificate. Obtained through ancestry.com. For what it's worth, the certificate listed Mike's profession as "messenger boy."
20 *"All morning and early afternoon..."* Roger Birtwell, "$100 Down," *Collier's*, September 27, 1941.
21 *"I used to sit out there..."* Ibid.
22 *"He said, 'I can't compete financially..."* Barber talking with Robert Creamer, 1968. Creamer interviewed Barber at length that year for their book, *Rhubarb in the Catbird Seat*. The audio can be found on the website of the University of Florida Special & Area Studies Collections.
22 *"How can you expect a man to go out..."* George Kirksey, United Press, "Landis Assails Farm System of Major Leagues," December 6, 1929.

23 *"He knows the Midwest so well..."* John B. Foster, "Famous Baseball Scouts," syndicated, *Ithaca Journal*, January 26, 1931.
23 *"Boys wishing tryouts..."* "Boys From St. Louis District Will Have Cardinal Tryouts," *St. Louis Post-Dispatch*, September 20, 1936.
24 *His pay was sixteen dollars per week.* Birtwell, *Collier's*, 1941.
24 *"Do you want to want to play pro baseball?"* Ibid.
24 *"I told my father..."* Honig, *Baseball When the Grass Was Real*, p. 288
24 *"Well, I want to talk to you too,"* Ibid.
25 *"You know, when Pete got that contract..."* Farrington, *The Sporting News*, February 6, 1941.

Chapter 3: Gentlemen's Agreement
26 *Pete Reiser is having a drink...* Tuber interview, 1981.
26 *I wanted to be a Cardinal."* Ibid.
26 *Pete could refer to the baseball scrapbook...* Pages provided by Shirley Tuber.
27 *"Well, the best, ah..."* Tuber interview, 1981.
27 *"MacPhail and Rickey cooked up..."* Harold Parrott, *The Lords of Baseball*, Praeger Publishers, 1976, p. 141.
28 *"When my parents sold their house..."* Author interview, 2020.
28 *"There's a boy that's going to go places."* J. Roy Stockton column, *St. Louis Post-Dispatch*, February 26, 1939.
28 *"... the car lacked a heater."* "Round the Town with Regan," *St. Louis Star and Times*, March 5, 1936.
29 *"... he encountered a stray cow."* "From the Press Box," *Tucson Daily Citizen*, March 10, 1936
29 *"Stanley Frank Musial was still attending high school..."* Giglio, James N., *Musial: From Stash to Stan the Man*. Columbia and London: University of Missouri Press, 2001.
29 *"Charley Barrett's traveling buddy."* This account of Pete's travels with Barrett is drawn from several sources, including Pete's 1974 interview with Donald Honig and interviews he gave over the years to *The Sporting News*.
30 *"the Cardinals had a huge number of players..."* Information on the size and scope of the Cardinal farm system in the 1930s comes from the minor league affiliates pages on baseballreference.com. At its absolute peak in 1940, the Cardinals' farm system had thirty-one teams and a whopping seven hundred seventy-five players, the large majority of whom never sniffed a day in the big leagues. The system finally shrunk as a result of World War II forcing many minor leagues to shut down, along with cost-cutting by Cardinal owner Sam Breadon after Branch Rickey departed for Brooklyn.
30 *"Whenever we went into a town..."* Honig, *Baseball When the Grass Was Real*, p. 289.
31 *"Don't let anybody tell you..."* Bob Wilson, "Sport Talk," *Knoxville News-Sentinel*, May 25, 1936.
31 *"The boys are there..."* Ibid.
31 *"The Cardinals seemed to represent..."* Robert Creamer, *Baseball: An Illustrated History*, Knopf Doubleday Publishing Group, New York, 1996.
32 *"He started out at a Cardinal training camp..."* Reiser scrapbook.
32 *"I was assigned by the Cardinals..."* Frank Finch, "Pistol Pete—Gritty Busher to Big-Time Star, *The Sporting News*, April 25, 1962.
33 *"We couldn't live without her..."* Tuber interview, 1981.
33 *"I can remember nobody used to sit..."* Ibid.
33 *His best day came on...* "Two Homers Beat Pilots 2-1 Thursday," *Caruthersville Journal*, July 22, 1937.

33 "*Barrett personally paid his protégé's expenses...*" J. Roy Stockton column, *St. Louis Post-Dispatch*, February 26, 1939.
34 "*You are advised that, in accordance...*" Original letter sent by Judge Landis, in possession of Shirley Tuber.
34 "*Landis believed the Cardinals were using handshake deals...*" Information on Landis' decision to release 91 Cardinal farmhands and his rationale comes from "Landis Frees Players of Five Small Cardinal Farms," J. Roy Stockton, *St. Louis Post Dispatch*, March 23, 1938; "Landis Cracks Down on Cardinals, Releases 100 Farm Players," Associated Press, *St. Joseph News-Press*, March 24, 1938, and "Landis Cardinal Chain Decision Limits Farm System Expansion," *The Sporting News*, March 31, 1938.
35 "*He kept leagues alive...*" Tuber interview, 1981.
35 "*Charley Barrett had been tipped off...*" Joe Williams, "Vet Scout Sets Facts Straight on Pete Reiser," *Knoxville News-Sentinel*, March 30, 1960.
35 "*Charley Barrett was a good friend...*" Tuber interview, 1981.
35 "*In the event I am declared a free agent...*" Original contract in possession of Shirley Tuber.
36 "*If I was a kid breaking in today...*" Robert L. Burnes, "I'd Play the Same Way Again—Reiser," *The Sporting News*, January 15, 1956.
36 "*I could have hollered to Landis...*" Ibid.
36 "*Each time, McGrew almost had a heart attack...*" Finch, *The Sporting News*, 1962.
37 "*These guys were old and fat...*" Tuber interview, 1981.
37 "*Durocher bellowed, 'Stay fair!'*..." Turkin, "Dodgers Top Cards, 6-4," *New York Daily News*, March 23, 1939.
38 "*The kid has now faced six pitchers...*" The articles by Turkin, Holmes, Frank and McGowen all come from the March 24th editions of their respective newspapers.
38 "*The latest headline hero...*" Turkin, "Reiser 2nd Cronin!" *New York Daily News*, March 25, 1939.
38 "*Our incredible infant...*" Stanley Frank, *New York Post*, March 25, 1939.
39 "*I'll say one thing for him...*" Holmes, "Reiser, Stopped at Bat, Proves Flash at Second," *Brooklyn Eagle*, March 28, 1939.
39 "*They've been burying me all spring...*" Associated Press, *Berkshire (Mass.) County Eagle*, March 29, 1939.
39 "*He's definitely lost his speed.*" Jack Smith, "Gehrig Won't Start Unless He Improves," *New York Daily News*, March 30, 1939.
39 "*He's a natural hitter...*" Ibid.
39 "*The Dodgers needed ballplayers...*" Tuber interview, 1981.
40 "*as natural a hitter as you ever laid eyes on...*" Bill McCullough, "MacPhail Breezes in and Out of Brooklyn and Leaves Fourth-Place Feeling in the Air," *Brooklyn Eagle*, April 6, 1939.
40 "*On mornings after the Dodgers have lost...*" Taylor, *New Yorker*, July 12, 1941.
40 "*MacPhail, man, he would go wild.*" Interview of Barber by William J. Marshall, June 27, 1987. for the University of Kentucky's Desegregation of Major League Baseball Oral History Project. The project was named after former Kentucky senator Happy Chandler, who was commissioner when Jackie Robinson broke the color barrier. All the interviews conducted for the project can be found at kentuckyoralhistory.org.
41 "*DO NOT PLAY REISER AGAIN.*" Leo Durocher with Ed Linn, *Nice Guys Finish Last*, Simon and Schuster, 1975, p. 108.
41 "*In a somewhat legendary confrontation...*" We'll never know exactly what happened in this meeting, because the three principals gave such widely diverging accounts. MacPhail, talking to *The Sporting News* in 1963, depicted it as calm and orderly, with no yelling, no heat—and Durocher admitting he was wrong, which sounds un-Leo like. Durocher, in *Nice*

Guys Finished Last, said MacPhail began cursing the minute he walked through the door, fired him, kept on cursing and escalated things to the point where Leo leaped up and shoved MacPhail out of his chair. According to this account, when MacPhail pulled himself up, he had tears in his eyes, threw his arms around Leo and re-hired him on the spot. MacDonald's account, published in a 1943 *Saturday Evening Post* article, leans closer to Durocher's than MacPhail's but mentions nothing about a shove, tears or a conciliatory hug. If this author had to take a guess, I'd say Durocher's account is the most accurate one, given that both the Dodger manager and GM were such emotionally explosive individuals.

41 *"Reiser was just a kid..."* John Steadman, "MacPhail Retired? Don't You Ever Believe That," *The Sporting News*, October 26, 1963.
41 *"Twenty-fifth man on the squad..."* Turkin, "Dodgers in Fourth," *New York Daily News*, April 15, 1939.
42 *"Imagine, I had just taken infield practice..."* Finch, *The Sporting News*, April 25, 1962.
42 *"When they sent me back in '39..."* Tuber interview, 1981.
42 *"I wasn't impatient, I was good."* Ibid.
42 *"Reiser is fast and loose on the bases and afield."* Harry O'Donnell, *Elmira Star-Gazette*, April 27, 1939.
42 Pete injured his throwing arm. "Montreal Options Pitcher Malseed to Pioneers," *Elmira Star-Gazette*, May 8, 1939.
42 *"In one 11-10 victory..."* "Grays Invade Dunn Field for Twin Bill Tuesday," *Elmira Star-Gazette*, May 29, 1939. All game accounts of Pete with the Elmira team come from the local paper except where noted.
42 *"Everyone was commenting..."* "Elmira's 4th-Inning Uprising Routs Barons," *Wilkes-Barre Record*, June 8, 1939.
43 *"... isn't a good enough southpaw"* "Pioneers Seeking Outfielder to Replace Reiser," *Elmira Star-Gazette*, June 19, 1939.
43 *"When I came to after the operation..."* W.C. Heinz, "The Rocky Road of Pistol Pete," *True*, June 1958.
43 *"My arm has completely healed."* "Reiser Says His Arm's Okay Now," *Elmira Star-Gazette*, October 13, 1939.
43 *"No fungoed grounder passed him."* "Reese Joins Camp; Proves He's Good," *New York Daily News*, February 20, 1940.
44 *... twelve hits in twenty-five times at bat.* Reiser's skein calculated from April 1940 box scores in the *Montreal Gazette*.
44 *"I say, no way I can't play now."* Tuber interview, 1981.
44 *"What the hell's going on here?"* Ibid.
44 *"I thought, no sense in going home.* Ibid.
45 *"To make a long story short..."* Ibid.
45 *"... the trade made the front page."* For example, take the *St. Louis Globe-Democrat* of June 13, 1940. The war got the all-caps top headline: "GERMANS HAVE CUT PARIS OFF ON THREE SIDES, BERLIN SAYS." But right below that, in page-crossing large type: "Cardinals Trade Joe Medwick and Curt Davis to Brooklyn." In the *Eagle*, the war took the big headline but the picture below showed Dodger fans lining up to buy tickets after hearing that Medwick was joining the team.
45 *"[The writers] had gotten another glimpse at Reiser..."* Parrott, *Lords of Baseball*, p. 125.
46 *"I can't prove that I'm the player..."* Tuber interview, 1981.
464 *"Pete Reiser looked so well against our Miners..."* Chick Feldman, "Hatchin' Them Out," *Scranton Tribune*, July 10, 1940.
47 *"A team five games out of first place..."* Turkin, "Dodgers Buy Reiser," *New York Daily News*, July 24, 1940.

47 *"Couldn't sleep a wink, I was so excited."* Honig, *Baseball When the Grass Was Real*, p. 296.
47 *"Everything Goes Wrong..."* "Hex on Pete Reiser in Dodger Debut," *Brooklyn Eagle*, July 24, 1940.
47 *"When we start training next spring..."* "Durocher Sold on Reiser as '41 Regular," *Elmira Star-Gazette*, September 18, 1940.

Chapter 4: "Some Kind of Year, '41"

48 *"curled up on the ground next to home plate."* Accounts of Pete's beaning by Ike Pearson are drawn from several articles published April 24, 1941: Turkin, "Reiser Beaned, Saved by Helmet," *New York Daily News*; Jerry Mitchell, "Reiser Lost for Two Weeks, Head Injury Not Serious," *New York Post*; Lee Scott, "Pete Reiser Will Be Lost to Dodgers for Two Weeks or Possibly Longer," *Brooklyn Citizen*; and Holmes, "Reiser May Return in a Week," *Brooklyn Eagle*.
48 *"I was so scared I was sick."* Mitchell, *New York Post*, April 24, 1941.
48 *"You weren't any more scared..."* ibid.
49 *"Accusing Bowman of attempted murder."* Scott, "MacPhail Wants Bowman Barred for 'Deliberate Beaning' of Medwick," *Brooklyn Citizen*, and Turkin, "Medwick Beaned, Bowman Menaced," *New York Daily News*, both June 19, 1940.
49 *"He's a very lucky boy..."* Turkin, *Daily News*, April 24, 1941.
50 *"I don't know what just happened."* Ibid.
50 *Three days at Caledonian.* The *Eagle* reported Pete's release from the hospital on April 27.
50 *"Pete is more than satisfied..."* "Reiser Mails Signed Contract to Dodgers," *St. Louis Star and Times*, January 10, 1941.
50 *"I told Corriden to specialize..."* Turkin, "Durocher to Try Reiser in Center," *New York Daily News*, February 23, 1941.
51 *"Ever since Pete Reiser got back..."* Scott, "Dodgers Now Living up To Spring Training Form as They Beat Giants," *Brooklyn Citizen*, April 21, 1941.
50 *"We knew in spring training..."* Honig, *Baseball Between the Lines*, p. 94.
51 *"Everyone is asking me..."* "Stronger Pitching Staff Gives Dodgers Good Chance for Flag, Durocher Says," *Brooklyn Citizen*, March 28, 1941.
51 *"MacPhail has just bought..."* Whitney Martin, Associated Press, "Scribe Says MacPhail Using Sound Business Judgment," *Dayton Journal Herald*, May 8, 1941.
51 *"The nearly apoplectic crowd..."* "Dodgers Win in 9th, 4-3, for 9th in a Row," *New York Daily News*, May 1, 1941.
53 *"opening a two-inch long gash..."* Details on the catch and its aftermath come from "Reiser Plays Today Despite Cut in Back," *New York Daily News*, May 9, 1941; "Reiser Back in Drydock," *Brooklyn Eagle*, May 9, 1941. The headline on the *Daily News* article was wrong; Reiser would not play for ten days.
53 *"I believe that boy has really arrived."* John Kieran, "Around the Batting Cage," *New York Times*, May 14, 1941.
53 *"... couldn't have been more dramatic."* Louis Effrat, "Dodgers Stage Rally in Sixth to Triumph Over Phillies," *New York Times*, May 26, 1941.
54 *"mad lunge for the pitch."* Turkin, "Flock Wins 8-4, Reiser Hits Homer," *New York Daily News*, May 26, 1941.
54 *"a highly obscure Brooklyn pitcher."* Markus and McFeely's original script for "Captain America: The First Avenger" can be found online. In this version, Steve Rogers figures out that he's no longer in the 1940s because in his mind, Chipman *couldn't* have pitched to Workman—the Dodgers had traded him to the Cubs (for Eddie Stanky) before Workman joined the Braves. But in reality, Chipman did pitch for the Dodgers against Workman and the

Braves on May 2, 1944. Whatever the facts, this would have been a trivial and rather dull way for Captain America to realize he's been asleep for seven decades, and the final scene in the film with Reiser hitting the grand slam unquestionably has more dramatic punch.

55 *"Brooklynites... flocked to Ebbets Field."* Dodgers attendance in 1941 would top one-point-two million, a new club record, and nearly triple the team's attendance during the depths of the Depression. The attendance record would stand until after the war.

55 *"Brooklyn? Is Brooklyn still in the league?"* Those apparently were not Terry's precise words. When first reported in an AP story on January 26, 1934, Terry was quoted as saying "The Dodgers—are they still in the league?" Within a short time the quote morphed into the slightly altered form that most baseball historians are familiar with. I can't help but wonder if certain newspapermen and/or Dodger faithful deliberately altered the quote in the retelling, so it sounded like Terry was insulting not just the team but the entire borough, which would make a better story.

55 *"The starting lineup out of a hat."* Joe Williams column, *New York World Telegram*, March 28, 1939. The other "Uncle Robbie" stories come from Robinson's SABR biography (https://sabr.org/bioproj/person/wilbert-robinson/).

56 *"Three men on third base."* This is a familiar tale to most baseball historians. For the record, the incident featured prominently in newspaper coverage of the game but didn't grab the headlines. The *Brooklyn Citizen* did have a memorable subhead: "Traffic Rules Needed for Herman."

56 *"She never missed a game..."* Honig, *Baseball When the Grass Was Real*, p. 296.

57 *"You weren't back in the stands..."* Creamer interview of Barber, 1968.

57 *"a fertile talent for taking a bad situation..."* Rickey seems to have first uttered this quote in "The Lip," a story in the April 14, 1947 issue of *Time* magazine (which incidentally featured a smiling Durocher on the cover that week). He re-used it many times thereafter.

58 *"I would take him to manage any club."* Bill Van Fleet, "Things He Didn't Say Significant?" *Fort Worth Star-Telegram*, April 17, 1960. Rickey said this right after repeating his familiar line about Leo being good at making a bad situation worse.

58 *"Charming side, sometimes funny."* Leo's sense of comedy was good enough that he carved out a sideline career in showbiz. During the 1940s, he was a recurring guest on the top-rated radio shows of comedians Fred Allen and Jack Benny and appeared in a Red Skelton movie short. In the '60s, he played himself on television sitcoms like *Mr. Ed*, *The Donna Reed Show*, *The Munsters* and *The Beverly Hillbillies*.

58 *"When I came in, he said, 'Monte...'"* Irvin interviewed by William J. Marshall, May 12, 1977, for the University of Kentucky's Desegregation of Major League Baseball Oral History Project.

58 *"I've heard a lot of guys knock Leo..."* Honig, *Baseball When the Grass Was Real*, p. 304.

59 *"I don't know anybody with a better chance..."* Holmes, "Polo Grounds Series Puts Dodgers' Pitching to Test," *Brooklyn Eagle*, May 30, 1941.

59 *"... and he threw up in the dugout."* Si Burick, "All Time Record Crowd Sees Dodgers Tumble Reds to Fourth," *Dayton Daily News*, June 23, 1941.

59 *"Derringer's stopping you by..."* Raymond Schussler, "Diamond Theft," *Long Beach Press-Telegram*, October 10, 1971.

60 *"This is no early season streak he's having."* Dick McCann, "Durocher Calls Reiser His Greatest Find," *New York Daily News*, June 1, 1941.

60 *"I'm nuts about that kid."* Holmes, "Dodgers, Reds Both Improved," *Brooklyn Eagle*, April 29, 1941.

60 *"That Reiser is the best..."* Harvey Boyle, "Frisch Likes the Dodgers, *Pittsburgh Post-Gazette*, June 26, 1941.

60 *"There wouldn't be any pennant race..."* Schumacher, *Pittsburgh Sun-Telegraph* June 30, 1941.
60 *"On every bench in Ford Frick's domain..."* Arthur Patterson, *New York Herald Tribune*, June 1, 1941.
61 *"His average has remained far in advance..."* Jerry Mitchell, "Reiser's Playing Is Brilliant as Reds Drop Doubleheader," *New York Post*, June 23, 1941.
61 *"I know what another Ty Cobb means."* Grantland Rice column, syndicated, *New York Sun*, July 2, 1941.
62 *"I'll never forget the All-Star Game."* Daley, "Sports of the Times," *New York Times*, May 28, 1946.
63 *"It's a pretty tough thing to give up."* John Rosengren, *Hank Greenberg: Hero of Heroes*, New American Library, 2013, p. 221.
64 *"The vocal support of the faithful..."* Scott, *Brooklyn Citizen*, August 6, 1941.
64 *"So you thought Dixie was getting..."* Parrott, "Both Sides," *Brooklyn Eagle*, July 12, 1941.
64 *"If you see one, you know the other..."* Photo caption, *Brooklyn Eagle*, September 9, 1941.
65 *"We just clicked."* J.G.T. Spink, "Pee Wee and Pete—Pals," *The Sporting News*, September 11, 1941.
65 *"Pee Wee was a young kid."* Herman interviewed by Rod Roberts, 1990. Interview can found on the website of the Baseball Hall of Fame.
66 *"... want to throw the furniture."* Holmes, "Dodgers Worried? No, Fighting Mad!" *Brooklyn Eagle*, July 23, 1941.
66 *"MacPhail put him in a cab."* "Flock Loses Reiser; Goes to Hospital," *New York Daily News*, August 5, 1941.
67 *"Pete would mischaracterize this incident..."* Honig, *Baseball When the Grass Was Real*, p. 293. As noted elsewhere in the text, Pete sometimes got details wrong when recounting events in his career. However, the story about Paul Erickson beaning him and putting him in the hospital seems to be a work of pure fiction. Paul Erickson faced Pete eighteen times in his career and did not hit him with a pitch even once. And there's no record of Pete needing medical care after the Dick Errickson beaning. The only beaning that put Pete in the hospital was the one by Ike Pearson. I suppose it's possible that Landis visited him after that incident, but if he did, there was nothing about it in the papers.
67 *"I can't recall any two teams..."* Grantland Rice column, syndicated, *St. Louis Globe-Democrat*, August 26, 1941.
67 *"I don't know whether to fine the kid..."* Holmes, "Flock Plan Did NOT Call for Reiser Homer," *Brooklyn Eagle*, August 19, 1941.
68 *"As Reiser ran in..."* Roscoe McGowen, "Dodgers Top Cubs with Early Attack," *New York Times*, August 23, 1941.
68 *"Anything I think I can get my bat on..."* "McKechnie Peeved at Sports Writers Who Blame Him for All-Star Game Loss," *Cincinnati Enquirer*, July 11, 1941.
68 *"I begged him..."* McCann, "Attendance Mark Set as Flock, Reds Play," *New York Daily News*, August 28, 1941.
69 *"You know what would happen..."* Jack Smith, "Are Giants in League? Sh! Lippy Won't Talk," *New York Daily News*, Sept 6, 1941.
69 *"showering the field with scorecards..."* Holmes, "Dodgers Off on Last Junket to 'Badlands,'" *Brooklyn Eagle*, Sept 8, 1941.
69 *"serenaded them with Frederic Chopin."* Ibid.
71 *"I don't see how they can keep the prize away..."* Chilly Doyle, "Chilly Sauce," *Pittsburgh Sun-Telegraph*, September 18, 1941.

71 "*Baseball still was a game to them . . .*" Meany, "Infields of the West Leave Mark on Flock," *PM Daily*, September 18, 1941.
72 "*. . . hundreds wandered onto the field.*" "Festive Fans of Brooklyn 'Take' City," *Philadelphia Inquirer*, Sept 22, 1941. This has to be one of the greatest examples of the visiting team's rooters taking over the home team's ballpark. The invading Brooklynites strung up banners in Shibe Park that read "Brooklyn the Champs of 1941" and "Our Dodgers the Greatest Team on Earth." Attendance for the September 21st doubleheader topped thirty-five thousand, then the largest crowd ever to see a baseball game in Philadelphia, and Dodger fans probably made up a majority of the crowd.
72 "*a telegraph operator in the press box . . .*" Meany, "Telegrapher's Key Clicks a Symphony," *PM Daily*, September 26, 1941
74 "*Some kind of year, '41.*" Honig, *Baseball When the Grass Was Real*, p. 296.
74 "*I don't see a vacant seat . . .*" Mutual radio broadcast, World Series Game One, October 1, 1941.
75 "*. . . Reiser and Reese will be nervous?*" Jimmy Powers column, *New York Daily News*, September 30, 1941.
75 "*You might not think it . . .*" Mutual radio broadcast, World Series Game One, October 1, 1941.
76 "*Right fielder Henrich goes back . . .*" Mutual radio broadcast, World Series Game Four, October 4, 1941.
77 "*Casey gets by Henrich, it's all over.*" Ibid.
77 "*It was like a punch on the chin.*" Joseph Richler, *The World Series: a 75th Anniversary*, Simon and Schuster, 1978, p. 162.
77 "*My mistake was . . .*" Richler, p. 184
77 "*I remember talking to him . . .*" Author interview, 2020.
77 "*He'd laugh . . .*" Ibid.
78 "*. . . a cross-country drive to California.*" Silent home movies taken by Reiser on the trip, courtesy Shirley Tuber.
78 "*I declined his invite because . . .*" Eddie Zeltner, "One King They Can't Get Out," Long Branch, New Jersey *Daily Record*, August 7, 1942.
79 "*In light of events of the past few days . . .*" "Feller Joins Naval Reserve," *Des Moines Register*, December 10, 1941.
79 "*We are in trouble . . .*" Associated Press, "Hank to Re-Enlist," *Detroit Free Press*, December 10, 1941.
79 "*I honestly feel that it would be best . . .*" The actual letter can be seen on the website of the Baseball Hall of Fame. (https://baseballhall.org/discover-more/stories/short-stops/keep-baseball-going)

Chapter 5: Hitting the Wall

81 "*At the end of Saturday's action . . .*" The raw numbers cited come from baseballreference.com. I determined Pete was leading the league in these categories by examining the batting leaders column published daily in many newspapers during this era.
82 "*But this doesn't account for Pete Reiser . . .*" Grantland Rice column, syndicated, *Baltimore Sun*, July 21, 1942.
82 "*And Brooklyn will be tougher . . .*" United Press, *Rochester Democrat and Chronicle*, July 24, 1941.
83 "*The clock atop . . .*" W. Vernon Tietjen, "Cards Beat Dodgers Twice, Trail by 6," *St. Louis Star and Times*, July 20, 1942.

83 "*Racing back at top speed,*" Martin J. Haley, "34,986 See Cards Trounce Dodgers Twice," *St. Louis Globe-Democrat*, July 20, 1942.
83 "*It might have been the greatest catch . . .*" Holmes, "Loss of Pete Reiser Would Be Ruinous," *Brooklyn Eagle*, July 20, 1942.
83 "*he crashed against the concrete . . .*" Tietjen, July 20, 1942.
84 "*Pete dropped to the ground . . .*" "Dodgers Lose Reiser, Casey and Ground in Rough Series in St. Louis," *Brooklyn Citizen*, July 20, 1942.
84 "*Dazed by the collision . . .*" McCann, "Cards Batter Brooks 8-5, 7-6; Reiser Injured," *New York Daily News*, July 20, 1942.
84 "*As Slaughter crossed the plate . . .*" McGowen, "Cards Down Brooklyn 8-5 and 7-6," *New York Times*, July 20, 1942.
85 "*Enos Slaughter leads off the inning . . .*" Honig, *Baseball When the Grass Was Real*, p. 285.
85 "*I'd hit fences before, but not like this . . .*" Bob Broeg column, *St. Louis Post-Dispatch*, May 15, 1962.
85 "*Dr. Hyland, who was a very good friend of mine . . .*" Honig, *Baseball When the Grass Was Real*, p. 303.
85 "*X-rays of Pete's head had come back negative.*" "Cooper Has Strained Ligament, Reiser Suffered No Fracture," *St. Louis Post-Dispatch;* Associated Press, "Reiser On the Mend," *Kansas City Star;* McGowen, "Cards Down Brooklyn 8-5 and 7-6," *New York Times*, all July 20, 1942, and Dick McCann, "Skull OK, Reiser Back in 10 Days," *New York Daily News*, July 21, 1942. Not until several years later did Pete and reporters start referring to his Sportsman's Park injury as a skull fracture. In an era where old newspaper articles weren't easily available and many reporters relied on plain memory for fact-checking, the inaccurate info took on a life of its own.
86 "*Pete's dad entered the clubhouse . . .*" Unbylined report found in Pete's Hall of Fame player file.
86 "*. . . well enough to wave and smile.*" Photo, *St. Louis Star and Times*, July 21, 1942.
86 "*Concussions occur when the brain hits . . .*" Author interview with Dr. Daniel Zimet, August 2021.
86 "*The science is still out on this . . .*" Ibid.
87 "*I don't like hospitals,*" Heinz, *True*, 1958.
87 "*I wasn't supposed to, but . . .*" Honig, *Baseball When the Grass Was Real*, p. 303.
87 "*He was never the same again.*" Daley, "Nostalgia Flashback to Another Spring," *New York Times*, March 2, 1972.
88 "*Leo saw me and he said . . .*" Heinz, *True*, 1958.
88 "*Reiser demonstrated there was nothing wrong . . .*" Scott, "Durocher Has Pitching Staff in Top Form for Series with Cardinals," *Brooklyn Citizen*, July 24, 1942.
88 "*MacPhail got incensed . . .*" Honig, *Baseball When the Grass Was Real*, p. 303.
89 "*Pete sat on the bench with the boys . . .*" Scott, *Brooklyn Citizen*, July 24, 1942.
90 "*Reiser was suffering headaches . . .*" Holmes, "Reiser Still Plagued by Dizziness, Rules Himself Out of Lineup," *Brooklyn Eagle*, August 5, 1942.
90 "*The team does not seem to be . . .*" Scott, "Brooklyn Team Sorely Misses Pete Reiser's Batting Punch and Speed," *Brooklyn Citizen*, August 8, 1942.
90 "*Reiser was one of their star players.*" Larry Powell, *Bottom of the Ninth: An Oral History on the Life of Harry "The Hat" Walker*, iUniverse, 2000, p. 42.
90 "*Another player would have stopped . . .*" Scott, "Pete Reiser's Return Big Help to Champs," *Brooklyn Citizen*, August 11, 1942.
90 "*This club isn't as good . . .*" Scott, "MacPhail Berates Dodgers for Not Showing More Hustle," *Brooklyn Citizen*, August 13, 1942.

91 "I was in pretty bad shape..." Gillespie, "Banged-Up Reiser Gets a 'Good Break,'" *The Sporting News*, January 5, 1949.
91 "Leo kept me in there." Honig, *Baseball When the Grass Was Real*, p. 304.
92 "And St. Louis is Petey's home town!" Fred Lieb, "Give Us Show and We'll Go," *The Sporting News*, September 3, 1942.
92 "It's too fidgety sitting around." John B. Chandler, Associated Press, "Pete Reiser, Resting Here, Pulls For (to Jinx) Cards," *Baltimore Sun*, September 2, 1942.
92 "It hurts only a little when I run." Turkin, "Reiser's Gotta Hit the Ball or Get a Pain in Side," *New York Daily News*, September 6, 1942.
93 "Many experts rate Harold Patrick Reiser..." Meany, *Saturday Evening Post*, September 1942.
93 "Reputations are pretty much punctured..." Meany, "Reese Didn't Fiddle While the Flatbush Empire Burned," *PM Daily*, September 21, 1942.
93 "Then there came the injury to Pete Reiser." Grantland Rice column, syndicated, *Baltimore Sun*, September 23, 1942.
94 "It was as heartbreaking and messy..." Parrott, *Lords of Baseball*, p. 136.
94 "I was always the kind of fellow..." Gillespie, *Sporting News*, January 1949.
94 "There's no question in my mind..." Honig, *Baseball When the Grass Was Real*, p. 304.
94 "I don't know how a person..." Author interview, August 2021.
94 "We don't need no crying towels." Holmes, "Dodgers Show Generosity in Series Shares," *Brooklyn Eagle*, September 28, 1942.
95 "I've lost some tough pennant races before..." Holmes, "Dodgers Didn't Lose Flag—Cards Won It," *Brooklyn Eagle*, September 28, 1942.
95 "... ready to go." "'I'm Ready' Says Reiser Here Confirming Draft Call," *St. Louis Star and Times*, December 11, 1942.
95 "Gotta go now fellas." United Press, "Pete Reiser, Dodgers Star, Signs Up as Buck Private," *Berkshire (Mass.) Eagle*, January 14, 1943.

Chapter 6: "A Wild and Frightening Beauty"
97 "May 25, 1991 at the Kingdome." Video of this Griffey catch and many others can be found on YouTube under various names. For this one, look for "Spiderman Catch."
98 "There was always talk..." Interview of Frey by Rick Tuber, early 1990s.
99 "You can run head-on..." Ibid.
99 "[He] stuck me in the outfield." Bill Whitehead, "Ken Griffey Jr. Talks Passion for Baseball With Campers at Jackie Robinson Complex in Vero Beach," TCPalm.com, July 29, 2019.
100 "I was running full speed..." Video of 1991 Griffey interview on YouTube, "Ken Griffey Jr. Breaks Down His Finest Catches."
100 "Number one, you count..." YouTube video of Reynolds interview with Griffey, 2017.
100 "All I can think of..." YouTube video of Scully broadcast, May 14, 2013.
100 "And if he's too sore to play..." Buster Olney, "Harper Can Learn from Pete Reiser," ESPN.com, May 14, 2013.
100 "Some people can feel the wall..." Hermanski interviewed by Rick Tuber, early 1990s.
101 "He played so hard..." Peter Golenbock, *Bums: An Oral History of the Brooklyn Dodgers*, 1984, p. 170-71.
101 "Reiser had blinding running speed..." Red Barber, "If and Might Cloud the Center Field Question," *Tallahassee Democrat*, June 1, 1975.
101 "He continually tries to build..." Holmes, "Reiser's Latest Wall Bout Is Not Serious," *Brooklyn Eagle*, May 20, 1946.
101 "It was frightening to see..." Barber, *Tallahassee Democrat*, 1975.

101 *"This is supposition, but...."* Tuber interview, 1981.
102 *"It was my way of playing..."* Heinz, *True*, 1958.
102 *"Why did all those fences happen to me?"* Jeanne Hoffman, "Coliseum Screen vs. Pete Reiser? Retirement 'Robbed' L.A. Fans," *Los Angeles Times*, June 1, 1960.
102 *"It was my style of playing."* Honig, *Baseball When the Grass Was Real*, p. 305.
102 *"It's hard to explain."* George Watkins, "Pete Reiser: He Nearly Gave His Life for Baseball," *The Californian*, August 16, 1980.
103 *"Reiser and I have collided..."* Mitchell, "Sports on Parade," *New York Post*, March 30, 1942.
103 *"He is motivated by a wonderful..."* Jimmy Cannon, "Freedom Means No Check," *Esquire*, June 1, 1949.
104 *"That's not unique to him."* Author interview of Zimet, August 2021.
104 *"It takes mental effort..."* Ibid.
104 *"I know that he was so focused..."* Author interview, September 2020.
104 *"He's great, great, great."* Cannon, *Esquire*, 1949.
105 *"[I] don't believe that it is fool-proof."* "Rubber Padding on Ebbets Fences to Protect Reiser," *Brooklyn Eagle*, March 14, 1948.
105 *"The Reiser case was familiar..."* Alex Kahn, United Press International, "Dodgers Stadium Outfield Wall Lined With Plywood," *Honolulu Advertiser*, May 27, 1962.
105 *"If we had a wall like this..."* Ibid.
105 *"I'm sure they won't have any trouble..."* Young, "Dodgers Recall Flatbush Era," *New York Daily News*, February 24, 1960.
105 *"He's only got half as many bones..."* Jim Murray, "Pete Was a Pistol," *Los Angeles Times*, April 5, 1964.
105 *"Wherever he is today..."* Murray, "The Career That Might Have Been," *Los Angeles Times*, October 28, 1981.

Chapter 7: Soldiering On
119 *"I had a comic-book biography..."* Jim Lehrer, *We Were Dreamers*, New York, Antheneum, 1975, p. 187.
120 *"I made Pop take me..."* Ibid.
120 *"...a strong Pete Reiser obsession."* The book I'm referencing is Lehrer's 2009 novel, *Oh Johnny*.
120 *"The definite loss of Reiser..."* John Drebinger, "Brooklyn Star Passes His Exam," *New York Times*, January 14, 1943.
120 *"But they'll not be able to replace..."* Holmes, "Replacing Reiser Stops Flock," *Brooklyn Eagle*, December 11, 1942.
121 *"...slower than snails with fallen arches."* Harry Grayson, "Sportswriter for NEA Picks Yanks, Cards," *Burlington Daily News*, April 21, 1943.
121 *"Rickey did not come cheap."* Terms of Rickey's 1942 contract with the Dodgers can be found in the Branch Rickey papers, stored at the Library of Congress in Washington.
121 *"...the gift to run and the urge to go."* Parrott, "Rickey Demands Loyalty Above All from His Aides," *Brooklyn Eagle*, November 2, 1942.
121 *"He didn't think he'd be drafted."* 1993 interview of Patricia Reiser by Rick Tuber.
122 *"I'm sittin' on a bench with the other guys..."* Heinz, *True*, 1958.
122 *"I heard a doctor tell Reiser..."* Holmes, "Athletes Get No Breaks in Draft," *Brooklyn Eagle*, November 5, 1952.
122 *"Fort Riley was in rough country."* Powell, *Bottom of the Ninth*, p. 72.

Notes

123 *"Pete gets K.P and detail..."* "Even Hap Can't Get Owl to Screech in Mayflower," *Louisville Courier-Journal*, March 21, 1943.
123 *"Feeling better?"* Honig, *Baseball When the Grass Was Real*, p. 309.
123 *"a voice squawked over the PA."* Ibid and Heinz, *True*, 1958.
124 *"They want me to discharge you."* Ibid.
124 *"The regular doctors examined me."* William Mead, *Even the Browns*, Contemporary Books, 1978, p. 108.
125 *"They said, 'You'll never go overseas..."* Interview of Walker by William J. Marshall, May 11, 1988, for the University of Kentucky's Desegregation of Major League Baseball Oral History Project.
125 *"No one in authority in the service..."* Holmes, "Branca's Pitching is Tonic for Leo," *Brooklyn Eagle*, August 10, 1945.
125 *"occasional publicity tasks."* "Skeletons From Various Closets," *Marysville (Kansas) Advocate*, April 29, 1943.
125 *"We whomped everybody..."* Honig, *Baseball When the Grass Was Real*, p. 310.
126 *"We made up for that one..."* Al Warden, "Patrolling the Sport Highway," *Ogden Standard-Examiner*, July 26, 1944.
126 *"slid headfirst into third so hard..."* Bob Maisel, "Take It From Rex Barney, Pistol Pete Was the Best," *Baltimore Sun*, November 21, 1981.
126 *"An officer told him he couldn't play..."* Honig, *Baseball When the Grass Was Real*, p. 310.
127 *"I'd have to say Ted Williams, Musial..."* Rod Roberts interview of Barlick, July 22, 1991, for the Baseball Hall of Fame.
127 *"It's close, but..."* Parrott, "Olmo Gives Dodgers Life in Outfield," *Brooklyn Eagle*, August 14, 1943.
127 *"He's the only one in the league..."* Hy Hurwitz, "Shotton Says Reiser Can Be Great, But Didn't Want to Play for Rickey," *Boston Globe*, December 16, 1948.
127 *"I thought Reiser would be..."* Joe King, "Diamond Dossier... Pee Wee Reese," *The Sporting News*, October 15, 1952.
128 *"If you concede that..."* Daley, *New York Times*, May 27, 1946.
128 *"Reiser, on furlough..."* McGowen, "Lanier Triumphs Over Brooklyn, 5-1," *New York Times*, September 25, 1943.
128 *"Once when we were driving..."* Leighton Housh, "Kicks It Away—Steals It Back," *Des Moines Tribune*, September 23, 1946.
129 *"Considering what a lot of guys did..."* Heinz, *True*, 1958.
129 *"given leave to see Pat."* Tuber interview of Pat Reiser, 1993.
129 *"Probably the most unhappy..."* Tom Bernard, "Ace of Diamonds," *The American Magazine*, July 1947.
130 *"I like the Army fine..."* *Marysville (Kansas) Advocate*, April 29, 1943
130 *"I miss hearing Hilda's cowbell..."* Associated Press, "Reiser Has His Say," Manhattan, Kansas *Morning Chronicle*, June 12, 1943.
130 *"I'll never complain about playing..."* Walt Dobbins, "I May Be Wrong" column, *Lincoln Star Journal*, January 3, 1944.
130 *"Finally, Reiser turned his head."* Jim Montgomery, "In Bad Blue Ink, Reiser Lives On," *Cincinnati Enquirer*, October 31, 1981.
130 *"Pat filed a petition for divorce."* "Pete Reiser's Wife Sues for Divorce," *St. Louis Star and Times*, February 2, 1944; "Pete Reiser Sued for Divorce," *St. Louis Globe-Democrat*, February 3, 1944; and "Pete Reiser, Brooklyn Star, Sued for Divorce," February 3, 1944, *St. Louis Post-Dispatch*. The latter reported on February 14 that the divorce had gone through and listed the terms of alimony and child support payments.

131 *"As you are well aware . . ."* January 9, 1945 letter to Rickey from Pete, stored with the Branch Rickey papers at the Library of Congress. On the back of the letter, someone, possibly Rickey's secretary, wrote down the amount of the Dodgers' loans to Pete: $1,000 on January 24, 1944 and $250 on June 30, 1944.
131 *"I was glad to have your letter . . ."* Rickey letter to Pete, dated January 12, 1945.
133 *"It's not for us."* Harry Feeney Jr., "Dodger Brides Give Real Lowdown on Reese and Reiser," *New York Post*, July 1942.
133 *"I know all about Pete Reiser . . ."* Oscar Ruhl, "Reiser? Rickey Calls Him Well - 'A Good Boy,'" *The Sporting News*, January 22, 1947.
133 *"He liked the guys."* Author interview, September 2020.
133 *"You know how close I was . . ."* Garagiola interview by Rick Tuber, 1989.
134 *"The only player . . ."* Shirley Tuber email to author, August 2020.
134 *"I was born at third base . . ."* Jim McCulley, "Weep for the Browns," *New York Daily News*, October 7, 1944.
134 *"Pete found himself promoted."* I haven't found the exact date of the promotion but it happened sometime in the spring of '45. In April, Louisiana newspapers referred to Pete as a corporal; in May they started calling him a sergeant.
134 *"bleachers standing stark and empty"* The photo appeared in *Barksdale Bark*, the newspaper of the Barksdale Field air base (now Barksdale Air Force Base) in northwest Louisiana.
135 *"Running back at full speed . . ."* "Camp Pats Blast Lee Team, 9-2," *Newport News Daily Press*, August 2, 1945.
135 *"Pete ran right through it . . ."* Pete described running through the fence or hedge on many occasions, including interviews with newspaper reporters, *The Sporting News*, W.C. Heinz and Donald Honig. The exact date of the incident remains elusive. I can find no daily newspaper accounts of him playing in Camp Lee games after August 1, 1945. August '45 issues of the Camp Lee weekly, the *Lee Traveler*, make no mention of Reiser playing after then either. However, New York-area newspapers reported that he made a visit to Ebbets Field on August 10, 1945 and worked out with the Dodgers before the game. That would suggest his arm was still okay at that point, but there's no way to be sure. Maybe it was already injured and he avoided making long throws that day. What's clear is that Pete had stopped playing by the second half of August. There is no published record of him doing any type of baseball activity between then and the start of spring training the following year.
135 *"The X-ray examination showed no injury."* Les Conklin, International News Service, "Bums Base Stealing Champ Reveals His Success Secret," *Muncie (Ind.) Journal*, October 25, 1946.
136 *"Pete played some baseball."* "Pete Reiser on Millville Visit," *Millvale Daily*, October 30, 1945.
136 *". . . not be back until 1947."* "Army Keeps Reiser," *Binghamton (N.Y.) Press and Sun Bulletin*, September 13, 1945.
136 *"Now it's November . . ."* Heinz, *True*, 1958.
137 *"Joe Garagiola, this kid catcher . . ."* Tietjen, "Pete Reiser May Become 'Lefty' Thrower," *St. Louis Star and Times*, December 8, 1945.

Chapter 8: "He's the Difference, Brother"

138 *"Pete had lunged up the line . . ."* Cannon, "Reiser Is Brooklyn's Hero," *New York Post*, April 19, 1946.
138 *"With a clenched-teeth . . ."* Without exception, all photos of Pete stealing home show his teeth tightly clenched as he slides across the plate.
139 *"Peace and contentment . . ."* Daley, "Echoes From Ebbets Field," *New York Times*, April 19, 1946.
139 *"I looked around me . . ."* Cannon, *Post*, April 19, 1946.

139 *"This is very disturbing."* Burr, "Reiser's Proposed Shoulder Surgery Has Rickey Jittery," *Brooklyn Eagle*, December 6, 1945.
139 *"He worked out with us last summer . . ."* Howard Pierce, "Along the Sidelines," *Elmira Star-Gazette*, December 13, 1945.
140 *"The St. Louis boy is dissatisfied . . ."* Sid Keener column, *St. Louis Star and Times*, February 11, 1946.
140 *"Pete Reiser is to the Brooklyns . . ."* Grayson, "Was Reiser's Throwing Arm Hurt?" syndicated article, *Evansville Courier and Press*, January 20, 1946.
140 *"No sir, absolutely not . . ."* "Rickey Here, Snubs Reiser," *St. Louis Star and Times*, March 6, 1946.
141 *"In the flick of an eyelash . . ."* Arch Murray, "Reiser Still Clouts 'Em," *New York Post*, March 16, 1946.
141 *"Reiser isn't a total stranger to third base."* Burr, "Pete Reiser Is Installed as Dodgers' Third Baseman," *Brooklyn Eagle*, March 30, 1946.
141 *"The shoulder I fell on . . ."* Burr, "Dr. Kildare Needed for Ailing Dodgers," *Brooklyn Eagle*, April 1, 1946.
141 *"If my right whip . . ."* Holmes, "Pete's Throwing 'Arms' Are Vital," *Brooklyn Eagle*, April 9, 1946.
142 *"He told me it wouldn't do any harm . . ."* Burr, "Behrman Proves Valuable Player: Dodgers Open Ebbets Field Today," *Brooklyn Eagle*, April 12, 1946.
142 *"How about that Reiser?"* Cannon, *New York Post*, April 19, 1946.
142 *"The pain is killing me . . ."* Scott, "Pete Reiser's Bat Plays Important Role in Victory," *Brooklyn Citizen*, April 23, 1946.
143 *"I had a good season last year . . ."* United Press, "Olmo Goes to Mexico If Flock Bid Is Topped," *New York Daily News*, February 6, 1946.
143 *"For the first time in my life . . ."* Monte Irvin with Jim Riley, *Nice Guys Finish First: The Autobiography of Monte Irvin*, New York. Carroll and Graf, 1996, p. 101.
144 *"We are building seven ballparks . . ."* Gillespie, "Pasquel Has $30,000,000 to Pour Into Mexican Baseball," *St. Louis Star and Times*, February 26, 1946.
144 *"He can go to Mexico . . ."* Burr, "Someone Takes Flock for Mexican Hayride," *Brooklyn Eagle*, April 3, 1946.
145 *Loussac first offered a five-year contract . . .* Details on the Pasquel's efforts to woo Reiser come from: "Reiser Weighing Bid to Play in Mexico; Wants More Time," Associated Press, *Cincinnati Enquirer*, May 4, 1946; "Rojek, Dodger, Jumps to Mexico; Reiser Considering a Big Offer," McGowen, *New York Times*, May 4, 1946; and Burr, "Reiser Weighs Mex Offer of $100,000," *Brooklyn Eagle*, May 4, 1946.
145 *"Sure, I'm considering their offer . . ."* McGowen, *New York Times*, May 4, 1946.
145 *"I don't know what to do . . ."* Associated Press, *Cincinnati Enquirer*, May 4, 1946.
145 *There's a magnificent car downstairs . . .* Burr, "Reiser, Rojek Rescued from Mexican League by Rickey Word Barrage," *Brooklyn Eagle*, May 5, 1946.
146 *"Are you going to cut my throat?"* Burnes, *The Sporting News*, 1956.
146 *". . . a man without a country."* Burr, "Mexican War On As Rickey Fires Injunction," *Brooklyn Eagle*, May 7, 1946.
146 *"I think I did the wise thing . . ."* Associated Press, "Reiser to Stay With Dodgers," *Tampa Bay Times*, May 5, 1946.
146 *"A two thousand five hundred dollar raise . . ."* Gillespie, *The Sporting News*, 1949.
147 *"Hughes was paying him little attention."* Burr, "Reiser's 9th Inning Homer Gives Dodgers 12-11 Win Over Phillies in Wild Tilt," *Brooklyn Eagle*, May 12, 1946.
147 *"Shades of Ty Cobb and Max Carey!"* Turkin, "Flock Dupes Phils, 6-3," *New York Daily News*, May 14, 1946.

148 *"Kiner and Johnny Barrett both froze..."* Cornelius Ryan, United Press, "Dodgers Fumble Way to Front," *Dayton Daily Herald*, May 18, 1946.
148 *"Most other managers..."* "One Year Contract Gives Rickey Tight Rein on Durocher," NEA syndicate, *Muncie Evening Press*, November 29, 1946.
149 *"He can't hit, he can't run..."* The oft-quoted line about Stanky originated in a July 2, 1946 Associated Press profile of the Dodgers' second baseman: "On mechanical ability alone, Stanky might be lucky to stick with a good AA club. Rickey admits he can't hit, can't throw, and would have a hard time outracing his granduncle. But, says Rickey, his fighting spirit makes him one of the most valuable players on the team."
149 *"It's lucky that I stumbled..."* Holmes, "Reiser's Latest Wall Bout Is Not Serious," *Brooklyn Eagle*, May 20, 1946.
150 *"Durocher can thank Pete..."* Lundquist, United Press, "Pete Reiser Big Factor In Stopping Cardinals From Sweeping Series," *Brooklyn Citizen*, June 13, 1946.
150 *"Other base runners have to be watched..."* Burr, "Dodgers Open Long Home Stand Tonight." *Brooklyn Eagle*, June 14, 1946.
150 *"He worries the pitchers..."* J.G. Taylor Spink, "Looping the Loops," *The Sporting News*, July 17, 1946.
150 *"When Pete was on..."* Cannon, "Reiser Is the Best in National," *New York Post*, July 5, 1946.
150 *"I rely on the pitcher's fear..."* Spink, "Looping the Loops," *The Sporting News*, October 2, 1946.
151 *"The doctor said if it became worse..."* Murphy, "Reiser Is Dodgers' Hope, *New York Sun*, June 11, 1946.
151 *"... even a one-armed Reiser."* Herbert Goren, "Reiser Is Contented and Eager," *New York Sun*, February 4, 1947.
151 *... there is the big question."* Spink, *The Sporting News*, July 17, 1946.
152 *"The peg was perfect..."* Burr, "Hatten Proves Flock Hurler Can Go Route," *Brooklyn Eagle*, June 20, 1946.
152 *"Terrible, just terrible."* Daley, "Conversation in the Brooklyn Manner," *New York Times*, July 5, 1946.
152 *"... didn't want to be the one to advise the Dodgers."* Young, "Ailing Arm Worries Reiser as Dodgers Face Cubs," *New York Daily News*, June 19, 1946.
152 *"It should be mentioned here..."* Ibid.
154 *"Without him the all-star game..."* Cannon, *New York Post*, July 5, 1946.
154 *"I don't think it's fair..."* "Ask to Drop Pete From All-Stars," *New York Daily News*, July 2, 1946.
154 *"The Nationals displayed no fight."* Jim McCulley, "The Shame of It!" *New York Daily News*, July 10, 1946.
154 *"Pete is pretty depressed..."* Young, "Reiser Rises to Stardom Despite Many Injuries," *New York Daily News*, July 7, 1946.
154 *"In Chicago I stole home..."* Heinz, *True*, 1958.
155 *"Pete isn't hitting those long drives..."* Burr, "Dodgers Seek Aid of Farm Clubs as Lead Shrinks to 3 ½ Games," *Brooklyn Eagle*, July 13, 1946.
155 *"Reiser hurt us badly..."* Holmes, "Durocher Discusses the State of the World," *Brooklyn Eagle*, July 25, 1946.
155 *"Practically jet-propelled."* Turkin, "Dodgers Rip Reds 7-3; Reiser Hits 3-Run HR," *New York Daily News*, July 30, 1946.
156 *"He missed—and once again paid the price."* The account of Reiser's crash is drawn from: Burr, "Ebbets Left Field Wall Plays Prominent Role in Flatbush Setback by Gashouse

Gang," *Brooklyn Eagle;* Young, "Reiser In Hospital; KO'd By Wall Crash," *New York Daily News,* and a photo of Pete and his wife published in the *Binghamton Press and Sun-Bulletin,* all August 2, 1946.

156 *"I don't think it's anything serious."* Young, *New York Daily News,* August 2, 1946.

156 *"In view of his eagerness to go home..."* Goren, "Reiser Is Back to Aid Dodgers in Flag Race," *New York Sun,* August 7, 1946.

156 *"it was enough to burn his fingers."* Young, "Reiser Lights Gas—Dodgers Lose Reiser," *New York Daily News,* August 7, 1946.

157 *"When Reiser plays..."* Lee Scott, "Reiser Demonstrates Real Value to Dodgers," *Brooklyn Citizen,* August 9, 1946.

157 *"Bill Voiselle of the Giants challenged me."* Spink, *Sporting News,* October 1946.

158 *"It's not a secret the odd collection..."* Harman Nichols, United Press, "Dodgers Head Into Series With Cubs Tied for Top," *Dunkirk Evening Observer,* August 28, 1946.

158 *"A born gambler through and through..."* Leonard Cohen, "Cards' Class vs. Leo's Bums," *New York Post,* September 12, 1946.

158 *"... the Dodgers wear a hungry look."* Goren, "Will to Rally Dodger Asset," *New York Sun,* August 13, 1946.

159 *"It felt as though every muscle..."* Young, "Will Risk Operation Throw Lefty: Reiser," *New York Daily News,* September 4, 1946.

159 *"What good am I like this?"* Ibid.

159 *"The towering Mr. Gee..."* Burr, "Giants Stage Circus Act for Ebbets Fans," *Brooklyn Eagle,* September 9, 1946.

160 *"Pete got up limping."* Martin J. Haley, "Brooks Rout Munger, Whip Cards 4-3," *St. Louis Globe-Democrat,* and Burr, "All's Well in Flatbush as Ole Higbe Stops Cards in Relief Role," *Brooklyn Eagle,* both September 14, 1946.

160 *"It was a grand exhibition of pure guts."* Young, "Swish Grand Slam Sets Flock Back 2 Games; Cubs Cop 10-7," *New York Daily News,* September 17, 1946.

161 *"Jesus Christ."* Honig, *Baseball When the Grass Was Real,* p. 312.

161 *"I knew right away that this finished Reiser."* Holmes, "Misfortune Fells Reiser Once More," *Brooklyn Eagle,* September 27, 1946.

161 *"I tried to slide back in a way..."* Ibid.

162 *"I just can't watch a game I'm not in."* Young, "Reiser Sees One Frame, Can't Stand Suspense," *New York Daily News,* October 2, 1946.

163 *"In the last month of play..."* Grantland Rice column, syndicated, *St. Louis Globe-Democrat,* October 3, 1946.

163 *"... we just couldn't make the grade."* Associated Press, "Stanky Says Reiser's Loss Cost Pennant," *Tampa Tribune,* October 23, 1946.

163 *"Pete Reiser came near wrecking himself..."* Grantland Rice column, syndicated, *St. Louis Globe-Democrat,* October 2, 1946.

163 *"Had I been able to play every game..."* Spink, *Sporting News,* October 2, 1946.

Chapter 9: The Other What Ifs

165 *"It's defeatist to harp on..."* Oliver Burkeman, "Man of Steel," *The Guardian,* September 17, 2002.

166 *"Rushin conjured up a scenario..."* Steve Rushin, "What Might Have Been?" *Sports Illustrated,* July 19, 1993.

167 *"forty-six thousand towel-twirling Redbird fans..."* Video of 2014 National League Championship Series game 2. Watching Taveras' home run, it's easy to see why many thought he was destined for greatness. The home run came on a beautiful, powerful, utterly natural swing.

When he returned to the dugout, every member of the team gave him a hug or a handslap, and the crowd kept roaring until he came out for a curtain call. Sadly, he got only more hit before his death, a pinch-hit single in Game Four.

168 *"neck-risking outfielder"* Si Burick column, *Dayton Daily News*, May 24, 1948.

168 *"American League's Pete Reiser."* Lundquist, United Press, "Macks' Elmer Valo Unable to Practice What He Preaches," *Scranton Tribune*, March 18, 1951.

168 *"When that ball comes out there . . ."* Ibid.

168 *". . . the fellow who runs into walls."* Daley, "Fire Ravages a Memorable Landmark," *New York Times*, August 25, 1971.

168 *". . . chased a long fly into the brick outfield wall."* Davis' catch is preserved on an old WGN broadcast. Starting from mid-center field, Eric the Red sprints back to the warning track, extends his glove to grab the long drive off the bat of the Cubs' Brian Dayett, then slams shoulder-first into the ivy-covered wall. "I don't know what other center fielder could have made that play," exclaims Harry Caray as Davis walks off the field, looking groggy.

169 *"the best hitter, best runner . . ."* This is one of those quotes that pops up every time people discuss Eric Davis. It seems to be genuine; I've never heard O'Neill disown it, and it's been used in many newspapers and websites. Only thing is, I can't find the original source for the quote, which is a frustrating thing to a journalistic stickler like me. I decided to use it here, because the sentiment is certainly defensible; in his early days, Davis was very possibly the best player in the National League. But still, I'd like to know when O'Neill said this, and to who.

170 *"It's unfair to name just a few . . ."* C. William Duncan, "Who Is Baseball's Greatest Player?" *Louisville Courier-Journal*, July 5, 1931.

170 *"He had a magnificent arm . . ."* Bozeman Bulger, "What Made Great Ball Players Great," New York World syndicate, *Springfield News-Leader*, April 6, 1924.

170 *"Ferguson's pitching completely puzzling . . ."* "A Good Beginning," *Philadelphia Inquirer*, May 2, 1884.

170 *"I left because I feared . . ."* *The Sporting News*, September 27, 1886.

171 *"The great feature of both contests . . ."* "Remarkable Ball-Playing," *The Times*, October 10, 1886.

171 *"Ferguson thinks his salary . . ."* "Both the Local Clubs Getting Down to Solid Work," *The Times*, March 20, 1887.

171 *"detained in the east."* Diamond Dust," *San Francisco Examiner*, December 5, 1887. I've seen it reported elsewhere that Ferguson took part in the western tour with his teammates. And in fact, notices in two Los Angeles newspapers announced he was going to pitch games the afternoons of December 23-26. However, I can find no box score or any mention of his actual participation in those games or any others on the tour. He didn't go.

171 *"Ferguson is not seriously ill."* "Base Ball Notes," *The Times*, April 14, 1888.

171 *"Ferguson will be badly missed . . ."* "The Phillies in Bad Shape," *The Times*, April 17, 1888.

172 *"He is very thin . . ."* *Pittsburgh Press*, April 26, 1888.

172 *"several Philly players lifted his casket."* "Pitcher Ferguson's Funeral," *The Times*, May 1, 1888.

173 *"I never did care much . . ."* Ron Fimrite, "A Call to Arms," *Sports Illustrated*, October 16, 1991.

173 *"you've finally caught on . . ."* Hugh Fullerton Jr., Associated Press, "Sports Roundup," *Ottawa Journal*, January 31, 1942.

173 *"Camp Wheeler went all the way . . ."* "Camp Wheeler, Ga. Spokes Beat Enid's Fliers to Gain Title," *Wichita Eagle*, August 30, 1943.

174 *"very good playing shape."* Guy Butler, "Sgt. Cecil Travis Here, Fears for Major Careers of Older Players, *Miami News*, February 9, 1944.

Notes

174 "Heck, you was in that snow..." Gary Bloomfield, *Duty, Honor, Victory: America's Athletes in World War II*, Lyons Press, 2004, p.81.

174 "...drove all night to get to Washington." Associated Press, "Cecil Travis Home; Joins Washington," *Cincinnati Enquirer*, September 7, 1945.

174 "found it difficult to run..." International News service, "Say Greatest Problem for Returning Athletes Is Getting Legs in Condition," Waterloo, Iowa *Courier*, October 23, 1945.

174 "I was just dead last year." Denmon Thompson, "Travis in Poor Shape but Convinced He'll Regain His Speed," *Washington Evening Star*, February 25, 1946.

174 "My problem when I got back..." Todd Newville, "Cecil Howell Travis, Shortstop, Super Senator," *Baseball Digest*, May 2003.

175 "If it had not been for the war..." Jeff D'Alessio and Furman Bisher, "Only War Could Keep Him From the Hall of Fame," *Atlanta Journal Constitution*, December 17, 2006.

175 "There are a lot of players..." Furman Bisher, "The All-Stars From Fayette County," *Atlanta Journal Constitution*, July 11, 2000.

176 "He took a second to admire the hit." Video of Marlins vs. Braves, September 11, 2013.

177 "Tonight we didn't win because..." Bill Verigan, "Bird Flies, 2-1, as Reggie Loses One," *New York Daily News*, June 21, 1977.

178 "I've been in baseball for 35 years..." ABC broadcast, Tigers vs. Yankees, June 28, 1976.

178 "I thought, 'That really looked weird.'" Doug Wilson, *The Bird: The Life and Legacy of Mark Fidrych*, Thomas Dunne Books, 2013.

178 "All of the sudden, he couldn't..." Ibid.

178 "I was throwing great." Jim Benagh, "Ailing Fidrych Hears Boos," *Detroit Free Press*, July 13, 1977.

180 "That was it." Lawrence Ritter, *The Glory of Their Times: the Story of the Early Days of Baseball Told by the Men Who Played It*," William Morrow & Co., 1966, p. 166.

180 "It was in a cast..." Ibid.

180 "I stayed on the farm because..." Don Amore, "Smoky Joe Wood Provides a Voice From the Past," *Hartford Courant*, June 17, 2013.

181 "Hitting is very nice..." Ibid.

181 "I just didn't want to see..." Marc Lancaster, "Rays Gain Ground on Road Trip," *Tampa Tribune*, August 18, 2008.

181 "Hamilton had been blessed genetically..." Tim Stevens, "Hamilton's Story Is One of Promise, Pain and Redemption," *Charlotte Observer*, April 30, 2017.

181 "Then he'd fall back." Hamilton's struggles with his addictions are chronicled in his 2010 autobiography, *Beyond Belief*, written with Tim Keown.

182 "Standing at home plate..." Mark Feinsand, "Just Out of Sight," *New York Daily News*, July 15, 2008.

182 "He told me, 'You haven't hit one...'" "Say What?" *New York Daily News*, October 30, 2011.

183 "Surround yourself with good people..." Jeff Wilson, "Hall-Bound Hamilton Talks New Life, Addiction," *Fort-Worth Star Telegram*, May 21, 2019.

184 "Casey Stengel told Ferrell..." Joseph Wancho, SABR Biography of Herb Score, https://sabr.org/bioproj/person/herb-score/

184 "You know, maybe I was fortunate..." David Budin, *Coshocton Tribune*, "Herb Score: He No Longer Pitches But He Still Delivers," April 8, 1994.

185 "He was the best pitcher in baseball..." Jerry Crowe, "A Cruel Stroke for J.R. Richard," *Los Angeles Times*, June 29, 1987.

185 "I felt like I was the baddest lion..." Tyler Kepner, *A History of Baseball in Ten Pitches*, Anchor Books, 2019, p. 21.

185 *"the team physician insultingly suggested..."* Lou Maysel, "Basketball Schedule Juggled at UT," *Austin American-Statesman*, July 17, 1980.
186 *"I'm not working out twice a day..."* Jack Lang, "J.R. Richard Rejects Idea to Pitch in Minors," *New York Daily News*, June 7, 1981.
186 *"Virdon organized a simulated game."* Ray Didinger, "Dub Him Richard the Lion-Hearted," *Philadelphia Daily News*, September 8, 1981.
186 *"He doesn't look like he's been sick..."* Jim Elsleger, "Richard Arrives in Tucson," *Arizona Daily Star*, August 5, 1982.
187 *"God said love everybody..."* Associated Press, "Faith Helps Ex-Houston Astro J.R. Richard After Stroke and Homelessness," *The Daily Review* (Morgan City, Louisiana) August 14, 2018.
188 *"He could play third base like..."* Monte Irvin, *Few and Chosen*, Triumph Books, 2007, p. 65.
188 *"With Willie Wells at short..."* Buck O'Neill, *I Was Right on Time*, Simon and Schuster, 2007, p. 145.
188 *"There is a Negro shortstop down here..."* Jimmy Powers column, *New York Daily News*, July 10, 1946.
188 *"You fellows are from the South."* Gordon Cobbledick, *Cleveland Plain Dealer*, June 22, 1946.
189 *"I thought about it a lot."* Will Grimsley, Associated Press, "Drive Launched for Black Baseball Leagues Museum," *St. Louis Post-Dispatch*, November 7, 1980.
189 *"I told our scout, 'Why don't you..."* William J. Marshall interview of Maglie, May 25, 1981 for University of Kentucky's Desegregation of Major League Baseball Oral History Project.
190 *"... an emergency appendectomy."* Photo, *Minneapolis Star Tribune*, July 17, 1951.
191 *"Ray was considered several times..."* Jules Tygiel, *Baseball's Great Experiment*, 1983, p. 264
191 *"I said to Horace Stoneham..."* William J. Marshall interview of Dandridge, November 12, 1979 for University of Kentucky's Desegregation of Major League Baseball Oral History Project.
191 *"I want to sincerely thank..."* Dandridge Hall of Fame induction speech.

Chapter 10: Jackie and the Last Rites

193 *"Dodgers Trip Braves, 5-3..."* All the headlines and articles about Robinson's debut come from the April 16, 1947 editions of the cited New York newspapers.
193 *"If Pete Reiser can play a full season..."* The Red Barber Show, CBS Radio, April 15, 1947. A low-quality recording can be found online (www.oldtimeradiodownloads.com/sports/red-barber-show/red-barber-show-1947-04-15).
194 *"My ankle hurts a little..."* Herbert Goren, "Reiser Shows Old-Time Form," *New York Sun*, April 16, 1947.
194 *"He'll be all right."* Bill Roeder, *New York World-Telegram*, April 16, 1947.
194 *"If he wasn't..."* Oscar Fraley, United Press, "Not the Minors," *Elmira Star-Gazette*, April 16, 1947.
194 *"What a player that man is."* Ibid.
194 *"The writers are all gathered around..."* Bill Roeder, "He Put the Head in the Headlines," New York Baseball Writers Association dinner program, February 1, 1976.
195 *"He said, 'You can play ball..."* Fred Lieb, "Reiser's Newest Gripe: Dodgers Won't Talk," *The Sporting News*, January 15, 1947.
195 *"I am sure that Pete will throw..."* Young, "Reiser Arm Operation Success," *New York Daily News*, December 18, 1946.
195 *"Reiser knows what it is like..."* "Pete Reiser Named Sport King of March of Dimes," *Brooklyn Eagle*, January 14, 1947.

Notes

195 *"I'm supposed to be one of the valuable players . . ."* Lieb, *Sporting News*, January 15, 1947.

195 *"I understand that Reiser believes . . ."* Joe Trimble, "Robinson's Flock Future Up to Players: Rickey," *New York Daily News*, January 14, 1947.

196 *"Rickey had launched a secret plan . . ."* Branch Rickey's master plan to integrate major league baseball has been comprehensively covered in several books. Readers wanting to learn more about Rickey's maneuverings should consult Arthur Mann's *Branch Rickey: American in Action* (1957), Murray Polner's *Branch Rickey: A Biography* (1982), Lee Lowenfish's *Branch Rickey: Baseball's Ferocious Gentleman* (2007), Jonathan Eig's *Opening Day* (2007) and Jimmy Breslin's *Branch Rickey* (2011). These books and the movie *42* also give a comprehensive view of Robinson's debut season with the Dodgers.

197 *"I don't mind trouble but . . ."* The original letter can be seen on the National Archives website (www.archives.gov/publications/prologue/2008/spring/robinson.html).

197 *"Pete could find no fault . . ."* W. Vernon Tietjen, "Pete Reiser May Become 'Lefty' Thrower," *St. Louis Star and Times*, December 8, 1945.

197 *"long as he isn't with the Dodgers . . ."* United Press, "Negro Player Question Meets Wide Reaction," *Pittsburgh Post-Gazette*, October 25, 1945.

198 *"Mr. Rickey, do you really think . . ."* This quote, which has appeared in many a story and book about Robinson, has a slightly murky history. Its earliest appearance in print appears to be a May 13, 1950 *Saturday Evening Post* article, "The Truth About the Jackie Robinson Case," written by sportswriter and Rickey's assistant Arthur Mann. Mann reports the conversation between Hopper and Rickey as though he observed it first-hand. That's certainly possible but seems unlikely, as Mann did not join the Brooklyn staff until after the 1946 season. More likely, he got the quote from his boss, who sometimes pointed to Hopper as an example of how racists in baseball, and in general, could change their views. For what it's worth, Hopper never confirmed nor denied that he made the comment.

198 *"You're a great ballplayer . . ."* Jackie Robinson and Alfred Duckett, *I Never Had It Made*, HarperCollins, 1972, p. 71. I can't find that exact quote from Hopper in any 1946 paper but here's one from the August 13, 1946 *Windsor Star* in Ontario that comes pretty close: "Jackie's got all the guts in the world. He proved that to me during the season. He's a big-league ballplayer, a team hustler and a real gentleman."

198 *"go up and stay up."* "Racine Predicts Better All-Round Baseball Club," *Montreal Gazette*, March 19, 1947.

198 *"It would be a crime not to bring . . ."* Burr, "Robinson May Be Dodgers' 1st Sacker After Royal Series," *Brooklyn Eagle*, March 17, 1947.

198 *"We the undersigned will not . . ."* Roger Kahn, *Rickey & Robinson*, Rodale Books, 2013, p.117. I should add that others have said there was no actual petition, that Walker and company just talked about starting one. But Pete and Pee Wee Reese both said an actual petition was passed around.

199 *"Pee Wee Reese and I were the last ones . . ."* "Petitions Couldn't Stop His Debut," *Pittsburgh Courier*, November 4, 1972.

199 *"I'd had an experience when . . ."* Honig, *Baseball When the Grass Was Real*, p. 312.

199 *"He grew up in North St. Louis . . ."* Author interview, September 2020.

199 *"I wasn't trying to think of myself . . ."* Pee Wee Reese, "What Jackie Robinson Meant to an Old Friend," *New York Times*, July 17, 1977

200 *"He seems to be all for Robinson . . ."* Wendell Smith, "The Sports Beat," *Pittsburgh Courier*, April 12, 1947.

200 *"Stanky: He appears to be prejudiced . . ."* Ibid.

201 *"They'll call me a louse . . ."* Lee Lowenfish, *Baseball's Ferocious Gentleman*, University of Nebraska Press, 2007, p. 413

*201 "Threatened to boycott the team." * "Durocher Hit as CYO Quits Knot-Hole Club," *Brooklyn Eagle*, February 28, 1947.
201 "Where does MacPhail come off..." International News Service, "Durocher Charges MacPhail Has Gamblers In His Box," *St. Louis Star and Times*, March 10, 1947.
201 "I hate like hell to see him go." Dan Noonan, "Chant of 'Bring Leo Back' Rings at Knot Hole Dinner," *Brooklyn Eagle*, April 11, 1947. The Reese and Reiser quotes come from the same article.
202 "Sure, it hurts during the game." Young, "Ankle Up, Pete Down, but He'll Face Braves," *New York Daily News*, April 21, 1947.
202 "Though he still covers considerable ground..." Ibid.
203 "The first time I watched Robinson..." Burr, "Shotton Changes His Mind About Robinson Speed," *Brooklyn Eagle*, April 23, 1947.
204 "Pete Reiser went out of his way..." "Dodger Dust," *Pittsburgh Courier*, May 31, 1947.
205 "Pete Reiser isn't getting the jump..." Burr, "Herman Plays Dodger Opener Under Protest," *Brooklyn Eagle*, June 4, 1947.
205 "Back flew Reiser..." Young, "Reiser Hurt Crashing Fall, Flock Wins 9-4," *New York Daily News*, June 5, 1947. Descriptions from Goren, Burr, Johnson, Laney come from their respective papers that same day, while Lundquist's account was a wire story.
207 "He was bleeding pretty badly." Herbert Goren, "Reiser Is Expected Back With Dodgers in a Week," New York Sun, June 5, 1947.*
207 "Someone hits a hell of a shot." Rick Tuber interview of Gene Hermanski, date unknown.
207 "I got to Pete first and saw the ball..." Mike Santangelo, "Dixie Walker Facing His Toughest Opponent," *New York Daily News*, March 2, 1982.
208 "... stayed there for another four days." Associated Press, "Reiser Released From Hospital," *Syracuse Post-Standard*, June 10, 1947.
208 "King inadvertently barreled into the pair." Associated Press, "Hardluck Reiser Hurt Again, *St. Louis Post-Dispatch*, June 16, 1947 and Young, "Reiser - The Kid They Can't Miss," *New York Daily News*, June 17, 1947.
209 "He did go to Hopkins, but not until June 24." Burr, "Reiser Flies to Baltimore for Checkup at Hopkins," *Brooklyn Eagle*, June 24, 1947.
209 "... not serious enough to warrant hospitalization." Associated Press, "Reiser Out Two More Weeks," *New York Daily News*, June 27, 1947.
209 "That's why they sent me home." James L. Toomey, "Reiser Wants Cinder Path to Warn Fielders," *St. Louis Star and Times*, July 8, 1947.
209 "We are going to ask Pete..." Burr, "Reiser's Presence Tonic for Dodgers," *Brooklyn Eagle*, July 11, 1947.
211 "Robinson is the principal factor..." United Press, "Ben Chapman Lauds Play of Robinson," *Elmira Star-Gazette*, June 21, 1947.
211 "It's what the doctor ordered." Burr, "Reiser's Presence Tonic for Dodgers," *Brooklyn Eagle*, July 11, 1947.
212 "I think its dislocated." Burr, "Flock Loses Reiser for Red Series," *Brooklyn Eagle*, July 22, 1947.
213 "I know I played both of them badly..." Burr, "Reiser Dizzy Spells New Flock Headache," *Brooklyn Eagle*, August 7, 1947.
213 "took a knee to the groin area." Burr, "Chicago Shifts Jeers from Dixie to Pete," *Brooklyn Eagle*, September 10, 1947.
213 "lost the ball in the late-afternoon sun." Young, "Flock Quells Cards 8-7; Soars to 5 ½ Lead," *New York Daily News*, September 14, 1947.
215 "I couldn't point to any one player..." Burr, "Relax Guys n' Gals, the Dodgers Are In!" *Brooklyn Eagle*, September 23, 1947.

Notes

215 *"I like this ballclub of Shotton's."* Ibid.
216 *"Have a box seat at the World's Series."* Namm's advertisement, *New York Daily News*, September 28, 1947.
216 *"The Dodgers have no power to match..."* United Press, "DiMag Gives Yanks Edge in Outfield," *Pittsburgh Press*, September 27, 1947.
216 *"A sound Reiser would come closest..."* Harry Grayson, "DiMaggio, Henrick Give Yankees Outfield Edge," NEA syndicate, *Ogden Standard Examiner*, September 28, 1947.
216 *"I consider the Dodgers..."* Al Buck, "Across the Table Story of MacPhail Quotations," *The Sporting News*, September 17, 1947.
217 *"Favorites have been beaten before..."* Burr, "Shotton Sure Flock Will Capture Series," *Brooklyn Eagle*, September 27, 1947.
217 *"Pete then hit a one-bouncer..."* As seen in baseball's official 1947 World Series film.
217 *"arching his back and accelerating."* This is also in the World Series film, seen in freeze-frame to show how Reiser avoided the tag. The description of Pete's center field fiascos in Game Two also come from the film.
218 *"I've seen better outfielders than Reiser..."* Jim McCulley, "Yankees Sympathize with 'Goat' Reiser," *New York Daily News*, October 2, 1947.
218 *"I don't think the fellow..."* Young, "Change Lineup? 'Could Be' Says Burt, *New York Daily News*, October 2, 1947.
218 *"I won't be able to play tomorrow..."* Turkin, "Injury to Reiser May Bench Him," *New York Daily News*, October 3, 1947.
219 *"The doctor X-rayed it..."* Honig, *Baseball When the Grass Was Real*, p. 311.
220 *"What are you doing here?"* Roger Birtwell, "Inside Story of an Inning That Hit the Peak of Drama," *The Sporting News*, October 15, 1947.
220 *"Ain't you going to volunteer to hit?"* Barber, *1947: When All Hell Broke Loose in Baseball*, p. 324-325.
221 *"You don't just put that winning run..."* "The Way It Was," PBS, aired August 6, 1975.
221 *"You've got the tying run on second..."* James Dawson, "Bevens Disconsolate, Admits Bases on Balls Deprived Him of Series Glory," *New York Times*, October 4, 1947.
221 *"Barney [Shotton] sent up his best..."* Burr, "Happy Vetoes Lip Series Cut," *Brooklyn Eagle*, October 4, 1947.
221 *"DiMaggio told me years later..."* Honig, *Baseball When the Grass Was Real*, p. 312.
222 *"I would have rather have seen them lose..."* Milton Richman, United Press, "Brooklyn Mourns Bums Defeat; Looks to Next Year for Revenge," *Scranton Tribune*, October 8, 1947.
223 *"Pete Reiser is not for sale or trade."* McGowen, "Dodgers Are Firm on Keeping Reiser," *New York Times*, March 14, 1948.
223 *"Pete Reiser will always be getting hurt."* Whitney Martin, Associated Press, "Padding Is Added to Protect Pete," *Raleigh News and Observer*, January 29, 1948.
223 *"I'll believe that when I see it."* Young, "Reiser Returns Dodger Pact; 18Gs Not Enough," *New York Daily News*, February 8, 1948.

Chapter 11: Baseball Afterlife
224 *"In '48 Rickey didn't want me..."* Honig, *Baseball When the Grass Was Real*, p. 314.
224 *"poor Pete has been banged around..."* Holmes, "Branch Rickey and the Revolving Door," *Brooklyn Eagle*, August 19, 1948.
225 *"If I don't get more money now..."* United Press, "Reiser Rejects Dodger Pay Hike," *Pittsburgh Press*, February 15, 1948.
225 *"At the first workout yesterday..."* Burr, "Signing of Reese, Stanky Peps Flock," *Brooklyn Eagle*, March 2, 1948.

225 *"I don't want to take off the winter fat..."* Burr, "Reiser Vetoes Switch-Hitting Plan, Fast Workouts on Beef Removal," *Brooklyn Eagle*, March 3, 1948.
225 *"Leo Durocher's wife is here..."* "Wife Banned, Pete Wins Rebellion," *New York Daily News*, March 10, 1948.
225 *"I always admired the spunk..."* Laraine Day, *Day With the Giants*, Doubleday & Company, 1952, p. 67.
225 *"He lacks height..."* Grayson, "Reiser at First No Surprise," NEA syndicate, *Ogden Standard Examiner*, March 23, 1948.
226 *"It's obvious that as a first-sacker..."* Young, "Appendix Fells Flock's Taylor," *New York Daily News*, April 29, 1948.
226 *"Pete's too fat..."* Burr, "Hugh Casey Faces Full-Time Job Putting Out Fires for Dodgers," *Brooklyn Eagle*, April 21, 1948.
226 *"If I don't get word from Reiser..."* Young, "Hurling, Reiser Worry Rickey," *New York Daily News*, June 19, 1948.
226 *"The Brooklyn organization's patience..."* Bob Curley, "Curley Cues," Ridgewood. New Jersey *Sunday News*, June 20, 1948.
226 *"Pete Reiser is a great guy..."* Jimmy Powers column, *New York Daily News*, June 11, 1948.
226 *"running only to doctors these days..."* Young, "Flock Tries to Run Out of 6th," *New York Daily News*, May 29, 1948.
227 *"I think I'll quit."* Young, "Dodgers Edge Giants 13-12 With 4 in 9th," *New York Daily News*, July 5, 1948.
227 *"This one was only a single..."* Ibid.
228 *"I get a new third baseman..."* Burr, "Reiser Shines at Third, Then Is Sidelined Again," *The Sporting News*, September 22, 1948.
228 *"I'll play anywhere..."* Young, "Reiser Dislikes Brooklyn; He'll Go Anywhere Else," *New York Daily News*, October 23, 1948.
228 *"I don't think I've ever felt better..."* Grantland Rice column, syndicated, April 14, 1949.
228 *"I'm not worried..."* Ibid.
228 *"Practically everybody you meet down here..."* Joe Williams, syndicated, "Pete Reiser Made the Key Man in 3-Way National League Race," *Wilmington News-Journal*, March 21, 1949.
229 *"hit it to the parking lot..."* Young, "Reiser 4-Run HR Hikes Boston Over Flock, 7-6," *New York Daily News*, May 29, 1949.
229 *"Reiser has had more ailments..."* Bob Holbrook, "Cooney Indicates He May Drop Southworth Shift Policy," *Boston Globe*, August 18, 1949.
230 *"Maybe if he had been a catcher..."* Associated Press, "Reiser Gets Last Chance as Catcher," *Pittsburgh Post-Gazette*, March 16, 1951.
230 *"is broken in body..."* Bob Broeg, "Patched and Wired Pete Reiser Says He's Not Sorry He Took Dangerous Way," *St. Louis Post-Dispatch*, September 2, 1951.
230 *"I don't see how Reiser..."* Jim Schlemmer, "Indians Sign Reiser; Lemon is Next," *Akron Beacon Journal*, February 7, 1952.
231 *"I like his fire and desire."* Associated Press, "Reiser Makes Grade as One-Man Bench for Cleveland Club," *Cincinnati Enquirer*, March 12, 1952.
231 *"I can't throw or swing anymore."* Burr, "Injury Fails to Stop Campy," *Brooklyn Eagle*, July 15, 1952.
231 *"It's no secret that Reiser ruined himself..."* Jimmy Powers column, *New York Daily News*, July 23, 1952.
231 *"There were times when other kids..."* Herbert Kamm, "Fence-Crashing Pete Reiser Bears Big Personal Burden," *Pittsburgh Press*, March 30, 1959.

232 *"I played in class D, didn't I?"* Furman Bisher, "The Road Back to Brooklyn," *Atlanta Journal Constitution*, April 20, 1955.
232 *"You know, I'm really happier today..."* Associated Press, "Reiser Happier Working With Youngsters," *Elmira Star-Gazette*, March 8, 1959.
232 *"When Pete came through the gate..."* Heinz, *True*, 1958.
233 *"Pete started me from scratch..."* Maury Wills with Steve Gardner, *It Pays to Steal*, Prentice-Hall, 1963, p. 52.
233 *"They say in every man's life..."* Wills, p. 53.
234 *"I know that was a great highlight..."* Shirley Tuber email to author, 2020.
234 *"wanted to leave the hospital..."* United Press International, "Dodgers' Pete Reiser Suffers Heart Attack," *Fresno Bee*, April 17, 1964.
235 *"Leo was very good to Pete..."* Author interview with Rick and Shirley Tuber, September 2020.
235 *"Oh, don't talk about it!"* Ibid.
235 *"I was visiting dad in Chicago..."* Shirley Tuber email to author, 2020.
235 *"The whole season has been going too good..."* Tom Fitzpatrick, "Stag Party Proves It: Leo Owns the Town," *Kenosha News*, June 6, 1969.
236 *"... Leo hadn't been ill."* "Tribune Traces Durocher Trip in Two-Day Absence," *Chicago Tribune*, July 29, 1969.
236 *"It would be nice to win this year..."* Lee Remmel, "Pete Reiser Serves as Cubs' Disciplinarian," Appleton, Wisconsin *Post-Cresent*, August 10, 1969.
237 *"I just remember the feeling..."* Author interview with Tubers, September 2020.
237 *"I believe I have a nack..."* Pete's January 1945 letter to Rickey, in the Branch Rickey papers at the Library of Congress.
238 *"He just didn't want to see a suitcase..."* Shirley Tuber email to author, 2020.
238 *"He'd had a couple of heart attacks..."* Ibid.
238 *"... an unexpected visit from W.C. Heinz."* The full story of Heinz's 1979 visit with Pete can be found in his book *Once They Heard the Cheers*.
238 *"They've really slowed me down."* George Watkins, "Pete Reiser: He Nearly Gave His Life for Baseball," *The Californian*, August 16, 1980.
238 *"I'm starting to like it."* Ibid.
239 *"He was laboring so for breath..."* "Pete Reiser, former Dodger Outfielder, Dies at Age 62," *The Desert Sun*, October 27, 1981.
239 *"This is quite a loss."* "Funeral Services Held for Ex-Dodger Reiser," *The Desert Sun*, October 29, 1981.
239 *"I have a warm smile on my face."* Anthony Sciretta, *Arizona Daily Star*, Letters to the Editor, November 8, 1981.

Chapter 12: Legacy
240 *"The notion that he was so good..."* Daniel Brown email to author, 2021.
241 *"I heard Krukow say..."* Ibid.
241 *"a career that left him cast in plaster..."* Daniel Brown, "Mike Krukow on Pistol Pete Reiser, Leo the Lip and other links to baseball's glorious past," *The Athletic*, March 17, 2021.
241 *"... could have been the greatest."* Furman Bisher, "Fearless Pete Reiser: if not for a wall, he'd be in the Hall," *Atlanta Journal-Constitution*, May 19, 1997.
242 *"As Bump ran for it..."* Bernard Malamud, *The Natural*, Harcourt, Brace and World, New York, 1952.
242 *"The old Brooklyn Dodgers were our heroes..."* Karen Heller, "Malamud's Long View of Short Stories," *USA Today*, August 19, 1983.

242 *"As a Dodger fan I preferred Reiser..."* Phillip Roth, *Goodbye, Columbus*. New York, Houghton Mifflin, 1959, p. 236.
243 *"You can call me anything."* Jim Lehrer, *Oh Johnny: A Novel*. New York, Random House, 2009, p. 51.
243 *"He looks okay, boychik."* Pete Hamill, *Snow in August*. New York, Little, Brown and Company, 1997, p. 298.
243 *"He play baseball good?"* Pete Hamill, *The Christmas Kid and Other Brooklyn Stories*, New York, Little, Brown and Company, 2012, p. 25.
243 *"... sweet ball players but ignorant punks."* Cary Nelson and Jefferson Hendricks, *Edwin Rolfe: a Biological Essay and Guide to the Rolfe Archive at the University of Illinois at Urbana-Champaign*, the University of Illinois Library, 1990, p. 107. Hemingway did not expand on what Pete and Pee Wee said or did to bring on such a harsh judgment. His opinion of three other Dodgers: "Freddy Fitzsimmons could have been a company union guy. Larry French is a good guy; smart and mean and educated.... [Hugh Casey] is as mean as the south is and has many of the south's good qualities."
244 *"There are some things, though..."* W.C. Heinz, "What Is Sought Can't Be Given," *New York Sun*, July 31, 1946.
244 *"I didn't see the old-timers...."* Heinz, *True*, 1958.
244 *"He was the best I ever had..."* Ibid.
245 *"Every ballpark in America..."* Murray, *Los Angeles Times*, 1964.
245 *"When you watch the World Series..."* Murray, *Los Angeles Times*, 1981.
246 *"I think that only real baseball fans..."* Shirley Tuber email to author, 2020.
247 *"Pete Reiser would be in the Hall of Fame..."* Murray, *Los Angeles Times*, 1981.
247 *"The least they could have done..."* Bisher, *AJC*, 1997.
247 *"At least every year at Hall of Fame induction time..."* Shirley Tuber email.
248 *"I wouldn't play any differently..."* Broeg, *St. Louis Post-Dispatch*, 1951.
248 *"Sure, if I could have avoided bouncing off fences..."* Burnes, *Sporting News*, 1956.
248 *"If I had it to do over..."* Dave Anderson, "Pete Reiser," *New York Times*, February 1, 1976.
248 *"No, I don't have any regrets."* Honig, *Baseball When the Grass Was Real*, p. 315.
248 *"The one thing I do remember..."* Shirley Tuber email.

Harper, Bryce, xii, 100, 263
Harris, Bucky, 217, 219, 221-22
Hassett, Buddy, 5
Hatten, Joe, 158, 268
Head, Ed, 142
Heinz, W.C., vi, 43, 86-88, 102, 122, 124, 137, 232-33, 238, 243-45, 249, 257, 262-66. 268, 276-78
Hemingway, Ernest, 243, 278
Henrich, Tommy, 39, 76-78, 102, 220, 242, 261
Herman, Babe, 56
Herman, Billy, xvi, 52-54, 58-59, 65, 69-71, 84, 95, 136, 142, 147, 149,158, 173, 243, 260, 274
Hermanski, Gene, 100 139-40, 155, 158. 193, 202, 206-208, 215, 219-20, 222, 263, 274
Higbe, Kirby, 51, 65-66, 83, 134, 136, 198, 199, 201, 269
Hodges, Gil, 164, 222, 227, 236
Holmes, Tommy (writer), 3, 38, 83-84-90, 101, 120, 122, 129, 224, 252, 256, 258-65, 267-69
Holmes, Tommy (player), xvi, 6-7
Honig, Donald, vi, xii, 3, 6, 10, 15, 17, 19-20, 27, 74, 85, 94, 102, 124, 137, 199, 219, 221, 228, 240, 248-49, 251-55, 257-66, 269, 273, 275, 278
Hopper, Clay, 32, 198, 273
Howard, Frank, 232, 234, 240
Hubbell, Carl, 69
Hubbs, Ken, 166-67
Hyland, Dr. Robert, 43, 85, 87-89, 92, 122, 128, 137, 150-53, 195, 204, 226, 262

Irvin, Monte, 58, 143, 187-90, 259

James, Bill, 172, 247, 249
Jethroe, Sam, 190
Jorgensen, Spider, 192, 210, 213, 215, 219-220
Judd, Oscar, 147

Keller, Charlie, 77, 102, 106, 136
Kieran, John, 75, 241, 258
Killefer, Bill, 44-46
Kiner, Ralph, 148, 152, 205, 267
King, Clyde, 208, 210

Klein, Lou, 144, 163
Koufax, Sandy, 165, 184, 234
Kurowski, Whitey, 31, 33-34, 106, 119, 256, 244-45

Landis, Judge Kenesaw Mountain: declares Reiser a free agent, 34-35; opposition to farm systems, 22. Also 21, 26-27, 36, 67, 79, 108, 126, 144, 200, 254-56, 260
Lanier, Max, 58, 82-83, 144, 163, 188, 265
Lavagetto, Cookie, 47, 51, 56, 58, 69, 72, 76, 120, 132, 158, 204, 221-22, 227
Lehrer, Jim, 119-20, 243, 249, 264, 277
Lindell, Johnny, 136, 218-19
Lombardi, Ernie, 92, 138, 247
Lopez, Al, 152, 231

Magerkurth, George, 154
Malamud, Bernard, xxi, 241-42, 249, 277
Mantle, Mickey, x, xvi, 98, 183, 247
Marion, Marty, 31
Martin, Fred, 144, 163
Martin, Whitney, 52, 66, 76, 258
Mays, Willie, x, xvi, 101, 168, 187, 190, 242, 244, 247
MacPhail, Larry, vi, 4, 27, 35, 39-42, 44-52, 57-58, 65-66, 70, 73, 79, 88-94, 100, 110, 121, 201, 216, 252, 255-58, 260, 262, 273, 275
McCann, Dick, 84, 259, 262
McCarthy, Joe, 39, 102
McCormick, Frank, 59, 247
McCormick, Mike, 153, 228
McDonald, John, 41
McGowen, Roscoe, 9, 38, 84, 252, 256, 260, 262, 265, 267, 275
McGrew, Ted, 35-36, 46, 256
McKechnie, Bill, 60, 62, 70, 102, 260
Medwick, Joe, xv, 8-9, 11, 21-22, 27, 45-46, 49, 51-52, 54, 66-67, 69, 80, 82-83, 107, 139, 248, 253, 258
Meany, Tom, 3, 9. 15. 71, 93 251, 254, 260-61, 263
Mitchell, Jerry, 61, 258-59, 264
Miskis, Eddie, 221

Mize, Johnny, 31, 53, 62, 82, 247
Moore, Terry, 4, 213
Murray, Arch, 141, 151, 267
Murray, Jim, 85, 105, 239, 241, 245-47. 264, 278
Murphy, Edward T., 151, 252-53, 268
Musial, Stan, xv, xvi, 27, 29, 71, 82, 127-28, 130, 142, 144, 155, 160, 162, 204, 213, 240, 247, 255,

Newcombe, Don, 164, 227

Ott, Mel, 62, 82, 247
Owen, Mickey, xv, 10, 31, 51-52, 69, 77, 144, 188

Parrott, Harold, 27-28, 40, 45-46, 57, 94, 133, 199, 249, 255, 257, 260, 263-65
Pasquel, Jorge, 143-46, 187, 267
Pearson, Ike, 48-49, 52-54, 89, 112, 122, 147, 154, 245, 258, 260
Pollet, Howie, 150, 162, 213
Powers, Jimmy, 147, 188, 226, 231, 241, 261, 272, 276

Reese, Pee Wee, friendship with Pete, 64-65, 78-79; struggles in 1941, 65, 73; support for Jackie Robinson, 199-200; Also vi, xi, xv, 43, 51-52, , 70-71, 75-76, 84, 90, 103, 111, 113, 115, 121, 127, 129
Reiser, George (father), baseball career, 13-14; 15-17, 23-25, 42, 50, 86, 253
Reiser, John (grandfather), 13, 15
Reiser, Mike (brother): influence on Pete, 17-20; 107, 254
Reiser, Pat (wife), 78-79, 113, 130-32, 214, 225, 264-65
Reiser, Pete: All-Star Games, 10, 11, 62-63, 107, 154; appendicitis, 43; beaning by Ike Pearson, 48-50; bone chips removed, 43; birth, 15; broken ankles, 161-62, 218-29; in Captain America movie, xii, 54-55; childhood, 15-17; collisions with walls, 52-53, 83-86, 135, 149-150, 156, 205-207; death 238-39; dislocates shoulder, 212;

Index

Allen, Johnny, 3, 70, 77, 83, 85
Alston, Walter, 233

Barber, Red, xiii, xvi, 6, 40, 54, 57, 72, 74, 76, 101, 193, 221, 239, 249, 251, 254, 256, 259, 263, 272, 275
Barlick, Al, xvi, 127, 148, 155, 265
Barrett, Charley, signing of Reiser, 23-25; travels with Reiser 29-31. Also: 27-28, 35, 37, 46, 237, 255-56
Barrett, Johnny, 89, 148, 267
Bavasi, Buzzie, 105, 232
Behrman, Hank, 158, 214, 220, 267
Berra, Yogi, 17, 93, 168, 216, 220-21
Bevens, Bill, 219-221, 227, 275
Biederman, Les, 241, 252
Bisher, Furman, 241, 246, 271, 276-78
Boggs, Wade, 247
Bostock, Lyman, 167-68
Bowman, Bob, 49, 258
Branca, Ralph, 101, 139, 205, 210, 216, 265
Breadon, Sam, 121, 164, 255
Brewer, Jack, 138
Broeg, Bob, 241, 262, 276, 278
Butcher, Max, 67, 71
Burr, Harold, 66, 150, 152, 155, 159, 202, 205-206, 211, 225, 266-69, 273-76

Camilli, Dolph, 9, 40, 51, 59, 64, 66-67, 69, 71-73, 76, 78, 80, 83, 129, 139
Campanella, Roy, 143, 164, 187, 227
Cannon, Jimmy, 83, 103-104, 138-39, 142, 150, 152, 154, 157, 241, 264, 266-68
Casey, Hugh, 51, 59, 65-66, 69-71, 77, 120, 136, 198, 214, 220, 243, 261, 276, 278

Chandler, Happy, 144, 200-201, 256, 262
Chandler, Spud, 76
Chapman, Ray, 48, 206
Chester, Hilda, 56, 139
Chipman, Bob, 54, 154, 258
Cobb, Ty, xv, 2, 4, 10, 61-62, 147, 170, 233, 251, 260, 267
Cobbledick, Gordon, 188-89, 272
Cohen, Leonard, 158, 163, 218, 269
Corriden, Red, xv, 10, 50, 258
Cooper, Mort, 31, 58, 68, 82, 164, 262
Cooper, Walker, 31, 52, 164
Cox, Billy, 205, 227-28

Daley, Arthur, 5, 74, 87, 128-29, 139, 152, 159-60, 163, 241, 252, 260, 265-66, 268, 270
Dandridge, Ray, 143, 187-91, 272
Daniel, Dan, 163
Davis, Curt, 45, 69, 83, 243, 257
Davis, Eric, 168-69, 270
Davis, Tommy, 232, 234
Derringer, Paul, 59, 70, 259
Dean, Dizzy, 21, 27
DiMaggio, Joe, i, xv, 3-4, 11, 60, 62-63, 71, 75, 77-78, 82, 102, 107, 130, 140, 146, 172, 216, 218-19, 221, 240, 247, 251, 274-75
Dressen, Charlie, 59, 69, 127
Drysdale, Don, 234
Durocher, Leo: conflict with MacPhail, 40-41; jump to Giants, 227; praise of Reiser, 2, 39, 47, 60-62, 104; reputation 57-58; support for Jackie Robinson, 199-200; suspension from baseball, 200-201; managing Cubs, 234-37. Also xv-xvi, 3, 5-6, 89, 37-39, 43, 45-53, 55, 59, 52, 65-70, 72-73, 83, 88, 92-94, 106, 110-, 128-30, 139, 141-42, 145, 148-54,

157-58-, 160-63, 190, 199, 203-204, 207, 222, 227, 239, 241, 244, 249, 251, 256-59, 267, 273, 275, 277

Edwards, Bruce, 158-59, 215, 220, 222
Elliott, Bob, 8-9
Elson, Bob, x, 76-77

Feller, Bob, x, 62, 79, 136, 144, 175, 183, 261
Ferguson, Charlie, xi, 169-72, 270
Fernandez, Jose, xi, 175-77
Fidrych, Mark, xi, 177-79, 271
Fitzsimmons, Freddie, 51, 139, 278
Frank, Stanley, 37, 75, 256
French, Larry, 1, 89, 120, 278
Frey, Lonny, vi, 60, 98-99, 126, 133, 134, 155, 263
Frick, Ford, 60, 203, 259
Frisch, Frankie, 2, 8-9, 60, 251, 259,
Furillo, Carl, 139, 140, 148, 158, 160, 198, 202, 204, 208, 210, 215, 217, 219-20, 227

Galan, Augie, 88, 91, 93, 120, 140-41, 148-49, 160, 226, 246
Garagiola, Joe, vi, 17, 126, 133, 137, 160, 204, 214, 266
Gehrig, Lou, 39, 98, 187, 217, 256
Gionfriddo, Al, 220-21, 251
Gomez, Lefty, 39, 74
Gordon, Joe, 11, 76-77, 82, 93, 107
Gowdy, Curt, 220-221
Greenberg, Hank, xv, 63, 79, 136, 140, 205, 212, 230, 250, 260
Griffey, Ken Jr., 97-100, 183, 247, 263

Hamill, Pete, 243, 249, 277
Hamilton, Josh, xi, 181-84, 271

Index

drafted into army, 95-96, 122; free agency, 34-36; heart attack, 234; as major league coach, 233-37; marriage 78-79, 130-31; Mexican League offer, 143-46; as minor league manager, 232-33; in 1939 spring training, 37-39; in 1941 World Series, 75-78; in 1947 World Series, 217-222; playing style, x, 4-5, 10; promotion to majors, 47; religion, 16; salary battles, 140-41, 196, 224-25; signs with Cardinals, 23-25; signs with Indians, 230; signs with Pirates, 230; support for Jackie Robinson, 194, 197, 199-200, 204; trade to Braves, 228
Reiser, Sally (daughter), 117, 129-30, 209, 231, 239
Reiser, Stella (mother), 15-16, 19, 25, 253
Rice, Grantland, xv, 2, 61, 67, 82, 93, 167, 241, 251, 260-62, 263 269, 276
Richard, J.R., xi, 184-86, 271-72
Rickey, Branch: becomes Dodger GM, 121; becomes Pirates GM, 230; creation of farm system, 22-23; padding Ebbets Field walls, 233; plan to integrate baseball, 196-98; relations with Reiser, 32, 131-32, 139-141, 145-46. 152-53, 195-96, 224, 226. Also vi, xv, 22-23, 27, 29, 35, 39-40, 45-46, 57, 105, 110, 133, 136, 143-44, 149, 151, 153, 164, 195, 200-203, 208, 210-212, 215, 219, 221, 223-28, 237-38, 248-49, 255, 259, 264-68, 272-73, 275-77
Rickey, Branch Jr., 195
Rikard, Cully, 106, 205-207
Ritter, Lawrence, xii, 180, 240, 250-51, 271
Rizzo, Johnny, 31, 55, 83, 88, 243
Rizzuto, Phil, 76, 218
Robinson, Jackie: army experience, 196-97. baserunning, 200, 210-211, debut with Dodgers, 192-94; first encounter with Pete, 126; racist attacks on, 192, 203;

rookie of the year, 215. Also xi, 27, 32, 126, 164, 187-88, 198-99, 202-204, 213, 217, 220, 222, 225, 240, 249-250, 263, 272, 273-74
Robinson, Wilbert, 55, 170, 252, 259
Rolfe, Red, 77
Rossi, Dr. Dominic, 156, 206
Roth, Philip, 242, 250
Ruffing, Red, 75, 124, 136
Ruth, Babe, x, 2, 40, 44, 57, 61, 98, 169-70, 180, 217
Ryan, Nolan, 182, 184

Sain, Johnny, 159, 193-94
Schaeffer, Glen, 232
Schultz, Howie, 162
Schumacher, Gerry, 3, 60, 252, 254, 259,
Score, Herb, xi, 183-84
Scott, Lee, 51, 88-90, 142, 157, 248, 260, 262, 267, 269
Scully, Vince, 100, 246, 263
Seminick, Andy, 147-48, 202, 204
Sewell, Rip, 67, 71, 154
Shotton, Burt, 127, 203, 208, 210-11, 214-15, 217-22, 225, 227-28, 264- 274-75
Simmons, Al, 281, 247
Slaughter, Enos, 31, 52-53, 82-85, 106, 119, 142, 155, 160, 162, 213, 262
Smith, Red, x, 85, 239, 241, 251
Snider, Duke, 164, 202, 206, 208, 210, 227
Southworth, Billy, 58, 71, 84, 116, 228-29, 230, 276
Stanky, Eddie, 147, 149, 157, 162-63, 190, 193, 198, 200, 203, 210, 213, 219, 222, 225, 258, 267-69
Stargell, Willie, 99
Stengel, Casey, 5, 53, 60, 68, 80, 184, 271
Stockton, J. Roy, 28, 255-56
Stoneham, Horace, 189, 191, 272
Suzuki, Ichiro, 247

Taveras, Oscar, 167, 269
Terry, Bill, 3, 55, 69, 73, 259
Thompson, Hank, 189-91
Thomson, Bobby, xi, 190-91
Tietjen, W. Vernon, 83-84, 137, 197, 261, 266, 273
Travis, Cecil, 62, 172-75, 270-71

Tuber, Rick, vi, 16, 26, 77, 104, 118, 133, 207, 235, 237, 253, 263-64, 266, 274
Tuber, Shirley Reiser, vi, 4, 16, 18-19, 28, 36, 77, 134, 199, 231, 234-35, 238-39, 246-48, 252, 254-56, 262, 266, 277-78
Turkin, Hy, 10, 38, 147, 251-53, 256-58, 263, 267, 275

Vander Meer, Johnny, 158, 160
Vaughn, Arky, 8, 200, 220, 222, 247
Valo, Elmer, 135, 168, 245, 269

Waitkus, Eddie, 213
Walker, Dixie, vi, 50-51, 53-54, 59, 64, 66, 72, 76,92, 103, 124, 140, 142, 147, 149-151, 153, 155, 158, 161-62, 193, 197-200, 202, 204, 206-208, 210, 213-14, 217, 219-220, 273-74;
Walker, Harry, 83, 90, 121, 124-26, 262, 265
Walters, Bucky, 66, 70 , 155

Waner, Paul, 50, 247
Wendler, Dr. Harold, 202, 212, 218
White, Ernie, 58, 66
Wilkie, Lefty, 8, 60
Williams, Joe, 35, 229, 241, 250, 256, 259, 276
Williams, Ted, x, xv, xvi, 3,4,11, 62-63, 81, 93, 98, 107, 127, 140, 144, 146, 154, 162, 172-73, 175, 190, 240, 247, 252, ,265
Wills, Maury, 233-34, 250, 276
Wood, Smoky Joe, xi, 179-81, 271
Wyatt, Whit, 51, 58-59, 66, 72, 78, 86, 139

Young, Dick, xvi, 85, 105, 152, 154, 160, 162, 201-203, 205, 211, 216, 226, 227-28, 239, 241, 252

Zimet, Dr. Daniel, 86, 94, 104, 262, 264

About the Author

Dan Joseph is an editor by day and an author by night who lives in the Washington, D.C. area. A Pittsburgh native and graduate of Indiana University, Dan has worked for more than 20 years at the Voice of America, most as an editor in VOA's central newsroom, running the Africa desk. His first book, *Inside Al-Shabaab* (co-authored with Harun Maruf), was a revealing account of the inner workings of the Somali terrorist group. His second, *Last Ride of the Iron Horse*, tells the tale of Lou Gehrig's final year in the Yankee lineup, 1938, as he battled the early effects of the fatal disease ALS. A member of the Society for American Baseball Research (SABR), Dan uncovered the long-lost radio clip of Gehrig saying yes, Babe Ruth DID call his shot in the 1932 World Series. He is also one of the youngest people alive to have attended a Pittsburgh Pirates World Series game. Learn more about him at DanJosephauthor.net.

www.ingramcontent.com/pod-product-compliance
Lightning Source LLC
Chambersburg PA
CBHW031559110426
42742CB00036B/257